Object-Oriented Application Development
Using the Caché Postrelational Database

Springer-Verlag Berlin Heidelberg GmbH

W. Kirsten • M. Ihringer • M. Kühn • B. Röhrig

Object-Oriented Application Development Using the Caché Postrelational Database

Second, Revised and Updated Edition

With 121 Figures and 82 Tables

Springer

Dr. Wolfgang Kirsten
University of Frankfurt
Center of Medical Informatics
Department of Documentation and
Information Technology
Theodor-Stern-Kai 7, 60590 Frankfurt, Germany
w.kirsten@add.uni-frankfurt.de

Michael Ihringer
InterSystems GmbH
Hilpertstr. 20a, 64295 Darmstadt, Germany
ihringer@intersystems.de

Mathias Kühn
SYNERVA GmbH
Ludwig-Scriba-Str. 1, 65929 Frankfurt, Germany
kuehn@synerva.de

Dr. Bernhard Röhrig
Singerstraße 96, 99099 Erfurt, Germany
autor@roehrig.com

Translation of the German title "Objektorientierte Anwendungsentwicklung mit der postrelationalen Datenbank Caché, 2. Auflage" by W. Kirsten, M. Ihringer, M. Kühn and B. Röhrig
©Springer-Verlag 2003, ISBN 978-3-540-00960-3

Translated by Anthony S. Rudd, BSc, MSc

Additional material to this book can be downloaded from http://extras.springer.com

ISBN 978-3-540-00960-3

ACM Computing Classification (1998): H.2, D.1.5, D.2.2, D.3.2-3, E.1-2

Library of Congress Cataloging-in-Publication Data
[Objektorientierte Anwendungsentwicklung mit der postrelationalen Datenbank Caché. English]Object-Oriented Application Development Using the Caché Postrelational Database W. Kirsten...[et al.].-2nd rev. and updated ed.
    p.cm.
    Includes bibliographical references and index.
     ISBN 978-3-540-00960-3   ISBN 978-3-642-55516-9 (eBook)
     DOI 10.1007/978-3-642-55516-9
     1. Object-oriented programming (Computer science) 2. Application-software-development
     3. Caché (Coputer file) I. Kirsten, W. (Wolfgang), 1948-

QA76.64.O28413 2003
005.1'17 – dc22   2003057370

http://www.springer.de

© Springer-Verlag Berlin Heidelberg 2003
Originally published by Springer-Verlag Berlin Heidelberg New York in 2003
Softcover reprint of the hardcover 1st edition 2003

Cover design: KünkelLopka
Typesetting: Camera-ready by the authors
Printed on acid-free paper   33/3142 ud   543210

Prolog

"Object technology has slowly but steadily developed from an interesting 'buzzword' to a powerful technology taken seriously by professionals in information technology (IT). As this development unfolds, the choice of database system used to store objects becomes increasingly important."

When we introduced our preface to the first edition with these sentences in 2001, one did not have to be a prophet to make such a prediction. Like many others, however, we have been surprised by the speed with which object-oriented application development has gained acceptance. Today, very few development projects are not fully based on object technology, and products that are completely object-oriented have long dominated the market for development tools.

However, every software developer now faces the dilemma of how to store the object-oriented data of his application in a database. If he chooses one of the established relational database systems, which is suited for saving simple data, then comprehensively structured objects can only be mapped with great effort. To overcome the "impedance mismatch," i.e., the object-related paradigm break, extensive manual mapping or the use of middleware is required with the consequent unavoidable losses in performance and semantics. Some purely object-oriented databases resolve this dilemma by directly storing persistent objects; however, they have not gained acceptance because they do not provide the performance and reliability required by performance-critical enterprise applications with vast amounts of data.

Caché—the postrelational database product from InterSystems—is designed to overcome these restrictions for both relational and object-oriented databases. Its *Unified Data Architecture* provides a single layer for both object and SQL access to data stored efficiently in a transactional multidimensional database engine.

In this book, we do not wish to discuss the postrelational concepts of Caché at a merely theoretical level, but rather also show its practical uses for application development. Hence, the book guides the reader step-by-step through the development of postrelational applications.

Likewise, we felt it important to include extensive practical notes and a complete set of software on the CD-ROM that accompanies this book. We hope that you augment the study of this book with your own practical use of the Caché system.

This second edition of the book reflects the extensive development of Caché for version 5. New chapters provide detailed discussions on topics such as programming with ActiveX, object interaction with Java, and Web development with Caché Server Pages, XML, and Web Services. The remaining chapters have been reviewed and revised extensively; new material includes descriptions of the new Class Definition Language (CDL), the modernized Caché Studio, and numerous new and extended Caché concepts. The new content reflects the current state-of-the-art of modern Caché applications

We made the conscious decision to omit the description of Caché Basic, a new scripting language introduced into the Caché architecture with version 5. Instead, reference is made to all the literature available for Basic. The explanations and examples contained in this book therefore all refer to Caché's own scripting language, Caché ObjectScript.

Many colleagues contributed to the creation of this book by helping us with valuable suggestions and fruitful discussions. Here, we would like to especially mention Karin Schatz and Sebastian Huber. We profited greatly from their extensive experience with Caché.

We would also like to thank many Caché experts who checked the manuscript with particular attention to its practical use. In particular, Philip Russom and Jonathan Ostrowsky expended much care and knowledge in editing the final manuscript, and so resolved a number of remaining errors and inconsistencies.

Finally, our special thanks go to Dr. Hans Wössner from Springer-Verlag, who supported the project with enthusiasm from the beginning, and his colleague Ingeborg Mayer, who helped us build this revised and updated edition on the firm foundation of the editions of 1999 and 2001, and who courteously attended to our many wishes.

One of these long-time wishes was to provide the book's text in a searchable Adobe Acrobat Reader format and the examples as importable files on the enclosed CD-ROM, which was realized in this edition.

And all this would not have been possible without Anthony Rudd, who translated the often-difficult technical language from German into English.

The aims of this book are to provide a thorough introduction to application development with Caché, and to contribute to its successful adoption by serving as a useful everyday work and reference tool.

Darmstadt, June 2003   The Authors

Table of Contents

1 First Steps

1.1 Introduction

Because you are reading this book, we assume you are interested in object-oriented application development in general and the Caché postrelational database from InterSystems in particular. And because you have chosen a practical manual with a CD-ROM, we further assume that your interest is more than theoretical and that you wish to use it to gain practical experience as fast as possible.

Therefore, let us postpone, for the moment, a detailed description of object-oriented principles and go straightaway into application development. In this chapter we install Caché and other software products from the accompanying CD-ROM, become acquainted with basic system administration, and develop a small object-oriented application with Caché.

Installing Caché and developing the first object-oriented application

In Chapter 2 we shall return to the principles of object-oriented development. If you wish to skip this introductory chapter, you can jump to Chapter 2. Even so, you should install Caché before proceeding to later chapters that cover in detail the specific aspects of application development with Caché. You will find it easier to follow the examples given in this book if you run them for yourself with the software installed from the accompanying CD-ROM.

But before you unpack the CD-ROM and install the software, we must first answer one basic question:

What is Caché—the postrelational database?

InterSystems Corporation—a database vendor headquartered in Cambridge, Massachusetts—introduced Caché at the end of 1997. InterSystems refers to Caché as a "postrelational" database, which is primarily a time reference. In this sense, all databases designed and developed after the relational model could be called postrelational. The term is often used in this manner. For example, Vossen [1994] uses "postrelational" to group all databases no longer based on normalized, flat tables, and mentions nested-relational, multidimensional, and object-oriented databases as examples.

Postrelational database models

But a definition based on time alone does not suffice. To understand the content of a postrelational database, you must appreciate the changed demands made on modern database systems, which, for example, Currier [1997] describes impressively. Current applications are normally developed to support complex information flow and comprehensive work processes in companies. A developer's principal task here is to correctly determine the structures of the macro-cosmos and represent them as appropriate models in the micro-cosmos of information technology.

It is obvious that corporate applications are affected by the business processes they model. Object-oriented technologies are ideal for real-world business process modeling, and this is the main reason for their increasing popularity. (Chapter 2 provides a detailed description of the object-oriented technologies.)

It became apparent only later that the models in which information is stored also needed to be updated. Vaskevitch [1992] wrote in an article for BYTE magazine:

Postrelational databases reflect an image of the real world

> *Relational databases still make sense for many kinds of applications that lend themselves to expression as simple sets of simple tables. However, to build applications that reflect the real world, you will have to find a way to take another two steps forward this time to a postrelational world.*

In this sense, the postrelational model from Caché helps software developers represent the relationships of "real world" data in information technology without oversimplification. This book shows how you can quickly develop reliable, sophisticated applications using Caché.

1.2   System Requirements

To successfully install and run the software on the accompanying CD-ROM, your system should satisfy the following minimal requirements:

- Intel Pentium CPU
- Windows 95, 98, ME, NT 4.0 (SP4, 5 or 6), 2000 (SP2), or XP
- 128 MB main memory
- 100 MB free disk space
- Configured TCP/IP stack
- CD-ROM drive

1.3   Installation

The accompanying CD-ROM contains an automatic setup program that provides the following options:

- Read Book Online
- Install Acrobat Reader
- Install Caché 5
- Caché Documentation and Tutorials
- Book Examples

If the CD-ROM does not start automatically when you insert it, the autostart function for your CD-ROM drive has been deactivated. You can manually start the installation program by double-clicking the specified items in the following sequence: *My Computer*, the CD-ROM drive symbol, and the *autostart.exe* program.

1.3.1 Read Book Online

The enclosed CD-ROM contains the complete text of this book, including the code examples. Due to copyright restrictions, you cannot print the book from the CD-ROM; however, you can read and search the text with the Adobe Acrobat Reader. If Adobe Acrobat Reader is not installed on your system, you can install it from the CD-ROM.

1.3.2 Installing Caché

To install Caché, select the *Install Caché 5* option from the menu. (Note: to install Caché under Windows NT, 2000, or XP, you must be logged on as administrator.)

Install to the default path and select *8-bit* as the installation type when prompted. Be sure that all Caché components needed for the examples in this book are installed.

The installation is complete when the following display appears on the screen. Under some circumstances, the system will need to restart; the installation routine will tell you if this is the case.

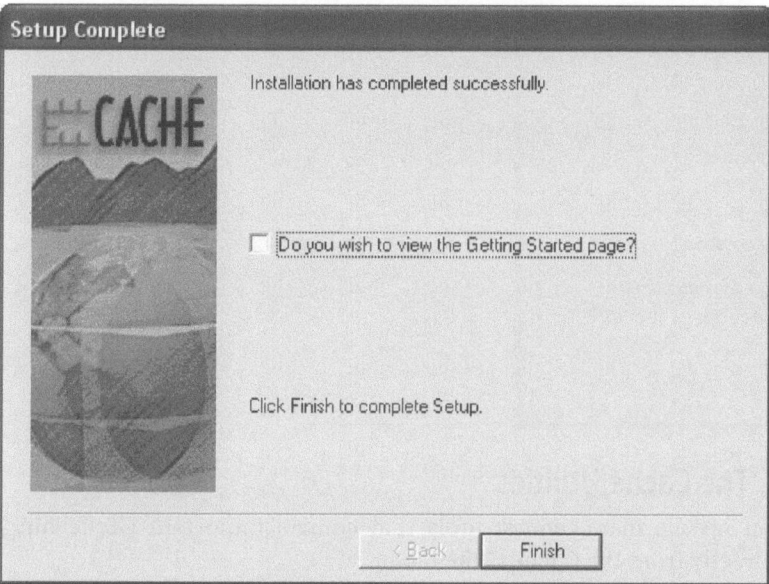

Figure 1.1 Successful installation

1.3.3 The Book Examples

The code examples used in the book can be imported as files from the CD-ROM. Use the setup program's menu option *Book Examples* to open Windows Explorer, which then shows subdirectories with the example files.

1.4 Using Caché

1.4.1 The Caché Cube

After a successful installation, Caché is ready to run. If no restart was necessary, Caché will already be running. To see whether Caché is running, check the system tray—this is the right-hand area of the taskbar at the lower edge of the screen. This displays the Caché Cube, an icon in the form of a cube. If the icon is colored, Caché is already running. If the cube is outlined in gray, Caché needs to be started, which you can do with the *Start Caché* option.

Figure 1.2 The Caché Cube

Click the Caché Cube icon to open a menu in which you can administer Caché. The second and third menu items are used to start and stop Caché.

Figure 1.3 The Caché Cube menu

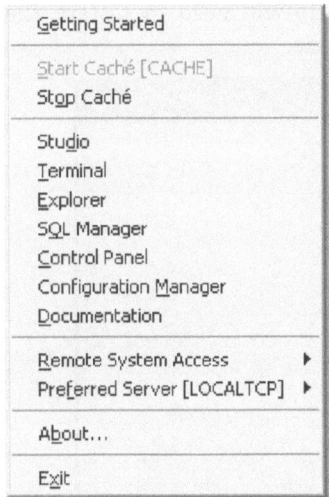

1.4.2 The Caché Utilities

Management tools for Caché

You can invoke management tools that control important Caché functions directly from the Caché Cube menu.

Table 1.1 The Caché utilities

Menu option	Description
Getting Started	Shows the "Getting Started" document with shortcuts to important Caché online documentation and tutorials.
Start Caché	Starts Caché.
Stop Caché	Stops Caché and optionally initiates a restart.
Studio	Caché Studio is a graphical editor you use to create classes, CSP pages and routines with Caché ObjectScript or Caché Basic.
Terminal	Caché Terminal provides a terminal emulation screen that you can use to logon in command mode to local or remote Caché systems.
Explorer	Caché Explorer manages databases and namespaces together with their associated classes, globals, and routines.

SQL Manager	Caché SQL Manager helps you manage all aspects of relational access to Caché.
Control Panel	Caché Control Panel administers the running Caché system and its processes.
Configuration Manager	The Configuration Manager defines the system and network configurations for Caché.
Documentation	Accesses the Caché online documentation and tutorials.
Remote System Access	When you invoke a utility here, you can specify a server other than the preferred server.
Preferred Server	Sets up the Caché servers and selects the preferred server. For a single-user installation, the local server (LOCALTCP) has been set up automatically during installation.
About	Displays the copyright and version information for Caché.
Exit	If you close the Caché Cube with this option, you can use the Start menu later to reactivate it at any time.

1.5 Step-by-Step Through the First Example

Once you have installed Caché and are familiar with its basic operations, it is time for an introduction to application development. We will use Caché to design and implement a small object-oriented application. This easy task can be accomplished in just 10 minutes.

Small object-oriented application with Caché

1.5.1 The Task

We start with a simple person class as an example. A person should have properties for family name, first name, and date of birth (DOB). We will let Caché create the associated methods that store and retrieve persons in the database. We also want to provide a query for selecting all stored persons. Schematically, our model has the following form:

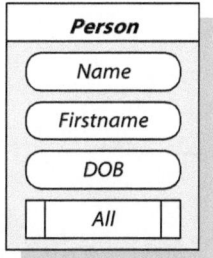

Figure 1.4 Person object class

1.5.2 Caché Studio

We now start Caché Studio to define this object class. Click the Caché Cube in the taskbar and select *Studio*. A window appears with the only existing connection, Local, and the namespace User already selected. Click *Connect* to accept these defaults.

Figure 1.5 Selecting a connection

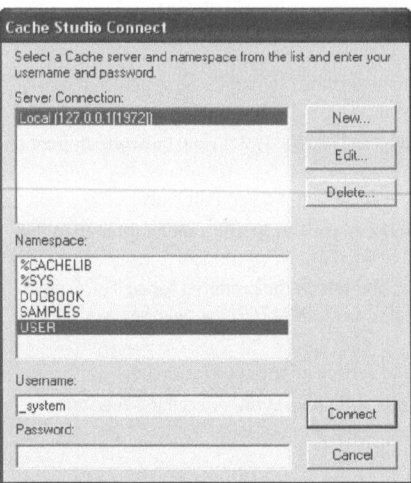

The Caché Studio main window that now appears shows an empty project with the name *Project1*.

Figure 1.6 Caché Studio

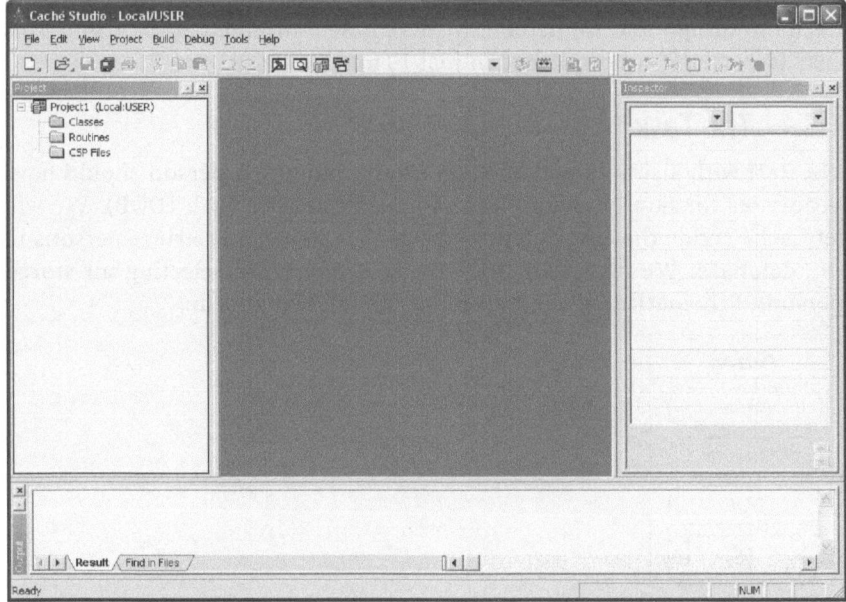

1.5.2.1 Creating a Class Definition

Caché provides a wizard for creating new classes. Right-click *Classes* and select *Create New Class* in the context menu that opens. The *New Class Wizard* appears. Now specify the name and description of the new class.

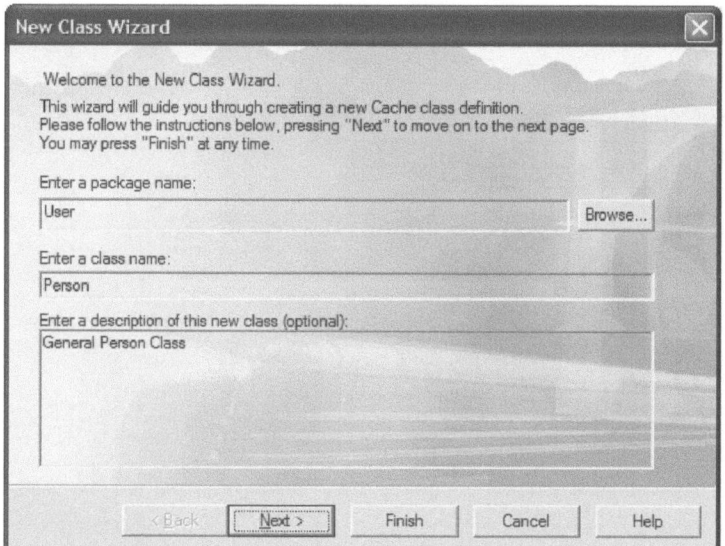

Figure 1.7 Creating a new class in the *New Class Wizard*

Keep the default package name, User. Specify Person as the name of the class, and enter a short description. Then click *Next* to proceed to the next step in which you specify the class type.

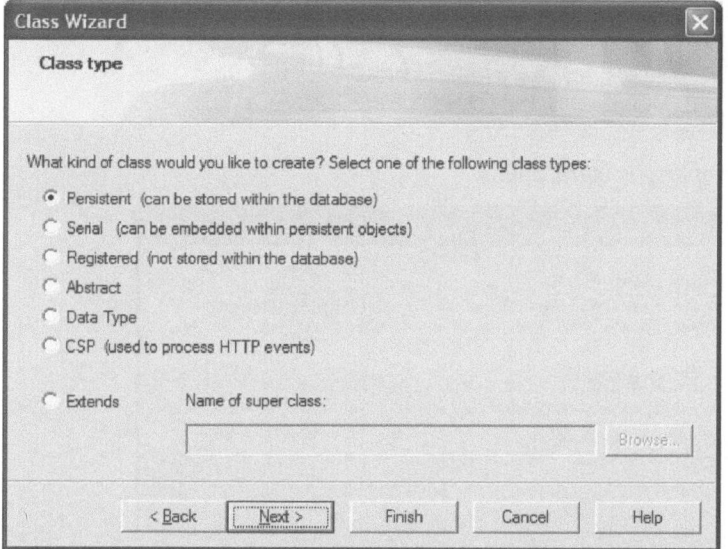

Figure 1.8 *Class type*—Selecting the class type

We keep the default class type, *Persistent*. Caché will now automatically store and fetch objects for this class.

Click *Complete* to skip the remaining steps of the wizard. The *Class Wizard* creates the new class, which now appears in the Caché Studio project hierarchy.

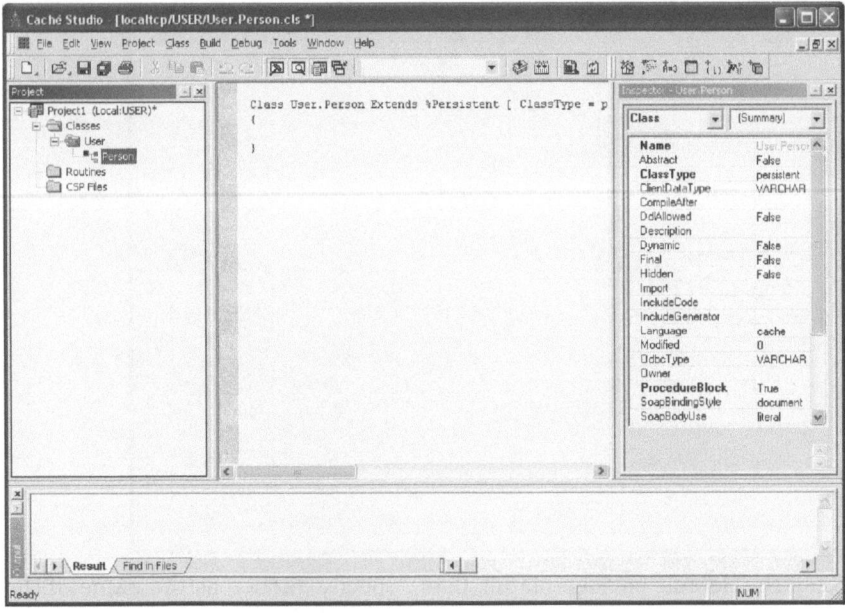

Figure 1.9 The newly-created class

1.5.2.2 Creating Properties

To define the properties of the class, click the *New Property* button.

Figure 1.10 The *New Property* button

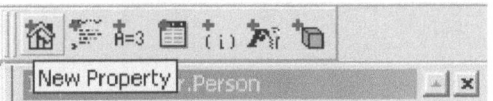

The *New Property Wizard* opens.

Figure 1.11 Creating a new property with the *New Property Wizard*

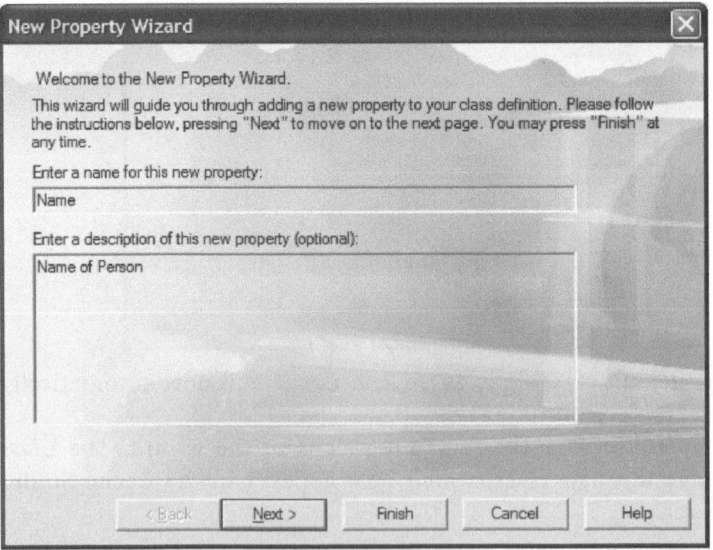

First we create a property for the person's name. Enter Name in the *Property name* field and specify a short description in the description field.

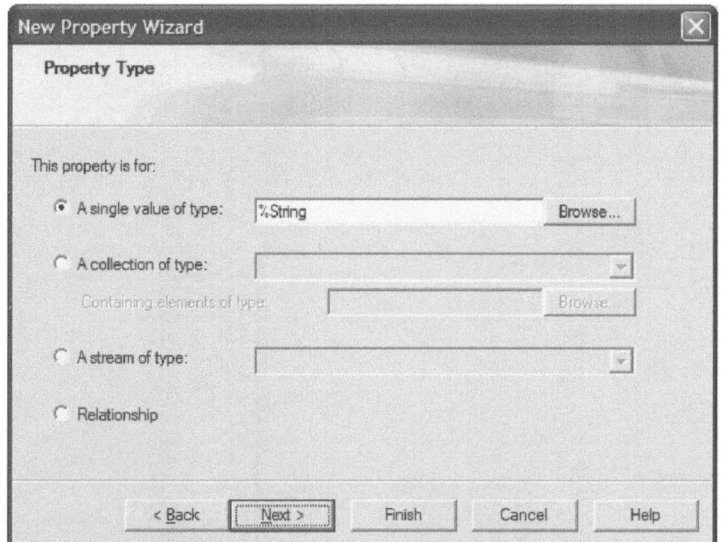

Figure 1.12 *Property Type*—Selection of data type

Retain the default type, %String, and click *Next*.

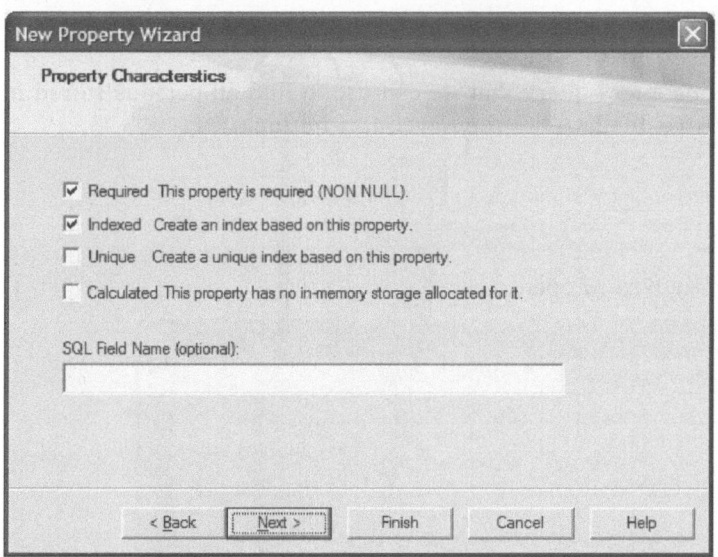

Figure 1.13 *Property Characteristics*—Characteristics of the Property

Check the *Required* and *Indexed* characteristics to specify that a name is mandatory and the name search is to be optimized, respectively. No other characteristics are necessary, so click *Finish*. The new property is now defined.

In the same way, we define the Firstname (without the *Required* and *Indexed* characteristics) and DOB (with the data type %Date) properties. Once we have defined these properties, the class definition has the following appearance:

Figure 1.14 The class definition in Caché Studio

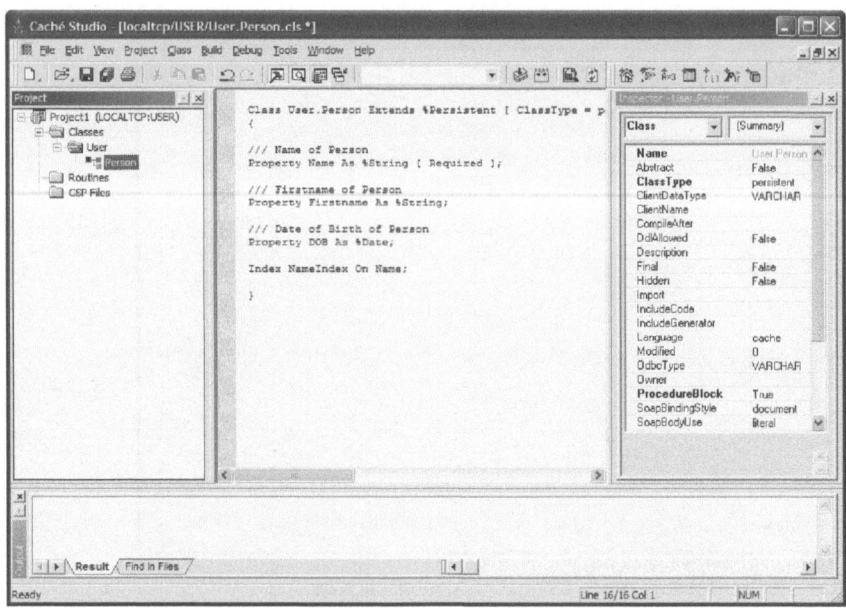

Figure 1.14 The class definition in Caché Studio

1.5.3 Creating the Query

We now define a new query that we can use to find all persons stored in the database. To do this, click the *New Query* button.

Figure 1.15 The *New Query* button

The *New Query Wizard* opens.

Figure 1.16 Creating a new query with the *New Query Wizard*

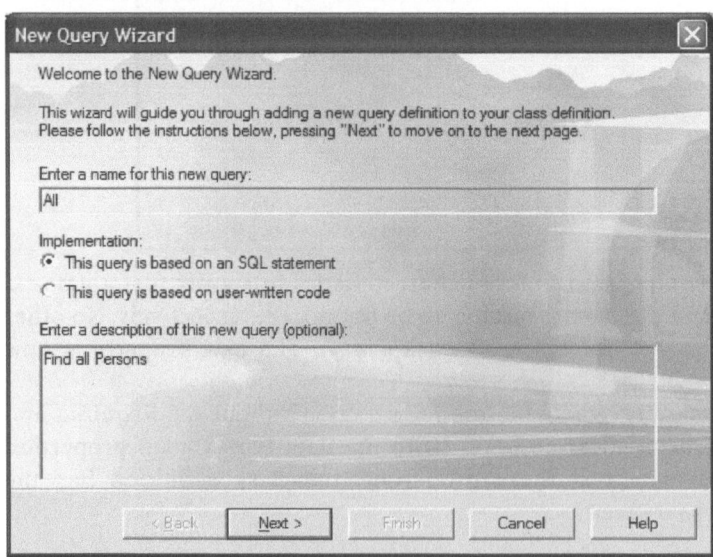

We enter All as the name of the query, and a short description in the field below. We keep the default, SQL statement, for the Implementation selection. Clicking *Next* displays the definition for the request parameter, which we do not need, so click *Next* to skip it. In the next step we specify the fields that the query is to supply.

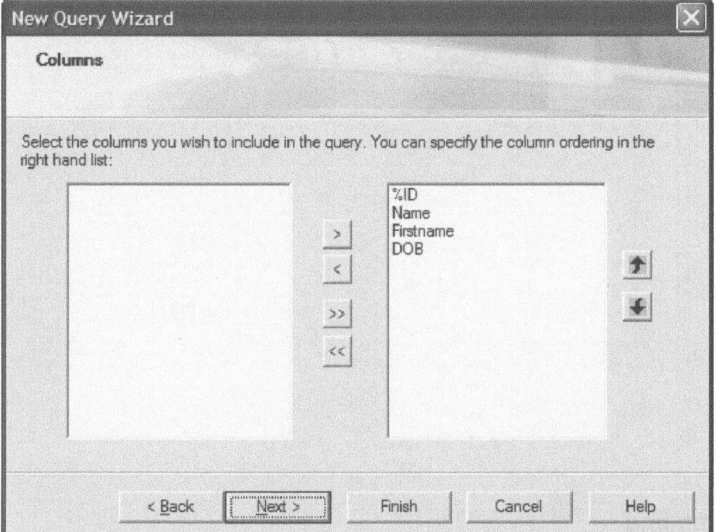

Figure 1.17 *Columns*—Selecting the query fields

On the left-hand side you see a list with all the properties of the object class and an additional ID field. Select each of the %ID, Name, Firstname, and DOB fields and click the > arrow to move each field into the right-hand list. When you are finished, click *Next*. The next step sets a query condition. Because we do not need to set this, click *Next* to proceed to make the selection for the sorting sequence.

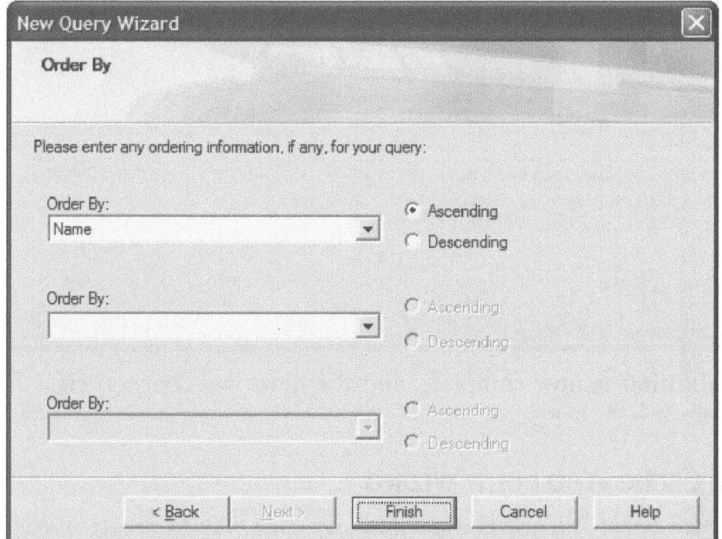

Figure 1.18 *Order By*—Defining the query's sorting sequence

Because we wish to sort the selection of persons by name, we choose the *Name* field from the *Order By* list. When we click *Finish,* Caché Studio shows the Person class with its properties and the new query.

Figure 1.19 Person class with its properties and the new All query

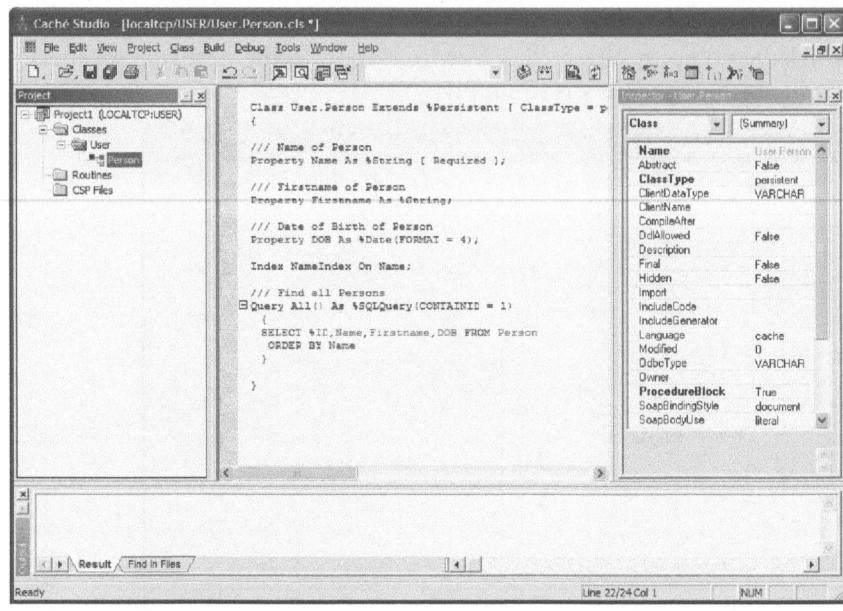

1.5.3.1 Compiling

A new class must be compiled before it can be used in Caché. To do this, click the *Compile* button.

Figure 1.20 The *Compile* button

After the compilation has completed, you see a message in the *Result* window that looks similar to the one shown in Figure 1.21.

Figure 1.21 Successful compilation of a class

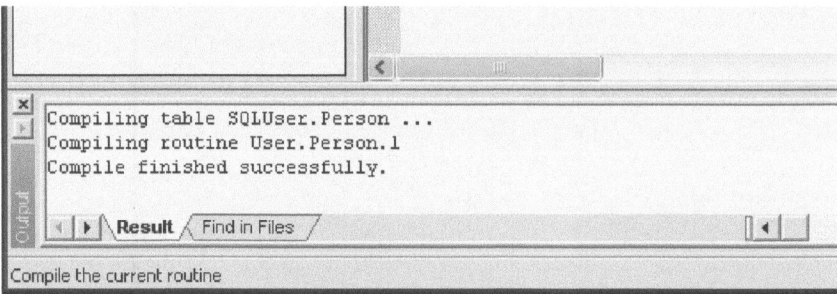

The class definition is now complete, and the new User.Person class is ready for use.

1.5.4 The Caché Web Form Wizard

The *Caché Web Form Wizard* is a particularly easy way to create a Web front end for a Caché class definition with Caché Server Pages (CSP). We will use it to populate our person class with data.

First, we must create a CSP form. Right-click on *CSP Files* in the Caché Studio project hierarchy. Select *Create New CSP File* in the context menu that opens. Caché produces a new CSP form and displays it.

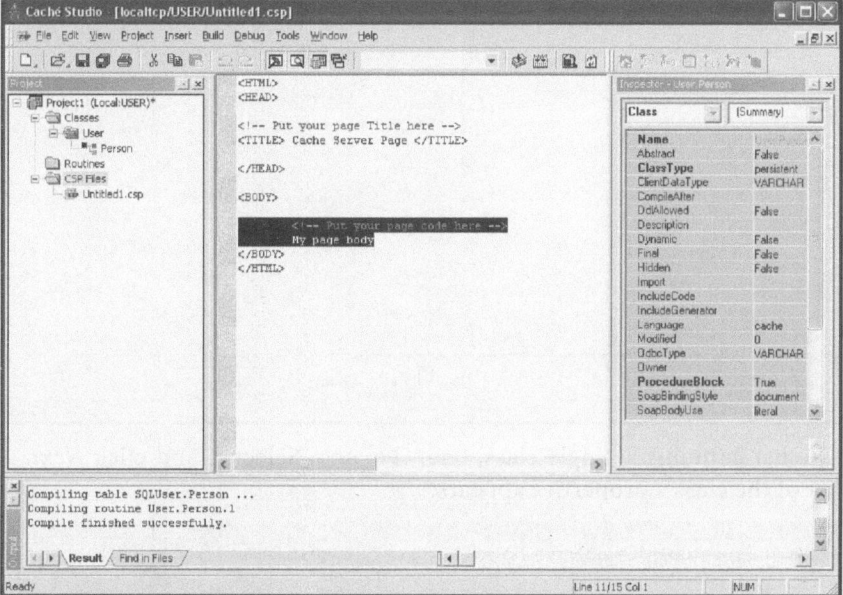

Figure 1.22 The newly-created CSP form

Mark the prepared default code between the <BODY> and </BODY> tags, then open the *Insert* menu and click the *Form Wizard*. A new window with the *Caché Web Form Wizard* opens.

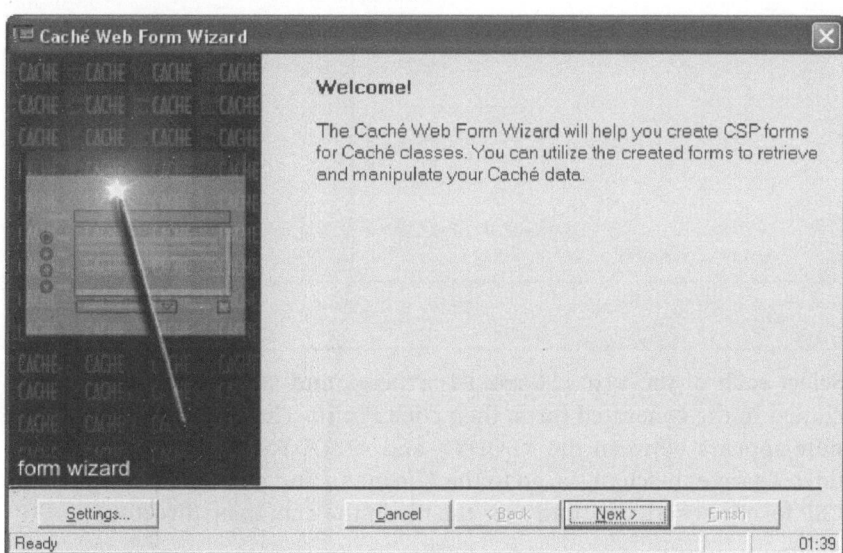

Figure 1.23 The Caché Web Form Wizard

Click *Next* to display a list of the available classes.

Figure 1.24 Selecting a class

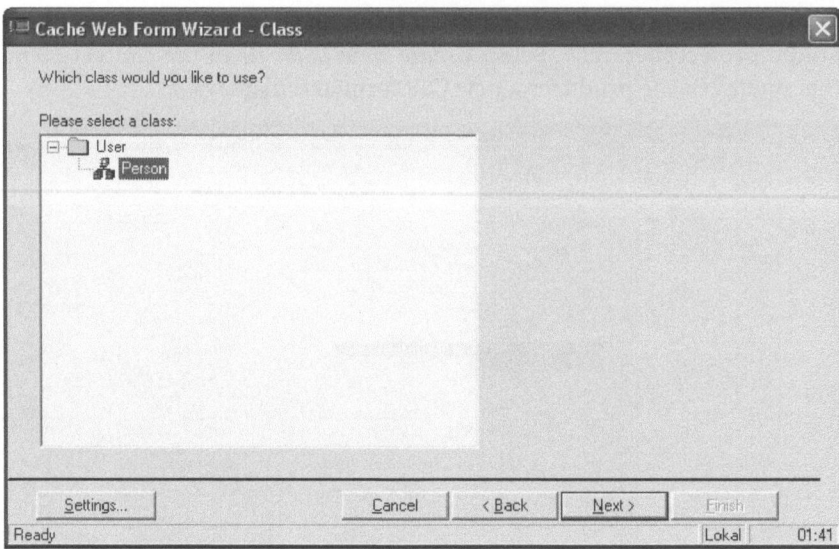

The list contains a single class, User.Person. Select it and click *Next*. A list of the class's properties appears.

Figure 1.25 Selecting properties

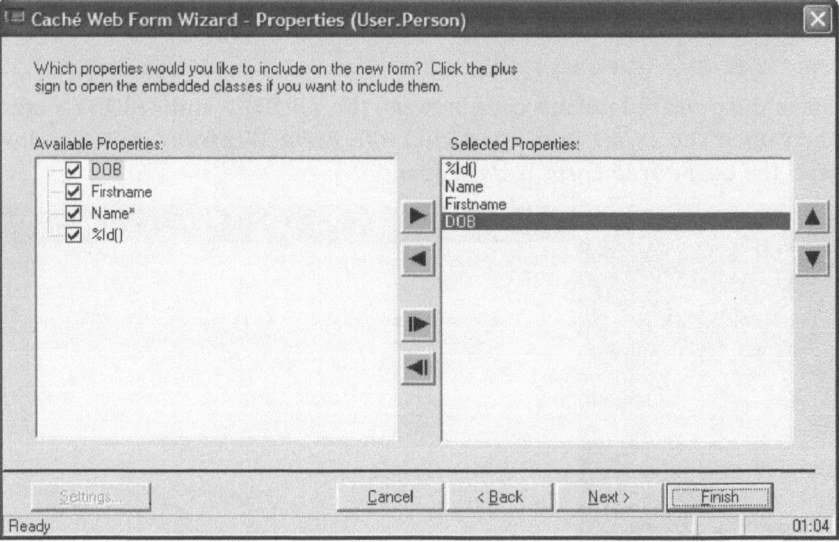

Select each of the %Id(), Name, Firstname, and DOB properties to be included in the generated form, then click *Finish*. The newly generated code now appears between the <BODY> and </BODY> tags in the code window. To save the changes, go to the *File* menu and click *Save As*. Name the CSP form person.csp, and save the file in the csp/user directory.

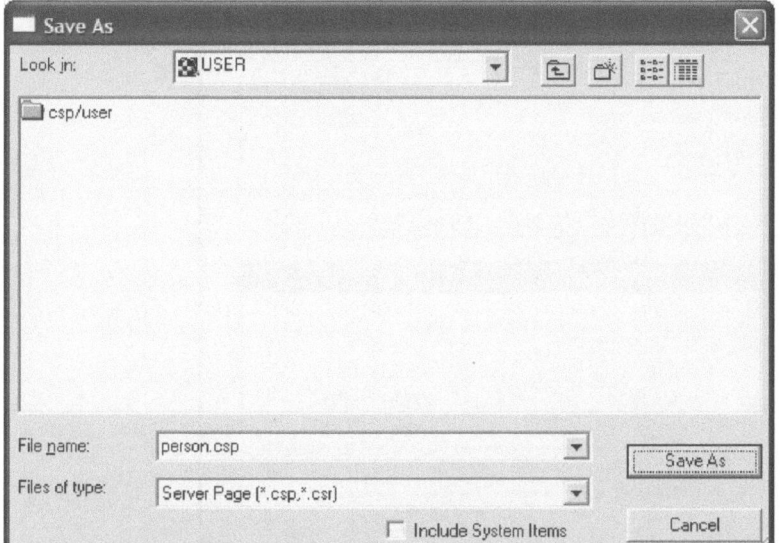

Figure 1.26 Saving a CSP form

To view the new Caché Server Page, click *Web Page* from the *View* menu. The Web browser opens, and the automatically generated form for our person class appears.

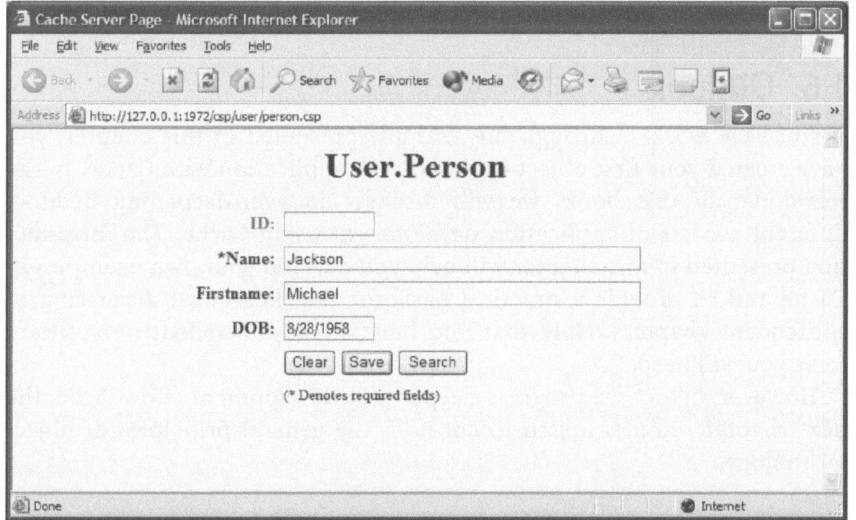

Figure 1.27 The automatically generated form in the Web browser

After you have used the wizard to create several persons, click the *Search* button to select a person to edit or delete.

Figure 1.28 Using the generated search function

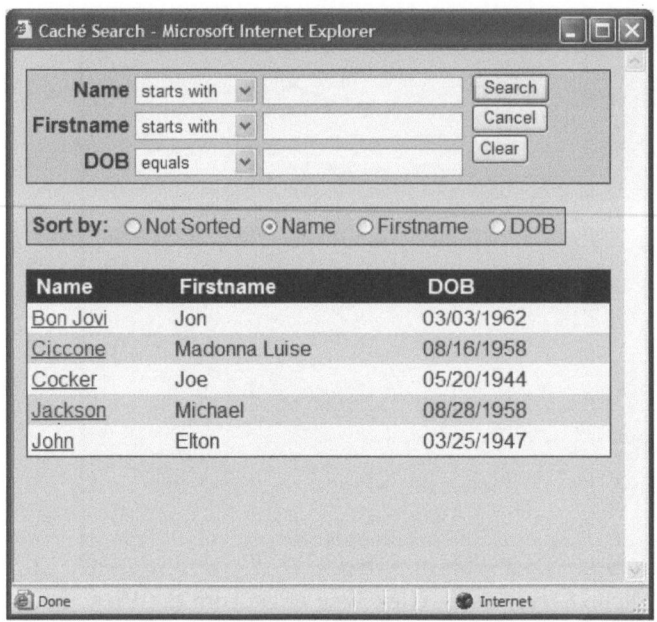

The form created by the *Caché Web Form Wizard* provides a general prototype that you can use for your own development projects. You can now edit and refine the code in Caché Studio according to your needs.

1.6 Outlook

Your first object-oriented Web application created with Caché

If you have worked through the example presented in this chapter, you have created your first object-oriented Web application with Caché. In the remainder of this book, we will discuss—in ever-deepening detail— different aspects of application development using Caché. The introduction presented in this chapter will help you develop your own examples in Caché and so provide a practical basis for the theoretical discussion in subsequent chapters. Note that you have already installed the software tools you will need.

However, before we progress deeper into development with Caché, the next chapter retraces a step to consider the general principles of object technology.

2 Introduction to Object Technology

2.1 Overview

In the introduction to the first chapter, we discussed the need to allow developers to represent the real world without changing paradigms. Object-oriented (OO) technology (or object technology) was invented especially for this purpose.

Object technology was developed to represent the real world with software

At the end of the 1960s, the software designers Dahl, Myhrhaug, and Nygaard at the Norwegian Computing Center developed a system for simulating complex industrial and social processes, which they called "Simula." Then, as today, software development was dominated by a procedural approach in which a problem is described in the language of the solution. In a traditional programming language, you define exact algorithms that a computer executes later.

The first OO language was Simula, developed in the 1960s in Norway

Simula took a revolutionary approach: describe the problem, instead of the solution. Objects appeared like actors on a virtual stage, possessing their own knowledge (i.e., data) and capabilities (algorithms or methods). Simula was initially used to build models that simulate real systems. However, its decisive advantages soon became apparent, and this new technology was applied to programming in general:

Object technology has decisive advantages

- Compared with the procedural approach (in which the program language code is written in structured forms such as routines, functions, and blocks), object technology also applies structuring to information. Hence, OO programming practices automatically segment large software systems into easily understandable units that can be developed and maintained independent of each other.

Objects are modular

- Objects have well-defined interfaces through which they communicate with other objects. Objects interoperate through these interfaces regardless of each other's internal structures.

Objects are interoperable

- Because objects are modular and interoperate through generalized interfaces, they can be reused in applications that require the same units.

Objects are reusable

- The OO concept models information structures, not algorithms. Because structures change slowly, OO software tends to have life cycles that are significantly longer than those of procedural programs.

Objects have a long life cycle

Once those advantages were recognized, Simula rapidly developed into a general-purpose programming language. Through the following years, other programming systems based on the object-oriented concept were designed and developed. In addition to C++, Smalltalk, and Java, the

Caché ObjectScript language described here belongs among the object-oriented languages of the 1990s. All modern OO languages are based on a number of common fundamental principles and concepts, which Taylor [1990 and 1995] discusses in detail. The following section provides a general introduction to these common fundamentals.

2.2 Objects, Properties, Methods, and Messages

Encapsulation means the secrecy principle

The most important concept in object technology is the *object* itself. This describes an encapsulated unit with properties and methods. *Encapsulation* means that the internal implementation is covered by a secrecy principle. Thus, neither program code nor variables are visible outside the object. Rather, objects have a public interface, which is described as a number of methods and properties. Whereas *methods* define the behavior of an object, *properties* are its "knowledge" or its data. Strictly speaking, properties cannot be manipulated directly (but only through data access methods), so they do not belong to the public interface. However, in many modern OO environments, such data access methods are provided automatically and invoked implicitly. Thus, for all practical purposes, object properties in such systems belong very much to the public interface.

Figure 2.1 An object

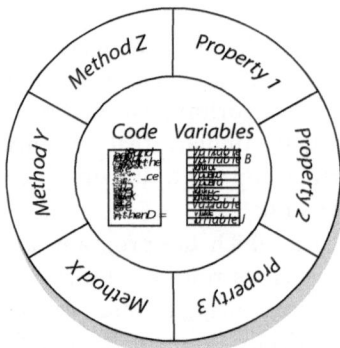

Executing a method

If you wish to execute a method, you cannot simply invoke its code, because this would violate the secrecy principle. Instead, you send the object a *message* requesting to execute a specific method. The message includes any parameters the method may require. The object itself decides what internal code to execute, invokes it, and passes parameter values appropriately.

Figure 2.2 Sending a message to an object

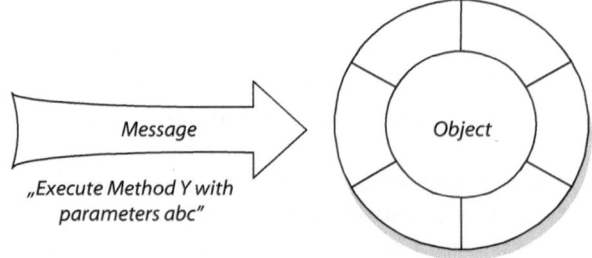

2.3 Object Classes and Instances

An object system usually contains a number of similar objects, which are grouped into so-called *object classes*. The incarnations of these object classes (the individual objects) are called *instances* of the class. For example, from the object-oriented viewpoint every human individual can be considered an instance of the "human" class.

The object class defines the properties, methods, and interface common to all instances. This definition serves as a framework that every instance can fill individually with its own values. Thus, the instances are of the *type* of their associated class. Instances also have an object identity that is independent of the values. Thus, two instances (even with identical values for all properties) are still clearly distinguishable examples of this type. In the previous example, it means that identical twins represent two individuals or instances, even when they exhibit exactly the same properties.

The object class defines properties and methods common to all instances

Instances of a class differ only in the values of their properties, not in their methods. The class definitions specify this binding for all instances. This means that all members of a class have an identical interface and, therefore, also exhibit an identical behavior. Even so, a fundamental differentiation can be made between instance methods and class methods, which determines whether an associated method refers to a specific instance of the class or acts independently of the instance.

Instance methods and class methods

As an example, let's consider a "triangle" that requires methods such as "draw," "delete," and "move," and properties such as "position," "size," and "color". The class defines the methods and contains the code with which a triangle is drawn, deleted, or moved from one position to another. Individual instances have values for the properties, namely for a specific position, size, and color. If you wish to delete a specific triangle, you use its "delete" method. Although this is defined in the object class, it is available as an instance method in each individual instance and so refers to that particular triangle in which it is invoked.

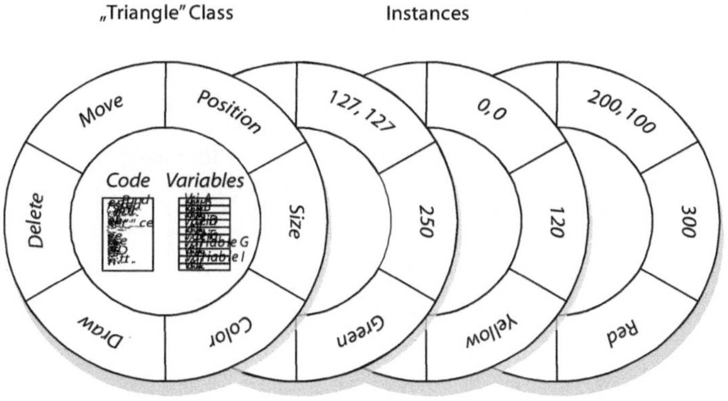

Example of a "triangle" class

Figure 2.3 A "triangle" class and its instances

But how do you create a new triangle? Up to now we know an object class only as a *container* for objects. Actually, it also has a second important significance: that of an *object factory*. This means that you can instruct an

Containers and object factory

object class to create a new instance through a special constructor function. Because this cannot yet apply to a specific instance, it is implemented as a class method which is simply called "new" in most systems.

2.4 Class Hierarchies and Inheritance

Substitutability

The term *inheritance* means that one object class is derived from another. A subclass has an "is a" relationship to the super class from which it inherits all its properties and methods. Thus, the subclass has the same interface as the super class and can be used in its place. This principle is called *substitutability* and means that every message you can send to an instance of the super class is also valid for instances of the subclass.

Specialization of subclasses

The subclass can be further specialized by adding properties and methods that the super class does not have. Similarly, you can overwrite methods so the subclass behaves differently than the super class. However, it is not possible to remove properties and methods that are present in the super class, because substitutability would no longer apply.

A further subclass can be derived from a subclass, and another from this; theoretically, there is no limit to the depth of an inheritance hierarchy. In some object systems, all classes are derived from a single base class that provides general system-wide object functionality. Each node of the inheritance hierarchy further specializes the classes.

With *multiple inheritance*, which not all object systems support, a subclass can be derived from two or more super classes simultaneously. Although this provides additional flexibility in building class hierarchies, it also creates potential for conflicts. For example, rules must specify what happens when different methods with the same name are inherited from multiple super classes.

Figure 2.4 Inheritance in a class hierarchy

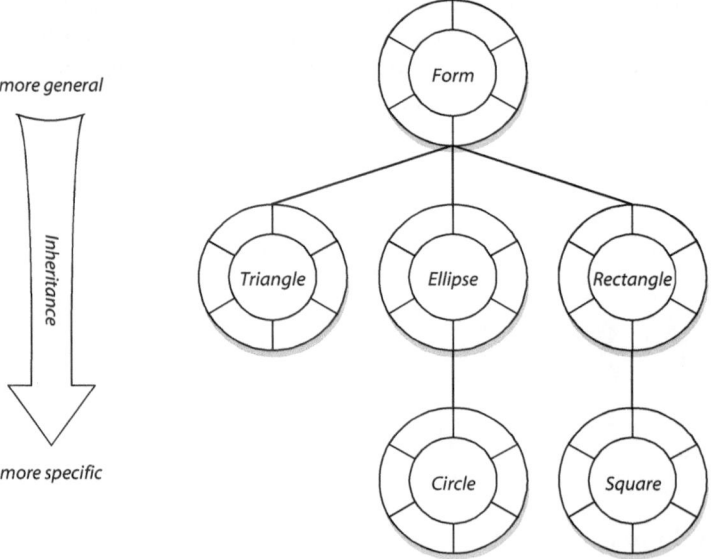

Let us assume that we wish to extend our triangle example with additional geometric forms. It would be useful to generalize the existing class hierarchy that currently consists of just a single class so that it can handle arbitrary forms. We achieve this with a "form" super class. This can contain the "draw," "delete," and "move" methods already defined for triangles. However, it's difficult (perhaps impossible) to write code that can draw arbitrary geometric forms. Consequently, we leave the "draw" method empty in the "form" super class and add suitable code to each of the "triangle," "ellipse," and "rectangle" subclasses.

Further geometric forms

However, the empty method definition in the super class is an important achievement. Namely, it is an interface through which we may draw any geometric form. Substitutability means that we can send the message "execute the 'draw' method" to any instance of an arbitrary subclass of "form." Thus, the ability to fill methods with code on a per-subclass basis (as well as the ability to add methods and properties to subclasses) enables an increasing *specialization* in a class hierarchy. The high-level definition of the interface makes it simple to extend an application. If an application can process objects of the type "form," it can automatically support all subclasses of "form." For example, a new "pentagon" form added to the class hierarchy is supported immediately.

Specialization in the class hierarchy

Let us now consider the "circle" and "square" classes as subclasses of "ellipse" and "rectangle." Both are special cases of an associated super class, but can contain additional rules. For example, the edge length of all sides must be the same for a square. Thus, you first describe the general case in a class hierarchy, and then implement the deviating *exceptions* in subclasses.

2.5   Abstract and Final Classes

In the previous example, we introduced a super class called "form" that contains a general definition of geometric forms. It would not make much sense to create instances of this without knowing the associated form. You can designate a class as *abstract*, meaning that it can serve only as a template for defining subclasses. Abstract classes cannot have instances.

Template for the definition of subclasses

Similarly, there are some classes from which no further subclasses should be created. These are designated as *final*. However, it is more common to define individual methods or properties as final; in this case, you can create subclasses, but the associated methods and property definitions can not be overwritten in subclasses.

2.6   Polymorphism

Polymorphism is where a general public interface hides differing behaviors. We have already encountered polymorphism in the example: the "draw" method applies to any object, although triangle, rectangle and ellipse subclasses use different code when drawing. Calling the draw method works regardless of the subclass type. We could even add a "pentagon" subclass to the class hierarchy, and calls of its draw method would

Using methods on an arbitrary object

work automatically (with no modifications to the application), assuming that it provides the appropriate code for pentagons.

Thus, polymorphism enables an important benefit of object-oriented applications: they can be modified and extended easily and with limited risk of error.

2.7 Complex Objects

Circles and rectangles serve as good introductory examples, but when we work with objects from the real world, data types tend to be more complex.

Figure 2.5 A complex object

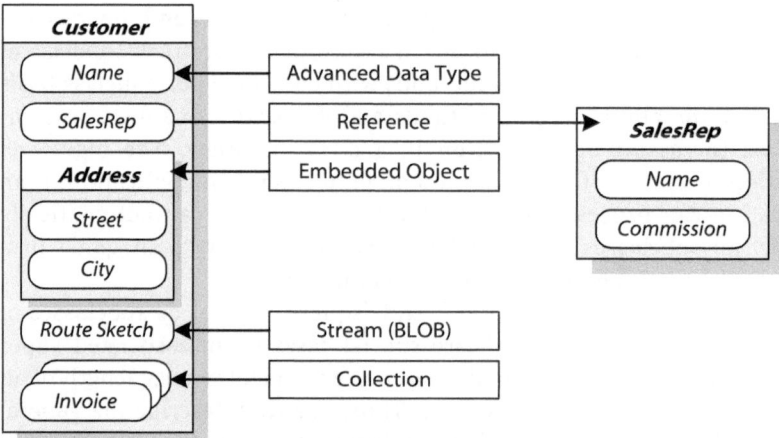

Advanced Data Types

Consider a business application with customers that we wish to represent in a "customer" object class. A customer has simple properties of type string or integer, as well as a "name" property consisting of a last name, a first name, and possibly additional names, titles, and academic qualifications. Such combined or derived data types can be defined in extended object systems as *Advanced Data Types (ADTs)* and used in the same manner as the supplied base data types. The data type definition is here a special case of a class definition.

Every object class is a valid data type

Similarly, every object class is also a valid data type. For example, if we store sales representatives with their names and commission rates in a "SalesRep" class, the customer object can possess a property of type "SalesRep" and thereby represent a *reference* to the associated sales rep. Alternatively, it would have been possible to implement this as a bi-directional *relationship* between the "Customer" and the "SalesRep" classes.

Because, in contrast to a sales representative, the address should not have its own identity independent of the customer, one would represent it as an *embedded object*. Its "street" and "city" properties then exist only in the context of the customer, but have their own class definition that can also be reused for other purposes (e.g., for suppliers). An embedded object can itself contain other embedded objects; theoretically, there are no limits to the levels of nesting.

Large quantities of unstructured data are stored as streams or binary large objects (*BLOBs*). This mechanism can be used here to save the route to the customer as a graphic image.

Finally, properties can occur more than once independent of their data type; this is called a *collection*. For example, a "customer" object can have an unlimited number of invoices as embedded objects; similarly, a collection can also contain simple values like strings, advanced data types, or references to objects.

2.8 Persistence and Other Database Requirements of Object Technology

Streams (or BLOBs) and collections

Various concepts are available when you wish to use object technology not only for processing but also for the permanent storage of data. (Blaha [1997] contains a detailed discussion of the requirements of object technology on a database system.) In all circumstances it is desirable that the object system exhibits a behavior that permits an automatic *persistence* of objects. If so, it suffices to mark an object class as persistent (in contrast to transient), and the object system itself ensures permanent storage for that class in a database system.

This case requires that the database system itself operates as an object-oriented system. If this is not the case, an *impedance mismatch* (or a paradigm break) occurs. For example, relational databases cannot necessarily store application data modeled as objects, because relational databases operate only on flat, normalized tables. When objects are stored in a purely relational database, the database must expend a significant effort converting from one model to the other. In many systems today, middleware products (or, in the case of "object-relational" products, even the database itself) perform these conversions. However, the basic problem remains, namely the decomposition of complex objects into their component parts. Critics call this *relational decomposition*.

A well-known quotation from the author and industry observer Esther Dyson impressively describes the associated effort:

> *Using tables to store objects is like driving your car home and then disassembling it in the garage. It can be assembled again in the morning, but one eventually asks whether this is the most efficient way to park a car.*   (quoted by Orfali et al. [1996], page 164)

Finally, we should recall that objects are not merely data (i.e., properties); they also exercise behavior (through methods). Generally, only object-oriented databases permit the direct execution of method code for objects stored in the database management system.

Object model and problem analysis

2.9 The Process of Object-Oriented Software Development

As we have already seen, the class hierarchy typical of object-oriented methodology forms the backbone of an application. Consequently, building the class hierarchy requires a certain amount of planning. However, this process is closely connected with problem analysis, because an object model describes the problem, not the solution. The market offers various tools that enable object-oriented analysis and modeling for application developers. Many of these tools are based on UML, a standardized analysis and design method; Grady Booch [1996] played a significant role in its development.

Framework for object-oriented implementation

Once a developer creates an object model and users approve it, the model provides a framework for object-oriented implementation. In fact, a good modeling tool can generate a class hierarchy automatically from the model.

Once a class hierarchy is in place, we have a complete definition of the modules (i.e., objects) and interfaces for an application. The actual development work can now begin: at this point, developers write code for object methods, thus fleshing out a functioning application from a model. The grid provided by the class hierarchy helps structure this process and, if necessary, subdivide it over a larger development team.

Finally, developers can create a front end with graphic tools such as Visual Basic for a Windows GUI or Dreamweaver for a browser-based user interface. The user uses this front end to communicate with the application.

The procedure for developing object-oriented applications

In closing, the procedure for developing object-oriented applications can be summarized as four somewhat simplified steps:
1. Create an object model
2. Define object classes
3. Write methods
4. Write a front end

Those are exactly the steps we followed in Section 1.5 to create our first Caché application. The subsequent chapters will look at each step in detail.

3 The Caché Object Model

3.1 Introduction

Most developers today are eager to apply various types of object technologies to the design and implementation of new business applications. The reality, however, is that most business environments have legacy and other installed applications that rely on relational databases, and the relational data model cannot be ignored when designing new applications that must integrate with this existing environment.

Another barrier to the adoption of object-oriented approaches to data management concerns queries. Structured query language (SQL) is a popular standard widely used by developers and application interfaces. SQL is essential to important IT functions such as reporting and data analysis, and it is a common component of high-performance online transaction processing (OLTP) systems.

Consequently, many database architects and application developers view their decision as "SQL versus objects." Either they decide that data requirements merit an object database (which usually means that application development must start from scratch) or they decide to retain their investment in relational databases (in which case, the advantages of object technology are limited from the outset).

SQL versus objects?

To resolve this dilemma, Caché integrates the two worlds: *Unified Data Architecture* provides an integrated description layer for objects and tables, which are represented directly in a transactional multidimensional database engine. By supporting data views and interfaces for both object and relational data models, UDA provides native data access for new and existing object or relational applications.

Unified Data Architecture

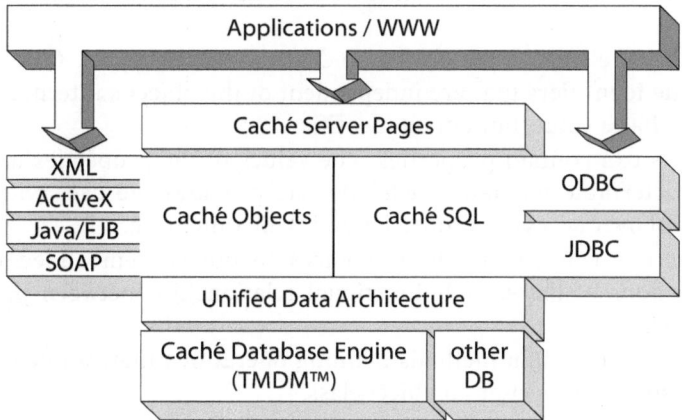

Figure 3.1 Caché system architecture

This chapter describes the object-oriented aspects of Unified Data Architecture (as a group also referred to as "Caché Objects"). Chapter 6 describes the use of persistent objects. Chapter 8 provides a detailed description of Caché SQL.

3.1.1 Characteristics of Caché Objects

ODMG Standard of the Object Data Management Group

The Caché object model adheres to the ODMG Standard from the Object Data Management Group (Cattel et al. [1997]). The basic operations for Caché Objects are based on object classes defined in Caché Studio and the subsequent compilation of these to produce runtime executables. Caché supports all principles of modern object technology for creating, storing, loading, and manipulating object instances:

Inheritance means the capability of deriving one object class from another. The new, subordinate class has an "is a" relationship to the higher-level class and inherits all general properties and methods. These can be further specialized, and new properties and methods that apply only to the derived class can be added. Caché Objects also support multiple inheritance in which a class can be derived from more than one higher-level class.

Polymorphism means that a single method can be included in objects of different classes so that the method executes differently per class. Polymorphism makes Caché Objects applications fully independent of the internal implementation of methods in each object class.

Several types of object persistence

Persistence is the most important property of an object database. It means that objects are permanently recorded on storage media and can be retrieved quickly and easily when needed. Caché Objects supports several types of object persistence—automatic storage in the multidimensional data model of Caché, user-defined storage in arbitrary structures, and storage using Caché SQL Gateway in tables of external relational databases. This enables developers to choose the optimal storage solution for each class, depending on the customer's requirements.

In addition to these basic concepts, the Caché object model has the following characteristics:

- Classes are determined by class definitions stored in the class dictionary.
- The basic elements are objects and literals (data types). Objects have unique identifiers that are independent of the object's internal state. A literal has a value, but not an identifier.
- Classes can contain properties. The values of the properties of an object determine its state. Caché Objects provides the user with direct control over access to properties and their validation.
- Properties can be literals, references to objects, embedded objects, collections of these, or bidirectional relationships between persistent objects.
- Classes can contain methods defining operations that can be executed for a specific object or an object class.

- Classes can contain method generators. These special methods are used for the compilation of classes to generate the actual method code that the class uses at runtime.
- Caché can automatically manage many general behavior characteristics of the objects (registered classes). Alternatively, the user can largely define the behavior (non-registered classes).
- Caché Objects stores persistent objects in the database using a storage strategy specified by the user.
- Classes can be further specialized using additional keywords and parameters.

3.1.2 Components of Caché Objects

The following table specifies the Caché Objects components:

Component	Description
Caché Studio	Caché Studio is an integrated GUI development environment for defining classes, their properties and methods. These definitions can either be made using forms and menus, or be programmed in the Caché Class Definition Language (CDL). In addition, Caché Studio can be used to create CSP pages and to program routines in Caché ObjectScript or Caché Basic.
Class Dictionary	The Class Dictionary serves as a universal repository that contains the definitions of all Caché classes. The remaining Caché Objects components use an API (Application Program Interface) to communicate with the Class Dictionary. The Class Dictionary can be created with Caché Studio or generated from XML, CDL, DDL or other file formats. It can also be exported in various formats.
Class Compiler	The Class Compiler compiles a class definition into application code that can be executed as a runtime module.
Macro Preprocessor	The Macro Preprocessor processes all source code written in Caché ObjectScript. It is responsible for resolving macros and embedded SQL, and replacing these with valid Caché ObjectScript code.
Caché Object Server for ActiveX	Caché Object Server for ActiveX is an ActiveX Automation Server that represents Caché objects externally as native ActiveX objects. The use of the ActiveX interface makes it possible for development tools such as Visual Basic, C++ , etc., to work with Caché objects, to set their properties, and to execute their methods.
Caché Object Server for Java	Caché Object Server for Java makes Caché objects available for Java applications.

Table 3.1 Components of Caché Objects

3.2 Class Types

Caché always differentiates between data type classes and object classes. Data type classes represent literals such as strings, integers, or other data types defined by the user.

Figure 3.2 Caché class types

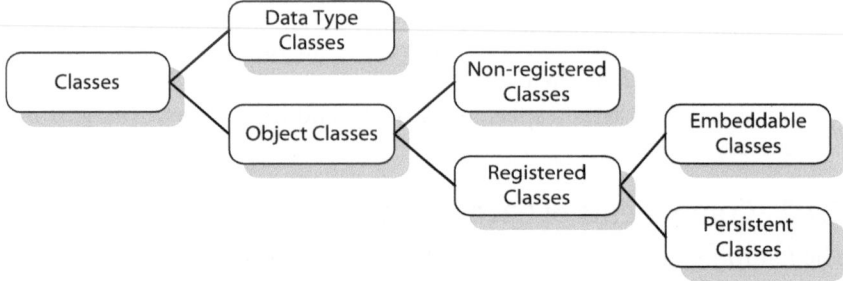

Object classes contain objects and are further subdivided into registered and non-registered classes. Non-registered classes do not provide their own behavior; the developer must create all the associated methods. In contrast, Caché provides registered classes with a comprehensive set of built-in functions. For example, the method %New() creates a new instance of a class.

A registered object class is transient, in that it has no code to store information in the database. Caché automatically creates storage methods for embeddable and persistent classes.

Whereas objects of embeddable classes can be stored only embedded in a persistent object, persistent objects have their own object identifier and so can be stored independently in the database.

3.2.1 Data Type Classes

Data type classes are special classes that define and maintain literal values. In contrast to object classes, data types have no independent identity and cannot be instantiated. They exist only as properties for objects that contain these literals.

Methods for the validation and conversion of values

Data type classes provide a specific set of methods for the validation and conversion of values. They cannot contain properties.

3.2.2 Object Classes

The creation of an object is called instantiation

An object class defines the data structure and the behavior of objects of a type. These objects are called instances of their associated class; the creation of an object is called *instantiation*.

Each object class has a unique class name, as well as properties, methods, and keywords that determine the general behavior of the class.

3.2.3 Non-Registered Object Classes

Object identity and object reference

Caché does not automatically manage instances of non-registered classes. Here, the developer is responsible for the provision and administration of the object identifier (OID) and the object reference (OREF). Because self-administered OREFs are not registered in Caché, non-registered classes have a few limitations:

- The system does not allocate storage for the values of the object.
- Swizzling (the automatic reloading of referenced objects) is not supported.
- Polymorphism is not supported.
- Variables that contain references to non-registered objects must be declared explicitly with the associated class type.

3.2.4 Registered Object Classes

Registered object classes have a complete set of methods that control the object behavior in storage. They automatically inherit these methods from the `%RegisteredObject` system class. Because instances of registered object classes exist only temporarily in the memory area of a process, these are called transient objects. In contrast, the embeddable and persistent object classes described in the following two sections are stored permanently in the database.

%RegisteredObject system class

Caché handles the creation of newly registered objects and the management of the storage space. It also provides an object reference (OREF) that can reference the object in memory. Registered classes support polymorphism.

3.2.5 Embeddable Object Classes

The instances of embeddable object classes can be stored temporarily in memory, as well as permanently in the database. These classes inherit their behavior from the Caché `%SerialObject` system class. This behavior allows instances to exist in memory independent of other objects. However, they can be stored in the database only embedded in other objects. Caché provides embeddable object classes with two capabilities:

%SerialObject system class

- The capability to create a string that contains the complete state (the values of all properties) of the object. The creation of this string is called *serialization*.

Serialization

- The capability to automatically read a serialized string from the database when needed and to represent it as an independent object in memory. This automatic reloading of associated objects is called *swizzling*.

Swizzling

Embedded objects are treated differently in memory as compared to the database:

Different treatment in memory and in the database

- An embedded object in memory is treated as a separate object and does not differ from a reference to any other object type. The value of an embedded object in memory is the object reference (OREF) to the representation of the object in memory.

• An embedded object in the database is stored serialized as part of the enclosing object. The object does not have its own identity (OID) and cannot be used by other objects without the enclosing object.

Figure 3.3 "Address" embedded object class

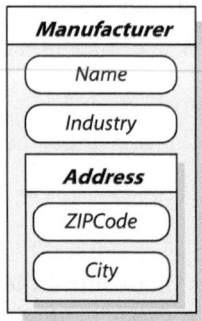

"Manufacturer" object class

A "Manufacturer" object class serves here as an example. A manufacturer has properties such as "Name" and "Industry," as well as an address with "ZIPCode" and "City." Naturally, you could define these properties of the address directly as a number of properties of the "Manufacturer" class. Initially, this appears to be sensible, because the address also represents a property of the manufacturer and should not exist independent of it. However, other objects also have addresses—for example, suppliers, customers, or persons. Consequently, defining the "Address" concept once enables its reuse in various object classes.

Modification effort is minimized

This is achieved when the definition of the "Manufacturer" class embeds a previously defined "Address" object class. On the one hand, the "Address" object class can also be used in the "Supplier," "Customer," and "Person" classes, and so create a standard for application development. On the other hand, modification effort is minimized should the format of the postal code change or a new property need to be added (such as "email," for example).

3.2.6 Persistent Object Classes

%Persistent system class

Persistent object classes have a comprehensive behavior for the permanent storage of their instances in the database. They inherit this behavior from the Caché system class %Persistent.

Persistent objects have an object identity and a unique object identifier (OID). Each persistent object can be stored independently in Caché. The use of a persistent object as a property of an object class is called a reference to a persistent object.

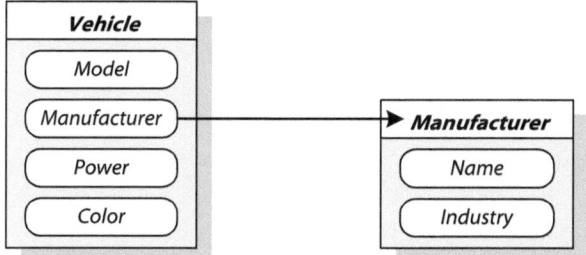

Figure 3.4 Reference to the "Manufacturer" persistent object

Thus, for example, the manufacturer of a vehicle is defined as a persistent "Manufacturer" object class. If you give the "Manufacturer" property of the "Vehicle" class the "Manufacturer" type, you are referencing a persistent object. Every instance of the "Vehicle" class can now reference an instance of the "Manufacturer" class. However, every manufacturer exists independent of whether and by how many vehicles it is referenced.

From the viewpoint of the "Vehicle" class, the properties and methods of the referenced manufacturer can be used in the same manner as its own properties and methods. When needed, Caché uses *swizzling* to bring the referenced objects into memory.

3.3 Elements of Classes

A class definition determines the type of the class and its behavior. This definition always consists of the properties and methods of the class. (Note because data type classes cannot be instantiated, they possess methods but no properties.) However, the complete definition of a class requires additional functional elements such as queries and indexes, and qualifying parameters and keywords. The complete list of the elements of a class definition (altogether called *class members*) includes:

List of the elements of a class definition

- a unique class name
- keywords—a number of keywords that modify the class definition
- properties—these contain the data (also called state) of the instances of a class. Properties can be literals, references to persistent objects, embedded objects, or bidirectional relationships between persistent objects. Data type classes do not contain any properties.
- methods—code that provides functionality
- parameters—values that modify the behavior of the class during compilation (typically using method generators)
- queries—set operations on object instances
- indexes—storage structures that optimize the access to objects

Every element of a class is identified by a unique name. Although Caché Objects supports uppercase and lowercase alphabetic letters (to increase readability), it normalizes names to uppercase. Hence, naming conventions must take this into consideration. Names prefixed with the percent character are reserved for system classes.

Identification through the use of unique names

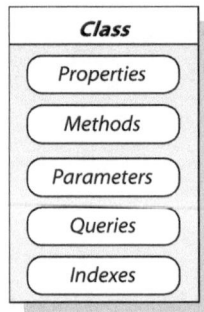

Figure 3.5 Class elements

3.3.1 Keywords

A number of keywords can modify the definition of a class. All keywords are optional and have a default value when they are omitted.

Keywords in the Class Definition Language (CDL)

Keywords are primarily required for the development of class definitions using Caché's Class Definition Language (CDL). Because Caché Object Architect represents the keywords with user interface controls (such as selection fields, checkboxes, etc.), you do not need to remember the names of keywords.

In addition to keywords for classes, the Caché object model also has keywords for properties, methods, queries, and indexes.

3.3.2 Properties

Properties represent the state of objects

Properties represent the state of an object. When representing state with contained values (either literal values or object references), these are called properties. Alternatively, properties can be used as relationships to maintain bidirectional connections between persistent objects. The Caché object model and its class definitions permit access to and manipulation of both kinds of properties.

Principles of public properties

Some object-oriented languages—such as Java and C++—do not support an equivalent concept of properties. Instead, these languages support a combination of private variables and public methods that are used to access properties. Caché provides a rich object model with public properties according to the following principles:

- Properties can be literals, references to persistent objects, embedded objects, streams (also known as binary large objects or BLOBs), collections of literals or objects, or bidirectional relationships between persistent objects.
- The properties have a set of automatically created methods used to validate and store values.
- Transparent format conversions and other data transformations can be performed during access to the values of properties and their storage.
- Referenced and embedded objects are automatically brought into memory when an access is made to the associated properties (called swizzling).

Properties have a unique name, a data type, an optional list of keywords, and an optional list of parameters valid for each data type.

3.3.2.1 Visibility of Properties

Properties can be designated as being either *public* or *private*. When a property is private, only methods of the same object class as the property can access it. Public properties—the default—can be accessed without restriction.

Properties: public or private

Private properties are inherited and are also visible within subclasses. Some other languages call this behavior *protected*.

3.3.2.2 Behavior of Properties

A number of methods are automatically associated with properties. These methods are not derived using simple inheritance. Rather, Caché has a special mechanism to create these special properties methods.

Every property inherits its own set of methods from two different sources:

- The general behavior, depending on the type of the property, is inherited from a properties class. These are, for example, the required Get(), Set(), and validation methods.

Properties class

- Type-specific behavior, depending on the data type of the property, is inherited from a data type class. Many of these methods are method generators, which, for example, also permit a minimum and maximum value to be specified for an Integer type property.

Data type class

Figure 3.6 Class compiler and the behavior of properties

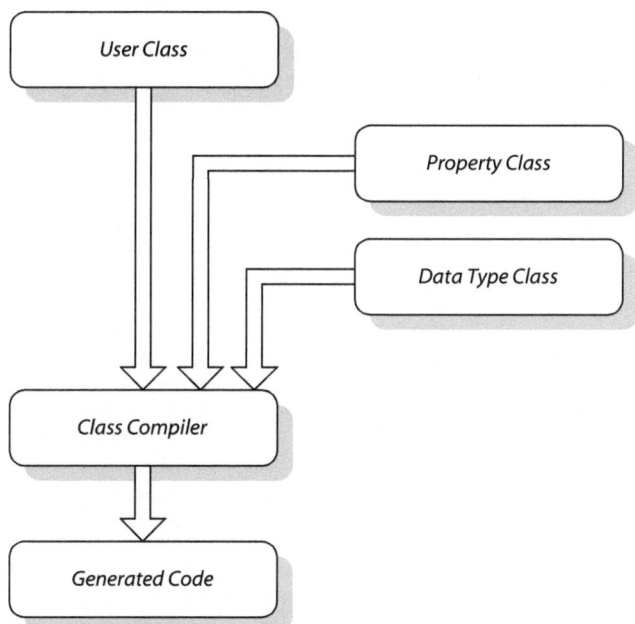

All properties classes are system classes. The user cannot specify or change the behavior of these classes.

3.3.2.3 Data Types

Caché supports an unlimited number of data types for the properties of object classes, where each data type also represents a class. Developers can implement their own data types (so-called Advanced Data Types or ADTs) by defining the appropriate data type classes. Data type classes also control the behavior of object properties when these are represented as columns of relational tables using SQL.

Data type classes provide the following functionality:

- They perform the necessary conversions of literal values between storage (in the database), logical (in memory), and display formats.
- They perform a validatino of literal values which can be further specified using parameters of the data type class.
- They ensure interoperability with SQL, ODBC, ActiveX, Java, and XML by providing required logical operations and data transformations.

Although data types are a special form of a class definition, they exhibit some fundamental differences compared to object classes:

- Data type classes cannot be used to form instances.
- Data type classes cannot contain properties.
- The data type interface hides data type class methods.

Caché base data types

Caché provides a number of base data types. The following table provides an overview:

Table 3.2 Caché base data types

Data type	Meaning	Optional parameters
%Binary	Binary data	MINLEN—minimum length in bytes MAXLEN—maximum length in bytes, default: 50
%Boolean	Boolean value (truth value, 0 or 1)	
%Currency	Currency	MINVAL—minimum value MAXVAL—maximum value FORMAT—format as argument of the $FNumber function (refer to Section 5.1.4.2)
%Date	Date (the logical format represents the number of days since December 31, 1840)	MINVAL—minimum value MAXVAL—maximum value FORMAT—format as argument of the $ZDate function (refer to Section 5.1.4.4)
%Float	Floating-point number	MINVAL—minimum value MAXVAL—maximum value FORMAT—format as argument of the $FNumber function (refer to Section 5.1.4.2) SCALE—number of decimal digits
%Integer	Integer	MINVAL—minimum value MAXVAL—maximum value FORMAT—format as argument of

		the $FNumber function (refer to Section 5.1.4.2)
%List	Data in the Caché-specific $List format	ODBCDELIMITER—delimiter used when the value is provided by ODBC as a list separated by delimiters, default: ","
%Name	Name in the format "last name, first name"	MAXLEN—maximum length, default: 25
%Numeric	Fixed-point value	MINVAL—minimum value MAXVAL—maximum value FORMAT—format as argument of the $FNumber function (refer to Section 5.1.4.2) SCALE—number of decimal digits, default: 2
%Status	Status/Error Code	
%String	String	MINLEN—minimum length in characters MAXLEN—maximum length in characters, default: 50 TRUNCATE—1, when the string is to be truncated to the maximum length (default), otherwise 0 PATTERN—permitted format as argument of the pattern match operator (refer to Section 5.1.2.2)
%Time	Time (the logical format represents the number of seconds since midnight)	MINVAL—minimum value MAXVAL—maximum value FORMAT—format as argument of the $ZTime function (refer to Section 5.1.4.4)
%TimeStamp	Timestamp consisting of date and time (YYYY-MM-DD HH:MM:SS)	MINVAL—minimum value MAXVAL—maximum value

Data formats and transformation methods for data type classes

Caché distinguishes between four different data formats in processing literals. The following table provides an overview:

Data format	Meaning
Display	The format with which information is presented to or entered by the user.
Logical	The internal representation of information in memory; also the basis for operations such as data comparisons.
Storage	The format used to store information in the database.
ODBC	The format used by ODBC and SQL to represent the information.

Table 3.3 Caché data formats

When the "logical" data format is considered as being the center, there are six transformations to and from the other three formats:

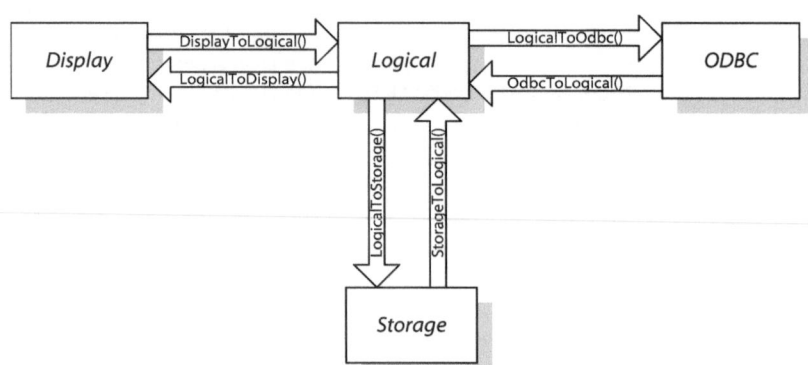

Figure 3.7 Data formats and their transformations

Caché automatically provides the appropriate transformation methods for the supplied base data types. If a developer defines a new data type class, the developer must give it the following transformation methods:

Table 3.4 Transformation methods for data types

Method	Meaning
DisplayToLogical()	Transforms a displayable value into internal format.
LogicalToDisplay()	Transforms an internal value into display format.
LogicalToOdbc()	Transforms an internal value into ODBC format (optional).
OdbcToLogical()	Transforms an ODBC value into internal format (optional).
LogicalToStorage()	Transforms an internal value into database format (optional).
StorageToLogical()	Transforms a database value into internal format (optional).

These methods serve as the basis for the creation of properties methods in the associated object classes. For example, consider a Person object class with a DOB property of the %Date data type. Caché automatically generates the DOBDisplayToLogical() methods, etc., for the Person class and uses these for the corresponding transformations.

Validation methods for data type classes

IsValidDT() *method*

In addition to the transformation methods, every data type class also has an IsValidDT() method that checks whether a specified value is valid for the particular data type. The first character of the value returned by the method contains 1 (for "valid") or 0 (for "invalid").

Table 3.5 Validation methods for data types

Method	Meaning
IsValidDT()	Checks whether the value is valid for the data type.

When the data type is used to define a property for an object class, Caché creates an appropriate properties method. In the Person object class example described above, this would have the name DOBIsValidDT(). Caché automatically invokes this properties method to validate values.

Client data types, ODBC types and SQL categories

The definition of data types assumes special importance when data are exchanged with other applications using Java, ActiveX, ODBC, or SQL. This requires that the data type of the associated application type is defined for each Caché data type. Certain keywords are used in the Caché data type classes for this purpose.

Keyword	Meaning
CLIENTDATATYPE	Specifies the data type in which values are to be displayed for Java or ActiveX clients.
ODBCTYPE	Specifies the ODBC data type to be used to exchange values using ODBC.
SQLCATEGORY	Defines the SQL category that SQL Tools use to compare data, for sorting, etc.

Table 3.6 Keywords for data type classes

Developers who define their own data types must specify these keywords. The keywords have defaults for the Caché built-in base data types:

Caché data type	CLIENTDATATYPE	ODBCTYPE	SQLCATEGORY
%Binary	BINARY	BINARY	STRING
%Boolean	INTEGER	INTEGER	INTEGER
%Currency	CURRENCY	CURRENCY	CURRENCY
%Date	DATE	DATE	DATE
%Float	DOUBLE	DOUBLE	DOUBLE
%Integer	INTEGER	INTEGER	INTEGER
%List	LIST	VARCHAR	STRING
%Name	VARCHAR	VARCHAR	NAME
%Numeric	NUMERIC	NUMERIC	NUMERIC
%String	VARCHAR	VARCHAR	STRING
%Time	TIME	TIME	TIME
%TimeStamp	TIMESTAMP	TIMESTAMP	TIMESTAMP

Table 3.7 Predefined keywords for Caché data types

Multiple-choice values

Caché has a convention for defining properties with multiple-choice values (so-called enumerated properties, which are selected from a list of predefined values). The following table illustrates this technique using the VALUELIST and DISPLAYLIST class parameters:

Class parameter	Meaning
VALUELIST	This contains the list of internal values. The first character of the list is also the delimiter. Example: "*C*M*Y*K"
DISPLAYLIST	This contains the list of values that can be displayed. The first character of the list is also the delimiter. Example: ",cyan,magenta,yellow,black"

Table 3.8 VALUELIST and DISPLAYLIST class parameters

Multiple-choice values function by convention, meaning that user-written LogicalToDisplay(), DisplayToLogical(), and IsValidDT() methods must check the existence of the two class parameters and use their value lists. The methods for Caché's built-in data type classes function accordingly.

3.3.2.4 Property Types

Properties can be literals (that is, simple values of data types), as well as references to objects, embedded objects, streams (BLOBs), various types of collections or multidimensional values, or bidirectional relationships between persistent objects.

Literals

%Integer, %Date and %String types

In its simplest form, a property can have the type %Integer, %Date, %String, or any other Caché built-in data type class or user-defined data type class. The data type class linked with the property controls the behavior of these literals.

Most data type classes also contain parameters that further specialize the data type. For example, using Class Definition Language (CDL), you can specify that the maximum value of a Count integer property be 100, as in the following example:

```
Property Count As %Integer(MAXVAL = 100);
```

References to objects

Every class is a valid data type in Caché

Every class is a valid data type in Caché. If (instead of a data type class), you define a property using a persistent class, you make a reference to a persistent object. In this case, the values of the property are references to the instances of the object class. For example, you can define a Manufacturer property that makes a reference to a persistent User.Manufacturer object class:

```
Property Manufacturer As User. Manufacturer;
```

Embedded objects

Embedded objects function similarly to references to objects. The principal difference is that, as a data type, they use an embeddable object class instead of a persistent object class.

Thus, the values of this property reference the corresponding object embedded in the referencing object instead of an independent object instance. Syntactically, the definition is identical to a reference to an object class:

```
Property Address As User.Address;
```

Streams

CHARACTERSTREAM and BINARYSTREAM data types

A stream (also called a *binary large object*, or *BLOB*) is a large unstructured data object that is stored in a database. Streams are typically used to store documents, technical drawings, and pictures. Because they can be very large, Caché does not handle streams as atomic information; instead, Caché provides methods that applications can use to read and write the data in a block-oriented fashion. According to their content, Caché distinguishes between streams of the type CHARACTERSTREAM (consisting of characters) and BINARYSTREAM (consisting of binary data).

Depending on a property's definition, Caché automatically stores streams in the database or in files at the operating system level. Setting the STORAGE parameter to the value GLOBAL or FILE makes this distinction. By setting the parameter LOCATION, you can specify the name of the database global or the file system directory where you want the streams to be saved.

STORAGE *and* LOCATION *parameters*

Collections

Caché represents properties with repeated values as collections. There are two kinds: array collections (sorted using a key) and list collections (sequenced lists). Collections can contain literals, embedded objects, and references to objects.

A collection inherits its basic behavior from a special system class that is dependent on the type of the included data:

Type	Array Collection	List Collection
Literal	%ArrayOfDataTypes	%ListOfDataTypes
Embedded object	%ArrayOfObjects	%ListOfObjects
Reference to object	%ArrayOfObjects	%ListOfObjects

Table 3.9 Collection types

Array Collections

Caché orders elements in an array using a key.

Key	Value
Hart	7/24/1960
Hoffmann	6/30/1963
Huber	8/7/1942
Meier	9/29/1959
Miller	2/13/1958
Smith	10/21/1958
Schulz	6/1/1950
...	...

Table 3.10 Array Collection with literals

The following definition specifies the array used in the previous example:

```
Property DOB As %Date [ Collection = array ];
```

Caché provides a method that adds new elements with a key to an array at the appropriate position. Other methods read an element from its position determined by a key and locate the next or previous element.

Elements can be embedded objects or references to persistent objects. The next example shows references to persistent objects:

```
Property Person As User.Person [ Collection = array ];
```

In this example, the elements of the array collection are references to objects of the Person (persistent) class, instead of the literals seen in other examples.

Table 3.11 Array Collection with references to objects

Key	Reference
Hart	Person 5
Hoffmann	Person 4
Huber	Person 2
Meier	Person 6
Miller	Person 3
Smith	Person 7
Schulz	Person 1
...	...

List Collection

A list collection represents an ordered list of elements in which every element is determined by its position.

Table 3.12 List Collection with literals

Position	Value
1	Meier
2	Miller
3	Hoffmann
4	Smith
5	Hart
6	Schulz
...	...
n	Huber

The following example defines the above table:

```
Property Name As %String [ Collection = list ];
```

Adding new elements

Caché provides methods for inserting new elements at any position in a list or appending elements at the end of a list. Other methods return an element located at a specific position, find the next or previous element, and determine the position of an element.

Elements of a list collection can also be embedded objects or references to persistent objects. The following example illustrates elements that refer to persistent objects:

```
Property Person As User.Person [ Collection = list ];
```

Table 3.13 List collection with references to objects

Position	Value
1	Person 6
2	Person 3
3	Person 4
4	Person 7
5	Person 5
6	Person 1
...	...
n	Person 2

Multidimensional properties

Properties can be multidimensional. A multidimensional property behaves like a multidimensional variable, namely the code can traverse and parse it with $Order and other functions usually applied to multidimensional variables. (Refer to Section 7.1 for a discussion of multidimensional variables.)

For example, consider a multidimensional property called Children.

Operations on multidimensional properties

```
Property Children As %String [ MultiDimensional ];
```

All functions that are typically applied to multidimensional variables can also be applied to the multidimensional property Children.

```
$Data(person.Children)
Set person.Children(2)="Sophie"
$Get(person.Children(1))
$Order(person.Children(""),-1)
Merge children=person.Children
Kill person.Children
```

Multidimensional properties are transient by default, that is, they do not have an automatic database representation. Furthermore, you cannot store multidimensional properties in SQL tables or represent them as fields in SQL tables. Because of these restrictions, the use of multidimensional properties is largely limited to representing existing multidimensional data structures. For developing new applications, it is often better to use Collections instead, as these are not subject to the previously mentioned restrictions.

Use of multidimensional properties vs. collections

Relationships

Relationships are bidirectional connections between persistent objects. In many respects, a relationship is similar to two persistent objects that use references to refer to each other. However, because relationships automatically guarantee referential integrity, deleting one object does not result in the other one referring to a nonexistent object.

Caché supports two types of relationships: *one-to-many* (independent objects) and *parent-child* (the child object is dependent on the parent object). On each side of the relationship is a persistent object class, which can be one and the same class.

Types of relationships

Within each respective object class, the relationship behaves like properties that form an object reference. One side (*many* or *child*) is just like a simple property; the other side (*one* or *parent*) is like a collection, and is managed from the %RelationshipObject system class. Relationships are completely transparent: a change made to one side immediately affects the other side as well.

3.3.2.5 Storage of Properties

The Caché object model gives users control over the storage of values for object properties. By default, Caché stores the value of a property—irrespective whether literal, embedded object, or reference to a persistent object—as part of the on-disk representation of the object. The value is also part of an object's representation in memory, although the value has a different format for each location. The value is stored on disk in a storage format, whereas its representation in memory is in an internal or logical format.

The two formats are usually identical. Even so, the representation of an object instance in the database can differ completely from the representation in memory. Furthermore, the use of different keywords for properties can affect the formats of the value both in storage and in memory.

Table 3.14 Representation of properties in memory and in the database

Type of the property	In memory	On disk
Simple	Internal format	Storage format
Transient	Internal format	N/A
Calculated	N/A	N/A
Multidimensional	Multidimensional array	N/A

Transient properties

Transient properties can store temporary values

Individual properties of persistent classes can be *transient*. These properties are then not stored with an instance when it is stored in the database. Transient properties are particularly useful when you need to store temporary values while working with an instance of a persistent class. Obviously, you could also use local variables in this situation, but the local variables would not be assigned to a specific instance.

Calculated properties

Calculation of a property at runtime

A property can also be *calculated;* in other words, the value of the property is calculated at runtime; the developer must provide an appropriate Get() method. For example, you could define an Age property that does not have a stored value, but each time it is accessed it calculates a person's age from his or her date of birth and the current date. The property must have an AgeGet() method that performs the appropriate calculation.

3.3.3 Methods

Methods designate the operations that an object or an object class can execute. Every method has a unique name, a formal specification of its arguments and return value, and the method code.

3.3.3.1 Arguments and Return Values for Methods

Formal list of the arguments

Every method has a formal list of arguments that are passed to it when the method is invoked at runtime. The list specifies all possible arguments, each with its expected data type and an optional default value. If no data type is specified, %String is assumed. The list can be empty, in which case the method expects no arguments. On the other hand, not all arguments need to be specified for the call, in which case they remain undefined or—when present—are assigned a default value.

By default, arguments are passed as values using a *call by value*. If you prefix an argument in the formal list with an ampersand (&), the call is expected to be made as a *call by reference*, namely with a reference to the passed variable.

3.3 Elements of Classes

In addition to the arguments used to pass values to a method, every method can also have a return value that it returns to its caller. The return value can have any data type. The frequently used %Status type can return information about the success of the method call.

Type %Status

3.3.3.2 Visibility of Methods

Methods can be defined either as being *public* or *private*. When methods are *private*, they can be invoked only by methods that belong to the class. In contrast, methods declared as *public* can be invoked without restriction.

In the Caché object model, *private* methods are inherited, visible, and usable within the subclasses. Some other languages designate this method behavior as *protected*.

3.3.3.3 Class Methods and Instance Methods

Methods are further subdivided into class methods and instance methods. The normal case is the instance method, which is usually called simply "method." Instance methods are always invoked for a specific object instance; the reference is passed implicitly. A reference to "self" is available within instance methods using the ##this syntax.

In contrast, the execution of class methods does not reference a specific object instance. Because class methods are called without passing an object reference, certain restrictions apply:

##this *syntax*

- They do not have ##this syntax.
- There is no access to object properties.
- Instance methods cannot be executed.

However, class methods can access class parameters.

%New() and %Open() are typical representatives of class methods. They create a new object instance and form an instance for a stored object, respectively. Because they themselves must first create the associated instances, it is obvious that these methods cannot be instance methods.

%New *and* %Open

3.3.3.4 Method Languages

The functionality of a method is implemented as program code. Caché supports three programming languages for writing such method code:

- Caché ObjectScript
- Caché Basic
- Java

The associated programming language is selected per method; within a class; methods can be implemented in different programming languages.

Caché ObjectScript and Caché Basic are translated into executable Caché code that runs in the Caché runtime environment. Method code written in Java is exported by the Caché Java binding together with the Java class definition, and run within the Java Virtual Machine.

In this book, we work almost exclusively with Caché ObjectScript.

3.3.3.5 Method Types

The Caché object model provides four different types of methods:

- Code methods
- Expression methods
- Call methods
- Method generators

The method types determine the form of the code generated for methods.

Code methods

Executable code

A code method contains executable code written in Caché ObjectScript, Caché Basic, or Java. In the case of Caché ObjectScript or Caché Basic, the class compiler uses this code to produce an executable routine that is invoked for method calls. Caché ObjectScript code can also contain macros, embedded SQL, embedded HTML, and embedded JavaScript. Java code is executed outside Caché.

Expression methods

Execution of an expression

An expression method contains just a Caché ObjectScript or Caché Basic code expression, not a complete routine. The compilation of the class replaces the method call with this expression, which is then executed at runtime.

An invocation using *call by reference* is not valid. Also, the expression cannot contain any embedded SQL, HTML, or JavaScript.

Call methods

Invoking an existing Caché routine

Call methods invoke an existing Caché routine. Their primary purpose is to enable you to incorporate legacy code in new object-oriented applications. (A call method is sometimes called an *object wrapper*.)

Method generators

Method generators are special methods that contain Caché ObjectScript code which, when executed, generates more Caché ObjectScript code. Method generators are used during the compilation of classes to create the runtime version of the method. They can access settings for class parameters in order to produce appropriate code.

Figure 3.8 Operation of a method generator

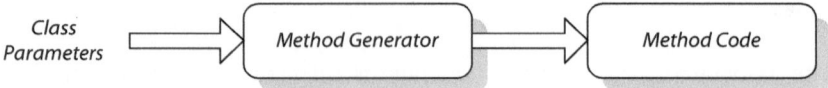

Method generators play an important practical role in the internal use of Caché data type classes and storage classes.

3.3.4 Class Parameters

Class parameters are constants, namely values that are defined for all objects of a class when the class is defined. The value of class parameters cannot be changed at runtime.

In contrast to properties, class parameters can be used within class methods. The values of class parameters are inherited and can be overwritten or extended with additional class parameters in derived classes.

Method generators typically use class parameters during compilation. Method generators use class parameters to control the generation of methods and, optionally, to specialize the behavior of data types.

Each registered object class has, for example, a PROPERTYVALIDATION class parameter. This specifies whether and (if appropriate) when the values of the properties are to be validated. The PROPERTYVALIDATION class parameter can have one of three values:

Validation of data types

- 0 means "no validation"
- 1 means "validate on update"
- 2 is the default and means "validate on save"

If you change these class parameters and recompile the class, the method generators insert the corresponding validation code at the correct location. Thus, class parameters are used to adapt the behavior of classes to the special requirements of the application.

3.3.5 Queries

Queries provide set operations on instances of object classes. If you consider all instances of a class as being a total set and the result of a query as a specific subset of this superset, you can see that queries form a *filter* for objects.

Set operations on instances of object classes

You can write queries in Caché ObjectScript, Caché Basic, or SQL. Caché Studio contains a user-friendly *New Query Wizard* that helps you to create SQL queries.

Caché groups the results of a query as a *result set*, which represents a special interface for processing query results in Caché ObjectScript, Caché Basic, ActiveX, or Java. Queries can also be exposed as *SQL Stored Procedures* or *Views* and so be further processed with SQL.

3.3.6 Indexes

Indexes represent an access path to the instances of a class. Indexes optimize the processing of queries when they are executed.

Access path to the instances of a class

Normally, indexes apply to all instances of a class and its subclasses. Thus, the index of a Person class (which has a Student subclass) includes both persons and students. However, an index of the Student subclass would contain only students.

Every index is sorted according to one or more properties of an object class that define the sorting criteria. The possible sorting criteria include:

- EXACT (exactly as specified)
- UPPER (normalized to uppercase)
- ALPHAUP (normalized to uppercase and all punctuation characters removed)
- SQLSTRING (leading blank spaces removed and empty values sorted as SQL empty string)
- SQLUPPER (leading blank spaces removed, normalized to uppercase and empty values sorted as SQL empty string)
- STRING (leading blank spaces removed; normalized to uppercase and all punctuation removed and empty values sorted as SQL empty string)
- SPACE (force alphabetic sorting, even for numbers)
- PLUS (force numeric sorting, even for strings)
- MINUS (reverse numeric sorting)

In addition to applying properties to sorting, the index can include additional properties as data fields. This makes their values accessible from the index with the consequent performance improvement by avoiding additional data accesses.

3.4   Inheritance

Inheritance is an object-oriented technique for which existing class definitions can be reused in a branched, increasingly specialized class hierarchy. The Caché object model supports all aspects of single and multiple inheritance.

Inheritance of all specifications of an object class

A class inherits all specifications of its super class, including the properties, methods, class parameters, and keywords. In addition to the methods of the super class, every class also inherits special properties-methods from system classes that determine the behavior of properties in general and data types in particular. New elements can be added to a subclass and inherited elements can be changed, provided these have not been designated as *Final*. Note that inherited elements cannot be deleted from a subclass.

3.4.1   Single Inheritance

Single inheritance: inheritance from a single super class

In single inheritance, a class inherits its elements from a single super class.

Let us consider the following example: a Person class has Name and DOB properties. A Student class inherits from this class. That is, a student is also a person with name and date of birth. The subclass automatically inherits these properties (together with all other elements) from the Person class. In addition, student-specific properties, such as a matriculation number, are also defined in the Student class. Student is now a derived and further specialized class of the Person class.

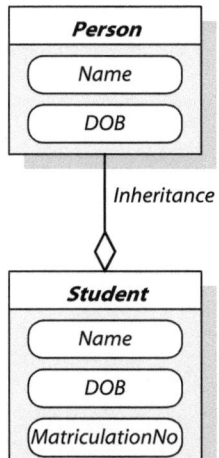

Figure 3.9 Example for inheritance

Every instance of a derived class is automatically also an instance of its super class. Consequently, we can now open an object of the Student class (derived from the Person class) and reference it as a person.

```
>Set pers=##class(User.Person).%OpenId(id)
>write pers.Name
Miller,John
```

Obviously, we can also access this object as a student:

```
>write pers.MatriculationNo
2002-09-016
```

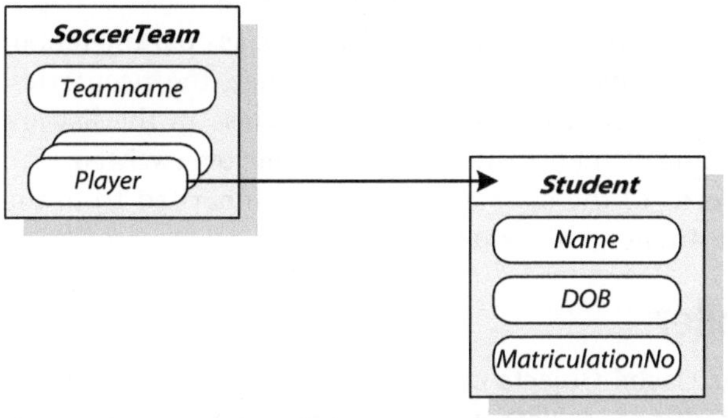

Figure 3.10 Use of the "Student" subclass in place of the "Person" super class

Similarly, we can reference a member of the Student class from a class that has a reference to the persistent Person class. There is a "student *is a* person" relationship between the Person super class and the Student subclass.

3.4.2 Multiple Inheritance

In multiple inheritance, a class inherits its behavior and structure from several super classes. We achieve this in Caché by specifying a list of super classes.

Multiple inheritance: inheritance from several super classes

Figure 3.11 Example of multiple
inheritance

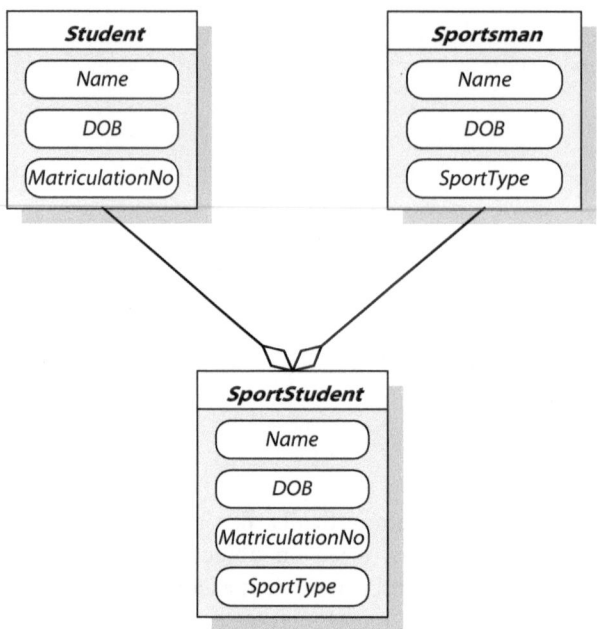

For example, a student can also be a sportsperson. When we create a new
SportStudent class with the Student and Sportsman super classes to
manage sports students, SportStudent inherits the properties and methods from both classes.

However, this introduces conflicts, in that both classes have the properties Name and DOB. How is this conflict resolved in Caché?

The keywords for classes, properties, methods, and class parameters of
the first super class in the list are inherited first. Then the properties,
methods, and class parameters from the next super class in the list are
inherited, and any existing elements with the same name overwritten.

Note that the keywords of the class are exclusively inherited from the
first super class and so are not overwritten.

3.5 Class Compiler

*Compile objects into executable
application routines*

The class compiler for Caché Objects compiles class definitions into executable application routines. A class must be compiled before it can be
used.

The class compiler lets you select just those classes you want compiled.
You can specify a single class, modified classes only, or all classes. If a
single class is compiled, the class compiler first checks whether the super
classes for this class have been changed since the last compilation (or
have never been compiled). If necessary, any modified classes inherited
by the compiled class are also compiled automatically.

4 Defining Classes

4.1 Introduction

Object classes are typically defined in Caché using *Caché Studio,* an integrated development environment for defining object classes. Caché's *Unified Data Architecture* automatically generates tables (complete with columns and key fields) from all class definitions, their properties and methods. The complete definition is made using the Class Definition Language (CDL) of Caché and is stored in the database in some internal format. Export functions are available for various class definition formats commonly used in the OO world. Additionally, *RoseCachéLink* provides a direct bidirectional interface to *Rational Rose*, the visual modeling tool (based on the object-oriented standard language *UML*) from Rational Software.

Caché Studio

Data definitions in Caché do not need to adhere to the object-oriented paradigm. Unified Data Architecture allows definitions of existing relational tables to be imported, from which it automatically creates an appropriate class hierarchy. When designing relational data structures for Caché, developers typically depend on the *Data Definition Language (DDL)* that Caché fully supports. If you wish, you can use third-party relational modeling tools to design a data model for Caché. However, if you intend only to apply existing definitions and data to Caché, a more practical method is available: Caché SQL Manager provides a special *Data Migration Wizard* that uses ODBC to import existing table definitions and data directly from relational databases (refer to Section 8.4).

Migrating existing relational tables

4.2 Caché Studio

You start Caché Studio from the Caché Cube in the system tray of your Windows desktop. It requires a connection to a Caché server. Readers who completed online the example presented in Chapter 1 already have established this connection for the local server.

Caché Studio is a central workbench that Caché developers use to perform all tasks, starting with creating and managing classes, routines and CSP pages, and ending with debugging and managing the source code.

Central workbench for Caché developers

Figure 4.1 Caché Studio

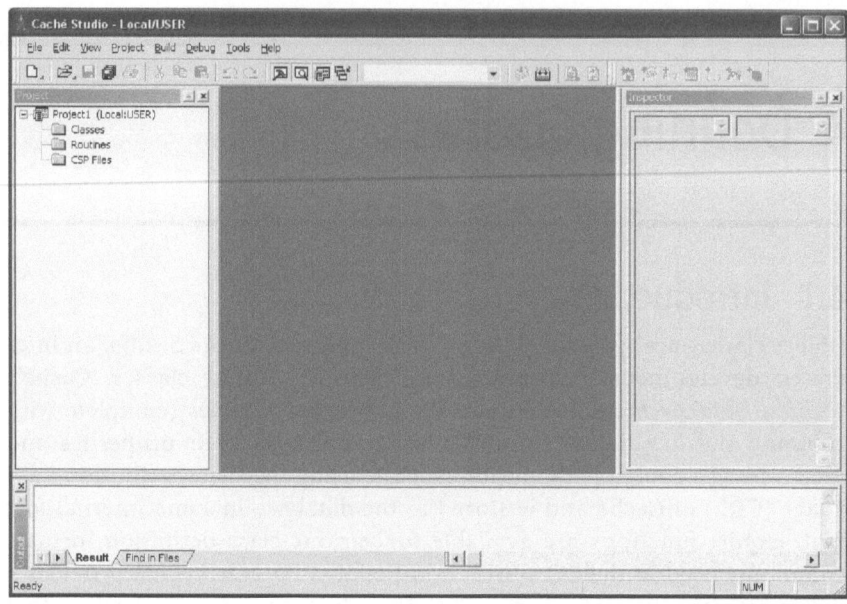

Projects   When Caché Studio is started, it opens a window that is divided into four
sections. On the left-hand side, the current project is shown with its contents displayed in a tree-like hierarchy. Projects in Caché Studio enable
you to group different components that constitute an application or other
development project and to manage them as a unit. Projects can contain
classes, routines and CSP files, all of which must originate from the same
namespace. Any of these elements can also be concurrently part of several
projects.

The large, middle area of the main window is empty when a new project is opened. This is Caché Studio's workspace, and is the only area that
cannot be hidden. As soon as a class, routine, or CSP page is opened, the
corresponding code is displayed here where it can be edited.

On the right-hand side, the *Inspector* displays the definitions of the object classes and their elements in table form.

The *Output* window is located at the bottom of the main window. It
displays the results of several Caché Studio actions, such as the compiling
classes.

You can show or hide the different areas from the *View* menu by clicking *Project, Inspector, Output,* and *Watch* (another window that is hidden
by default and is used for debugging purposes).

Wizards   At the top of the window, under the menu bar, another tool bar contains several groups of buttons. For example, the group on the far right
represents the *Wizards* that we will use to define classes.

4.2.1 Packages

Before we start defining classes, we need to discuss *packages*, a concept
used in Caché to group related classes under a common name. For example, an application may include an Accounting system and an Inventory

system. The classes that form these applications could be organized into an "Accounting" package and an "Inventory" package, as follows:

- Accounting
  - Invoice
  - Item
- Inventory
  - Warehouse
  - Item

Any of these classes can be referred to by its full name (which consists of a package name and a class name), represented in Caché's dot syntax as Accounting.Invoice or Inventory.Item. If the package name can be determined from context (refer to Section 4.2.1.3), then it can be omitted, as in Invoice.

Package names can be omitted

A package is simply a naming convention; it does not provide additional capabilities beyond how classes are named.

4.2.1.1 Package Names

Package names are simple strings. Although package names may contain period characters (but no other punctuation), there is no package hierarchy. For example, if you name a class Test.Subtest.TestClass, this indicates that the name of the class is TestClass and the name of the package is Test.Subtest (which is mapped for SQL purposes to the Test_Subtest schema, as described in Chapter 8).

There is no package hierarchy

There are several limitations on the length and usage of package names:

- Two packages cannot share the same first 25 characters.
- Within a package, the first 25 characters of each class name must be unique.
- The complete name of a class, including its package, must be less than 56 characters.

4.2.1.2 Defining Packages

The name of a class implies a package. An easy way to create a package is to select *New* from Caché Studio's *File* menu, then choose *Caché Class Definition* and use a name for the new class that also contains a new package name. Once the new class is created, the new package also exists. Similarly, when the last class with this package name is deleted, the package is automatically deleted.

Packages are automatically created and deleted

4.2.1.3 Determining the Package Name from the Context

Backward compatibility is achieved through two "built-in" packages:

- %Library—All % classes are implicitly part of the %Library package. (The actual class name does not have the % character.)
- User—All non-% class names without a package are implicitly part of the User package.

%Library and User built-in packages

For example, any reference to the `Person` class internally references `User.Person`. The Caché system class `%Library.Persistent` can be abbreviated as `%Persistent`.

4.2.2 Class Definition Language (CDL)

In Chapter 1, we created a class definition using the wizard that offers helpful forms and menu options for guiding the developer through the definition process. You can also create a class definition directly in Caché Studio's main window using Caché's Class Definition Language (CDL). You can also switch back and forth between the code-based view in the main window and the forms-based view in the Inspector window as you wish.

Whitespace   CDL has been designed to give the developer the greatest possible freedom in formatting code. *Whitespace* (also called empty space), tabs, and row delimiters generally do not have any syntactical meaning. Code can be inserted and structured into meaningful blocks. Note that Caché does not store the CDL text of the class definition, but creates an internal representation in the database. Thus small deviations in formatting can occur when the class definition is viewed later.

Caché ObjectScript code   For Caché ObjectScript code embedded in CDL (for example, as method code), the slightly more restrictive formatting rules of Caché ObjectScript apply (refer to Chapter 5).

Comments   Comments in CDL code use the following syntax:
- `//` means that the rest of the line is considered to be a comment.
- All text between the delimiters `/*` and `*/` is considered to be a comment, regardless of its length.

Comments in Caché ObjectScript code use the syntax described in Chapter 5, meaning they can alternatively also be preceded by a semicolon (;).

4.2.3 Defining Classes

Using the *New Class Wizard* is the easiest way to create a new class definition in Caché Studio. The wizard guides the developer in several easy steps through the definition of a new Caché class.

You can start the wizard either by selecting the *File* menu and clicking *New,* then *Caché Class Definition*, or by selecting *Create New Class* from the *Classes* context menu in the project window.

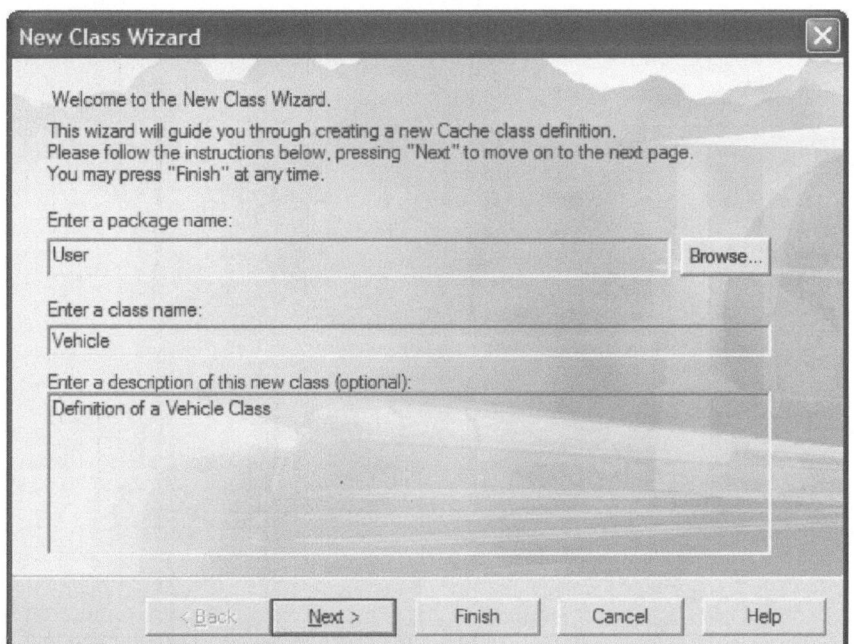

Figure 4.2 The New Class Wizard

In the *package name* field, enter the name of the package to which the new class should belong. You can choose the name of an existing package or create a new name.

Enter the class name in the next field. Note that names starting with the percent symbol (%) are reserved for the Caché system class.

You can enter a description of the class in the *Description* field; the text of the description can use HTML formatting. Descriptions are optional, but are recommended for describing the class's purpose and use, especially when several developers are working on the project. Descriptions are passed to the system documentation automatically created in Caché. In practice, the complete class hierarchy is often created at the beginning of a project, and documented before the programming phase starts; object functionality is then added step-by-step as each new method code is added.

Figure 4.3 Defining the class type

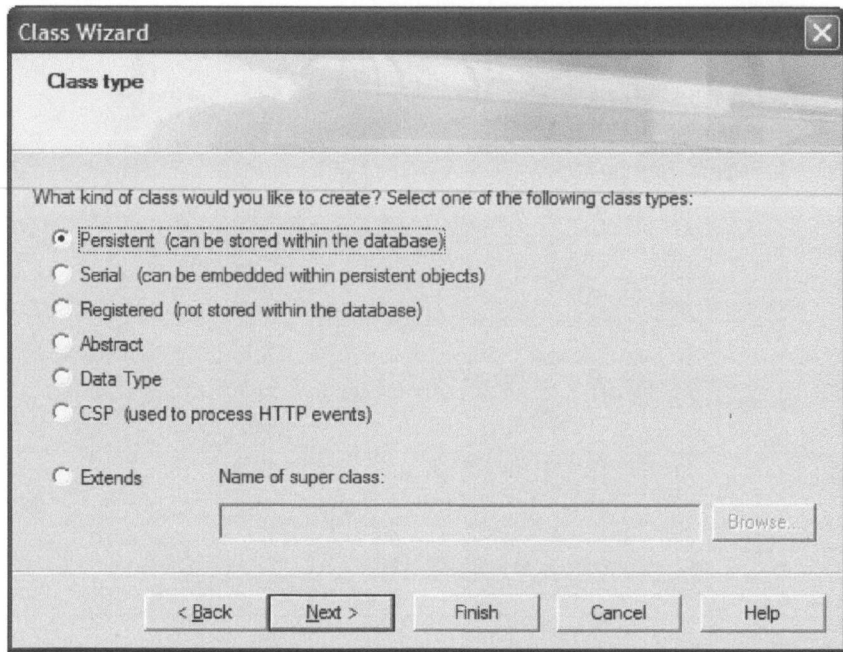

Next you specify the class type, which is typically *Persistent* or *Serial* for persistent classes or embedded objects, respectively. *Registered* classes are transient, meaning they receive no method to load or to store values in the database. *Abstract* classes serve as templates used to derive sub-classes. *Data Type* classes have a set of methods—the so-called data type interface—which defines the behavior of properties that use this data type. *CSP* classes are used as Caché Server Pages.

Super classes   If you specify a *super class*, classes inherit elements from that super class. You can enter the names of several super classes, each separated by commas, to create multiple inheritance. All elements (properties, methods, etc.) can be inherited from the classes in the list; if there is a name conflict, the elements from the last super class in the list are used. The only exception is the class keyword, which is always inherited from the first super class in the list.

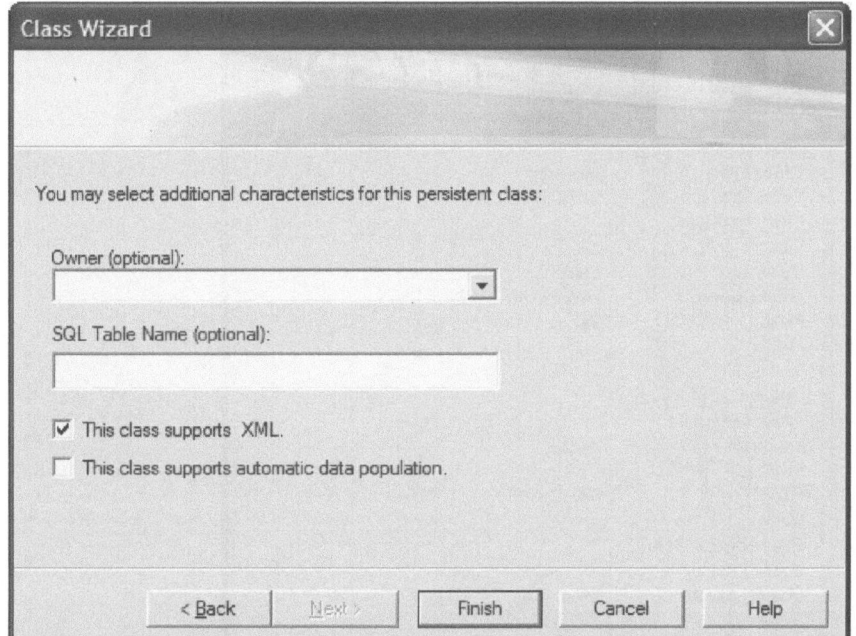

Figure 4.4 Additional characteristics of a persistent class

If you specified the class as persistent, the wizard prompts for additional characteristics. You can indicate an owner of the class if you wish to use SQL security. Under *SQL Table Name* you can specify the name used to map the class as an SQL table. This is necessary if the name of the class is an SQL reserved word or contains an underscore, which is not permitted in SQL names.

The two checkboxes that follow can be used to inherit behavior from the classes. *This class supports XML* directs Caché to automatically include methods for XML projection; *This class supports automatic data population* specifies that methods are made available to populate the class with random test data.

The class definition is now complete. The main window of Caché Studio that now appears displays the new class definition as CDL code and a tabular summary in the Inspector window.

Figure 4.5 Inspector window for the class

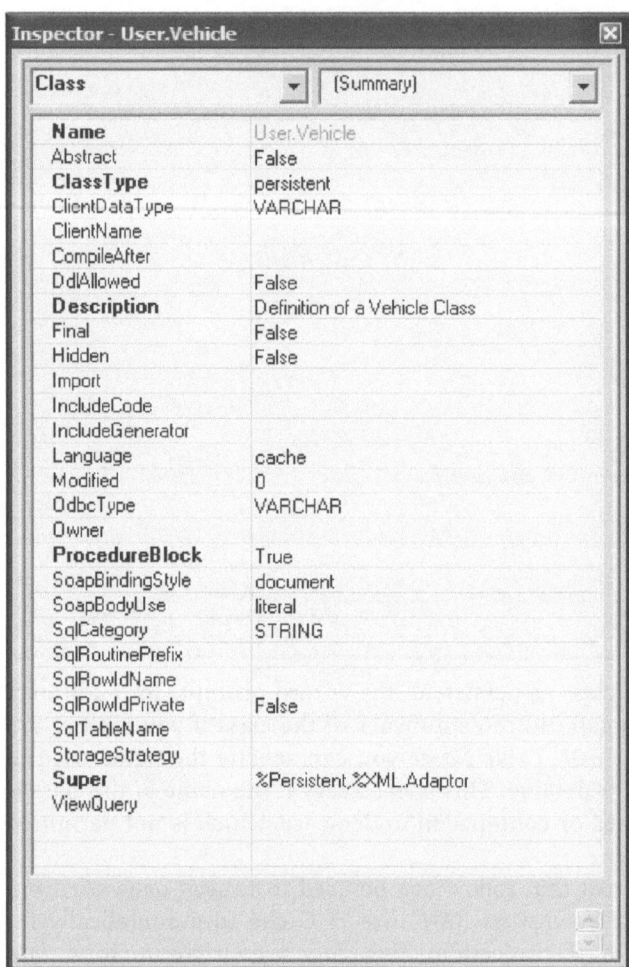

The class definition in CDL

```
/// Definition of a Vehicle Class

Class User.Vehicle Extends (%Persistent, %XML.Adaptor)
                [ ClassType = persistent, ProcedureBlock ]
{

}
```

4.2.4 Properties

To define a new property, choose the *New Property Wizard* button below the menu bar or click *Add* and *New Property* in the *Class* menu.

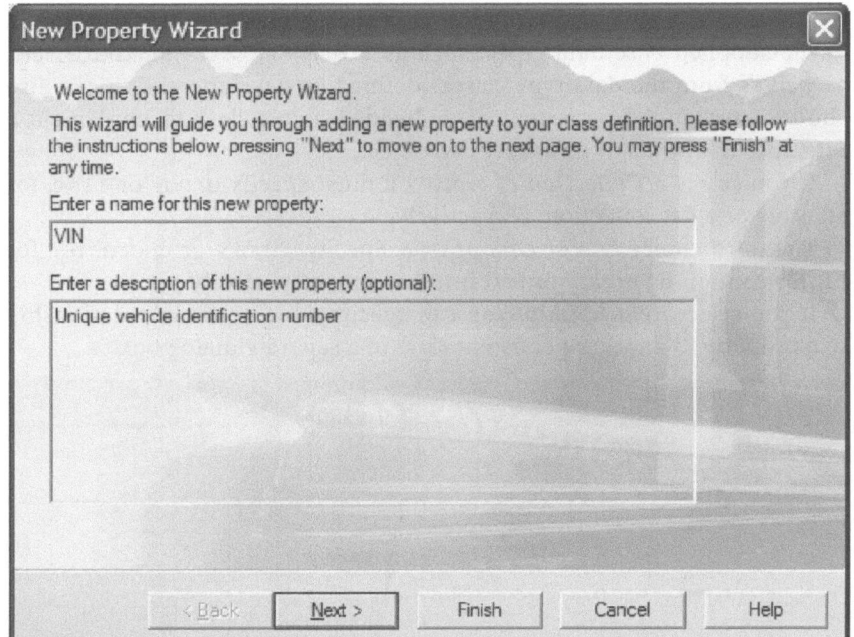

Figure 4.6 The New Property Wizard

Enter the property name in the first field. Optionally, you can enter a description of the class in the *Description* field; the text of the description can use HTML formatting.

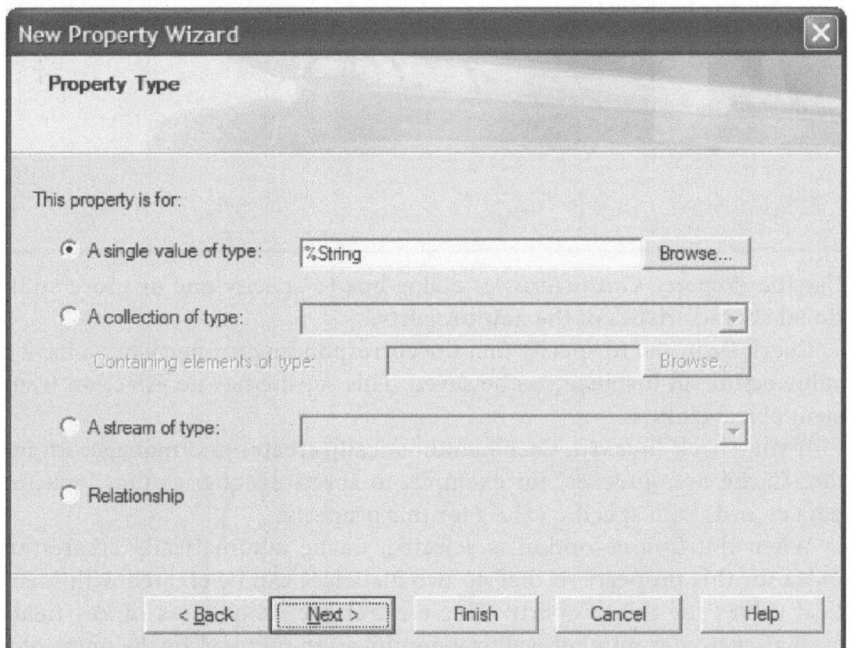

Figure 4.7 Selecting the property type

In the next step you choose one of four property types. (For a detailed description of data types, refer to Section 3.3.2.3.)

If you select *A single value of type,* you can choose from a list of all Caché-supplied base data types, such as %Integer, %String, %Date, etc. as well as from the data type classes defined by developers. You can also choose any defined persistent or embedded object class to implement a reference to objects or an embedded object.

If you select *A Collection of type,* you must specify array or list, for an array or a list collection, respectively.

The third choice is *A stream of type.* Specify binary or character for BLOBs containing binary or text information, respectively.

If you select *Relationship,* you can specify a bidirectional relationship to a property of another persistent class in a separate dialog box.

Figure 4.8 Property Characteristics

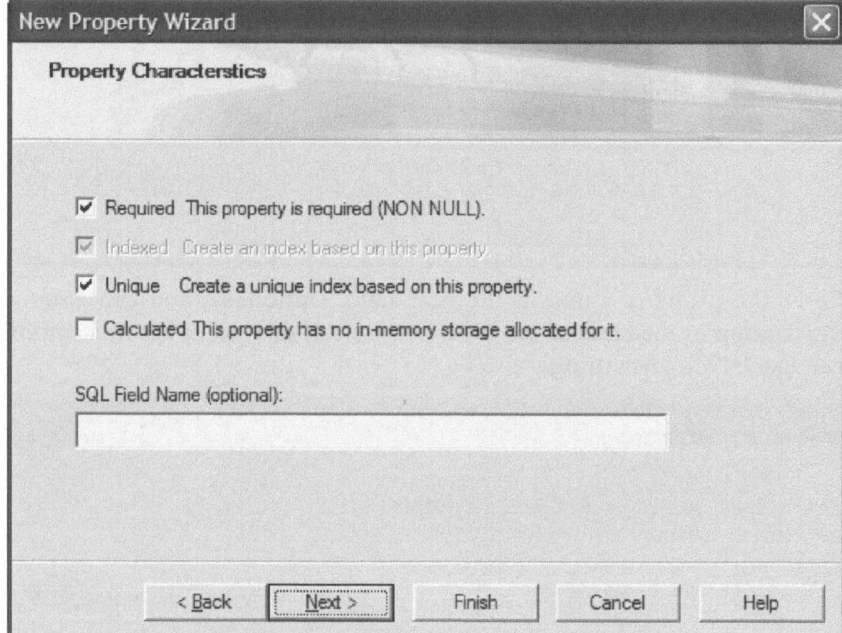

Use the *Property Characteristics* dialog box to specify one or more additional characteristics of the new property.

Check *Required* to specify that the corresponding property must have a value before an instance can be saved. This setting has no effect on transient object classes.

If you check *Indexed,* Caché automatically creates and manages an index. Caché uses indexes, for example, to speed up queries that look for data records with specific values for this property.

When the *Unique* option is selected, Caché automatically creates an index for this property so that no two instances can be created with identical values for this property. This ensures the uniqueness of key fields such as customer number, vehicle identification number, or the name of a document.

A property marked as *Calculated* has no value but rather is calculated at runtime as needed.

If you enter an optional *SQL Field Name,* the name is used for the corresponding table column in the SQL projection of the class. If you leave the field blank, the column has the same name as the property. If the property name is an SQL reserved word, you must specify a different name.

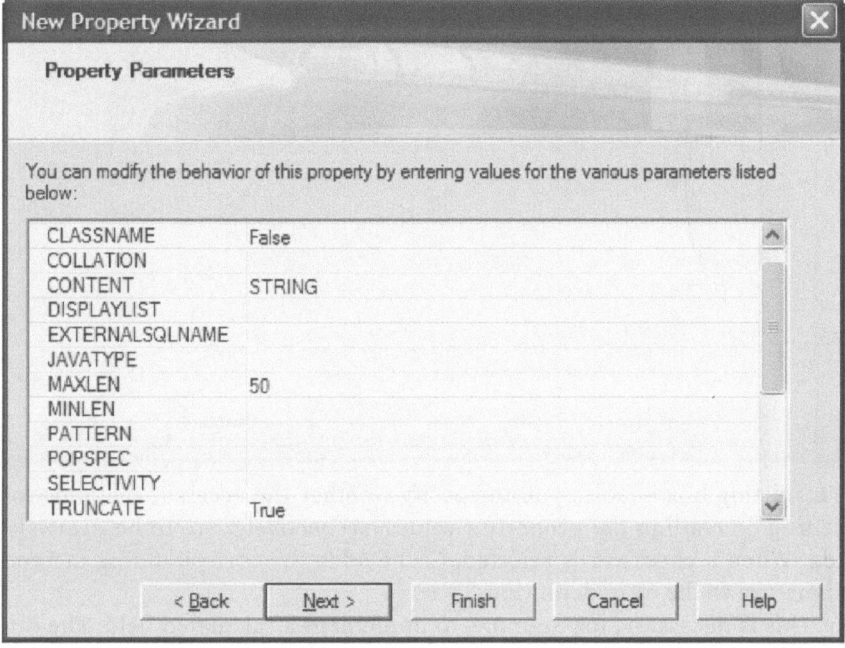

Figure 4.9 Property Parameters

The *Property Parameters* dialog box lists the parameters defined for the data type of the property (refer to Section 3.3.2.3 and the *Caché Objects Class Reference*). These have values inherited from the data type class. You can overwrite these inherited values to further specialize the data type. For example, you can specify the maximum length for a string (50 characters in the example) or the minimum or maximum value for a number. When the class definition is compiled, Caché uses the definitions of the data type and the values of the parameters to create the specific validation code for this property.

Figure 4.10 Overwriting accessor
methods

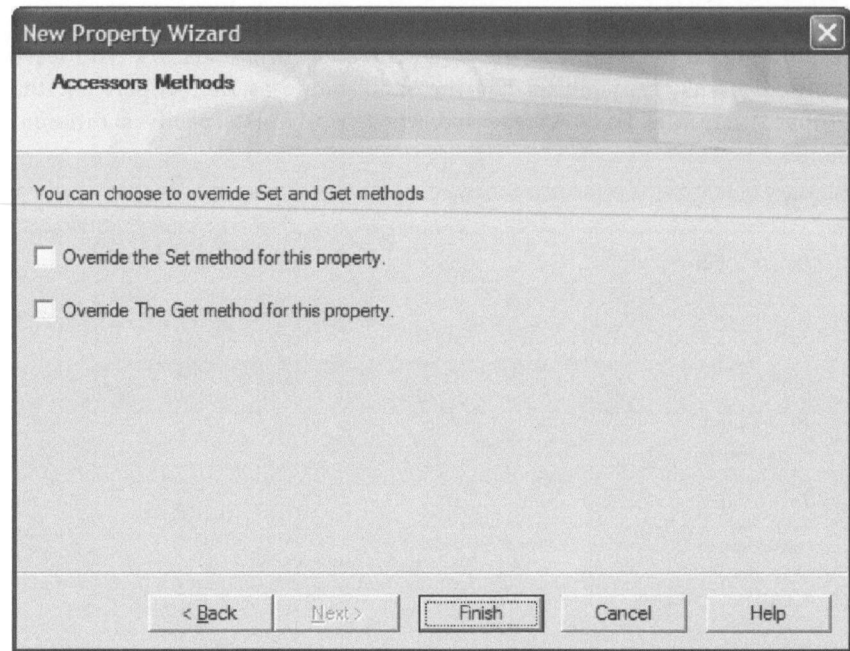

This dialog box enables you to specify whether the accessor methods for setting or reading the property's values, respectively, are to be overwritten. When a checkbox is selected, Caché adds the corresponding method signature to the class definition.

Calculated field in the object view

This is necessary, for example, to implement a calculated field. The calculation, as far as it concerns the object view, appears in the property method with the name PropertyGet(). For a VAT (value-added tax) calculated property, the method is called VATGet(). It has no parameters, and its return value is the value of the calculated property.

Calculated field in the SQL view

Note that the definition of calculated fields in the SQL view differs from that of the object view. The reason that Caché supports two different approaches to these definitions is that SQL access represents a set operation for which the process data records are not instantiated as objects. However, the Get() method is an instance method, and cannot be executed within SQL.

Instead, we mark the property as SqlComputed in CDL, and write the corresponding code in the procedure block with the keyword SqlComputeCode. This requires a special syntax to reference the SQL fields: these are placed in curly brackets. This syntax saves the result of the calculation in the SQL field. For example:

```
Property AgeInYears As %Integer [ Calculated,
SqlComputeCode = { Set {AgeInYears} =
    $Horolog-{DOB}\365.2425}, SqlComputed ];
```

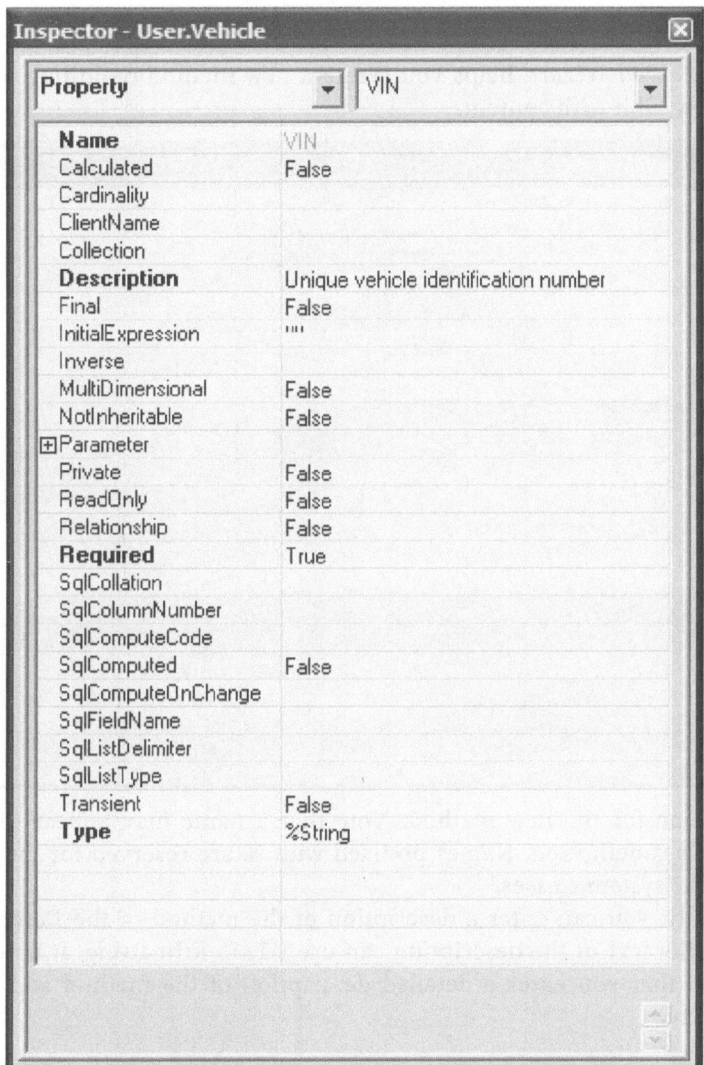

Figure 4.11 Inspector window for the property

The property definition in CDL

```
/// Unique vehicle identification number
Property VIN As %String [ Required ];
```

4.2.5 Methods

The *New Method Wizard* helps you create a new method definition and immediately fill it with contents.

Figure 4.12 The New Method Wizard

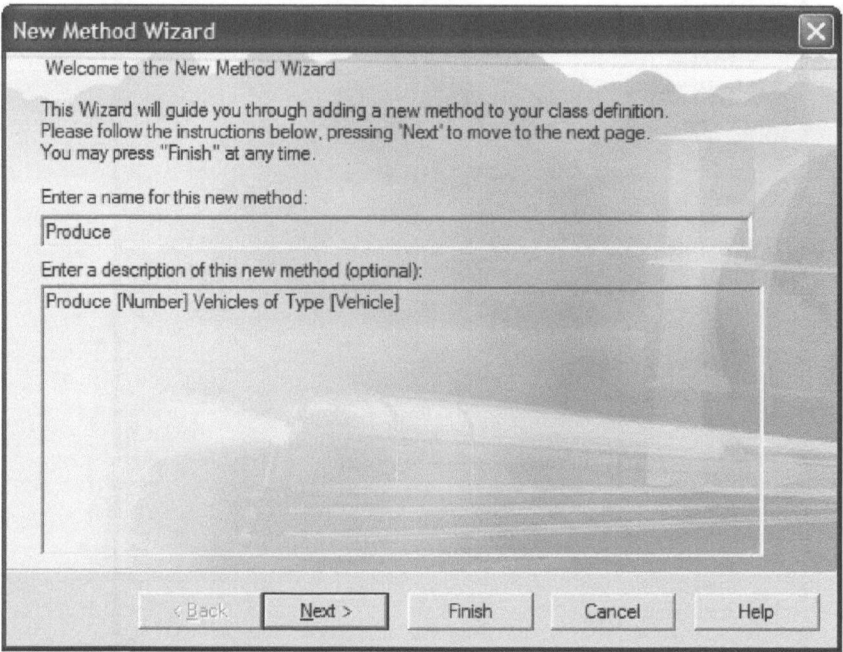

Enter a name for the new method. Note that a name may appear only once per class definition. Names prefixed with % are reserved for methods of Caché system classes.

Optionally, you can enter a description of the method in the *Description* field; the text of the description can use HTML formatting. It is recommended that you enter a detailed description of the method and its purpose here.

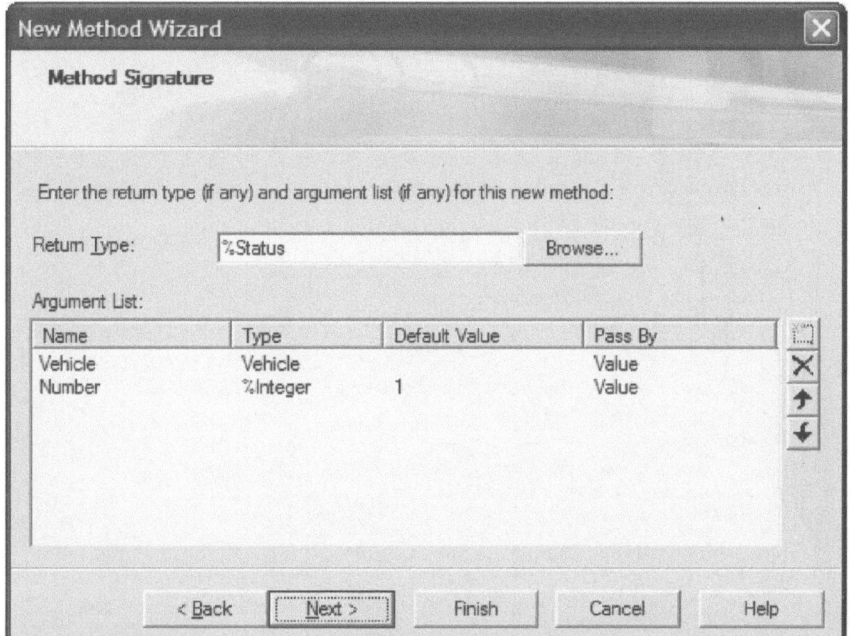

Figure 4.13 Method Signature

The next dialog box lets you specify the method signature. The signature describes the method's interface, namely the number, meaning and types of its arguments, and the return value.

The *Return Type* field provides a selection list from which you select the data type of the method's return value. All Caché data types are allowed. %Status is often used to return information regarding the success or the failure of the execution.

The *Argument List* is where you enter method's arguments. It is initially empty when a new method is created. Click the top box on the right-hand side of the list to add a new argument; clicking the red X deletes a marked argument. The up or down arrow moves a marked argument to the top or bottom of the list, respectively.

Double-clicking an argument opens a new window with the associated definition. *Name* represents the formal name of the argument with which it is referenced in the method. *Type* specifies the argument's data type; *Default* provides the argument's default value, the *Reference* or *Value* entry for *Pass By* specifies whether the argument is to be passed as a reference or as a value, respectively.

Figure 4.14 Method Characteristics

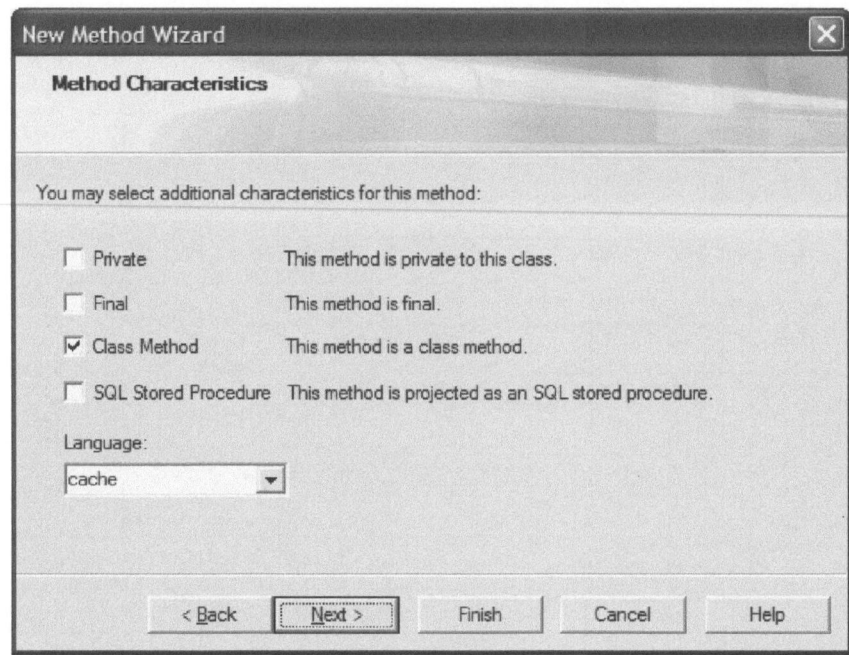

The *Method Characteristics* dialog box provides four checkboxes that enable you to specify further characteristics for a method.

Marking *Private* specifies that this method cannot be used outside its own class or classes derived from it. Methods without this checkbox being marked are *public,* and can be called without restriction.

Checking *Final* ensures that the method cannot be overwritten in subclasses.

Check *Class method* to mark a method as being a class method. Unlike instance methods, it then does not refer to a specific instance of the class and can therefore be used without the class being instantiated.

SQL Stored Procedure can only be marked for class methods, and specifies that the method can be called from SQL as a stored procedure.

Finally, under *Language* you can select the programming language used to write the method. The choices are basic, cache (the default), and Java.

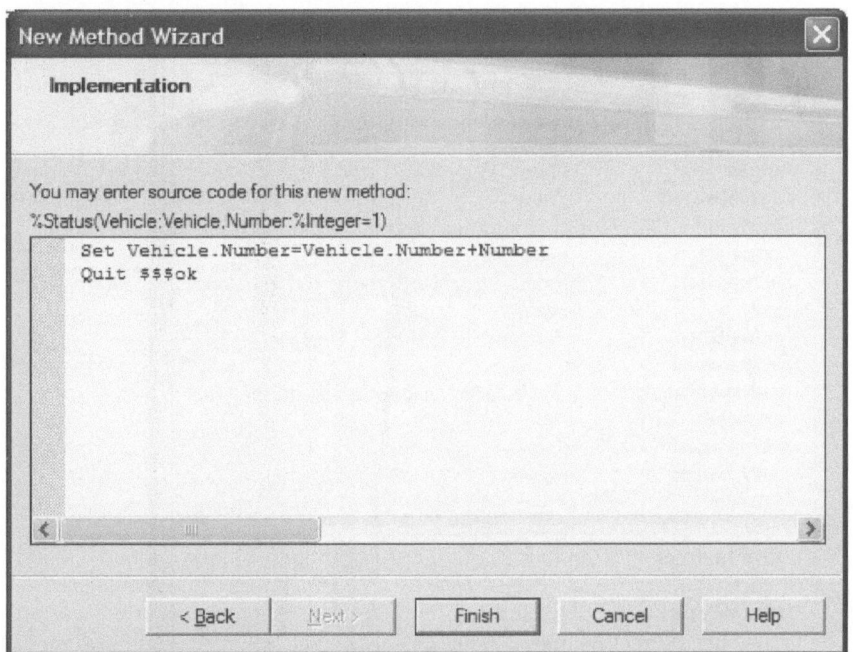

Figure 4.15 Method implementation

The method can now be implemented in the selected programming language. The Quit command is used to exit a Caché ObjectScript method and assign its return value.

Figure 4.16 Inspector window for the
method

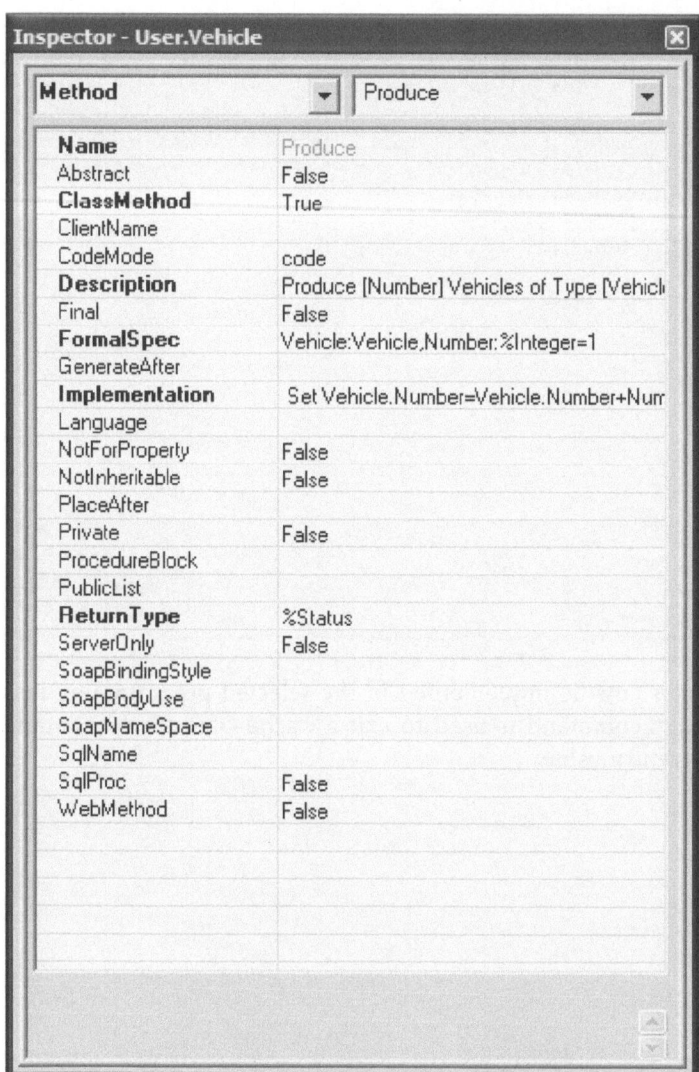

The method definition in CDL

```
/// Produce [Number] Vehicles of Type [Vehicle]
ClassMethod Produce (Vehicle As Vehicle,
                     Number As %Integer = 1) As %Status
{
 Set Vehicle.Number=Vehicle.Number+Number
 Quit $$$ok
}
```

4.2.6 Class Parameters

Click the *New Parameter* button to use the *New Parameter Wizard* to define a class parameter .

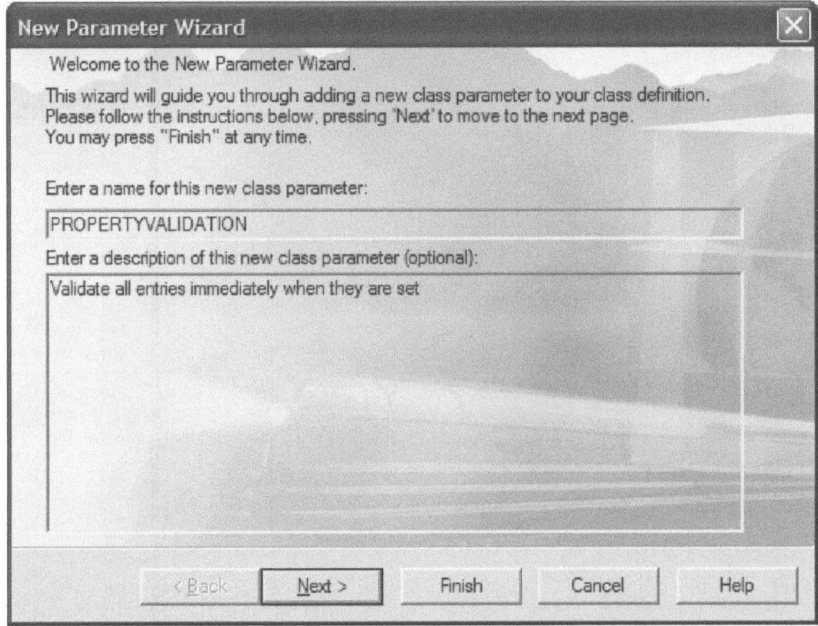

Figure 4.17 The New Parameter Wizard

Enter a name for the new parameter. Optionally, you can enter a description of the parameter in the *Description* field; the text of the description can use HTML formatting.

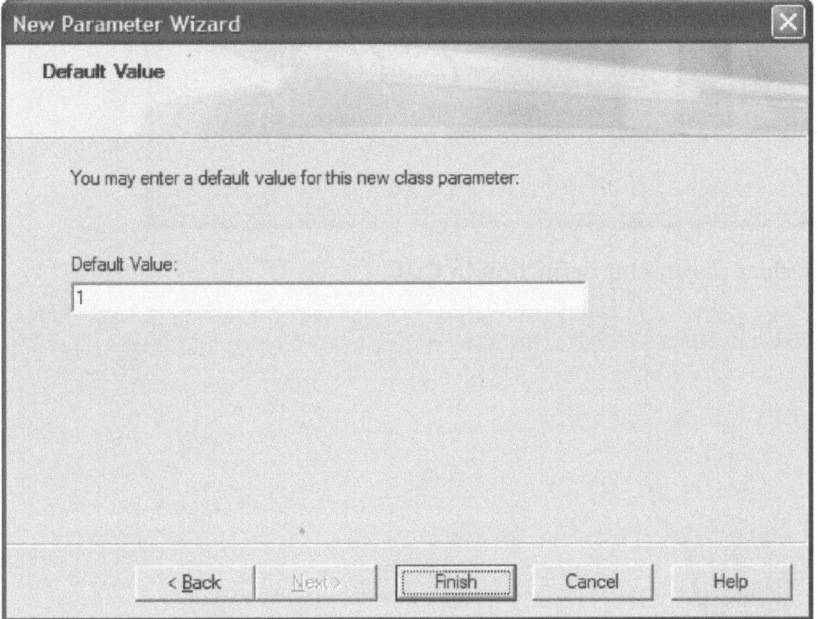

Figure 4.18 Parameter value

Enter the parameter's value in the next dialog box as *Default Value*.

Figure 4.19 Inspector window for the class parameter

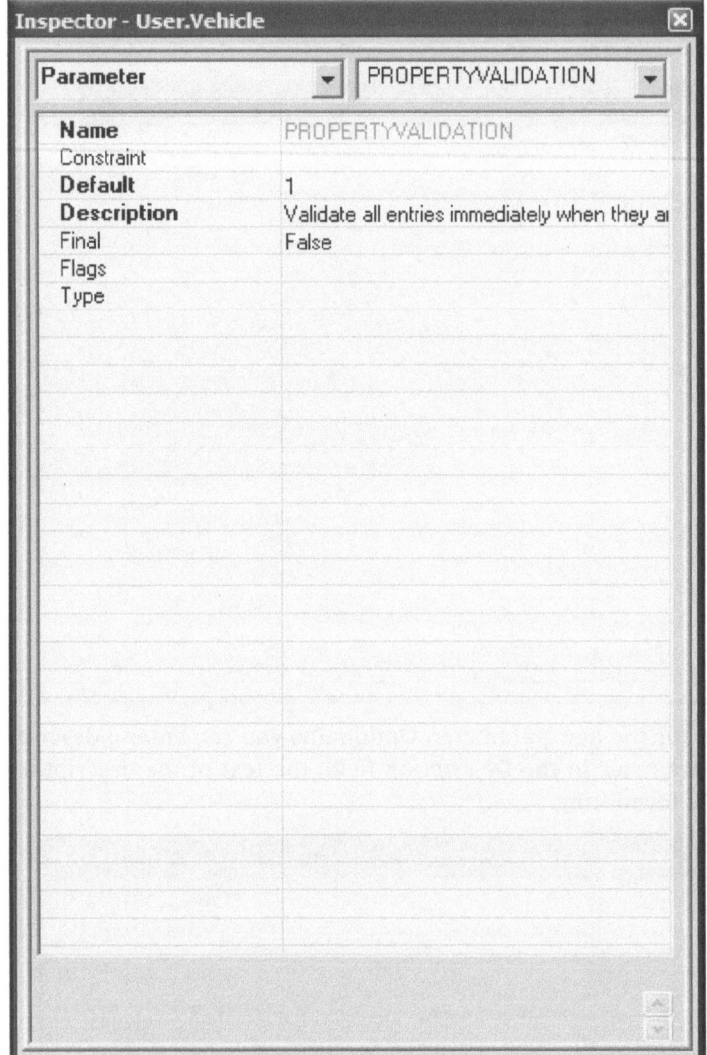

The class parameter definition in CDL

```
/// Validate all entries immediately when they are set
Parameter PROPERTYVALIDATION = 1;
```

4.2.7 Queries

Click the *New Query* button to open the *New Query Wizard* to guide you step-by-step through the definition of an SQL query.

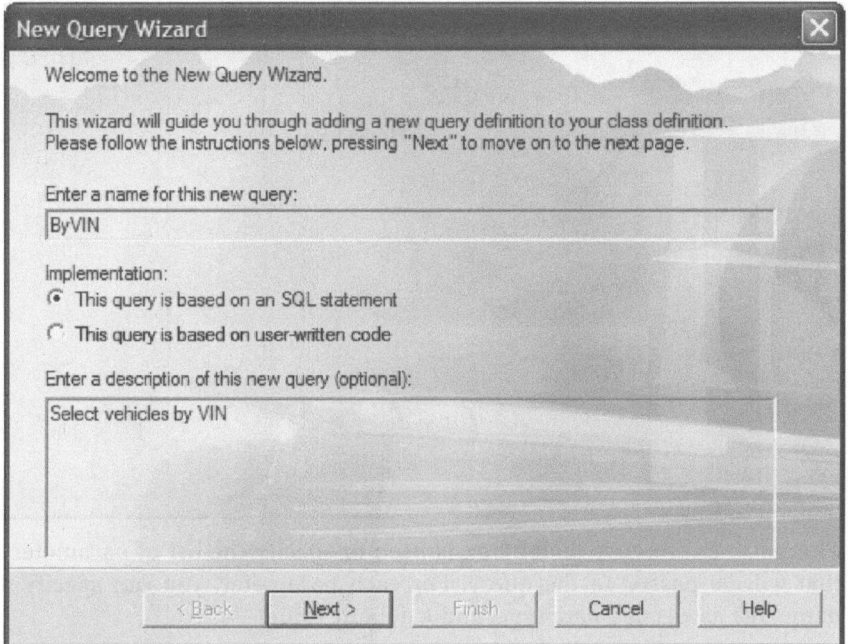

Figure 4.20 The New Query Wizard

First, the query must be assigned a unique name in the *Query name* field.

You now select how the query will be implemented. Choose *This query is based on an SQL statement* for a query defined in SQL, or *This query is based on user-written code* for a query written in Caché ObjectScript or Caché Basic. For the latter, you must program three class methods, QueryExecute(), QueryFetch() and QueryClose(), where Query is replaced with the actual name of the query.

Optionally, you can enter a description of the query in the *Description* field; the text of the description can use HTML formatting.

SQL query or query programmed in Caché ObjectScript or Caché Basic

Figure 4.21 Query parameters

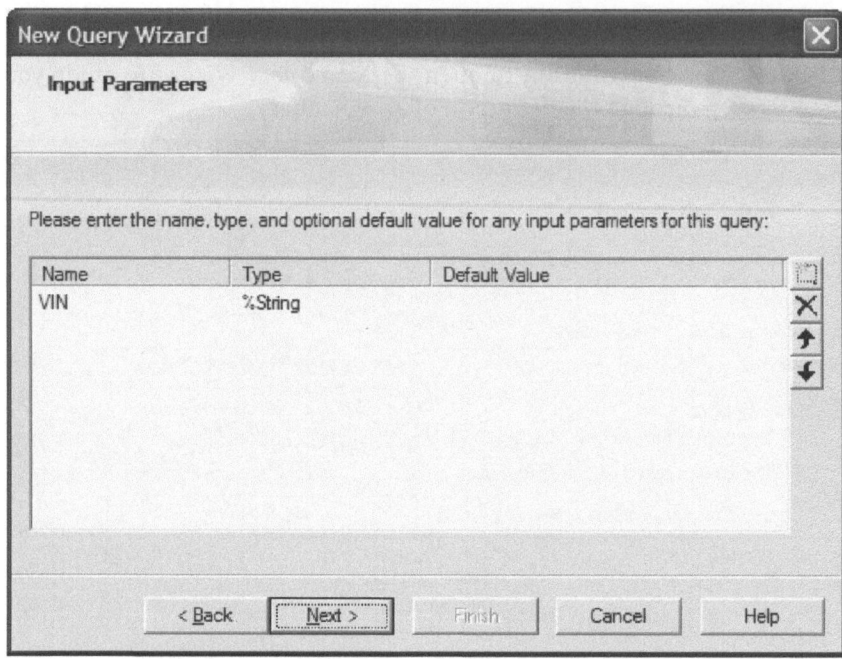

The *Input Parameters* dialog box is used to specify the list of parameters that will be passed to the query. For each parameter, you can specify a name, the associated data type, and a default value.

Figure 4.22 Query columns

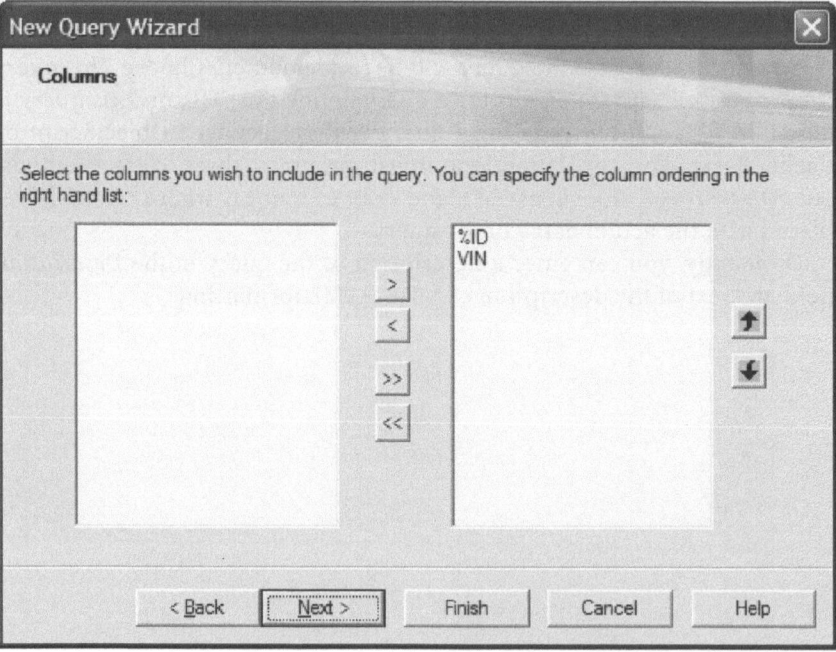

Use the *Columns* dialog box to select and order the columns you wish to include in the query result.

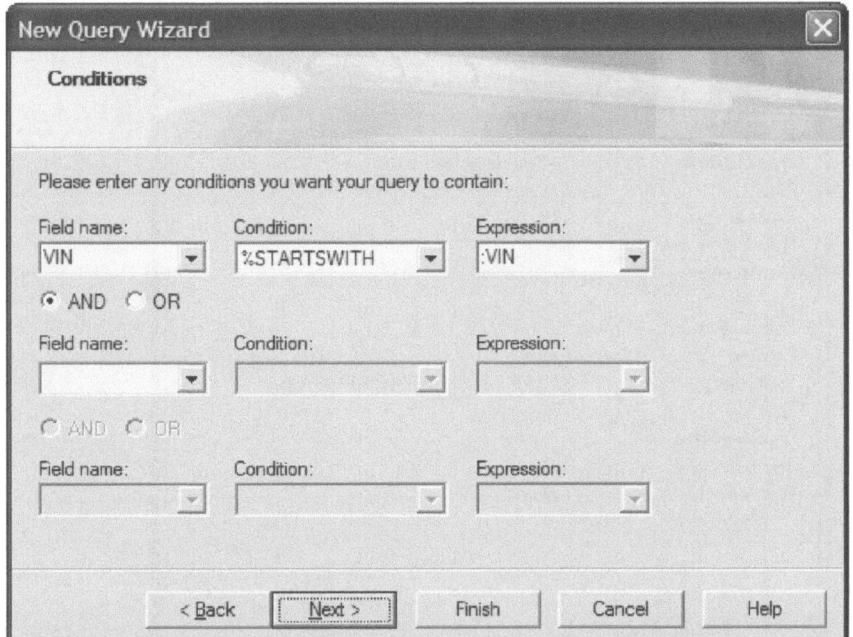

Figure 4.23 Query condition

Next, select any conditions for the objects to be included in the query result.

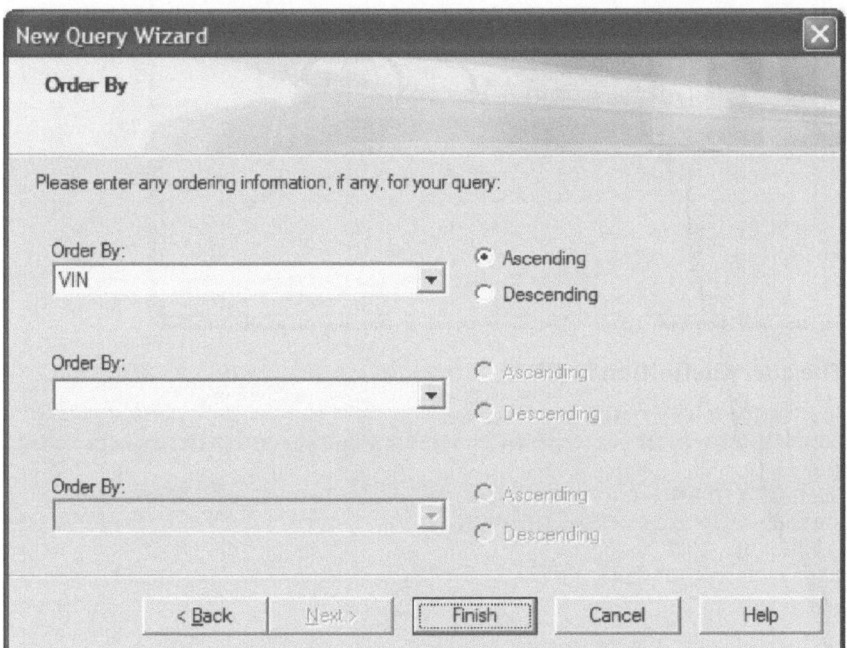

Figure 4.24 Sorting of queries

Finally, you select how the query result is to be sorted.

Figure 4.25 Inspector window for the query

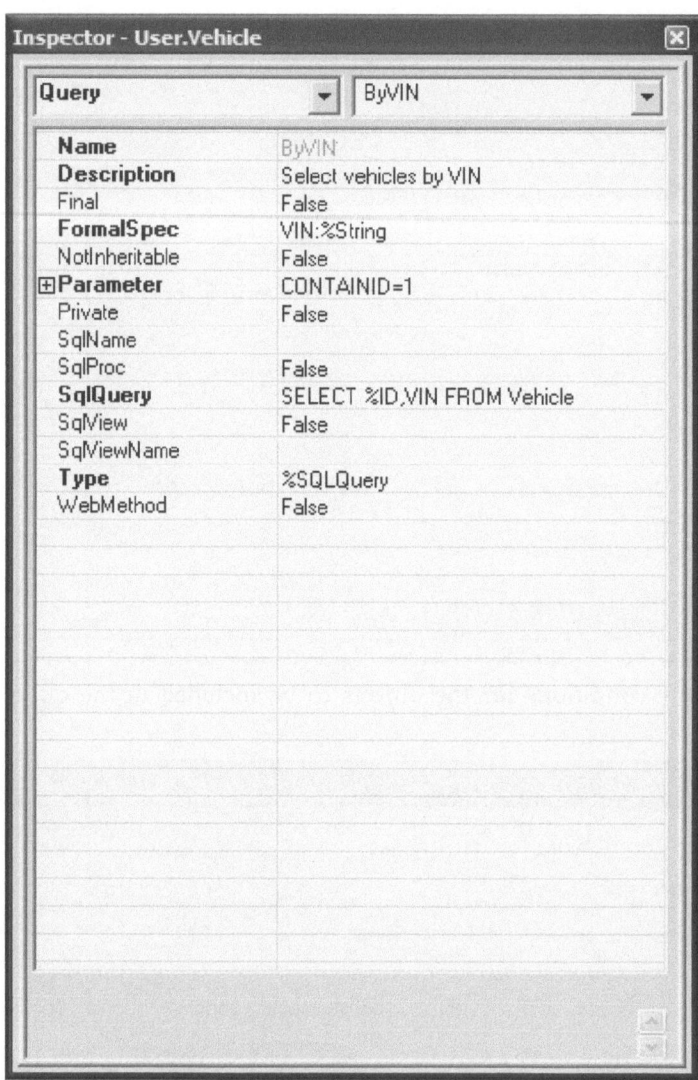

The query definition in CDL

```
/// Select vehicles by VIN
Query ByVIN(VIN As %String) As %SQLQuery(CONTAINID = 1)
{
SELECT %ID,VIN FROM Vehicle
 WHERE (VIN %STARTSWITH :VIN)
 ORDER BY VIN
}
```

4.2.8 Indexes

You can start the *New Index Wizard* by clicking the *New Index* button or by selecting *Add* and *New Index* from the *Class* menu.

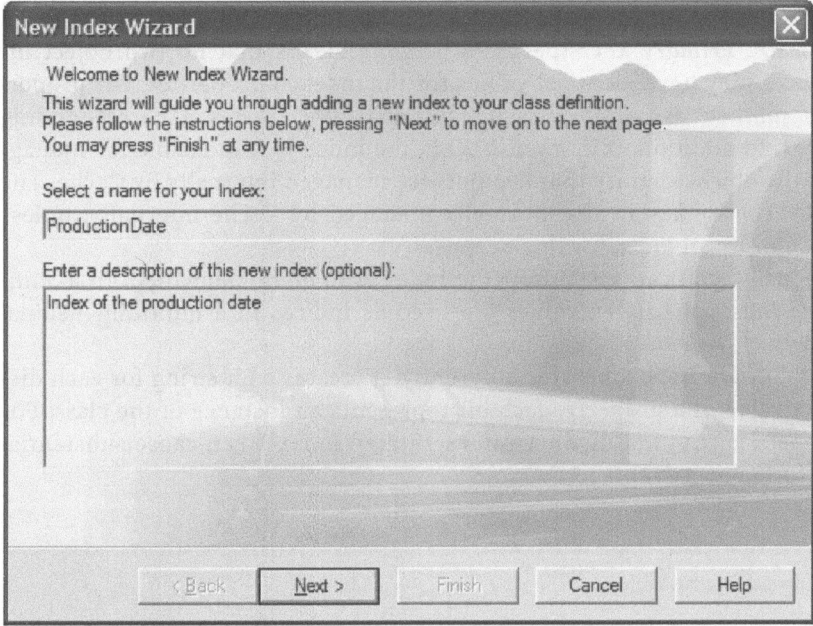

Figure 4.26 The New Index Wizard

Enter a unique name for the new index. Optionally, you can enter a description of the index in the *Description* field; the text of the description can use HTML formatting.

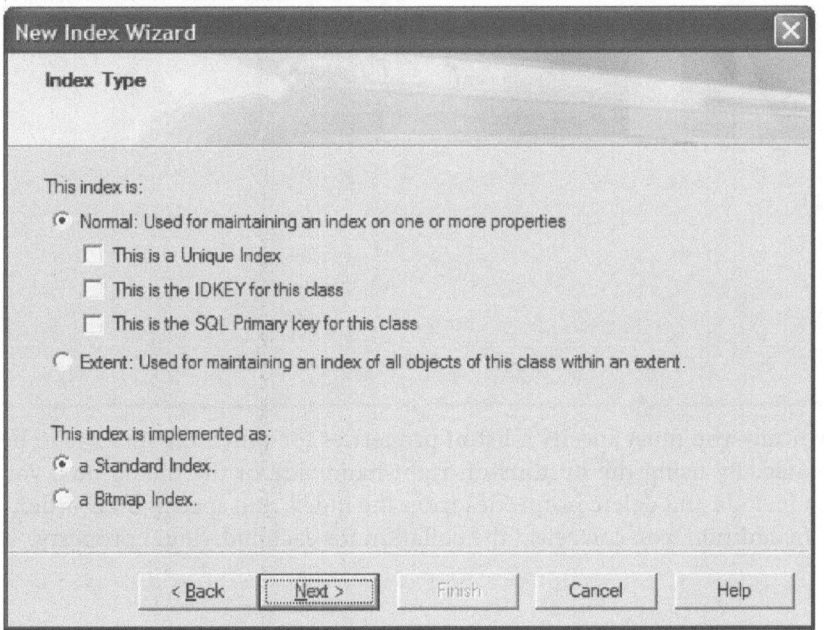

Figure 4.27 Index type

You specify the use of the index in the *Index Type* page. *Normal* creates an index for access optimization using one or more of the following checked options. An *Extent* index will find all objects of an extent. (An extent includes objects of the actual class and all subclasses).

Unique Index, IDKEY and SQL Primary key

You can select three options for a normal index: *Unique Index*, *IDKEY*, and *SQL Primary key*. Specifying *Unique* means that no two object instances may have identical values for the indexed properties. For properties marked as *unique*, Caché automatically creates a corresponding index. In addition, if marked *IDKEY*, the index is responsible for managing the object identity that is otherwise managed internally by Caché. The *SQL Primary key* is also normally managed by Caché internally, unless you specify an index for this purpose.

Index implementation

Finally, you can select how the index is to be implemented. In a *Standard Index,* the index values are used as indices in a multidimensional array.

Bitmap index

A *Bitmap Index* operates differently: it creates a bit string for each distinct value of a property, each bit represents an instance of the class. For properties with few distinct values, bitmap indexes can cause substantial performance advantages.

Figure 4.28 Index Properties

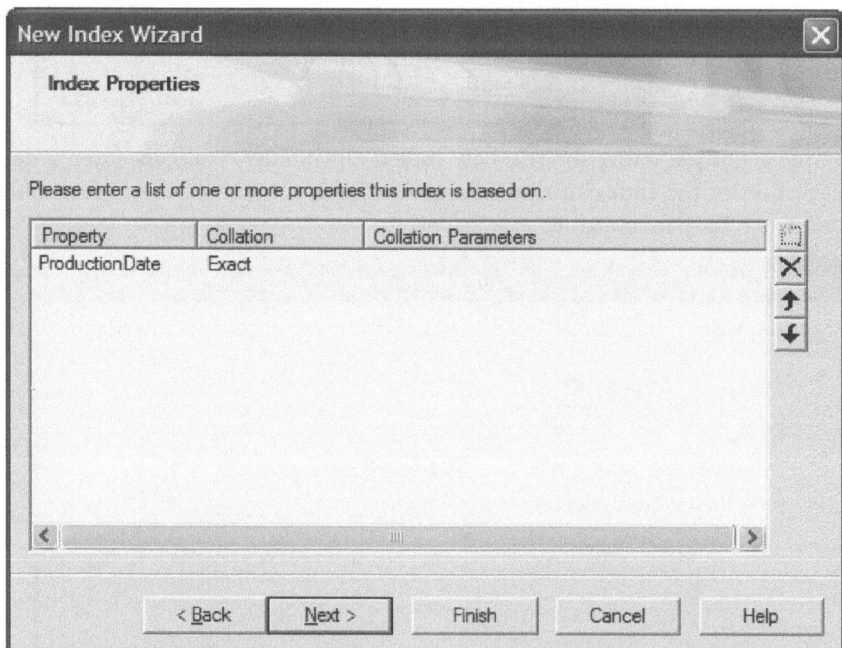

Typically you must specify a list of properties for which the index is to be created. By using the buttons on right-hand side of the dialog box, you can include and delete properties from the index, and specify their order.

In addition, you can select the collation for each individual property.

Collation of properties

When property data are included in an index, each value is typically used without change. This means the collation formed by the index depends on how these values are spelled (including the case). For example, the name "deSantis" would not appear between "Dannenberg" and "Dierendorf," because of its lowercase spelling means it would be sorted after all uppercase names—often an undesirable result.

However, a parameter can be specified for the property that influences how the properties in an index are to be collated. The corresponding parameter is COLLATION can assume one of the values listed in Table 4.2. Each COLLATION value represents a specified transformation rule applied to a value before it is inserted in the index. If a specific value is sought in the index, it is subject to the same transformation. Formats specified by COLLATION effectively normalize the values inserted in an index. A typical example is the ALPHAUP sorting that normalizes strings to a uniform uppercase form and removes any punctuation marks such as blanks, dashes, etc.

COLLATION parameter

Collation (COLLATION=)	Description
ALPHAUP	Replaces all lowercase characters with the corresponding uppercase characters, and removes all punctuation marks except question marks (?) and commas (,).
EXACT	Does not perform any transformation.
MINUS	Interprets all values (also character strings) numerically and inverts the sign.
PLUS	Interprets all values (also character strings) numerically.
SPACE	Interprets all values (also numbers) as character strings and inserts a leading blank at the front.
SQLSTRING	Removes leading blanks and sorts empty values as an SQL empty string.
SQLUPPER	Removes leading blanks, replaces all lowercase characters with the corresponding uppercase characters, and sorts empty values as an SQL empty string.
STRING	Removes leading blanks, replaces all lowercase characters with the corresponding uppercase characters, removes all punctuation marks except commas (,) and sorts empty values as an SQL empty string.
UPPER	Replaces all lowercase characters with the corresponding uppercase characters.

Table 4.1 Collation of properties

Figure 4.29 Additional Index Data

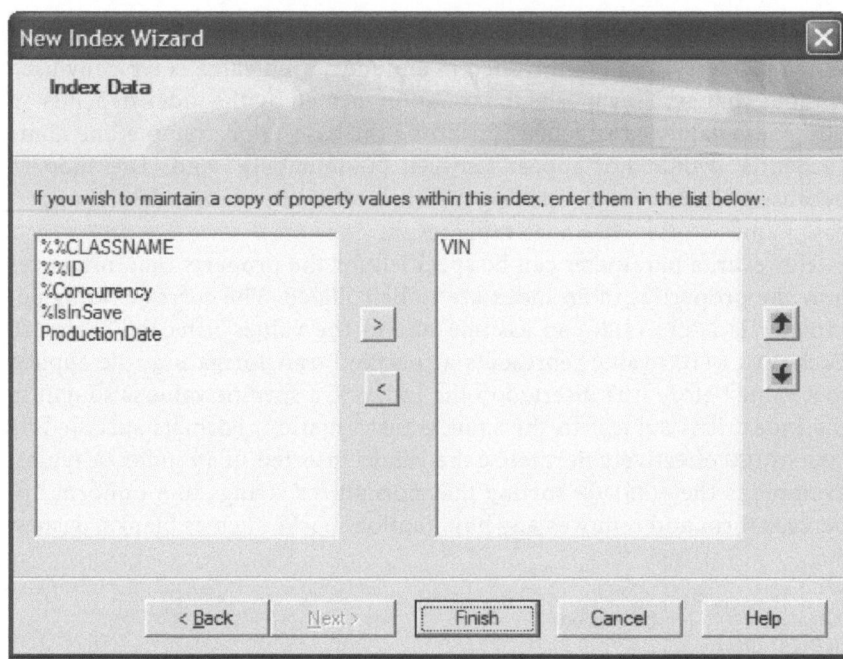

On the *Index Data* page, you can select any additional properties to be saved directly in the index. Of course, this means redundant data storage, but the runtime performance can be improved when the queries can be processed directly from the index.

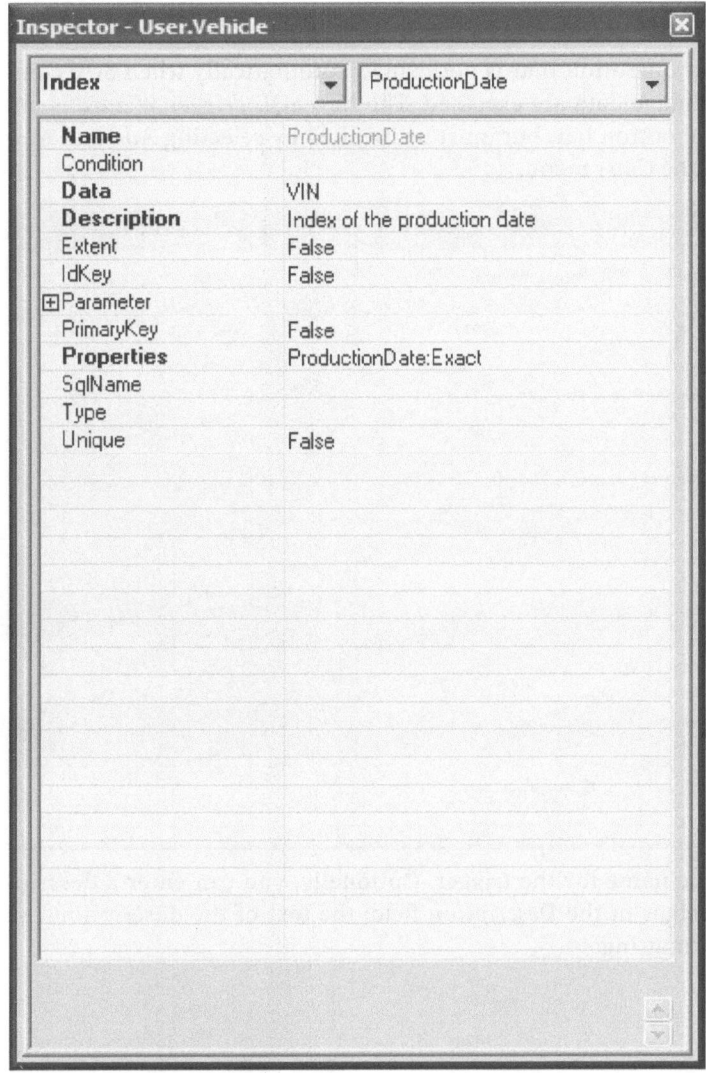

Figure 4.30 Inspector window for the Index

The index definition in CDL

```
/// Index of the production date
Index ProductionDate On ProductionDate As Exact
                                    [ Data = VIN ];
```

4.2.9 Triggers

A *trigger* is an operation that is performed automatically when SQL commands that change data are executed. The *New SQL Trigger Wizard* is not present on the button bar, but must be invoked by selecting *Add* and *New Trigger* from the *Class* menu.

Figure 4.31 New SQL Trigger Wizard

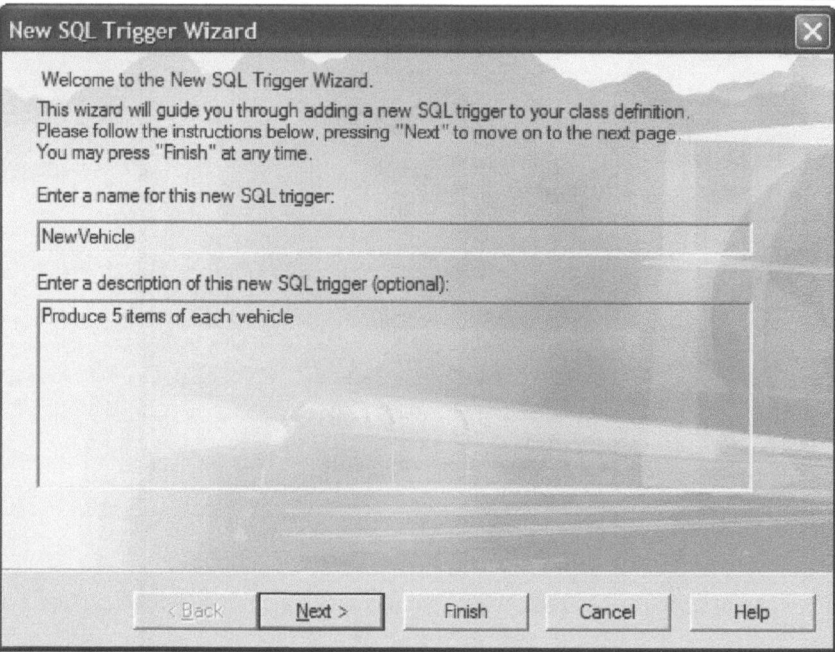

Enter a unique name for the trigger. Optionally, you can enter a description of the trigger in the *Description* field; the text of the description can use HTML formatting.

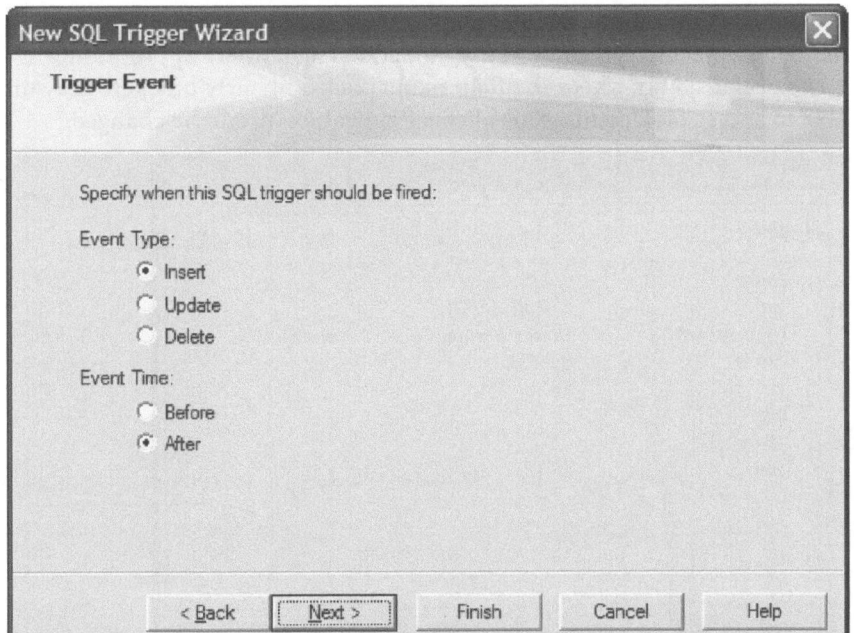

Figure 4.32 Trigger Event

Event Type defines when the trigger will be activated: at an INSERT (when a new data record is inserted into the database), an UPDATE (the change of an existing record) or DELETE (deletion of a record). A trigger always refers to one specific event; if necessary, several triggers can be defined.

Event Time specifies whether a trigger is activated *Before* or *After* the triggering event.

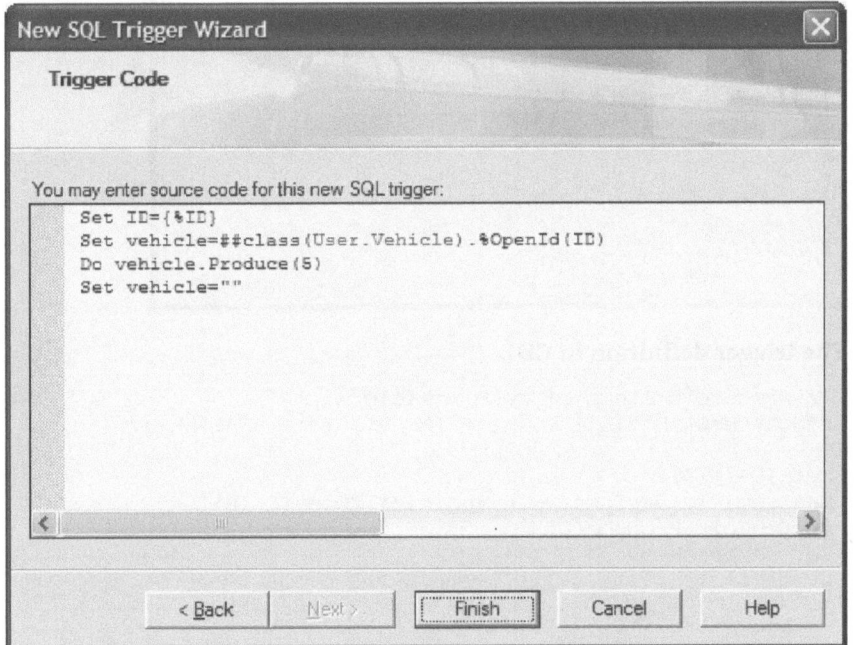

Figure 4.33 Trigger-Code

You enter the actual trigger code in this dialog box. Although it is written in Caché ObjectScript, you can use embedded SQL where appropriate.

A special syntax where the field name placed in curly brackets is available to access table fields. This allows field values also to be changed.

Figure 4.34 Inspector window for the trigger

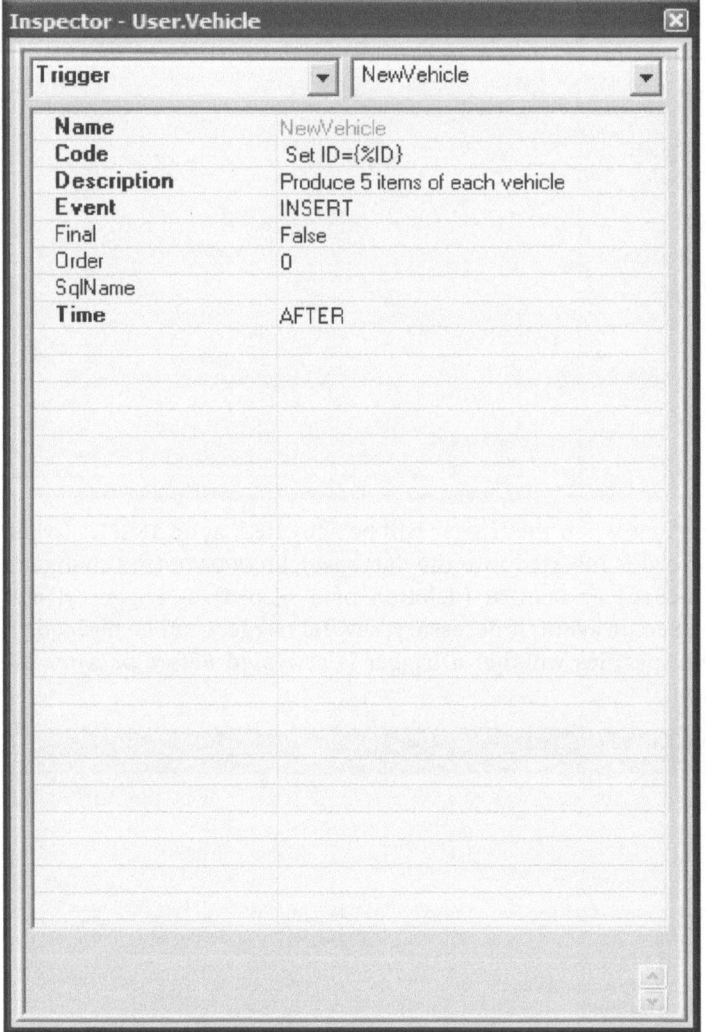

The trigger definition in CDL

```
/// Produce 5 items of each vehicle
Trigger NewVehicle [ Event = INSERT, Time = AFTER ]
{
 Set ID={%ID}
 Set vehicle=##class(User.Vehicle).%OpenId(ID)
 Do vehicle.Produce(5)
 Set vehicle=""

}
```

4.2.10 The Complete Example

The following example contains the complete CDL definition of the Person class that was defined as an example in Chapter 1. In addition, another calculated characteristic, Age, has been included with a corresponding display as SQL *computed field,* and the date of birth has been changed to European format:

```
/// General person class
Class User.Person Extends %Persistent
                [ ClassType = persistent, ProcedureBlock ]{

/// Name of person
Property Name As %String [ Required ];

/// First name of person
Property Firstname As %String;

/// Date of birth of person
Property DOB As %Date;

Property Age As %Integer [ Calculated, SqlComputeCode = {
Set {AgeInYears}=$Horolog-{DOB}\365.2425
}, SqlComputed, SqlFieldName = AgeInYears ];

Method AgeGet() As %Integer
{
 Quit $Horolog-..DOB\365.2425
}

Index NameIndex On Name;

/// Find all Persons
Query All() As %SQLQuery(CONTAINID = 1)
{
SELECT %ID,Name,Firstname,DOB FROM Person
 ORDER BY Name
}
```

4.3 Managing Classes with Caché Explorer

As we have already seen in this chapter, Caché Studio's step-by-step guidance makes it easy to define Caché classes. In addition to making new definitions, Caché Studio also includes basic functionality for exporting single class definitions.

Caché Explorer is a more extensive environment for managing Caché classes as well as routines and globals (the structures in which Caché stores programs and data).

Figure 4.35 Classes in Caché Explorer

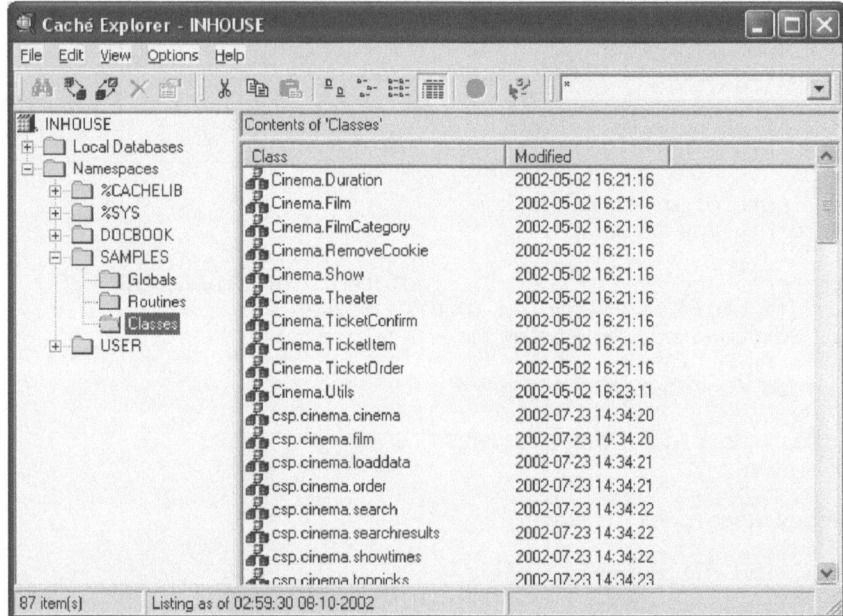

Caché Explorer consists largely of two frames: the tree structure in the left-hand frame represents a Caché system with its local databases, namespaces, and contained classes, globals, and routines; the right-hand side shows the corresponding contents.

For all these elements, Caché Explorer provides comprehensive functions for managing, importing, and exporting definitions and data. You can export and import a single element, groups of elements, or all elements. You can also use files to transfer elements from one Caché system to another.

Export formats for class definitions
Various formats are supported for exporting class definitions:

- Class Definition Language (CDL)—but be careful: this is the old format used in previous Caché versions!
- Java class definition
- Standard Object Definition Language (ODL)
- A class definition in XML format (XML)—this is the preferred format for the current Caché version.

You can use the XML format to transfer a fully functional class definition from one Caché system to another. The other formats are used primarily to pass class definitions from Caché to non-Caché development tools or for compatibility with previous Caché versions.

To transfer data associated with a class (that is, the stored object instances), you must export its corresponding *globals*. Globals (or global variables) are the *internal* storage structures for Caché. Globals are described in detail in Chapter 7. Note that two globals are used per class: *^package.class*D contains the data and *^package.class*I contains the indexes of the object instances, where the text string *class* in the global name is the same as the class name and *package* is its corresponding package name.

Because generated routines will be regenerated automatically on the target system after import, you do not need to transfer them. However, if user-written routines belong to the object definition (as well as so-called *macro includes* with the .INC file extension), they must also be exported and imported into the target system.

4.4 Caché Objects Utilities at the Command Level

This section summarizes Caché Terminal *(a command shell)*, the ^%apiOBJ utility program, and the $System special object that provide developers with various API calls for managing the Caché Objects environment.

4.4.1 Caché Terminal and the Command Level

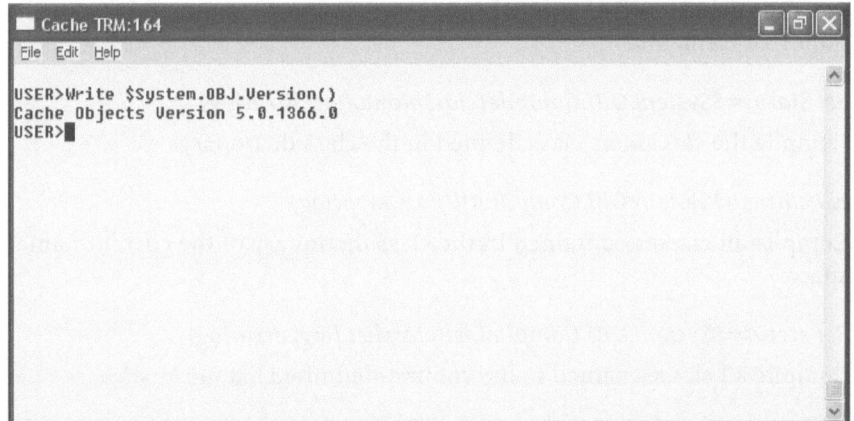

Figure 4.36 Caché Terminal

The Caché Cube menu contains a program with the name Caché Terminal. This is a terminal emulation window supplied with Caché that is suitable for executing text-oriented applications. (Refer to Chapter 13.) Many developers and system administrators use Caché Terminal for simple tests and to debug programs. When you start Caché Terminal, a terminal emulation window opens and the USER> system prompt appears. This prompt belongs to the Caché *command shell*; the text "USER" specifies the namespace in which you are working. You can enter any Caché ObjectScript code here and execute it immediately.

Example

```
USER>Write $System.OBJ.Version()
Cache Objects Version 5.0.1366.0
```

This example displays the version information for Caché Objects.

4.4.2 Loading and Compiling Class Definitions

The following list describes the API calls that load and compile CDL files into the Caché class dictionary:

List of API calls   *Set status=$System.OBJ.Load(filename,flag,.errorlog,.elements,listonly)*

Loading class definitions   Load one or more class definition files into the Caché class dictionary. *filename* is the name of the file to be loaded; *filename* can also be an asterisk-delimited list of file names. Caché automatically recognizes the file format by its extension. For an explanation of the optional arguments *flag* and *errorlog,* refer to Section 4.4.9. The optional *elements* argument contains a list of the imported elements. If the *listonly* argument is specified and true, instead of the data being imported, the elements are listed.

Set status=$System.OBJ.LoadDir(dir,flag,.errorlog,.recurse,.elements)

Load all CDL and XML class definition files from the specified directory into the Caché class dictionary. *dir* is the operating system directory where the files reside. If *recurs* is specified and true, then subdirectories are also included. The optional *elements* argument receives the list of the imported elements.

Set status=$System.OBJ.Compile(classname,flag,.errorlog)

Compiling classes   Compile the *classname* class defined in the class dictionary.

Set status=$System.OBJ.CompileAll(flag,.errorlog)

Compile all classes contained in the class dictionary of the current namespace.

Set status=$System.OBJ.CompileList(classlist,flag,.errorlog)

Compile all classes named in the comma-delimited list in *classlist.*

Set status=$System.OBJ.CompilePackage(package,flag,.errorlog)

Compile all classes that belong to the specified *package.*

Set status=$System.OBJ.CompileProject(project,flag,.errorlog)

Compile all classes (and other elements) that belong to the specified *project.*

4.4.3 Exporting Class Definitions

The following section describes the calls for exporting class definitions in the various file formats supported by Caché:

Set status=$System.OBJ.Export(items,file,flag,.errorlog)

Export the elements identified by *items* (single element or a comma-delimited list) as an XML file with name *file*. The extension specifies the type of the associated elements. Valid extensions are:

- .CLS—Class definitions
- .CSP—Caché Server Pages
- .CSR—Caché rule files
- .MAC—Macro routines
- .INT—Intermediate code routines
- .BAS—Caché Basic routines
- .INC—Include files
- .GBL—Globals
- .PRJ—Caché Studio projects
- .OBJ—Object code

If the User.Person and User.Student classes are to be exported, then the value for the items is User.Person.cls,User.Student.cls.

Set status=$System.OBJ.ExportPackage(package,file,flag,.errorlog)

Export all the classes belonging to the *package* as an XML file with name *file*.

Set status=$System.OBJ.ExportCDL(classlist,file,flag,.errorlog)

Export all classes listed in the comma-separated *list* as a CDL file with name *file*. (Note: this is the old CDL format from previous Caché versions!)

Set status=$System.OBJ.ExportCPP(classlist,file,flag,.errorlog)

Export all classes listed in the comma-separated *classlist* as a C++ file with name *file*.

Set status=$System.OBJ.ExportJava(classlist,dir,flag,.errorlog)

Export all classes listed in the comma-separated *classlist* as Java files in the directory *dir*. The files are named by classname with the extension .java.

4.4.4 Deleting Classes

There are two calls that can be used to delete a specific class or all classes in a package.

Set status=$System.OBJ.Delete(class,flags,.errorlog)

Delete the *class* and its generated routines from the current namespace.

Deleting classes

Set status=$System.OBJ.DeletePackage(package,flags)

Delete all classes of the *package* and their generated routines from the current namespace.

4.4.5 Indirectly Calling a Method

The following functions can be used to call a method indirectly. Unlike the usual method call or the class method call of with the ##class syntax described in Section 6.1.3.2, the class and method names are specified as variables here.

Set result=$ZOBJMETHOD(oref,method,parm₁,parm₂,...,parm₉)
Set result=$ZOBJCLASSMETHOD(class,method,parm₁,parm₂,...,parm₉)

Indirect method calls

Execute the object or class method of the class using *parm₁* to *parm₉* parameters.

4.4.6 Determining the Version Number

Write $System.OBJ.Version()

Determining the version number

Return the current version number of Caché Objects.

4.4.7 Default Settings for Concurrency and Transaction Mode

The following calls set the default settings for the concurrency and the transaction mode. Refer to Section 6.2.2.5 for a more detailed description of these concepts.

Write $$GetConcurrencyMode^%apiOBJ()

Concurrency

Returns the current default setting for the concurrency.

Write $$SetConcurrencyMode^%apiOBJ(mode)

Sets the default setting for concurrency to *mode*. The return value is the previously set mode. Permitted values for *mode* are 0, 1, 2, 3, and 4. If *mode* contains an invalid value, the function returns "InvalidConcurrencyMode" as result.

Example

```
Set oldsetting=$$SetConcurrencyMode^%apiOBJ(1)
```

Write $$GetTransactionMode^%apiOBJ()

Transaction mode

Returns the current default setting for the transaction mode.

Write $$SetTransactionMode^%apiOBJ(mode)

Sets the default value of the current process for transaction mode to *mode*. The return value is the previously set mode. Permitted values for *mode* are 0 and 1. If *mode* contains an invalid value, the function returns "InvalidTransactionMode" as result.

Example

```
Set oldsetting=$$SetTransactionMode^%apiOBJ(1)
```

4.4.8 Querying Error Messages

Do $System.DisplayError(status)

Shows the error message associated with the status code *status*. This call is useful for locating errors.

Evaluating status codes

Example

```
>Set status=Person.%Save()
>Write +status
0
>Do $System.OBJ.DisplayError(status)
ERROR #5802: Datatype validation failed: User.Person.DOB
```

4.4.9 The *flag* and *errorlog* Arguments

Many of the calls described in the previous sections have two optional arguments: *flag* and *errorlog*.

4.4.9.1 The *flag* Argument

The value for *flag* is a string that contains a number of compiler options. Each compiler option consists of a single character. The following table summarizes these options:

Flag	Meaning	Explanation
a	Application	Include application classes (these are all classes not marked as system classes). The a-flag is set as default.
b	Sub Classes	Include subclasses
c	Compile	For the Load*() methods, this flag specifies that classes are also to be compiled.
d	Display	Display the progress and any error messages during loading and compilation. The d-flag is set as default.
f	Force Compile	Force compilation of class(es), even if there are instances currently open in other processes.
k	Keep	During the compilation of classes, normally only the internal .OBJ code of the generated routines is retained. This flag ensures that .MAC and .INT code are also retained for debugging purposes.
r	Recursive	Include all super classes of a class and all data type classes used from this class.
s	System	Include system classes.
u	Update	Include only those classes whose definition has changed.

Table 4.2 Compiler options that can be set with the *flag* argument

The compiler options specified as a string in the *flag* argument can be specified in either uppercase or lowercase. Any option can be suppressed by prefixing a minus sign (–) to the associated alphabetic option. For example, the "cr-d" flags specify recursive compilation without displaying any status information.

Examples

```
Set status=$System.OBJ.LoadFile("C:\Book\Person.xml","cr-d")
Set status=$System.OBJ.LoadDir("C:\Book","c")
```

4.4.9.2 The *errorlog* Argument

To help in troubleshooting, you can specify an *errorlog* parameter for all the previously described calls. This is passed as *call by reference* to a local variable, which, after the execution, contains the number of errors and the individual messages in the following format:

Format of error messages

```
errorlog=n
errorlog(1)= error message 1
errorlog(2)= error message 2
...
errorlog(n)= error message n
```

If error messages are not displayed but only returned in errorlog variables, you must also deactivate the d-flag, as shown in the following example.

Example

```
>Set status=$System.OBJ.Compile("NotPresent","-d",.Error)
>ZWrite Error
Error=1
Error(1)=" ERROR #5351: Class 'User.NotPresent' does not
exist"
Error(1,"code")=5351
Error(1,"param")=1
Error(1,"param",1)="User.NotPresent"
```

5 Fundamentals of Caché ObjectScript

5.1 Basic Structures of Caché ObjectScript

5.1.1 Variables

Caché ObjectScript distinguishes between transient data (namely, data that exists only in memory) and persistent data (i.e., data stored permanently in the database). Both transient and persistent data can exist as scalar or multidimensional structures. The latter, being persistent data, provides the basis for the high-performance *multidimensional access* of Caché ObjectScript. Chapter 7 provides a detailed discussion of this together with multidimensionality.

Transient and persistent data

Let us consider transient and persistent data from another viewpoint. Transient data relates to a particular process and can never be accessed by another process. Transient data are local to this process, and thus is also called a *local variable*.

Local variables

In contrast, persistent data are multiuser data, namely, several processes can access a particular persistent data structure (given the appropriate authorization, of course). They are available system-wide, hence the term global variables, or *globals*. To distinguish them from local variables, all globals are prefixed with a carat symbol ("^").

Global variables

5.1.1.1 Variables and Variable Names

Caché ObjectScript does not limit the length of local or global names. However, only the first 31 characters are significant. The first character must be a lower or uppercase alphabetic character or the % symbol. Characters after the first one can be any mixture of alphabetic characters and digits; no punctuation characters are allowed. The list of allowed alphabetic characters includes national characters such as umlauts etc. Note that all Caché ObjectScript variable names are case sensitive. Thus, locvar and LocVar represent different variables.

Syntax

Three commands define local and global variables: Set, Read, and For. The Kill command deletes variables. Section 5.1.3 provides details.

Examples

```
Set Article1="Trousers"
Read "Article — ",Article2
Kill Article1,Article2
```

The variables Article1 and Article2 receive specific values upon execution of the Set and Read commands, respectively. The variables and

Visibility scope of local variables

Special variables

Structured system variables

their contents are deleted upon executing the Kill command; the Article1 and Article2 variables are then undefined.

A programmer has several mechanisms in Caché ObjectScript for actively determining the visibility scope of local variables. These will be discussed in detail in Section 5.2.4.2.

Caché ObjectScript—in the following sense—is declaration free: the only external data type is the variable-length string. That is, all variables have the type String. However, variables are interpreted *internally* numerically or logically as the result of an arithmetic or Boolean operation. This is done using rules that are transparent to the programmer; these rules are shown in Section 5.1.2.4, together with typical applications.

Special variables represent another category. They are predefined in Caché ObjectScript, and can be set by a program in only a few cases. A dollar sign ("$") prefixed to the name of variable defines it as a special variable. A typical example is $Horolog, which supplies Caché's internal system time. Section 5.1.1.2 shows the most important special variables in a table.

Finally, we should mention a particular form of internal, low-level variables. These are structured system variables, and they can be considered as being a cross between the previously described special variables and global variables. The caret and dollar sign characters ("^$") are prefixed to a structured system variable name. Structured system variables contain low-level information. For example, the ^$Job structured system variable provides information about the current process. The Appendix of this book and the *Caché ObjectScript Reference* contain a list of these variables and their effects.

5.1.1.2 Special Variables

The table below summarizes the most important special variables. If part of a special variable name is shown in square brackets in the table, the variable can be abbreviated to the dollar sign and its first alphabetic character. Some special variables are not listed here, but are described later as they arise. These include the $TLevel special variable used for transaction processing and all special variables associated with the error processing. (Refer to Section 5.4.)

Table 5.1 Special variables

Special variable	Short description
$HALT	If $HALT is set to the name of a routine, this routine is called when a Halt command is executed.
$Horolog	$Horolog contains the date and the time as two counters separated by a comma. The first counter specifies the number of days since Thursday, December 31, 1840 (the day with the value 0). The second counter specifies the number of seconds since midnight today. Also refer to the $ZTimeStamp special variable that functions like $Horolog, but also provides milliseconds.

```
>Write $Horolog
57713,36814
>Write $Piece($Horolog,",",2)
36815
>Write +$Horolog
57713
```

$Io	$Io specifies the name of the input or output device currently being used.

```
>Use "TTA3:" Write $Io
TTA3:
```

$Job	$Job contains a positive integer that uniquely identifies each running process. $Job does not change while this process is active.

```
>Write $Job
1024
>Set ^temp($Job)="String"
```

$Key	$Key contains the character or the character sequence that the last Read command read. Also refer to its functional equivalent $ZB.

```
>Write $Key
<Return>
```

$Principal	Similar to $Io, $Principal contains the name of the device that the current process initially started.

```
>Write $Principal
/dev/tty05
```

$Quit	$Quit always has the value 1 in a called user-defined function, otherwise (namely in subroutines) the value is 0. Also refer to Section 5.2.7 (Extrinsic Functions).

```
>Write $Quit
0
```

$Storage	$Storage contains the size of the area, in bytes, available for the current process to store its local variables. Also refer to $ZStorage.

```
>Write $Storage
15845
```

$Test	$Test contains the value of the most recently calculated test switch. $Test is set for the line-oriented "If with argument" and for the Open, Lock, Read, and Job with Timeout commands. If and Else without arguments (and also a postcondition) do not change the value of $Test. $Test is saved when user-defined functions are called, special variables are accessed, and when the call of a program block includes a Do without argument. It is set back to the old value at the end of the call.

```
>If a=5 Write $Test
1  (if a=5)
>Open dev::10 Write $Test
1  (if Open was successful within 10 seconds)
```

$X	$X reflects the horizontal position of the cursor on an output device. Each output printable character increments the value of $X by 1.

```
>If $X>79 Write !
```

$Y	$Y reflects the vertical position of the cursor on an output device. Each new line (ASCII character 10) increments the value of $Y by 1.

```
>If $Y>59 Write #
```

$ZA	Status of the last Read command on the current device.

```
>Write $ZA#2
1
```

$ZB	Functionally equivalent to $Key. It contains the character or the character sequence that ended the last Read.

```
>Write $ZB
<Return>
```

$ZCHild	When the current Caché process starts a new process using the Job command, $ZCHild contains its process ID. The value is 0 when no process was started.

```
>Write $ZCHild
37
```

$ZEOF	$ZEOF indicates if the end of file is reached after reading from a sequential file. The value −1 indicates *end of file*.

```
>If $ZEOF Close file
```

$ZHorolog	$ZHorolog contains the time in seconds and milliseconds since Caché was started.

```
>Write $ZHorolog
2365.63
```

$ZIo	$ZIo contains information about the type of a terminal device's connection. For example for a Telnet connection, $ZIo contains the IP address of the *remote hosts* in the form nnn.nnn.nnn.nnn.

```
>Write $ZIo
192.9.200.79/1260
```

$ZJob	$ZJob contains a binary number that contains special information about the current job as bits.

```
>Write $ZJob
5
```

$ZMode	$ZMode contains the device parameters that were specified with the last Open or Use command.

```
>Write $ZMode
RY\ISM\
```

$ZName	$ZName contains the name of the currently loaded routine.

```
>Write $ZName
Rec112
```

$ZNSpace	$ZNSpace contains the name of the current namespace. It can be set to change the namespace and is then functionally equivalent to the ZNspace command.

```
>Write $ZNSpace
USER
```

$ZParent	$ZParent contains the process ID that the running process created with a Job command. The value is 0 if this was not created with a Job command.

```
>Write $ZParent
0
```

$ZPI	$ZPI contains the mathematical constant for π, namely: 3.141592653589...
>Write $ZPI 3.1415926535589793238	
$ZReference	$ZReference supplies a complete reference to the most recently accessed global variable.
>Set ^G(1)="Hello" >Write $Zreference ^G(1)	
$ZStorage	$ZStorage contains (or sets) the size of the working storage (in KB) that is available (or is to be made available) for a Caché process.
>Write $ZStorage 24	
$ZTimeStamp $ZTS	Like $Horolog, $ZTimeStamp contains a day and seconds counter, the latter expressed in milliseconds.
>Write $ZTS 57500,11608.52	
$ZTimeZone $ZTZ	$ZTimeZone contains the number of minutes west of GMT. Boston results in +300, Berlin in -60. After $ZTZ is set to a value (e.g., Set $ZTimeZone=n), the value of $Horolog reflects the change in time zone.
>Write $ZTZ 300	
$ZVersion	$ZVersion contains the current Caché version number.
>Write $Zversion Cache for Windows NT (Intel) 5.0	

5.1.2 Operators and Expressions

Operators are symbolic characters that specify the type of the operation to be executed. Caché ObjectScript distinguishes between unary and binary operations, depending on how many operands appear. A binary operation has the following general form:

Unary and binary operations

```
<Operand1><Operator><Operand2>
```

where the operands can be expressions, that is, they may themselves consist of a combination of other operations. The sequence of the processing for binary operators is strictly left to right. Unary operators are always processed before binary operators. When required, parentheses can be used to change the processing sequence.

Caché ObjectScript provides a wide range of operators, some of which are special operators that support the efficient, string-oriented programming for which ObjectScript is well-known.

Binary operators are grouped into:

- arithmetic operators, e.g., basic computation, such as raising a number to a power, etc.
- string operators, e.g., the concatenation operator, or the test whether one string contains another string
- logical operators, in particular, AND, OR, and NOT

- comparison operators, e.g., compare numbers for greater and less than, or compare two strings for equality.

There is also the operator for pattern matching (the meaning and use of which is described in the next section), as well as the indirection operator (which adopts a special status, as discussed in Section 5.1.3.4). The There are three unary operators: ' (NOT), + (plus), and – (minus). The result of each logical and comparison operator can be inverted with the Not symbol ('). The following general rule applies: A'<op>B is equivalent to '(A<op>B), where <op> represents one of the operator characters =, [, <,],]], >, &, !, or ?.

Examples

```
2'=3      corresponds to      '(2=3)      (logical TRUE)
6'<10     corresponds to      '(6<10)     (logical FALSE)
```

The combined operator '= is easy to recognize as the "not equal" operator and '< as a "not less than" or "greater than equal" operator.

5.1.2.1 Overview of Operators

Unary arithmetic operators (+, –)

The sign operators (+ and –) force a numeric interpretation of operands, for cases where they might otherwise be interpreted as text operations. (Refer to Section 5.1.2.4.) The sign is inverted in the case of the minus operator.

Expression	Value
--13	13
+"12ab"	12
+$Horolog	57731

The unary logical operator (')

The *not* operator inverts the logical value of the following expression. Its double use is equivalent to the single logical interpretation of its operand.

Expression	Value
'1	0
'0	1

Binary arithmetic operators (+,–,*, /,\, #, **)

In addition to the four basic arithmetic operations (+, –, *, /), there are also:

- integer division \, which returns the integer interpretation of a normal division
- power operator ** (with which you can use fractions as exponents to calculate the root of a number)
- Modulo operator #, which is formally defined as:

```
a#b corresponds to  a-(b*[a/b])
```

where [a/b] represents the largest integer less than or equal to a/b (in other words, the integer division of a by b).

Here are examples using the local variables and their values a=5, b=7, c=10

Expression	Value
a+b	12
a*b-c	25
c/a	2
2+a*b	49
2+(a*b)	37
3700#3600	100
c#a	0
9.123\1	9
3700\3600	1
2**5	32
9**.5	3
16**.25	2
4**(-2)	.0625

Arithmetic comparison operators (<, >)

These two operators compare two numeric values for greater than or less than. The comparisons initially convert the operands into numeric values before the comparison is performed. The result of a comparison is either 0 for "false" or 1 for "true".

When y=12, z=15

Expression	Value
y<z	1
z>"16abc"	0

String comparison operators (=, [,],]])

The = comparison operator compares two strings for equality. If you wish to test for numeric equality, you must force a numeric interpretation by prefixing a plus character to each operand (e.g., +number1=+number2).

The Contains operator [tests whether the right-hand string is contained in the left-hand string. The Follows operator] tests whether the left-hand operand follows the right-hand operand in lexicographic sequence. The "Sorts after" operator]] tests whether the left-hand operand sorts after the right-hand operator. (Refer to Section 7.1.1.2.)

When x=3, y="A", z="3.0"

Expression	Value
x="a"	0
x=z	0
"ABC"[y	1
x]y	0
y]x	1
z](x=y)	1
2]]19	0

Logical operators (&, !, &&, ||)

The logical *and* (&) is true when both operands are true. The logical *or* (!) is true when at least one operand is true.

When m=0, n=1

Expression	Value
(m=1)&(n=1)	0
(m=1)!(n=1)	1
'(m=1)&(n=1)	1
m=0'&(n=1)	1
m=0&'n'=1	1

Please note here that, in every case, the operations also evaluate the right-hand operands, even when the evaluation of the left-hand operand has already determined the final result.

&& and || operators

In addition to the two logical operators listed above, Caché Object-Script also provides two related operators, && (AND) and || (OR), which differ from & and ! in one important aspect: both omit the evaluation of the right-hand operand when the evaluation of the left-hand part of the operation has already produced the complete result. The latter is the case when the left-hand operand for the AND operation is FALSE or when it is TRUE for the OR operation.

Concatenation (_)

The effect of the concatenation operation is to combine two strings to form a single string.

When x="12"

Expression	Value
"AB"_"CD"	ABCD
"AB "_x	AB 12
x_"A"[2	1

5.1.2.2 The Pattern Match Operator

The question mark ("?") is the operator symbol for pattern matching. The left-hand operand is the string to be evaluated. The right-hand operand is a so-called "pattern" that consists of a number and one or more character classes. The result of the pattern match is a logical TRUE (i.e., the value 1) when the operand corresponds exactly to the pattern, otherwise 0. The number 348 (used here as an example) consists of three digits. Thus, the pattern match 348?3N (348 corresponds to the "three digits" pattern) returns a logical TRUE value.

One or more character classes

The basis of the pattern match is the character set used in Caché. The set is subdivided into individual character classes for the pattern match. Although Caché supports a range of different character sets (in its so-called National Language Support features), the 7-bit ASCII character set is well-suited to explain the basic principle of the pattern match. However, for an extension to other character sets, we must always ask to which character set(s) does a specified character belong.

Let us consider here the control characters as a character class that consists of ASCII characters with codes 0–31 and 127. Similarly, consider punctuation characters, digits, and alphabetic characters. Each of these classes has a short designation that indicates the characters used in the pattern match.

Character Class	Designation	ASCII Codes	Example
C	Control characters	0-31, 127	Bell
P	Punctuation characters	32-47, 58-64	!,$,%,&,/
N	Digits	48-57	5
U	Uppercase letters	65-90	A–Z
L	Lowercase letters	92-122	a–z
A	Alphabetic characters	65-90, 92-122	A–Z, a–z
E	All characters	0-127	

Table 5.2 Character classes and their meanings for pattern matching

The last two groups do not represent their own character classes but are combinations of other classes.

In the pattern match, the character class for each character of a string is tested. A pattern is built using a simple principle: it consists of a series of pattern elements without delimiters. Each of these pattern elements consists of a part that specifies a replication factor and a part that specifies which character class is to be used for the comparison.

Sequence of pattern elements

As an example, consider a date in the form mm/dd/yyyy (such as 11/29/1999) contained in the date variable. The following command line validates a date input:

```
If date?2N1P2N1P4N { Write "Date input valid" }
```

The contents of the date variable are checked to see whether they match the 2N1P2N1P4N pattern. This consists of five pattern elements, namely 2N, 1P, 2N, 1P, and 4N. Each pattern element consists of a replication factor and the specification of a character class. Thus, the 2N pattern

Replication factor

element recognizes exactly two successive numeric digits, whereas 1P recognizes exactly one punctuation character.

The result of the pattern match is a logical value, and is always 1 (TRUE) when the variable matches the pattern or 0 (FALSE) when this is not the case.

Date inputs of the form 310/5/1999 are recognized as being false, because three digits introduce this string rather than the third character being a punctuation character as required by the pattern.

Instead of general punctuation characters, you can also specify the exact character you wish to have in the date. For example, to require a slash as the delimiter, you specify the pattern element 1"/". Then you can more exactly formulate the pattern for a date, such as: 2N1"/"2N1"/"4N.

It is also possible to specify the minimum or maximum number of times that a character of a class can occur.

The following table summarizes permitted range formats.

Table 5.3 Formats of the repeat factor

Repeat Factor	Meaning
<number>	The pattern must occur exactly <number> times.
<number1>.<number2>	The pattern must occur at least <number1> times, but not more than <number2> times.
<number>.	The pattern must occur at least <number> times, but it can appear an unlimited maximum number of times.
.<number>	The pattern can occur a maximum <number> times.
.	The pattern can occur an unlimited number of times (or not at all).

You can use the following pattern match expression to fully validate the above date:

```
1.2N1"/"1.2N1"/"4N
```

Rather than validating whether a string matches a pattern, you often do the reverse. You test whether a string does *not* match a specified pattern. Then, you can display an error message and request the user to re-enter the string.

Typical uses of pattern matching

The following examples show typical uses of pattern matching.

Examples

A string that starts with an uppercase letter and followed optionally by letters or punctuation characters:

```
1U.AP
```

A German car registration plate, such as DA-DM 733:

```
1.3U1"-"1.2U1" "1.4N
```

A string to test for the presence of a control character:

```
.E1C.E
```

Finally, we must consider the concept of alternate patterns. A date is a good example, because users can enter it in many formats, all of which are recognizable as dates:

- Separator is dot: 11.29.1999
- Separator is slash: 11/29/1999
- Separator is dash: 11-29-1999

Mixed forms or other separators are not permitted. It is easy to see that the first two and the last four digits are fixed and the alternating part lies in between. The following pattern match validates the date examples, while permitting alternate separators:

```
1.2N1(1"."1.2N1".",1"/"1.2N1"/",1"-"1.2N1"-")4N
```

The bracketed series of patterns represent an OR situation: either the first or the second or the third pattern must be satisfied.

Please consult Caché manuals for further details about this very powerful variant of pattern matching.

5.1.2.3 Expressions

Fundamental to a deeper understanding of Caché ObjectScript is the <expr> term expression. The processing of expressions plays a central role in Caché ObjectScript.

Stated briefly, an expression is a syntactical element that produces a value in Caché ObjectScript. Multiplying a user-defined function with a global variable—such as $$Fun(a)*^G(1,2)—is an good example.

An expression is characterized through the connection of so-called expression atoms (as primary value-indicating elements), plus unary or binary operators. Consequently, you can imagine an expression atom as an elementary expression that cannot be further shortened. Bracketed expressions also represent expression atoms.

Table 5.4 shows the expression atoms that can be used in Caché ObjectScript.

Expression atom	Meaning	Example
<glvn>	Local or global variable	^G(1,2)
<svn>	Special variable	$Horolog
<function>	Function	$Length(a)
<exfunc>	User-defined function	$$X(1)
<exvar>	User-defined variable	$$H
<numlit>	Numeric literal	1.07
<strlit>	String literal	"abc"
<ssvn>	Structured system variable	^$Routine(name)
(<expr>)	Bracketed expression	($$F1(x1)_$$F2(x2))

Table 5.4 Expression atoms defined in Caché ObjectScript

An expression is processed in the following three steps:
1. Evaluate the left-hand expression atom.
2. Evaluate the right-hand expression atom, and perform the operation.
3. Proceed right, and repeat step 2 if necessary.

Individual operators have no priority

This statement means that there is no form of preference for specific operators. All binary operators are executed strictly from left to right. Consequently, 3+4*5 yields 35; bracketing can be used to obtain a different result, for example, 3+(4*5) yields 23. You can avoid parentheses in many cases by reordering the operations: for instance, 4*5+3 also yields 23.

In contrast, the unary operators (the + and – signs, and the logical negation ') are processed from right to left. In other words, the expression atom is calculated first (e.g., a function), and then the unary operations applied. In this regard, -''+$Length("abcde") equals –1. Note the double negation with the NOT operator.

Powerful instrument

What initially appears to be a hindrance, actually provides (together with the implicit type interpretation discussed in the next section) a powerful instrument with which experienced Caché programmers like to utilize. For example, the expression jjjj#4=0+28 represents the number of days in February, provided the variable jjjj represents a year between 1901 and 2099. In this time period, year numbers representing a leap year do not have a remainder when divided by four, and the comparison to 0 returns (logical) 1 to which the number 28 is added.

Spaces within expressions

Other than three clearly defined exceptions, expressions can contain any number of spaces.

Example

```
Set¬sum = x + y + z , mue = sum / 3
```

The symbol ¬ represents a single space that must be placed between a command word and the first argument of the command. Although we mentioned this exception earlier, we should point out here that commands without arguments must always be followed by at least two spaces (or a line end). The other two syntactic situations that cannot contain any additional spaces are:

- Names of variables, classes, objects, methods, properties, and routines, including labels, *cannot* contain spaces.
- Literal numbers (namely, constants) also *cannot* contain spaces.

5.1.2.4 Number Representation and Implicit Data Type Conversion

Non-typed languages

Non-typed languages (such as Caché ObjectScript) provide conventions in which a data type conversion is performed automatically according to the syntactic context.

For example, arithmetic operations performed on strings return numeric values that can be considered to be special cases of strings. There are unique rules for the interpretation of strings as numbers and also numbers as the Boolean truth values 0 and 1 in conjunction with the logical operators.

Numbers in Caché ObjectScript

It is essential to appreciate how numbers are represented in Caché ObjectScript. They can have the form of an integer (e.g., 4661), decimal numbers with decimal places (e.g., 2.1 or .57), or exponential forms, where the mantissa has one of the previously described forms and the exponent is a positive or negative integer (e.g., 3E7 or 31.4E-1). A lowercase "e" can also be used to represent an exponent. Thus, 1e9 and 1E9 are identical.

All of these numbers can have leading zeros (e.g., 001 or 03E-3). They can have any number of signs. Each minus sign changes the sign of the result; plus signs are ignored.

Caché ObjectScript performs the numeric interpretation of a string from left to right. It is terminated as soon as a character is detected that does not match the pattern specified above. The numeric value 0 is assigned to the string if no numeric interpretation is possible. The following examples illustrate that all numeric unary and binary operators force a numeric interpretation of a string.

Expression	Value
+"123abc"	123
--"314.159E-2xyz"	3.14159
+"This is a number = 1265"	0
+$Horolog	57123
"3 apples"+"4 pears"	7
1>"large"	1 (TRUE)
".3"="3E-1"	0 (FALSE)
+".3"=+"3E-1"	1 (TRUE)

Table 5.5 Examples of numeric interpretation

Whereas the first two examples are obvious, the third example does not contain a string at the start that can be interpreted as a number. (The numbers further to the right in the string are, therefore, not evaluated.) The fourth example shows how to get the day part of $Horolog. The fifth example is obvious. The sixth example illustrates that the greater-than operator is also a numeric operator (1 is larger than 0). This also applies for the less-than operator, but not for the equals operator ("="). The seventh example exhibits precisely this behavior: ".3" and "3E-1" are two different strings, even though their numeric content is identical. Checking the numeric equality of two variables requires forcing a numeric interpretation (as in the last example).

Finally, we can consider the logical evaluation of a string, which requires that the string be interpreted numerically. If the numeric interpretation of a string is nonzero, the logical interpretation is TRUE, namely 1. And vice versa: if the numeric interpretation is zero, the logical interpretation of this string is FALSE, namely 0.

Logical interpretation

Thus, the expression "abc"!"1 Pizza" is equivalent to FALSE OR TRUE, which represents a true statement.

5.1.3 Commands

Commands in Caché ObjectScript perform actions. For example, the Set command assigns a value to a variable, and the Do command invokes a routine. Caché ObjectScript provides a large number of commands for various actions.

The aim of this section is to explain the significant properties of most Caché ObjectScript commands. Some command classes we will cover in later sections of this book. These include the commands for program flow control, transaction processing, and command constructs that have their own syntax. (Refer to Section 5.3.)

5.1.3.1 Syntax of Commands and Special Features

The command Set ArtNo=12345678 assigns a special value to the ArtNo variable. In general, commands in Caché ObjectScript consist of command words (in this example, Set) and associated command arguments (in the example, ArtNo=12345678).

```
<commandword><blank>[<argument>,<argument>,...]
```

In a form of replication of the command word, you can specify a list of individual arguments separated by commas that are executed in sequence.

Abbreviation to the first letter of a command

A single blank must appear between the command and its first argument. All commands can be abbreviated to their first letter (or, in some cases, to the first two letters) to ensure uniqueness. Experienced Caché ObjectScript programmers make wide use of command abbreviations.

Examples

```
Set ArtNo=12345678,ArtDes="light-colored trousers"
Do ^P1(ArtNo,ArtDes),P2(ArtNo)
```

Several commands do not require arguments or can be used optionally with or without arguments. The most important are: Do, For, If, Else, and Quit. In these cases, at least two blank characters (or a line end) must follow a command with no argument before a new command can start.

Command post-condition

A special feature in Caché ObjectScript is the so-called *command post-condition*, a logical expression that decides whether a command is to be executed. The command is executed only when the logical expression evaluates to TRUE. The logical expression is suffixed to the command word with a colon. The syntax of post-conditions follows this general structure:

```
<command word><:><logical expression><blank>[<argument>,...]
```

Examples

```
Do:Sales>100000 ^SoBu(Sales),^Warehouse(type)
Set:var=1 var=2
Quit:i>31
Kill:t=9 var1,var2,var3
```

The associated post-conditions are underscored in the example, and the commands are executed only when the post-condition is logically TRUE. This applies to the command and all its arguments. The command post-processing is permitted for all commands except If, Else, and For.

Finally, it should be noted that device-specific parameters (written in parentheses and separated from the command argument with a colon) can determine device types for the input/output commands Open, Use, and Close.

5.1 Basic Structures of Caché ObjectScript

Commands are executed only when the post-condition is logically TRUE

Example

```
Open dev:(/CRT:/MARGIN=80)
```

You can omit parentheses when a command has only one parameter. (Refer to Chapter 13 for device-specific parameters.)

You can specify a so-called "timeout" for four commands: Read, Open, Lock, and Job. The timeout value is the number of seconds after which the command processing must have been completed. If it is not complete, the command is terminated automatically (and the value for $Test implicitly set to 0). (Refer to Chapter 13 for details about device-specific commands.)

Timeouts for Read, Open, Lock *and* Job

Examples

```
Read "Article Number: ",ArtNo:10
Open dev::0 Else  Write "Device not available"
```

The first example shows a typical use in conjunction with the Read command. If this command does not complete within ten seconds (usually by a mouse click or pressing the Return key), the system terminates the Read, and the ArtNo variable contains any text fragment that may have been entered up to that point. The use of a timeout with the Open command is common. If the program cannot *immediately* (timeout is 0) access the specified device, because, for example, it has been reserved by another process, the open attempt is terminated. Because the first colon separates the device-specific parameters, the Open command needs two colons.

Typical uses of a timeout

5.1.3.2 List of Important Commands

This section lists a series of tables that summarize the most important commands in Caché ObjectScript. Each table represents a group of commands that perform similar actions. Since commands for transaction processing are described in Section 7.3, they are not discussed here.

Every command can be abbreviated to its initial letter or letters. (Note that Section 5.1.3.4 discusses the @ indirection operator used in some of the following examples.)

Table 5.6 Groups of important Caché
ObjectScript commands

Command Group	Typical representatives
Control of program flow	`If`, `Else`, `For`, `Quit`, `Do`, `Goto`, `Break`, `Xecute`
Variable handling	`Set`, `Merge`, `Kill`, `New`, `Lock`
Input/output	`Read`, `Write`, `Open`, `Use`, `Close`
Miscellaneous	`Job`, `Hang`, `Halt`, `View`

The following table provides a short description of each program flow command.

Table 5.7 Commands for program
flow control

Command	Short description
`If`	`If` in this line-oriented form permits the conditional execution of the part of the program line that follows the command. The rest of the line is executed only when the logical interpretation of the `If` argument is TRUE (namely 1). `$Test` then receives the value 1. If the `If`-argument evaluates logically to FALSE, the execution continues with the next line and `$Test` is set to 0. `If` in the form without arguments executes the remainder of the line only when `$Test` is 1. *Instead of this old, line-oriented form, the use of the `If`/`Else`/`ElseIf` command construct is recommended; refer to Section 5.3.1.2.*

`If t=1`
`If age>30 If sex="m"`
`If  Set x=1`	

`Else`	`Else` permits the conditional execution of the part of the program line following the command depending on the `$Test` special variable. It is executed only when `$Test` has the value 0. Otherwise a branch is made to the next program line. `Else` has no arguments and does not change the value of `$Test`. *Instead of this old, line-oriented form, the use of the `If`/`Else`/`ElseIf` command construct is recommended; refer to Section 5.3.1.2.*
`If a<1 Do ^P1(t1)` `Else  Do ^P2(t1)`	
`For`	The `For` command causes the repeated execution of the complete program line that follows this command. The command has four formats. In the expression format, the control variable values are assigned from a specified list. In the range format, a control variable is increased from a start value by the increment until the end value is reached. In the third form, the end value is not specified, only the initial value and the increment. No control variables are specified for the fourth form without arguments. This variant must be ended with a `Quit` from the loop. A `Quit` can also be used to end the other forms. *Instead of this old, line-oriented form, the use of the `For` command construct is recommended; refer to Section 5.3.1.3.*

`For J=-9,5,7,36,-100`
`For i=1:1:10`
`For k="A","B",1:2:11`
`For l=1:1`
`For`	

`Quit`	`Quit` ends the associated innermost `For` loop and subroutines that were invoked with `Do` or `Xecute`, i.e., also program blocks. `Quit` does not have any argument for this usage form. User-defined functions and variables are ended with a `Quit` with argument (also refer to Section 5.2.7).

`Quit`
`Quit:t=10`
`Quit a*b`	

Do	In the form with arguments, Do executes successively the listed local or global subroutine. The execution of global subroutines starts in the first line when the routine name is not prefixed with a label. Otherwise, execution starts at the label. The next command after the invoking Do command is executed after processing the subroutine. A list of current parameters can follow the routine name. Each element can be an arbitrary expression or have the form .name, which serves to pass a reference to a variable. The current parameters are assigned to the formal parameters in the order of their appearance.

```
Do LoPro,^R1(1v,1v1)
Do ^Routine(a1,.a2)
Do:A=1 PROG:T=1
Do anam^ab
Do ^P1:C1
```

Goto	Goto terminates the sequential execution of programs and branches either to a line of the same routine or to a line of another routine, in each case without return. A post-condition on the command and arguments are permitted.

```
Goto loclabel
Goto:t A:s=1,B:s=2
Goto L1:C1,L2:C2
```

Xecute	The Xecute command executes a string as a single-line subroutine (without a label). Nested Xecute constructs, and the use of a post-condition for the command and the arguments, are also permitted. A Quit in an argument ends the execution of the argument.

```
Xecute a,^B
Xecute "S x=1"
Xexute:t["a" t(1,2):true
Xecute aa_"X ab"
```

Break	Break is a command for error processing. In the form without an argument, it sets a breakpoint (interrupt) and the program leaves execution mode. However, it is better to use the ZBreak command for this purpose. There are several variants of an argument of the Break command. Break 1 makes it possible to use <Ctrl-C> to set an interrupt; Break O deactivates this. An interrupt can also be set automatically after certain conditions, e.g., after every command execution with Break "S" (S indicates "single step") and several other arguments.

```
Break
Break 1
Break "S"
```

The following table provides a short description of each command that changes the value or state of a variable.

Command	Short description
Set	Set assigns values to variables. A value can be assigned to several variables by writing the variables within parentheses. Unless there are indexes on the left-hand side, the expression specified after the equal sign is always calculated first. Use Set $Piece or Set $Extract to replace parts of a string.

```
Set x=5,n(1)=4
Set ^FILE=3
Set:a>0 (i,j,k)=1
Set aa=ab+1
Set $Piece(v,"*",3)="A"
```

Table 5.8 Commands that change variables

Merge	Merge is used to copy complete subtrees of arrays into each other, whether they are defined locally or globally. Please refer to Chapter 7, which describes this important command in detail.

```
Merge a=b
Merge var(1)=^G(1,2)
```

Kill	Kill deletes the local or global variables specified in the argument list. In the form without arguments, all local variables are deleted. In the bracketed form, which can only be used for non-indexed local variables, all local variables not listed within parentheses are deleted. A Kill on a node of an indexed variable deletes the node and all its child nodes. Global variables and subtrees of multidimensional variables can be deleted only with the selective form.

```
Kill
Kill a,b,^C
Kill a(1,3)
Kill (v1,v2,v3)
Kill:bed p1,p2,@var
```

New	New hides the local variables specified in its argument list. Previously defined local variables with the same name are then undefined. If a value is assigned to a variable listed in the argument of the New command, this value remains available until a Quit command ends the current routine. A Kill is then performed automatically on these variables, and any previously defined values become visible again. In the form without arguments, all local variables are hidden. In the exclusive (bracketed) form, only those variables not listed within the parentheses are hidden. Only non-indexed variables can be listed in the argument of the New command. The effect applies only to the specified variable itself and all its (indexed) successors.

```
New
New a,b
New(x1,x2)
```

Lock	Lock is primarily used to lock global variables to reserve them temporarily for use by a Caché ObjectScript routine. The Lock command has four variants. Lock without arguments is used to release all locks. Lock with an argument without a plus or minus sign initially releases all locks, and then locks the variables specified in the argument. The argument can be either the name of a variable or a bracketed list of variable names. Finally, Lock with a plus sign prefixed to the argument requests additional locks for the variables specified in the argument; Lock with a minus sign prefixed to the argument releases the selective lock. The last two forms operate cumulatively: if the same variable, v, is locked more than once with Lock +v, it must be unlocked the same number of times with Lock −v before it becomes available to other processes. The locking of a node of a multidimensional variable also locks all child nodes. Neighboring nodes are not affected. A timeout can be specified and should always be used for the selective form. Also refer to Section 7.3.

```
Lock
Lock (a,^G)
Lock ^A(1,2)
Lock (b,^H):10
Lock +^A,-^PER(name)
Lock +(^P1,^P2)
```

The next table summarizes the commands used for input/output on the "home terminal" or on other attached devices. Note that Open, Use, and Close are platform-dependent commands, because device types and requirements vary per platform. (Refer to Chapter 12.)

Table 5.9 Device specific commands

Command	Short description
Read	Read assigns values read from an input device to local and global variables. An asterisk prefixed to the name of a variable reads a character whose ASCII code is assigned to the specified variable. A length restriction can be specified for the input and is separated with the number sign from the variable name. A timeout (to limit the input time) is also possible; it is introduced with a colon.

`Read x,^G1(ind)`
`Read "City: ",city`
`Read *z`
`Read:$Data(g) !,"Input? ",input#10`
`Read @a:10`	

Write	The Write command outputs data to the home terminal or the device specified with Use. An * signals the output of the ASCII equivalent. The format can be controlled with #, !, and ?, which force a form feed, line feed, and tab, respectively.

`Write "HELLO"`
`Write #!?10,*7`
`Write:'t a,b,!!,c+t/5_s`
`Write @a,@@v`	

Open	The Open command reserves a device or a file. Its execution results in the logical connection between program and device. It reserves the device for this program until a Close command is specified for the device. The type of use can be specified and is separated from the device name with a colon. It consists either of a single expression or a bracketed list of expressions. A timeout introduced with a further colon can be specified to place a time limit for the reservation attempt.

`Open device`
`Open 3,prnt::time`
`Open:'closed @tape`
`Open term:(Param):20`	

Use	Use regularly follows the Open command to declare a device as the current input/output device. Device parameters can be specified and are separated with a colon from the device name (possibly set within parentheses).

`Use device`
`Use:status="OPEN" dev`
`Use 3:(parameter)`
`Use @print`	

Close	Close releases all reserved devices specified as arguments. Device-specific parameters can follow the argument.

`Close "DEV",3`
`Close:bed>3 line`
`Close tty:(/DELETE)`	

The next table summarizes a miscellaneous group of Caché ObjectScript commands.

Table 5.10 Miscellaneous commands

Command	Short description
Job	Job starts one or more parallel Caché ObjectScript processes from the current program. The argument is the entry point of a local or global routine. Parameters can be transferred to the background process using a list of expressions set within parentheses. A colon can separate the specification of process parameters. These can be either a single expression or a list of expressions set within parentheses. A further colon can separate the specification of a timeout.

`Job ^A`
`Job B,A1^PROG`
`Job:g=1 J1::10`
`Job @var:(Parameter)`
`Job ^P1(4,x1,$Extract(name))`	

Hang	Hang pauses the execution of the current process for the number of seconds specified in the argument. Hang with a negative or 0 argument has no effect.

`Hang 10`
`Hang:t=1 b/4`
`Hang @i`	

Halt	Halt terminates the current process. Lock and Close commands (each without an argument) are performed automatically beforehand. Halt has no argument and so differs from the abbreviated form of the Hang command.
`Halt` `Halt:cancel`	
View	The View command processes the contents of working memory and the disk, i.e., viewed and changed. Consequently, only experienced Caché system programmers should use the View command. Refer to the Caché documentation for more details.
`View 6` `View O:ADDR:"WXYZ"`	

5.1.3.3 Overview of Z-commands

The next summarizes the group of Caché ObjectScript commands known as Z-commands (because their names begin with the letter Z).

Table 5.11 Caché ObjectScript Z-commands

Command group	Short description	Commands
Edit commands	Commands to edit routines in programming mode	`ZInsert`, `ZLoad`, `ZPrint`, `ZRemove`, `ZSave`, `ZWrite`
Error processing	Set breakpoints and error messages	`ZBreak`, `ZQuit`, `ZTrap`, `ZSYNC`
Low-level commands	Commands used to change some system settings, e.g., change the current namespace	`ZKill`, `ZNspace`, `ZZDUMP`

Edit commands   The edit commands provide experienced Caché programmers in certain circumstances with a quick means of editing routines directly in programming mode without invoking Caché Studio:

- load routines using ZLoad, e.g., ZLoad P1Calc
- add new lines in the routine using ZInsert, e.g.,
  ZInsert " Set x1=1,y2=2":+2 inserts this code after the second line as a new third line

- display the routine just changed using ZPrint (or the identical Print), e.g., ZPrint P1Calc
- store this routine using ZSave, e.g., ZSave P1Calc
- delete single lines or a complete routine from memory using ZRemove, e.g., ZRemove P1CalcOld
- display the current list of all local variables using ZWrite (without an argument) or display the value of a variable with all defined indexes, as with ZWrite a.

Note that ZLoad can be invoked only in programming mode and not, for example, from a routine. The interested reader should consult the Caché documentation for further information about this command group.

The command group used for error processing includes three other commands. We will discuss these in conjunction with error processing.

ZKill is an extension of the usual Kill command. ZKill permits the deletion of a subscripted variable *without* affecting any child nodes—namely subscripts at a lower level, as is the case with the Kill command.

Finally, ZNspace changes from one namespace to another by specifying the new namespace (possibly extended with a password) as an argument of the command.

5.1.3.4 The Indirection Operator @

The type conversion of a string into executable program code is performed explicitly using the a indirection operator in four clearly differentiated areas:

- Name indirection—type conversion into a name (e.g., of a variable).
- Argument indirection—type conversion into a complete command argument.
- Index indirection—type conversion into an indexed variable.
- Pattern indirection—type conversion into a pattern specification for pattern matching.

Type conversion of a string in program code

Short explanations (with examples) of these four forms of indirection follow.

Forms of indirection

Name indirection

Assume a variable v1 contains the name of a local variable as its value; for example, v1="locvar". The data type of the value of v1 obviously represents a string.

Because the Set command expects the name of a variable and not a string, the assignment Set "locvar"=4 produces an error message. However, the programmer can use the a indirection operator to force a type conversion into a name. For instance, Set av1=4 assigns the value 4 to the locvar variable. This form of indirection is called name indirection.

Name indirection can be used where Caché expects the names of variables (whether local, global, non-indexed, or an array) or routine references (such as label or label plus routine name).

Example

```
Set pname="^Prog1" Do @pname
```

This code invokes the ^Prog1 routine.

Argument indirection

In contrast to name indirection, argument indirection converts strings into arguments for commands. With the exception of the For command (with which argument indirection is not permitted), complete arguments or argument lists can be referenced indirectly.

Example

```
Set isetarg="x=1",@isetarg
```

The isetarg variable contains a syntactically correct argument of the Set command, which is executed using the indirection operator. Because "x=1" is not a permitted name, you can see a clear difference between name indirection and argument indirection. However, for many commands (e.g., Write, Read, Kill, New, etc.), the argument can be a name. In this case, the two forms do not differ. Here are examples in which the two forms are clearly different:

Examples

```
Set ikill="(e,f,g)" Kill @ikill
Set inew="(a,b,c)" New @inew
```

Subscript indirection

Expansion of local or global variables

Subscript indirection (a somewhat less frequently used form of indirection) expands local or global variables. The required pair of indirection operators makes it is easy to spot. The first operator converts its string into a variable name, whereas the second operator expands the name with the subscript (or subscripts) specified in parentheses. The following example illustrates the concept:

Example

```
>Set x(2,5,3)="SubInd" Set field="x(2,5)",d1=3
>Write @field@(d1)
SubInd
```

The code in the preceding example expands the variable by adding a third subscript level (with the value 3) to the x(2,5) field.

Pattern indirection

Pattern indirection can indirectly reference a complete pattern for a pattern match.

Example

```
Set lvpattern="1.3N" If input'?@lvpattern Do Error
```

Note that a string in the context of the pattern match is converted into a pattern using the "@" indirection operator.

5.1.4 Intrinsic Functions

Predefined functions—also called intrinsic functions—are a major part of most programming languages. Caché ObjectScript provides a large number of predefined functions for all processing areas. Functions can be referenced in any expression. A single value calculated from the specified arguments replaces the function call. Functions are recursive in Caché, meaning that they can contain themselves (or other functions) nested as arguments.

User-defined functions—the extrinsic functions—allow application developers to define their own functions. They are discussed in Section 5.2.7.

Intrinsic functions can be referenced in any expression

5.1.4.1 Characteristics of Intrinsic Functions

The names of all intrinsic functions in Caché ObjectScript begin with a dollar sign ("$"). The individual arguments of a function are enclosed within parentheses and separated by commas. Thus, in general, a function call takes the following form:

```
$functionname(Argument1,Argument2,...)
```

The function name can be written in uppercase, lowercase, or a mixture of both. With the exception of $ListBuild, a function must have at least one argument.

Examples

```
>Write $Extract("Summersmog",7,10)
smog
>Set d1=2*$Length("Summersmog") Write d1
20
>Set zk="Spring,Summer,Fall,Winter"
>Write $Extract(zk,8,$Length(zk))
Summer,Fall,Winter
```

Extracting a substring from a string (using the $Extract function) is a very common example of using an intrinsic function. Intrinsic functions often appear in expressions, and in fact arguments of functions can themselves be functions. The processing proceeds from the innermost element to the outermost.

Extract a substring from a string

Function names can be abbreviated. Generally, with the exceptions mentioned below, the name of an intrinsic function can be abbreviated, as long as the abbreviation is still unique compared with other function names.

Arguments represent arbitrary expressions

The *arguments* of various functions represent arbitrary expressions. Such expressions are evaluated differently depending on the function and the position of the argument.

The following expression types can occur:

Table 5.12 Caché ObjectScript expression types

Argument	Meaning
<expr>	indicates an arbitrary expression
<int expr>	indicates an expression interpreted as an integer
<num expr>	indicates an expression interpreted numerically
<log expr>	indicates an expression interpreted logically

The conversion occurs automatically. If, for example, an <int expr> is expected at some position in a function, but an arbitrary expression is there (e.g., 7**2*3.14159), then this expression is calculated first (producing 153.93791) and truncated to form the integer value 153, which is then used in the function calculation. The following example illustrates this:

Example

```
>Write $Extract("work assignment",2.5,3.5)
or
```

Note that the second and third arguments (specifying the start and end positions of the substring to be extracted from the string specified in the first argument) are decimal numbers, not integers, which the intrinsic function $Extract requires. $Extract automatically converts these (using implicit integer division with the number 1) to produce the numbers 2 and 3, respectively, before performing the string extract.

5.1.4.2 Grouping of Intrinsic Functions

The following table lists the intrinsic functions defined in Caché Object-Script. This section introduces these intrinsic functions, which are discussed in the sections that follow.

Table 5.13 Overview of built-in intrinsic functions in Caché Object-Script

Function class	Typical representatives	Comment
General	$Ascii, $CASE, $Char, $Random, $Select, $STack, $Text, $View	
Variable and data-base oriented	$Data, $Get, $Order, $NAme, $Query, $QSubscript, $QLength,$SORTBEGIN, $SORTEND	Described in detail in Chapter 7
String handling	$Extract, $Find, $Length, $Piece, $Reverse, $TRanslate	Refer to Section 5.1.5.2 for $Piece and $Length
Number formatting	$FNumber, $Justify, $INumber, $NUMber	

Lists	$LIst, $ListBuild, $ListData, $ListFind, $ListGet, $ListLength	Refer to Section 5.1.5
TP	$Increment	Refer to Section 7.3.2.4
Mathematics	$ZABS, $ZEXP, $ZLN, $ZSIN, etc.	
Date, time	$ZDate, $ZDateTime, $ZDateH, $ZTime, $ZTimeH	
Bit string	$BIT, $BITCOUNT, $BITFIND, $BITLOGIC, $ZBOOLEAN, $ZCyc	The previous functions ($ZBit, etc.) are still supported but should not be used in future.
General	$ISObject, $ZF, $ZHex, $ZISWide, $ZLAscii, $ZLChar, $ZName, $ZSEArch, $ZSEEK, $ZWAscii, $ZWBPack, $ZWBUnpack, $ZWChar, $ZWPack, $ZWUnpack	
String	$ZCONVert, $ZSTRIP, $ZPosition, $ZWidth, $ZZENKAKU	
Utility	$ZUtil(n)	Various utility functions defined for many integers n; some are platform-dependent

5.1.4.3 Overview of Functions

Caché ObjectScript intrinsic functions can be divided into six groups, according to the entities on which they operate:

- General functions needed for various purposes
- Variable-oriented functions, especially those that operate on the multi-dimensional variables typical for Caché ObjectScript
- String functions used to build, modify, and analyze strings
- Number-formatting functions
- List functions
- Functions for transaction processing

The following sections of this chapter present tables that summarize Caché ObjectScript intrinsic functions. Because the $STack function returns context information when an error occurs in the program, it is described in Section 5.4 in conjunction with error handling.

Function	Short description
$Ascii	$Ascii(<expr>) $Ascii(<expr>,<int expr>) $Ascii selects a character from a string (first argument) and returns the ASCII code for this character. The second argument specifies the position in the string. If the second argument is omitted, the first character of the string is assumed. If the string is null or the second argument is less than 1 or greater than the length of the string, $Ascii returns −1.

Table 5.14 General purpose intrinsic functions in Caché ObjectScript

```
>Write $Ascii("A")
65
>Write $Ascii("ABC",3)
67
>Write $Ascii("")
-1
```

$CASE	$CASE(<expr>,<expr>:<expr>[,...][,:default])
	$CASE(<expr>,<expr>:<name>[,...][,:default])
	In the first case, the value of the first expression is initially evaluated. The following expression pair <expr>:<expr> consists of a literal (numeric or string) followed by an expression. If the literal matches the first expression, the associated expression is used as function value. If none of the <expr> matches the first expression, the default value is used as function value, provided it exists, otherwise an error message is issued.
	As the second example shows, if $CASE is used as an argument for the Do or Goto command, a valid entry reference is expected instead of an arbitrary expression.

```
>Write $CASE(A,1:"One",2:"Two",3:"Three",:"something else")
>Goto $CASE(Input,"*":End,:^Process(Input))
```

$Char	$Char(<int expr>[,<int expr>,...])
	$Char is the inverse function of $Ascii and converts a number into the corresponding ASCII character. Negative arguments are permitted and produce the null string. The conversion is based on the ASCII character set. Also refer to $ZLChar and $ZWChar.

```
>Write $Char(65)
A
>Write $Char(65,66)
AB
>Write $Char(-1)
(the null string)
```

$Random	$Random(<int expr>)
	When the $Random argument is n, the function returns an integer random number in the range 0 to n−1.

```
>Write $Random(10)
5
```

$Select	$Select(<log expr>:<expr>[,<log expr>:
	<expr>] ...)
	Each argument for $Select is an ordered pair consisting of a logical expression and an arbitrary expression separated by a colon. The arguments are processed from left to right until a logical expression evaluates true. $Select then returns the value of the expression to the right of the colon. At least one logical expression must be true, otherwise an error message is issued.

```
>Set a=1
>Write $Select(a=1:5,a>1:0)
5
>Write $Select(a=2:5,1:0)
0
>Set min=$Select(s<t:s,1:t)
```

$Text	$Text(+<int expr>[^routine]) $Text(label[^routine]) $Text returns a line of code from a Caché ObjectScript routine, assuming that it is present in the source code. (If it is not present in the source code, $Text returns only the contents of the comment lines prefixed by two semicolons. The value of $Text is the null string for all other lines.) The first form of $Text references the relative line number (e.g., +3 for the third line). If this number is 0, the routine name is returned. In the second case, a label of a line present in a routine is specified, which then is output (with label). If the routine name is missing, Caché assumes the label to be in the currently loaded routine.

```
>Write $Text(+3)
 Read "Input: ",x
>Write $Text(+0)
P1Spec
>Write $Text(Label)
Label Set a=1,b=2
```

$View	$View(<expr>[,mode,<num expr>]) $View returns information about the contents of memory and is normally used to obtain very low-level system information in an error situation. Please refer to the *Caché ObjectScript Reference* for further details.

The following table lists Caché ObjectScript intrinsic functions that involve string processing.

Table 5.15 String functions

Function	Short description
$Extract	$Extract(<expr>) $Extract(<expr>,<int expr>) $Extract(<expr>,<int expr>,<int expr>) $Extract returns a substring of the first argument, for which the second and third arguments specify the start and end of the substring. If the third argument is not specified, the character specified by the second argument is extracted. If the second argument is also not specified, $Extract returns the first character of the string. If the second argument is greater than the third or greater than the length of the first argument, $Extract returns the null string. If the second argument is less than or equal to 1, $Extract extracts from the start of the string to the third argument. If the second argument is less than 1, the null string is returned. If the third argument is greater than the length of the string, $Extract extracts to the end of the string.

```
>Write $Extract("ABC")
A
>Write $Extract("XYZ",$L("XYZ"))
Z
>Write $Extract("AABB",2,3)
AB
>Write $Extract("Summer",3,255)
mmer
>Write $Extract("abc",5)
(the null string)
```

$Find	`$Find(<expr>,<expr>)` `$Find(<expr>,<expr>,<int expr>)`

`$Find` searches the first argument for the search string specified as the second argument. The search starts at the position specified by the third argument. If the third argument is missing, the search begins at the start of the first argument.

`$Find` returns the position of the first character after the found search string. If the search string is not found, the `$Find` value is 0. If a null string is specified as the second argument, the function value is always equal to the third argument or, if none was specified, to 1.

```
>Write $Find("ABC","A")
2
>Write $Find("XYZ","T")
0
>Write $Find("ABABAB","AB",3)
5
```

$Justify	`$Justify(<expr>,<int expr>)`
	`$Justify(<num expr>,<int expr>,`
	`        <int expr>)`

`$Justify` can be used to right-justify data fields and format numbers. The second parameter specifies the length of the output. If this exceeds the length of the data field, it remains unchanged. The third argument, if present, specifies the formatting of numeric data elements and forces a numeric interpretation of the first argument. It specifies the number of positions after the decimal point to be produced by rounding or inserting zeros. If the third argument is 0, neither decimal digits nor a decimal point is produced. Values greater than −1 and less than 1 are represented with a leading 0 before the decimal point.

```
>Write $Justify(12,3)
 12
>Write $Justify("Text",10)
      Text
>Write $Justify(12,3,2)
12.00
>Write $Justify(3.14,1,0)
3
>Write $Justify(.414,6,3)
 0.414
```

$Length	`$Length(<expr>)` `$Length(<expr>,<expr>)`

`$Length` returns the length of a string, expressed as the number of characters in the string. The length of a null string is 0. By specifying a string as the second argument, the function returns the number of occurrences of that string in the first argument plus 1. Thus, it counts the number of fields that include the substring specified in the second argument. If the second argument is a null string, `$Length` returns the value 0.

```
>Write $Length("ABCD")
4
>Write $Length("")
0
>Write $Length("AB/CD/EF","/")
3
```

$Piece	$Piece(<expr>,<expr>)
	$Piece(<expr>,<expr>,<int expr>)
	$Piece(<expr>,<expr>,<int expr>,
	<int expr>)
	$Piece considers the string passed as the first argument to be a series of fields, separated from each other by the delimiter character specified as the second argument. In its two-argument form, $Piece returns the first field. In the form with three arguments, it returns the field specified by the third argument. In the form with four arguments, it returns the fields in the range between argument three and argument four.
	If the string does not contain the delimiter, $Piece returns the complete string when the third argument is 1 or not present. Otherwise it returns the null string.
	The null string as delimiter always returns the null string as result. If the third argument is less than 1 or the fourth argument is greater than the number of fields in the first argument, the extraction is made from the first field or to the last field, respectively. If the fourth argument is less than the third or less than 1, or if the third argument is greater than the number of fields, $Piece always returns the null string.

```
>Set v="ABC/XYZ/123"
>Write $Piece(v,"/")
ABC
>Write $Piece(v,"/",2)
XYZ
>Write $Piece(v,"/",2,3)
XYZ/123
>Set $P(v,"/",2)="***" Write v
ABC/***/123
```

$Reverse	$Reverse(<expr>)
	$Reverse reverses the contents of a string.

```
>Write $Reverse("Rail")
liaR
```

$TRanslate	$TRanslate(<expr>,<expr>)
	$TRanslate(<expr>,<expr>,<expr>)
	$TRanslate converts the string specified in the first argument character-by-character using the rules specified by the second and third arguments. In the form with three arguments, it is determined for each character of the first argument whether and at which position it occurs for the first time in the second argument. If this is the case, it is replaced by the character that appears at the same position in the third argument. Excess characters of the second argument not translated in the third argument are removed from the first argument. The same applies when only two arguments are specified.

```
>Set u="EPUR",l="epur"
>Write $TRanslate("UPPER",u,l)
upper
>Write $TRanslate("train station","aeiou")
trn sttn
```

As implied in Table 5.13, Caché ObjectScript includes the $LIst function class, which creates and manages lists (Section 5.1.5 describes Caché ObjectScript's list functions.) $Increment is used for transaction processing, and is described separately in Section 7.3.1.4. The $INumber function is related to the $FNumber, and has only limited general significance. (Refer to the *Caché ObjectScript Reference* for a more detailed discussion.)

5.1.4.4 Overview of Z-Functions

Because of the large number of useful "Z-functions" in Caché ObjectScript, we can provide only an introductory description here. For more details, please refer to the *Caché ObjectScript Reference*. This introduction follows the grouping of Z-functions introduced with Table 5.13.

Mathematical Z-functions

Trigonometric functions, logarithmic functions, and the exponential function

Caché provides the repertoire of mathematical functions usual for a general programming system. These include:

- trigonometric functions $ZSIN, $ZCOS, $ZTAN, and $ZCOT
- arc functions $ZARCSIN, $ZARCCOS, and $ZARCTAN
- logarithmic functions $ZLN (natural logarithm) and $ZLOG (decimal-based logarithm)
- the exponential function $ZEXP

Date and time representation

ObjectScript includes a specific class of functions that either create a displayable date and time format from the internal system time or, in the reverse direction, convert a specified date and time to the internal system format. All functions can be called with a range of parameters to create the various formats, some of which are culture dependent.

The basis is the $Horolog special variable

The $Horolog special variable (refer to Section 5.1.1.2) forms the basis of Caché's internal date and time representation. This consists of a day counter and seconds counter separated by a comma. Some functions also use the $ZTimeStamp special variable, in which the seconds counter is extended with a milliseconds component (the remaining structure is the same as for $Horolog).

The first function discussed here is $ZDate, abbreviated to $ZD. The following example shows its general effect and most frequent use.

Example

```
>Write $ZDate(60000)
04/10/2005
```

The simplest form of $ZDate has one argument that is assumed to be in $Horolog format. By default, it displays a date in the American format MM/DD/YYYY, with the slash character as delimiter.

In the two-argument form of $ZDate, the second argument is a format parameter, as summarized in the table below:

2nd argument	Date format	Example	Comment
0	DD Mmm [YY]YY	10 Apr 2005	
1	MM/DD/[YY]YY	04/10/2005	
2	DD Mmm [YY]YY	10 Apr 2005	
3	YYYY-MM-DD	2005-04-10	ODBC format
4	DD/MM/[YY]YY	10/04/2005	European format
5	Mmm D, [YY]YY	Apr 10, 2005	
6	Mmm D [YY]YY	Apr 10 2005	
7	Mmm DD [YY]YY	Apr 10 2005	
8	YYYYMMDD	20050410	Numeric format
9	Month D, [YY]YY	April 10, 2005	

Table 5.16 Formats specified by the second argument of $ZDate

The third argument is useful for languages other than English. In cases where the second argument specifies a format that displays a month in abbreviated or full form, this month can be translated into the required language using a month name list.

Example

```
>Write $ZDate(60000,2," Januar Februar März ... Dezember")
10 April 2005
```

You can see that the third argument can specify a list of months in the required language.

Translating month names into a non-English language

Two final comments concerning $ZDate: first, an invalid parameter used in an argument produces an error message, in many cases <illegal value>. Second, although many % routines (*utilities*) also perform date and time conversions, intrinsic functions are more systematic and much faster than utilities. Consequently, we advise against the use of such routines.

$ZDateH (abbreviated to $ZDH) is the "reverse function" of $ZDate, in that it returns the day counter in $Horolog format for a date specified in one of the above formats.

Example

```
>Write $ZDateH("4/10/2005")
60000
```

From the example, you can see that the arguments of $ZDateH produce results very similar to those of $ZDate.

Caché ObjectScript's other time and date functions are listed below.

Table 5.17 Time and date functions

Function	Short form	Short description	Example
$ZDateTime	$ZDT	Similar to $ZDate but with the time specified in various optional formats	>Write $ZDT($H) 09/04/1998 10:13:19
$ZDateTimeH	$ZDTH	Similar to $ZDateH but the seconds counter is also created in $Horolog format	>Write $ZDTH("Jun⇦ ⇨ 13, 1997 15:19 ⇦ ⇨:23.539",5) 57142,55163.539
$ZTime	$ZT	Create the time in various optional formats from the seconds counter in $Horolog format	>Write $ZT(3600) 01:00:00
$ZTimeH	$ZTH	Create the seconds counter in $Horolog format from the specified time	>Write $ZTH("02:0⇦ ⇨0:00") 7200

Bit string functions

This section provides a brief discussion of the bit string functions. The *Caché ObjectScript Reference* contains further reference information.

A bit string is a series of on/off states

Bit operations are performed with four bit string functions: $BIT, $BITCOUNT, $BITFIND, and $BITLOGIC. A bit string is a series of on/off states specified by a sequence of ones and zeros, for example, [0,1,0,0,1,1,1,0].

$BIT produces a bit string or sets a bit value in a specified position . The form $BIT(bitstring,position) extracts the bit value at the identified position. The form $BIT(bitstring,position,bitvalue) returns the actual bit value at the specified position and assigns it a new value, bitvalue.

$BIT also exists in a left-side form. This can be used to set bit strings or change a single position of existing bit strings.

Example

```
Set a=""
Set $BIT(a,4)=1
```

This assignment initializes the variable a with the empty string and sets the fourth bit to 1; a then has the value [0,0,0,1].

$BITCOUNT is available in two different forms. In the one-argument form, $BITCOUNT(bitstring), it returns the number of bits in the bit string. If a bit value (0 or 1) is added as a second argument, the number of bits of the specified value in the bit string are counted.

The third bit string function, $BITFIND, searches for a bit value in a bit string and returns its position. For example, if a=[0,0,1,1,0], then $BITFIND(a,1) returns the number 3, since the bit value 1 appears for the first time in the third position. Adding a third argument to $BITFIND specifies the start position for the search. In the previous example, $BITFIND(a,0,3) returns the value 5, since the bit value 0 also appears at the fifth bit position.

The function $BITLOGIC performs bit operations on the bit string. Table 5.18 shows the four defined operators.

Operator	Operator symbol
AND	&
OR	|
Exclusive OR	^
NOT	~

Table 5.18 The four logic operators in $BITLOGIC

The general form of $BITLOGIC is

```
$BITLOGIC(bitstring_expression[,length)
```

where `bitstring_expression` represents a bit string expression constructed from the operators shown in Table 5.18. Thus the expression consists of either a sequence of AND and OR operations (for example, A&B|C) or only the NOT operator (for example, ~A). In this case, the bit complement of the bit string A is created by inverting all bit values. Brackets are allowed, for example, (A&B)|(B&C).

The second optional argument, `length`, returns the logical length of the resulting bit string.

The following examples assume that the A and B bit strings have the contents: A=[1,1], B=[0,1]

Examples

```
Set C=$BITLOGIC(~B)     // C has the value [1,0]
Set C=$BITLOGIC(A&B)    // C has the value [0,1]
Set C=$BITLOGIC(A|B)    // C has the value [1,1]
```

Another function, $ZBOOLEAN(arg1,arg2,bit-op), takes the byte representation of a symbol as reference and, depending on the value of the third argument, performs the specified bitwise Boolean operation on the first and second values. The name $ZBOOLEAN cannot be abbreviated. For further information, refer to the *Caché ObjectScript Reference*.

$ZBOOLEAN

General Z-functions

$ZF is used to call programs or functions written in languages other than Caché ObjectScript.

$ZF has the general form:

```
$ZF(-1,"commandline"[,arguments])
```

The second argument is a valid command line of the operating system. The optional third argument specifies a list of individual parameters that describe the details of the call. Full details can be found in the *Using Caché ObjectScript* manual.

$ZHex(<expr>) converts a hexadecimal string into decimal notation and vice versa. $ZHex can be abbreviated to $ZH. The next two examples illustrate the function:

Hexadecimal conversion

Example

```
>Write $ZHex(6840)
1AB8
>Write $ZHex(16_"H")
22
```

Appending a non-numeric character (e.g., "H") indicates that 16 is to be interpreted as hexadecimal.

Functions for Unicode symbol support

On operating systems that support the use of 16-bit Unicode symbols, $ZISWIDE(str) determines whether the str function argument contains a 16-bit symbol. If this is the case, the function returns 1 (true), otherwise 0. For example, $ZISWIDE($Char(71,300)) returns 1.

$ZLAscii and $ZWAscii, and the reverse functions $ZLChar and $ZWChar, are similar to the $Char and $Ascii functions. The only difference is that $ZLAscii and $ZWAscii operate on a four-byte string and a two-byte string, respectively. The abbreviations are (in the above sequence): $ZLA, $ZWA, $ZLC, and $ZWC.

The following examples illustrate the use of these functions. They are normally used for communications or general programming when binary information needs to be converted into ASCII characters.

Example

```
>Write $ZWCHAR(25185)
ab
>Write $ZWASCII("ab")
25185
>Write $ZLCHAR(1684234849)
abcd
>Write $ZLASCII("abcd")
1684234849
```

Validating names

$ZNAME(str,n) validates whether the str string complies with Caché ObjectScript's naming conventions. The parameter n specifies the type of name validation to be performed. For example, the value 0 can be used to test whether str is a valid local variable name. If str is a permitted name, the function returns 1 (true), otherwise it returns 0. The following table shows the possible values of n and the meaning of each value.

Table 5.19 $ZNAME parameter values

Parameter value	Meaning
0	Validation of a local variable name
1	Validation of a routine name
2	Validation of a label
3	Validation of a global variable name
4	Validation of a class name
5	Validation of a method name
6	Validation of an attribute name

$ZSEarch (abbreviated to $ZSE) is a function reserved for the Windows system platforms. $ZSEarch returns the complete file specification (the path and file name) of the file or group of files specified as the argument.

$ZWPack(str) and $ZWBPack(str) transform the argument str into two-byte characters. str may not contain any 16-bit characters; $ZISWIDE can be used to test for these characters. $ZWPack returns the so-called little-endian form, $ZWBPack the big-endian form. The inverse functions for these two functions are $ZWUNPack and $ZWBUNPack, respectively.

Z-string functions

The $ZConVerT(<expr>,mode) function (abbreviated to $ZCVT) greatly simplifies the conversion of uppercase characters to lowercase and vice versa. Its two modes are specified by the second argument as "u" (or "U") and "l" (or "L"). The first mode converts all lowercase characters present in the first argument to uppercase. The second mode operates in the reverse direction.

Example

```
>Write $ZConVerT("ABC123","L")
abc123
```

$ZCyc(<expr>) (abbreviated to $ZC) is relevant for data transmission or for communication between programs. It creates checksums that can be used to determine the validity of transferred data. The checksums are created bit-wise using XOR.

Create checksums

$ZSTRIP(<expr>,action,remove,retain) (no abbreviation allowed) is useful for removing and retaining individual characters or complete character classes in a given string. The character classes are specified in accordance with the systematic representation defined by pattern matching. (Refer to Section 5.1.2.2.) The following example illustrates how to strip all digits except 7s from an arbitrary string.

Example

```
>Set str="Jhfgsfg102nn7754ggiu"
>Write $ZSTRIP(str,"*N",,"7")
Jhfgsfg1nn77ggiu
```

The second argument specifies the action: remove all N (meaning numeric characters), whereas the fourth argument specifies which characters are to be retained. Although a third argument does not exist in the example, its comma must be present.

$ZUtil functions

$ZUtil(digit[,mode[,...]]) (abbreviated to $ZU) performs a number of quite different, often low-level operations, some of which, naturally, are platform dependent. Its operations apply to a broad range of individual numeric arguments. For further details on the availability of individual

Low-level operations

$ZUtil functions, refer to the *Caché ObjectScript Reference* and the *Release Notes*.

5.1.5 Lists

5.1.5.1 What are Lists?

A list consists of a series of individual values. Lists play a special role in both traditional and object-oriented programming, and assume the character of a dedicated data type. Consider a simple list, expressed in set-oriented notation:

Lists are series of values

```
L1={red,green,blue}
```

L1 consists of three elements. Although sets are unordered in set theory, the order of elements in a list is significant. The list L11={green,blue, red} is not the same as the list L1.
The list

```
L2={}
```

is empty and is called the null list.
A list can contain undefined elements, as the following example shows:

```
L3={red,green,,blue}
```

Note that the number of elements in this list is four, even though the third list element is not defined. Furthermore, L3 is not equivalent to the following list:

```
L4={red,green,"",blue},
```

because the third element in this list is defined as the null string.
Similarly, an element of a list can itself be another list:

```
L5={red,{light red,orange,cherry red},green,blue}
```

L5 contains four elements, the second of which is a list. L5 is an example of a *nested list*.

Concatenating lists

You can concatenate lists. The concatenation operator for lists in Caché is the underscore (_) character. The following instruction creates a six-element list with the listed elements:

```
{red,green,blue}_{brown,violet,black}
```

List processing plays an important role in Caché. The individual list elements are normally strings (except when a list element itself is a list). Typical tasks in list processing are:

- create a list
- determine the number of elements in a list
- extract one or more list elements
- search for a specific value in a list
- replace individual list values with other values.

Two different approaches are possible.

- You can manually create a list-oriented string. Delimiters separate the individual list elements from each other:

```
Set L1="red/green/blue"
```

The representation must be unique, namely, the selected delimiter may not appear as a character in any of the list elements. Caché Object-Script provides all language elements needed to create and manage these self-defined lists.

- Lists can also be created and managed using list functions. For example, the list L1 is created as follows:

List functions

```
Set L1=$ListBuild("red","green","blue")
```

Because the list functions represent a more systematic means of list management (compared to their hard-coded creation), we recommend the second method.

5.1.5.2 Self-administered List Management

As mentioned previously, a list is a structured string. Delimiters separate the individual elements in the list. Two examples:

```
Set list="spring/summer/fall/winter"
Set address="Wagner^John^2712, Washington Street^Cedar Rapi⇔
⇒ds/IA^52405^(319) 696-4521*(319) 694-6077"
```

The second example shows several features. First, *address* contains a string representing a data record expressed as a list, with the ^ character as delimiter. In addition, some fields (or rather, list elements) have sublists with other (sub)delimiters (such as the slash character between city and state or the asterisk character in the telephone numbers of the last list element).

This method uses three main language elements for managing lists (also refer to the definitions of language elements in Table 5.15):

Three language elements for list management

- The two-argument form of $Length determines the number of list elements.
- The $Piece function extracts individual list elements.
- A special form of the Set command (the form on the left-hand side) creates or replaces individual list elements.

Examples

```
>Write $Length(list,"/")
4
>Write $Piece(address,"^",3)
2712, Washington Street
>Set $Piece(address,"^",5)="52405-1966"
>Write address
Wagner^John^2712, Washington Street^Cedar Rapids/IA^52405-1⇔
⇒966^(319) 696-4521*(319) 694-6077
```

$Length returns the "length" of the list when you specify the list delimiter as the second argument. $Piece returns one (or more) list elements, where the delimiter is specified as the second argument.

The third example shows a special form of the Set command which replaces list elements. In the example, a new element to the right of the assignment sign replaces the fifth list element.

5.1.5.3 Creating Lists with $ListBuild

Caché ObjectScript defines six list functions. Because the length and type of the individual elements are specified in a list definition, these functions make list processing more systematic and faster compared to coding equivalent routines manually. Delimiters are not used.

The next table summarizes Caché ObjectScript's intrinsic functions for list processing.

Table 5.20 Short description of Caché ObjectScript's list functions

List function	Abbr.	Short description
$ListBuild	$LB	Creates lists
$ListLength	$LL	Returns the number of list elements
$LIst	$LI	Extracts one or more list elements from a list
$ListGet	$LG	Suppresses a <NULL VALUE> error when a reference is made to an undefined list element. Similar to $Get
$ListData	$LD	Logical pointer if a list element exists
$ListFind	$LF	Searches for a specific list element in a list

$ListBuild creates lists. The following examples refer to the lists L1 to L5 that we created at the start of this section:

Examples

```
Set L1=$ListBuild("red","green","blue")
```

L1={red,green,blue}

```
Set L2=$ListBuild()
```

empty list L2={}

```
Set L3=$ListBuild("red","green",,"blue")
```

L3={red,green,,blue}

```
Set L4=$ListBuild("red","green","","blue")
```

L4={red,green,"",blue}

```
Set L5=$ListBuild("red",$ListBuild("light
red","orange","cherry red"),"green","blue")
```

Nested list   A nested list is a list that contains another list as its second element.

$ListBuild arguments can represent any expression.

Example

```
Set list=$ListBuild(2*x1,3*x2)
```

This command creates a list with two numeric elements. Referencing an undefined variable in the $ListBuild function does not cause an error.

Example

```
Kill var Set list=$ListBuild(var,1)
```

This creates a list for which the first element is undefined and the second contains the value 1.

The concatenation operator can be used to concatenate lists. Thus

```
$ListBuild("a","b")_$ListBuild("c")
```

creates a list with the three elements "a","b", and "c".

Note that

```
$ListBuild("a","b")
$ListBuild("a","b")_$ListBuild()
$ListBuild("a","b")_$ListBuild("")
```

represent three different lists. The first list contains two elements. The second list contains three elements, where the third element is not defined. The third list also contains three elements, the third of which is the null string.

How many elements does a list contain? The $ListLength function answers this question. The following examples use the previously defined lists L1 to L5.

How many elements does a list contain?

Examples

```
>Write $ListLength(L1)
3
>Write $ListLength(L2)
1
>Write $ListLength(L3)
4
>Write $ListLength(L4)
4
>Write $ListLength(L5)
4
```

The examples are self explanatory. Note that $ListLength does not determine whether an element is itself a list, but counts only the number of primary list elements. Thus, $ListLength does not recognize elements in nested lists.

An error message <LIST> is displayed when an arbitrary string (instead of a list created with $ListBuild) is used as argument.

5.1.5.4 List Processing

The $LIst function extracts single or multiple elements from a list. It has the following general form:

Extracting elements from a list

```
$LIst(list[,position[,end]])
```

Note that list must represent a list created with $ListBuild, otherwise a <LIST> error message will be issued. In its single-argument form, $LISt extracts the first element from a list. position is the start position where the extraction is to be made. If no end-position is specified, just a single list element is extracted that is interpreted as being a string (provided it is not a sublist). If, however, an end-position is specified, at least one list element is extracted, which is also interpreted as a list. Thus, when L1 is defined as {red,green,blue},

```
$LISt(L1,2)   // results in the string "green"
$LISt(L1,2,2) // results in the list {green}
```

position and end can have the value –1, which is a shorthand notation for the last position. (You could also use the $ListLength(list) expression to obtain the last position.) Thus, the Set x=$LISt(L1,2,-1) call returns a list consisting of {green,blue}.

If position is 0, there are two possibilities:

```
$LISt(L1,0)   // <NULL VALUE> error message
$LISt(L1,0,2) // equivalent to $LISt(L1,1,2)
```

If position is less than –1, you receive a <RANGE> error message. The call has no effect when end-value is less than position. If position is greater than the list length (and no end-position is specified), the result is a null list, i.e., {}.

If you reference an undefined list element in the two-argument form of $LISt, you get a so-called <NULL VALUE> error. Because $LISt always returns a list, this cannot occur in the three-argument form:

```
Set L3=$ListBuild("red","green",,"blue")
Write $LISt(L3,3)     // <NULL VALUE> error, third element
                      // is undefined
Write $LISt(L3,3,3)   // no error message, result is the
                      // null list
```

Left-side form of $LISt

Similar to $Piece and $Extract, $LISt also has a so-called left-side form that can change individual or multiple list elements. For example, this form can create the missing third element in the list L3, as shown below:

```
Set $LISt(L3,3)="yellow"
```

The result is the list {red,green,yellow,blue}.

By extending this facility, sublists can be added to a list by placing the $ListBuild or $LISt function on the right-hand side of the instruction:

```
Set $LISt(x,pos)=$ListBuild(list)
Set $LISt(x,pos)=$LISt(list,pos,end)
```

$ListGet

The next list function, $ListGet, is an extension of $LISt. $ListGet is identical to the one- and two-argument forms of $LISt, except that it does not issue the <NULL VALUE> error. Consequently, it is similar to the $Get function. You can use $ListGet to extract a specific element from a list. If this list element is not defined, the two-argument form of the function returns the null string. When a third argument is specified, this is used as default value. For the next example, L3 has the definition {red,green,,blue} with a missing third element.

Examples

```
>Write $ListGet(L3,3)          // two-argument form
                               // the null string
>Write $ListGet(L3,3,"royal blue")
royal blue                     // three-argument form
```

How can you determine whether a list element is defined? The $ListData list function helps here. As with the other list functions, it should only be used on lists when you want to avoid a <LIST> error. The general form is:

```
$ListData(list,position)
```

$ListData uses the position parameter to reference *one* list element and determines whether it exists or is undefined. In the first case, the function returns 1, in the second case 0. Using our previous definition of L3, you can formulate the following examples.

Examples

```
>Write $ListData(L3,2)
1
>Write $ListData(L3,3)
0
```

Otherwise, the rules for the position parameter are the same as for the $LIst function.

The last list function we consider is $ListFind. It determines whether a particular list element appears in a list. Thus, it can search for and find the "green" element in the L3 list.

$ListFind

Example

```
>Write $ListFind(L3,"green")
2
```

$ListFind returns the position within the list or 0, when the specified list element is not present. It does not recognize substrings, such as "een," or elements in sublists.

The general form of $ListFind is:

```
$ListFind(list,searchvalue[,position])
```

It searches for searchvalue starting at the location position. This can have the value –1 when it refers to the last list field. If position is greater than the list length, the function returns 0.

You can use a For loop to find all occurrences of a specific list value. Assume the following list:

```
Lg={green,blue,ochre,green,red,black,green}
```

The following For loop finds the three positions of the "green" element:

5.1 Basic Structures of Caché ObjectScript

```
>Set x=0
>For  { Set x=$ListFind(Lg,"green",x) Quit:x=0  Write x,! }
```

As is usual for list functions, $ListFind can only operate on lists created with $LIst. You receive a <RANGE> error message when the value of the third position argument is less than −1.

5.2 Routines in Caché

5.2.1 Types of Routines

Caché recognizes four different types of routines used to create procedural code in Caché ObjectScript. The following table provides an overview.

Table 5.21 Different types of Caché routines

Extension	Routine Type	Explanation
.MAC	Macro code	Macro code can contain Caché ObjectScript code, macro directives, macros, embedded SQL, HTML, and JavaScript. It is compiled into intermediate code and this, in turn, into object code.
.INC	Macro include	Macro includes can contain any code also permitted in .MAC routines. They are used to build code libraries, and can be placed in macro routines with an Include statement, hence their name.
.INT	Intermediate code	Intermediate code is any valid Caché ObjectScript code. Macros and embedded SQL are first converted into intermediate code.
.OBJ	Object code	Before intermediate code can be executed, it must first be compiled into internal object code. Caché does this automatically when it stores an edited routine. Only the object code is needed at runtime; software houses normally supply their applications only in object code.

5.2.2 Creating Routines with Caché Studio

Caché Studio can be invoked from the Caché Cube menu. It contains a graphical routine editor that is a user-friendly means of creating object classes (including the creation of method code), Caché Server Pages, macro programs, macro includes, and intermediate code programs, as well as compiling these into executable object code.

Caché Studio provides aids to the programmer such as automatic syntax checking when the code is entered; different language elements are marked in color and syntax errors are shown. Caché Studio also contains a built-in debugger that can be used to find software errors in the application.

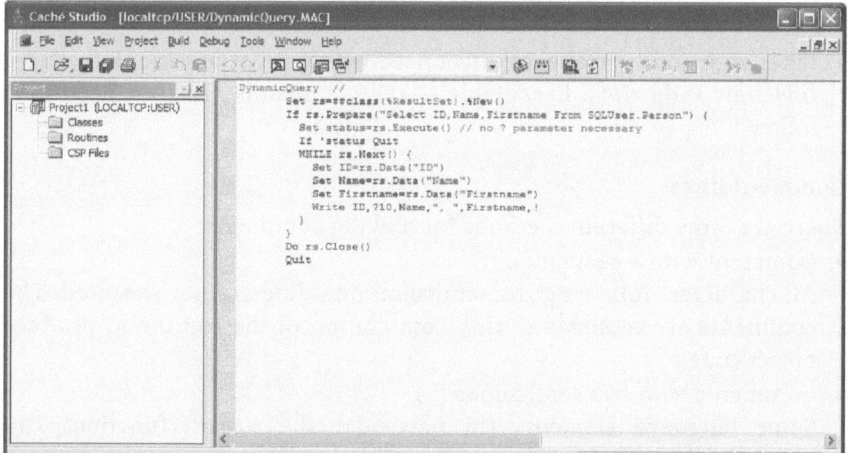

Figure 5.1 Editing a routine in Caché Studio

Programmers often use Caché Studio in conjunction with Caché Explorer, which provides comprehensive options for the administration of routines, including import/export and search functions.

5.2.3 Basic Structures of a Routine

Caché Routines consist of individual code blocks that are created and edited as source code, and are automatically compiled into a special object form when they are saved; this object code is not machine code, but rather a platform-independent p-code.

Individual code blocks

A routine name can be any combination of alphanumeric characters, but with three restrictions: the routine name cannot begin with a digit, the percent sign and the period cannot be used as the initial or the final character. Routines whose name begins with the percent sign are library routines that are not restricted to a single namespace; these names are reserved for Caché system routines. Although names are not subject to any length restriction, only the first 31 characters are used to distinguish names.

5.2.3.1 The Form of a Routine Line

A line is one of the basic structures within a routine, although you must keep in mind that a logical routine line can span several physical lines of code. Caché generally distinguishes four types of routine lines:

Lines with labels

- A label identifies a line within a routine. A label must always begin in the first column of a line. Permitted label names are the same as those for routines, together with digit combinations. Its length cannot exceed 31 characters. A label is always followed by one or more blanks or tabs, also called the *line start indicator*. Executable Caché commands can (but need not) follow.

Lines with code

- Lines with code are always introduced with at least one blank (called a *line start indicator*). Executable Caché commands can (but need not) follow.

Comment lines

Comments

There are three different methods for making comments:

- Comment with a semicolon (;)
  All characters following the semicolon on a line are not executed. The comments are removed during compilation of the routine to produce object code.
- Comments with two semicolons (;;)
  Some language elements (in particular the $Text function) can reference the text of a routine line. This is often used in combination with comments that store parameters or constants in the routine text. To allow this (even in cases where the source code of a routine is not available at runtime), comments separated by two semicolons are not removed in the object code. In other words, comments marked by two semicolons remain in the compilation, whereas those marked by a single semicolon are removed.
- C-conforming comments
  - Two slashes (//), equivalent to the single semicolon.
  - Comments that extend over several lines are introduced with /* and terminated with */. At least one space must lie between the last character of a command and the comment delimiter /*; two spaces are required for commands without arguments. This comment form can also be used within an argument list of a function, e.g.,

```
Write $Char( 65 /* 65 stands for the letter "A"  */)
```

Blank lines provide visual divisions in a routine and can improve readability. The first line of a routine cannot be a blank line.

An expression or command can extend over several routine lines. Obviously, the command word and the first argument cannot be split across lines.

Example

```
Set sum = x + y      // comment 1
 + z  ,              // comment 2
mue  =  sum  / 3     // comment 3
```

In the above example, comments occur at the end of each "subline."

In addition, a line is considered as a unit within the scope of the line-oriented form of the For, If, and Else commands, and thus cannot be split.

Maximum size of a routine line

The maximum size of a routine line is 4k.

5.2.3.2 Blocks in a Routine

A block is the routine structure that is next larger than a routine line. In general, Caché distinguishes between three different block structures:

1. "Dot" blocks called with a Do command without arguments, and introduced with one or more dots (that is, period characters) in a routine line
2. Procedure blocks enclosed within curly brackets and that can extend over several routine lines (discussed in detail in Section 5.2.6)
3. Command constructs with the commands for the flow control in a routine, in which the executable part also is enclosed within curly brackets (discussed in detail in Section 5.3).

Dot blocks extend the scope of a routine line. A Do command without arguments initializes this block. The dot block begins with a dot (after the *line start indicator*) at the beginning of the next line after the Do. Caché tracks nested dot blocks as hierarchy levels; for the first Do, Caché increments the Do stack by one (level 1). If another Do command without an argument appears in this level, the following line must begin with *two* points (level 2) and so on.

Do command without arguments

The individual blocks can, but need not, be terminated with a Quit command. A block dotted n times is terminated implicitly when a line dotted a number of times less than n appears.

End of a block

Note that, although a Goto or Do cannot be used to jump from a specific level to some other level, routines not contained in a block can be invoked locally or globally from a block.

The following example illustrates basic block structures.

```
<code>      /* This (main) area belongs to level 0
              It is undotted */
Do          // Do without arguments
.           // outer block, one dot, level 1
. <code>
. Do        // another Do without arguments
..          // inner block, two dots, level 2
.. <code>
.           // another level-1 block
.           // implicit end of the level-2 block
. <code>
            // no dot, main block
Quit
```

Two extensions of dot blocks should be considered here. First, each block level separately manages the $Test special variable. This means that a change made to $Test does not apply outside its level. (This differs sharply from a Do command that calls a routine name.) Second, as shown in the example above, the dots must also be included on comment lines to ensure that a block is not terminated prematurely.

$Test is stacked

133

5.2.4 Local Variables in Routines

5.2.4.1 General Routine Structure

A Caché routine typically consists of an entry label, individual routine lines that contain code, and a terminating Quit command. This structure can be repeated within a routine.

Example

```
P1      /* first line, with details relating to the
        creation/change of a routine */
        Set a=1
        Do P2
        Quit
P2      // first line of the P2 subroutine
        Set x=2,y=3
        Quit
```

This routine consists of two sections, the routine P1 and the routine P2 called from P1. A completely separate routine could use Do ^P1 to invoke P1 "globally," that is, load the routine from the routine directory on disk into memory and execute it there.

If the caret sign (the "global" character) is omitted, such as the call Do P2, the label is expected in the current routine. You can also call P2 as a subroutine of P1.

A "globally" called routine can be entered at a specific label. For example, the call Do P2^P1 invokes the (local) subroutine P2 in the routine P1.

Label+offset syntax

Finally, Caché ObjectScript supports a *label+offset* syntax to enter an invoked routine n lines (the so-called *offset*) after a *label*. For example, the call Do P1+3^P1 (applied to the example above) means branch three lines after the label P1 and start processing the routine there. In this case, bypassing the line Set a=1. Although this is flexible and useful in various situations (e.g., to test routines), it should be used with care, because editing a routine changes the arrangement of code lines, thus possibly redefining the *offset*.

Pass values to invoked routines

Note that you can call a label with a list of variables (contained in parentheses), which then serve as formal parameters in the subroutine invoked by the call.

Example

```
Invert(x1,x2,x3)    // Label with a list of formal
                    // parameters
```

Labels can be public or private, and are defined as such with a corresponding keyword. If the keyword is omitted, the default is public. Whereas public labels can be called from anywhere, private labels can be called only from the current routine.

```
Move(x) Private      /* private label can be called only
                        within the routine */
Rotate(x) Public     /* this label is public,
                        and can be called freely */
Invert(x)            /* ...this one as well */
```

Before leaving labels, let us now consider the implicit Quit command before a label with parameters.

Implicit Quit command

Examples

```
Start      //
           Write "Hello World",!
           // implicit Quit here
MySub(a)   //
           Write a,!
           // implicit Quit here
MyProc()   {
           Write "This is my procedure"
           // implicit Quit at the end of a procedure
           }
```

This implicit Quit command avoids "falling through" a routine when a Quit is omitted and a label with parameters is encountered. A Quit is forced because the parameters would not be defined.

5.2.4.2 The Scope of Local Variables

What is the visibility of local variables within a routine? In the Caché approach, all variables that have been set are initially visible throughout the *partition* of the current process; their scope is restricted only when expressly stated by the programmer. A partition is the data area of a process in Caché's working storage. In addition to the loaded routine and the defined local variables, a partition also contains process-specific details.

Data area of a process in working storage

Three variables are set in the sample routine below. The variable a set in routine P1 is also visible in routine P2 without this being stated explicitly. Furthermore, all set variables, namely a, x, and y, remain even after the execution of the routine.

This last situation is not always desirable. For software engineering reasons, you may wish to encapsulate routines, namely restrict the scope of variables to specific (sub)routines or procedures. (Refer to Section 5.2.6.)

Encapsulation of routines

Caché has various mechanisms for "cleaning up" local variables:

- Place the Kill command at the end of a routine (just prior to the terminating Quit command) to delete variables that are no longer required after leaving the routine.
- Use the New command to define a list of local variables for a routine and the subroutines it calls. Variables in the list are deleted automatically when the routine terminates.
- Pass values to routines. This is explained in Section 5.2.5.

• Define private and public variables for procedures as encapsulated blocks within routines. This is introduced in Section 5.2.6.

5.2.4.3 The New Command

Saving local variables

The idea behind the New command is that you specify a list of local variables for a routine that are defined only in this routine (and all subroutines it calls). Local variables listed in a New command are implicitly deleted when the routine terminates. Note that the New command is used only for local variables, not *global* variables (for which it returns an error message). The list consists of non-indexed local variables. The presence of a name also implies the saving of any defined *indexed* variables. For example, New a also saves any variable a(1) that might exist.

Previously defined variables of the same name as any listed in a New command are temporarily hidden and restored when the New command ends. This is a reliable means of avoiding name conflicts.

Example

```
P1      // first line, with details about the routine
        New a
        Set a=1
        Do P2
        Quit
P2      // first line of the P2 subroutine
        New x,y
        Set x=a,y=3
        Quit
```

In this example, a New command restricts the variable a (used in the routine P1) to P1 and the routine P2 (which P1 calls). The x and y variables are restricted to P2, and are deleted when P2 exits (that is, they cannot be used to pass values back to the calling routine).

Similar to the Kill command, the New command is also available in a form without arguments in which all variables are saved (which, however, has a certain overhead), and in the exclusive bracketed form—New (x)—in which all variables except x are saved.

5.2.5 Parameter Passing

Transfer of information

Parameter passing is an essential instrument for transferring information from a calling routine to a called routine (and back). Parameter passing is typically used in the following situations:
• calling a local or global routine
• calling a user-defined function
• calling a procedure

Caché provides two different forms of parameter passing:
• *call by value*—pass individual values to the called routine or procedure
• *call by reference*—establish a unique reference between variables of the calling routine and the called routine

In both cases, the maximum number of parameters allowed in the parameter list is 254.

5.2.5.1 Parameter Passing with *Call By Value*

In a call by value, an *actual* parameter list is passed by the call. The actual parameter list maps to the *formal* parameter list found at the entry to the called routine segment.

Actual parameter list

Example

```
        Set a=1,b=2,c=3
        Do P1(a,b,c)        // actual parameters are a, b, c
        ...
P1(r,s,t,)                  // formal parameters are r, s, t
        Set Sum=r+s+t       /* they receive the values from
                                a, b, c */

        ...
        Quit
```

Obviously, the actual parameters must exist. They can be any expressions that are evaluated and passed as values:

Example

```
Do ^P2($Length(x1)*2,^Order(custno))
```

The two values passed in this call represent expressions that must be evaluated before being passed. The first expression involves a function call, whereas the second expression obtains a value from a global variable.

Formal parameters are successively related to the current parameters and the value passed to this local variable. In the example, r, s, and t have the values 1, 2, and 3, respectively.

It is important to realize that the formal parameters are subject to an implicit New command at the start of the called routine. Similarly, an implicit K111 is also executed when the called routine ends. This means that the formal parameters exist only in the called routine and do not conflict with any variables with the same name that have been defined previously. This is a prerequisite for programming free of any side-effects.

Implicit New command

Writing routines without side-effects

Finally, two comments. Although specific actual parameters can be omitted, the separating commas in the list must be specified. The corresponding formal parameters are then undefined.

Example

```
Do ^P1(,p1,,p2,$Horolog+1)
```

The first and third parameters are omitted. The parentheses must remain, even when all parameters are omitted.

Any one variable name cannot appear more than once in the list of formal parameters:

```
P1(x,t,x,y,z)   // produces an error message !!
```

5.2.5.2 Parameter Passing with *Call By Reference*

Results can be returned from an invoked routine using the shared variable pool of the partition. However, this can cause an inadvertent double assignment of variable names. The *call by reference* form is more elegant and safer because it avoids this problem.

Relationship between variables

Here, a relationship between a variable in the calling routine and the called routine is established. Every change in the called routine is passed through to the associated variable; even if it is deleted with the Kill command.

The syntactic identification is a period prefixed to the variable name in the actual list. In contrast to the *call by value* method, the var variable can, but need not, exist.

```
        Kill var          // var no longer exists
        Do P1(.var)       // call by reference
        ...
P1(x)                     // formal parameter x
        Set x=0,x(1)=1,x(2)=2,x(3)=3
        ...
        Quit
```

Binding complete arrays

The *call by reference* can also bind complete arrays (that is, indexed local variables) to the called routine and vice versa. In the example routine, the indexed variables var, var(1), var(2), and var(3) exist after leaving P1. Thus, the var variable is equivalent to x. An array is passed to the called routine in the same manner.

Both *call by value* and *call by reference* forms can be mixed in a routine call.

Example

```
Do ^Sum(a,b,c,.sum)
```

5.2.6 Procedures

5.2.6.1 Structure of a Procedure

Section 5.2.4.2 explained the concepts that determine the scope of local variables in Caché. A New command in a subroutine can save the local variables used there and thus isolate it from the outside world. This means that the developer must create a list of all local variables to be saved. However, it is easy to overlook a variable. Although a New without an argument would avoid this situation by saving *all* variables, it represents a certain overhead and for performance reasons should be used sparingly.

To simplify the management of local variables, but also for general reasons, Caché supports *procedures*. A procedure consists of encapsulated code blocks defined within a routine. Procedures have the following form:

Formal structure of a procedure

```
<procedurename>  (<formal list>)  [<public list>]  <access> {
   code    ...
}
```

For example:

```
MyProc(X,Y) [A,B] Public {
      Write "X + Y = ", X+Y,!
      Write "A + B = ", A+B,!
}
```

This procedure, named MyProc, is *public* and has two formal parameters
(X and Y) and two "public" variables (A and B).

The principal syntactic components are:

Components of procedures

- The <procedurename> that identifies the procedure. It is a normal
  label that starts in column 1 and must conform syntactically to the
  rules for a routine name.
- The <formal list> that defines the parameters of the procedure. This is
  performed in the same manner as for subroutines or user-defined
  functions (refer to Section 5.2.3). Although the formal list cannot be
  omitted, empty brackets can be specified.
- An optional <public list> that defines the public variables used by the
  procedure.
- An optional <access> keyword (either *public* or *private*) that specifies
  whether the procedure can be accessed publicly or whether it is *private*.
- The curly brackets that enclose the procedure code. At least one space
  or the end of line must lie between the opening bracket and the start of
  the code. No executable code can lie after the closing bracket in the
  same line, although comments can.

The access keyword is either *public* or *private*. A procedure marked as
private can be called only from within the routine that contains this procedure. A procedure marked as *public* can be called from a different routine. If no keyword is specified, the default value *private* applies.

Access is either public *or* private

5.2.6.2 Procedure Code

The following list summarizes the most important principles of the program code in a procedure.

- A procedure must begin directly at the label of the procedure and not,
  for example, in a following line using the label+offset scheme. (This
  is possible with a Do or Goto command, although it is poor programming style.) Note that a label placed before an open bracket is interpreted as being within the brackets, i.e., the two following code
  fragments are equivalent:

```
MyProc ()                MyProc ()    {
label  {                 label
```

- All labels are *private* within a procedure and can only be addressed
  from within the procedure. *Private* labels are not visible to the outside
  world. The *private* keyword can be used for labels within a nested procedure, although this is not necessary. The *public* keyword cannot be
  used and causes a syntax error. $Text also cannot reference a private

All labels are private

label within a procedure; only the procedure label can be used as starting point using the `label+offset` scheme.

- Although identical label names are not permitted within a procedure, they are allowed in different procedures of the same routine. The same applies to a label name within a procedure and in the normal routine body, in which case the names can be identical.

- If a `Do` command or a call of an extrinsic function *without* routine name is used (i.e., the subroutine or the function is addressed locally using a label name), the subroutine or function body is initially expected within the procedure. If no such label occurs in the procedure, this label is then sought in the currently loaded routine.

- The previous rule must be modified slightly when a routine or function call *with* a routine name is used in a procedure, e.g., `LABEL1^ROU1`. It is obvious that initially the search is made for the label `LABEL1` in the `ROU1` routine. However, if you are already in the `ROU1` routine (i.e., this routine is currently loaded), this syntax always references a label external to the current procedure.

Goto only within the procedure
- If the procedure contains a `Goto`, only a *private* label within the procedure can be referenced. A `Goto` that references a label external to the procedure is not permitted.

- The "`label+offset`" syntax is not supported within a procedure. Exceptions:
  1. As mentioned previously, `$Text()` with `label+offset` is permitted.
  2. In programming mode, `Goto label+offset` can be used after a `Break` command (or an error) to jump to code within a procedure.
  3. `label+offset` can be used in conjunction with the `ZBreak` command, which allows the `label+offset` syntax to jump within a procedure.

- Changes to the special variable `$Test` made within a procedure are not visible externally, or, in other words, the value for `$Test` is the same at entry to and exit from the procedure.

- The closing bracket "}" can be placed at any position within a line, even in the first column. No code can follow the closing bracket on the same line.

- An implicit `Quit` is performed before the closing bracket that ends a procedure.

- Indirection and the `Xecute` command behave within a procedure as if they were performed outside the procedure. In other words, the `Xecute` command is processed like a subroutine *outside* the procedure.

If the indirection or the `Xecute` command references variables within a procedure, it is always assumed that these are *public*. This is the direct consequence of the fact that these two language constructs are executed outside the procedure, and private variables cannot be accessed externally. This rule continues when these two elements need to access labels. These must lie outside the procedure. Consequently, because a `Goto` command can only reference labels within the procedure, the Goto @A command is also not supported within a procedure.

Finally, let us consider the $CASE function, which is similar to $Select. In contrast to $Select, $CASE can be used to program a case differentiation *without* using indirection. Thus, $CASE within a procedure has adopted the role of $Select. Refer to Section 5.3.4 for details about the $CASE function.

$CASE function

5.2.6.3 Variables in a Procedure

Local variables in a procedure can be either *public* or *private*. Here, the variables specified in the <public list> are *public*, whereas all other variables referenced in the procedure are by default *private*. This is true even when the <public list> is empty. In this case, the list can be omitted.

In addition, variables with the *private* attribute are undefined on entry to the procedure and are implicitly deleted on exit from the procedure. Thus, they are similar to the variables that are saved with the New command. All %-variables (i.e., those prefixed with a % character) are implicitly *public*. For documentation reasons, they can appear in the <public list>this, however, is optional.

%-variables are implicitly public

If a subroutine within a procedure is now called from outside the procedure, the *private* variables assigned to the procedure are saved and reactivated on re-entry to the procedure. On the other hand, the called procedure or the called subroutine has access to variables with the *public* attribute or to %-variables (which are always *public*).

However, variables saved with a New command are not quite the same as variables with the *private* attribute. Generally, variables to be passed to another procedure or subroutine must be *public*. In other words, they must appear in the <public list>. A *public* variable of a procedure should be saved with a New command. This ensures that it is implicitly deleted when an (implicit or explicit) Quit command is executed.

Example

```
MyProc(x,y) [name] {
   New name
   Set name="John"
   Do ^Prog
   Quit
}
```

The name variable appears in the <public list> and thus is visible outside the procedure, hence, also in the called routine ^Prog. The name variable vanishes with the Quit command that ends the procedure.

The New command does not permit variables with the *private* attribute. Indeed, the command New x produces an error message when x is *not* a public variable (or a %-variable).

The above rules also apply to variables within the formal list of a procedure.

Example

```
MyProc(x,y) [x] {
  Do Customer^Prog1
}
```

In the example, x, but not y, is visible in the Customer^Prog1 routine.

5.2.7 Extrinsic Functions

User-defined functions

Functions that an application developer writes (in a manner similar to writing subroutines) are called user-defined functions. To differentiate these from intrinsic functions, they are called *extrinsic*. Although the two forms are similar, there are differences in their syntax and their use in expressions.

Because extrinsic functions have a structure similar to normal subroutines (for instance, in the way in which values are passed), we supply recommendations in the following sections when you should use a user-defined function and when a subroutine would be more appropriate.

5.2.7.1 Structure and Use

Two dollar signs

A user-defined function is invoked by its name. To distinguish it from a "normal" intrinsic function, an extrinsic function has *two* dollar signs prefixed to its name:

```
$$Name(Argumentlist)
```

Naming conventions for extrinsic functions follow the normal rules for a subroutine. The arguments are referenced either as *call by value* or *call by reference*. Function calls without arguments end with an empty pair of parentheses. Section 5.2.5 provides a detailed discussion of passing values to subroutines.

As mentioned previously, user-defined functions and subroutines are similar, although there are two important differences:

- The function calculation is ended as soon as a Quit *with* an argument occurs. The value of the Quit command's argument is the value returned by the function.
- The $Test signal variable is stored on entry to the function body and re-established after ending the function calculation. (Refer to Section 5.1.1.2 for more information about special variables.)

The basic structure of a user-defined function has the following format:

```
Name(<formal list>)
 <code>
 Quit <expr>
```

Difference at the end

Thus, the routine body of a user-defined function differs from that of a subroutine only in the way in which it ends. Otherwise the two are identical. Note although the inadvertent call of a user-defined function with a Do command does not produce an error in Caché, no function value is returned in such cases. By comparison, an inadvertent call to a normal subroutine as a user-defined function produces an error message. The following simple example shows the structure of a function body and the call of a user-defined function. Let us assume that you require a random integer in the range 100–200. The intrinsic function $Random(n) returns a random integer, but only in the range [0,n-1]. The following user-defined function solves the problem for any arbitrary interval [min,max]:

Example

```
Random(min,max)
 New diff,zz
 Set diff=max-min,zz=$Random(diff+1)+min
 Quit zz
```

As mentioned previously, the Quit command terminates a function and returns the value of its argument as the function value. In the above example, we could have avoided setting the zz variable by using the command Quit $Random(diff+1)+min.

Similar to subroutines, user-defined functions can be stored locally or "globally" in another routine. If the function code is contained locally in the current routine (say at the label Random(min,max)), then the following call suffices:

"Global" user-defined functions

```
Write $$Random(100,200)
```

If the $$Random function does not exist in the local routine (but is stored as a standalone routine), a caret sign must be added to the subroutine call:

```
Write $$^Random(100,200)
```

A third form of call is often used. In this case, several different functions are chained to each other in a routine body (which, for example, could be called function). The $$Random function is then called using the label within function as follows:

```
Write $$Random^function(100,200)
```

Thus, we reference the Random label within the function routine.

In contrast to intrinsic functions, the call can also contain *call-by-reference* parameters. As our next example, we extend the task of the above $$Random function as follows: ten integer random numbers should be created in the range [min,max] (repetitions are permitted), and these should be set in the locally indexed variable random(i), i=1(1)10. The routine now has the following form:

Call by reference

```
Random(min,max,x)
 New diff,i
 Set diff=max-min
 For i=1:1:10 { Set x(i)=$Random(diff+1)+min }
 Quit ""
```

The local array x(i) with ten random numbers is created in a For loop. Three parameters are passed with the function call, where the third parameter is referenced with *call by reference*.

This user-defined function is called, for example, with the following parameters:

```
Write $$^Random(100,200,.random)
```

The result of the function call is a null string, because the expression as argument of the Quit command is a null string. Hence, in this case, the Write command does nothing. However, the random(i), i=1(1)10 array was created with ten random numbers from the range 100 to 200; this array is available in the calling routine.

5.3 Procedural, Structured Programming

For controlling the flow within routines, a developer can choose between two methods in Caché ObjectScript:

- a line-oriented method based on the If, Else, and For commands familiar from previous versions of Caché
Command construct
- a *command construct* method based on the equivalent language elements in Java, C, and C++

Special circumstances aside, the two methods should not be mixed. Although to some extent they use the same command keywords (If, Else, and For), the corresponding commands differ syntactically and semantically. We strongly recommend that you use only the modern form of command constructs for new developments.

The four *command constructs* are summarized below:

- ```
  If <expr>[,<expr> ...] { code }
  ElseIf <expr>[,<expr> ...] { code }
  Else { code }
  ```
- `For <forparameter> { code }`
- `WHILE <expr>[,<expr> ...] { code }`
- `Do { code } WHILE <expr>[,<expr> ...]`

Code block
The so-called code block enclosed within curly brackets {} is important to the scope of the execution code. We emphasize that a general code block {} does *not* exist in Caché, but only in conjunction with these four command constructs (and naturally in conjunction with procedures). Section 5.3.2 describes the general rules for this block structure.

5.3.1 Command Constructs for Flow Control

5.3.1.1 The Expression List

Common structural features
The four command constructs have several common structural features. All have a {code} block that is described in detail in Section 5.3.2. In addition, the three If, WHILE, and Do/WHILE command constructs have an expression list <expr>[,<expr> ...] that consists of one or more expres-
  ```

sions separated by commas and which are processed from left to right. Examples of such expressions are:

```
(age>30)&&(sex="w")
$Piece(^G(1,typeno),"/",4)'?3N
r<5,s>2,t<10
```

Processing here means that the individual expressions are interpreted logically for their truth. The evaluation within an expression list terminates as soon as an expression is found that evaluates logically to FALSE (equals 0).

As soon as *all* expressions of a list are logically *true*, the associated code block is processed, possibly several times.

5.3.1.2 Alternatives: If/ElseIf/Else

In the most general form, this alternative has the following appearance:

```
If <expr>[,<expr> ...]{ code }
ElseIf <expr>[,<expr> ...]{ code }
Else { code }
```

Note here that the ElseIf and Else keywords are alternately optional. Thus, the following constructs are also useful:

ElseIf and Else are alternately optional

```
If <expr>[,<expr> ...] { code }
```

```
If <expr>[,<expr> ...] { code }
Else { code }
```

```
If <expr>[,<expr> ...] { code }
ElseIf <expr>[,<expr> ...] { code }
```

The ElseIf section can occur more than once, as in the next example:

Example

```
If b=5 {Set a=1} ElseIf b=6 {Set a=2} Else {Set a=4} Goto x
```

As is usual for alternatives of this type, only one code block is executed, either:

- the first code block in the If or ElseIf section whose expression list is true
- if none of the If or ElseIf conditions is true, the Else code block (when present)

The above example is easy to understand. However, note that the terminating Goto command is always executed because it is outside the If command construct. To improve readability, the example could be written as follows:

```
If b=5 {
  Set a=1
} ElseIf b=6 {
  Set a=2
} Else {
  Set a=4
```

```
}
Goto x
```

There are reasons to deviate from this easy-to-read form. For instance, the If command construct can extend over any number of lines, as long as the expression list starts in the same line following the If command construct and is separated by a single space.

Another example

```
If x<3,z>5 {
  Set a=1
  Do Label1
  Set b=2
  Do Label2
} Else {
  Do Label9
}
```

A Quit command within a code block acts as if the block were not present. Depending on the context in which the Quit command occurs, either a (sub)routine or a procedure will be ended or a For loop terminated.

A Goto command can jump to an address outside the If construct or to a label within this If construct, however, not in a different code block, irrespective of whether it is inside or outside the current block.

ElseIf and Else are not independent command words

Finally, note that ElseIf and Else are not independent command words, but form part of the If command construct. Thus, ElseIf and Else cannot be used without an introductory If. In addition, the value for $Test is stored on entry in a command construct and restored at its end.

5.3.1.3 Loops: For

The For, WHILE, and Do/WHILE command constructs each enables the repeated execution of a specific code segment. These are called repetitions or loops. The general form of the For command construct is:

```
For <forparameter> { code }
```

where the {code} code block is executed the number of times specified by the <forparameter>. Commands that follow the code block in the same line after the closing } bracket no longer belong to the For command and are executed just once.

The interesting feature of For in Caché is the broad variability of the For parameter. Four different formats are possible:

- *List* of arbitrary expressions in the form

```
For lv=<expr>[,<expr> ...] { code }
```

thus, for example:

```
For prime=2,3,5,7,11 { Write !,prime," is prime" }

For vowel="a","e","i","o","u" {
  Write !, vowel," is a vowel"
}
```

- Specification of a *numeric range* in the form

```
For lv=<num expr>:<num expr>:<num expr> { code }
```

where the numeric expressions are interpreted successively as start, increment, and end values, respectively. For example:

```
For i=1:1:10 { Write !,i," ",i**2 }
For delta=-2:.1:0 { Do ^function(delta) }
```

- Numeric format as above but without the specification of an end value

```
For lv=<num expr>:<num expr> { code }
```

thus, for example:

```
Set pa=1
For p=3:2 {
  If $$^PrimeTest(p) {
    Write !,p," is prime" Set pa=pa+1
    If pa>100 {
      Quit
    }
  }
}
```

- *Argumentless form.* Without arguments, there is no control variable, start value, or end value.

```
For  { code }
```

Thus, for example:

```
For  {
  Write $Char(7)
  Hang 1
  Quit:$Piece($Horolog,",",2)>72000)
}
```

A Quit command within a For loop ends the loop, as seen in the last two formats above. In many cases, the postcondition formulates a termination criterion (Refer to Section 5.1.3.1.) A Goto command ends a For loop when the jump goes outside the loop.

Quit command ending a loop

The following general rule applies to numeric loop forms with a control variable:

Numeric loop forms

- Start value, increment, and end value (if specified) are evaluated before the first loop passage, and they are assigned internally to the For loop. Changes made to these values within the loop do not affect the number of iterations.
- After the end of the loop, the control variable has the value of the last iteration.
- With conflicting formats (for example, when the end value for a positive increment is less than the start value), the iteration will not be executed.

Note that the various forms of the For construct can be mixed and nested freely.

Examples

```
For lv=2,5,49,1:1:15,1:2 { ... }  // mixed format

For i=1:1:3 {
  For j=1:1:5 {
    Set m(i,j)=0
    If i=j {
      Set m(i,j)=1
    }
  }
}
```

The first loop consists of three formats, namely list format (lv=2,5,49) followed by numeric range format (lv=1,2,...,15). A format without end value then follows (lv=1,3,5,...), meaning that this part of the loop must be terminated internally.

Nested For loop

The second example shows a nested For loop. A (3*5) unary matrix is created whose elements outside the diagonal are 0, but whose diagonal elements are to be set to 1.

As previously, the code block can extend over several lines. The next command after the code block will be processed when the loop ends.

5.3.1.4 Loops: WHILE and Do/WHILE

The two command constructs

- WHILE <expr>[,<expr> ...] { code }
- Do { code } WHILE <expr>[,<expr> ...]

Differences in loop termination

also form loops. The two differ in the way the condition for loop termination is tested. Whereas the test for WHILE is made at the beginning (head-controlled), Do/WHILE is tested after the code block (foot-controlled). In addition, all expressions in the lists must be logically true in order for the corresponding code block to be processed.

Example 1

```
WHILE x>3,y>4 {
  Set a=5
  Do Label
}
Write "complete"
```

Example 2

```
Do {
  Set a=5 Do Label
} WHILE y>4,y<10
Write "complete"
```

An important difference between the two is that the code block for Do/WHILE is performed at least once, but this is not the case for WHILE.

The `Write "complete"` command does not belong to the associated loop in the two examples.

As in other examples of the `For` command construct, a `Quit` within the code block terminates the loop.

A `Goto` command can jump to an address outside the block or to a label within this block level, but not in another code block, either within or outside the current block.

5.3.1.5 The CONTINUE command

The `CONTINUE` command can be used within a code block that follows a `For`, `WHILE`, or `Do WHILE`. This causes a jump back to the loop to check whether another execution of the code block follows. Thus, `CONTINUE` has the same effect as when the closing bracket of a code block is reached. `CONTINUE` can be used with a post condition. As an argumentless command, the command names must be followed by at least two blanks.

As an example we take the code segment from Section 5.3.1.3 that produces the first hundred prime numbers.

Example

```
Set pa=1
For p=3:2 {
  CONTINUE:'$$^PrimeTest(p)
  Write !,p," is prime" Set pa=pa+1
  If pa>100 {
    Quit
  }
}
```

If the `$$^PrimeTest(p)` function returns 0, then the current execution of the code block is ended. If it returns 1 to indicate that a prime number has been found, the condition is logically false and the `CONTINUE` command is skipped.

5.3.2 General Rules for {Code} Blocks

5.3.2.1 Rules

The following comments apply to code blocks within the command construct:
- A command construct can only be entered at its beginning, not by using a label within it
- Similarly, a code block can only be entered at its beginning
- A `Goto` within a code block can only branch
  1. within the same code block
  2. to a nested code block
  3. outside all other code blocks

A `Goto` cannot enter a new code block.

5.3.2.2 Examples for Code Blocks

Some commented examples help to understand the basic principles.

Example

Classic If/Else alternative in a line:

```
If x>3,y<4 { Set z=1 Do label1 } Else  { Set z=2 Do label2 }
```

Example

Functionally equivalent with the previous example, but spread over several lines:

```
If x>3,y<4 {
  Set z=1
  Do label1
} Else  {
  Set z=2
  Do label2
}
```

Example

A nested command construct in which the Do tag call is part of the For loop and is executed for each pass through the loop:

```
For y=1:1:10 {
  If abc(y)>0 {
    Set x=x+abc(y)
  } Else {
    Set x=x-abc(y)
  }
  Do tag
}
```

5.3.3 Line-Oriented Flow Control

Line-oriented variant

When the arguments of the If, Else, or For command words are not immediately followed by a code block, Caché recognizes the syntax as that of the classic line-oriented variant of these commands, where the scope of the command remains in effect to the end of the line. For stack management and code readability reasons, it is preferable not to mix the two forms (the classic line-oriented command form and the block-oriented command construct). Even so, there can be reasons to use both variants together, and thus the line-oriented flow control needs a more detailed discussion.

When a line-oriented If, Else, or For appears within a code block and the block end (i.e., the }bracket) occurs before the actual line end, it ends the scope of these line-oriented commands.

Example

```
If x<1 { Read "Name: ",name:5 Else  Write "Timeout" } Set x=1
```

The scope of the line-oriented `Else` command in the `If` code block is the code block of the `If` command. The `set x=1` is always executed.

The rule that the line can be broken does not apply to the `If`, `Else`, or `For` commands in their line-oriented forms. Thus, the line end is identical to the end of the effective scope of these commands. A command construct that starts within the scope of a line-oriented command must end on the same line.

Line cannot be broken

Example

```
If x<1,y<1 Set a=1 If z { Set b=2
Set c=3 } Else { Set k=5 }
```

This produces an error, because the first line begins with a line-oriented `If` command, which must all appear on a single line, even when (as in this example) a line-oriented form contains a block-oriented form. The two lines:

```
If x<1,y<1 Set a=1 If z { Set b=2 Set c=3 }
Else { Set k=5 }
```

also produce an error, because the `Else` command is not its own command construct. It belongs to the second `If` command on the first line. Therefore, the `Else` command must be on the same line that was initiated with the line-oriented `If` command.

The two following examples illustrate how a block-oriented `For` and a line-oriented `For` produce identical results despite their different constructs:

```
If x>3 {
  Set a=""
  For  {
    Set a=$Order(abc(a)) Quit:a=""  Set x=x+abc(a)
  }
  Set y=y+x
}
```

is identical with:

```
If x>3 {
 Set a="" For  Set a=$Order(abc(a)) Quit:a=""  Set x=x+abc(a)
 Set y=y+x
}
```

5.3.4 Alternatives with $CASE

Multiple permutations of the `If/ElseIf/Else` command construct can be formulated in Caché to achieve a wide variety of programming results.

Calling a routine based on the value of a variable is a common example:

Example

```
If a=1 {
  Do ^P1(3)
} ElseIf a=2 {
```

```
   Do ^P2(2)
 } ElseIf a=3 {
   Do ^P3(1)
 } Else {
   Do Error
 }
```

Variant of the $Select function

$CASE is a variant of the $Select function that allows a very efficient specification of multiple alternatives. The general form of $CASE is:

```
$CASE(<expr>,<expr>:<value>[,<expr>:<value> ...][,:<default>])
```

This form of $CASE has three argument categories. The first argument <expr> is interpreted as an expression, e.g., 2*x+1. A list of arguments <expr>:<value> now follows. Each element consists of two parts, where <expr> is an expression that is evaluated at runtime . The corresponding <value> is selected and becomes the value of the $CASE function when the <expr> matches the expression evaluated at the beginning. The last optional argument is selected only when none of the previous <expr> matches the initial expression.

Possible error condition

An error message is issued if the <default> argument is omitted and none of the previous arguments is satisfied. This means that $CASE (as $Select) should always include a default value.

Example

```
Set x=1
Set y=$CASE(2*x+1,1:"A",2:"B",3:"C",:"Z")
```

The initial expression in $CASE uses the set value of x to calculate the value 3. $CASE then finds the third case and returns its value ("C"), which is set into the variable y. If the initial expression evaluated to a non-specified case identifier, the result returned by $CASE would have been the default value "Z."

$CASE in connection with Do and Goto

Interestingly, the <value> argument part can be interpreted differently in the general definition of $CASE when used in conjunction with the Do and Goto commands. When $CASE is used as an argument for Do or Goto, the <value> is interpreted as an entry reference. In these cases, <value> must represent a valid label or a valid routine name (or both, and possibly with parameters). This means that it cannot be an expression that needs to be evaluated.

The next example shows another permutation of $CASE:

Example

```
Do $CASE(a,1:^P1(3),2:^P2(2),3:^P3(1),:Error)
```

Depending on the current value of the variable a, ^P1, ^P2, ^P3, or Error is called. An equivalent code line could be written with the Goto command.

Another equivalent is possible by using the $Select function, which, however, would require indirection. Because indirection is not allowed in procedures, $CASE is the preferred command within procedures.

5.4 Error Processing

5.4.1 Introduction

The terms *error handling, error trapping,* and *exception handling* are often used synonymously for error processing.

Together, they represent measures taken by a program when some form of error occurs that would terminate the process when there is no error processing. A popular example is—not only in Caché—an attempt to divide by 0. This situation can produce errors even from otherwise "correct" routines, causing them to terminate abnormally under certain circumstances.

An error without error processing results in the termination of the process

A programmer can easily become exasperated performing error testing during routine development, especially when changing to the so-called direct programming mode, where the developer can analyze the situations that caused the error and develop the appropriate corrective measures.

Caché itself generally supports this methodology with the Break command (also refer to Section 5.1.3.2), which switches from routine execution to the *programmer mode* or *debugger* level. The Break command allows various arguments that initiate different actions. The interested reader should refer to Chapter 8 of the *Caché ObjectScript Reference*, which provides a very detailed description of this topic.

Break *command*

Switching to *programmer mode* is certainly not acceptable for systems run by a customer. Rather, you need to store as much information as possible about the context in which an error may occur, and force the routine execution to continue at an appropriate location; this requires a routine entry reference where the execution of the routine can continue. In this way, Caché offers flexibility to the programmer by allowing the execution of *any* code after the occurrence of an error. Generally, a self-contained error processing routine is invoked. This routine could record the error (including the fault location), and also save the current status of the process and record values of individual variables.

Information about the context

5.4.2 Overview of Error Processing

The following information is important for a basic understanding of error processing:

- When an error occurs, Caché sets a corresponding error message in two special variables: $ECode and $ZError. An error-handling routine (called the "error handler") can analyze the contents of these variables and adopt appropriate measures.

- The string assigned to $ZError contains an error designation and the location where the error occurred (label and routine name), as in: <UNDEFINED>Lab1+3^routine.

- $ECode, on the other hand, contains a standardized error code enclosed within commas in accordance with ANSI X11.1 [1994]. For example, the error code for referencing an undefined global variable is:

$ECode *and* $ZError *special variables*

,M7,. The *Caché ObjectScript Reference* contains a list of standard error codes. If an error occurs that does not have a standardized entry, an error message is displayed in the same form, but beginning with Z (or, in some cases, U, for user-defined), such as: ,ZSTORE,

$ETrap or $ZTrap special variables

- Error handlers can be initialized by setting two special variables: $ETrap and $ZTrap. These differ from each other. $ETrap contains a complete command that is executed should an error occur. $ZTrap contains an entry reference to which the program execution branches in case of an error. $ZTrap has priority should both be set.

$STack or $EStack

- Nesting level is important for error processing. It increments by 1 when a subroutine, a user-defined function, or an Xecute-string is executed, and decrements again when a Quit (possibly with argument for $$ functions) terminates the current execution level. The current "depth" can be obtained by reading $STack or $EStack.

The following table summarizes the various language elements Caché provides for error processing.

Table 5.22 Language elements for error processing

Language element		Explanation
Special variables	$ECode	Is empty ("") or set with a standard error code. $ECode can be set to initiate an error and to check the error-processing logic.
	$ETrap	Contains the (arbitrary) code to be executed after an error.
	$ZTrap	Contains a branch address to which a jump is made after an error and where the processing continues.
	$STack	Contains the number of the stack level.
	$EStack	As $STack, but the New command can be used.
	$Quit	Is TRUE (1) when it is invoked in the context of a user-defined function, otherwise 0 in normal subroutines.
	$ZError	Caché error code after an error, e.g., <SYNTAX>Label+2^Prog1
Functions	$STack	Records the routine environment after an error in the various stack levels.
Commands	ZQuit	Deletes all or a specified number of stack levels.
	ZTrap	Can be set in a routine to simulate an error.

Four-level process of error handling

When an error occurs, Caché performs a four-step process:

1. If an error trap was set with $ZTrap, the execution stack is initially reset back to the point of setting $ZTrap. Caché then resumes execution of the routine at the line and in the routine specified by $ZTrap.
2. If an error trap was set with $ETrap, Caché executes the commands contained in $ETrap.
3. If no error trap has been set and you are in programming mode, Caché displays an appropriate error message. The execution stack remains unchanged, and you remain in programming mode. The programmer can resume execution of the routine later.

4. If no error trap has been set and you are in application mode, Caché displays an error message and executes a Halt command.

5.4.2.1 Error Trapping with $ETrap

As mentioned previously, error handlers can be based both on the $ZTrap special variable and alternatively on $ETrap. Here we focus on the mechanism of the $ETrap error handler.

$ETrap is a special variable and is set in the routine with a Set command. It contains the code that Caché executes when an error occurs. If, for example, the ErrorHandler1 error handling routine is to be executed after an error, set Set $ETrap="Goto ErrorHandler1". Note that this is a complete command (not just an entry reference, as with $ZTrap).

The term and concept "stack level" is important to error processing. *Stack level*
Every time a Do or Xecute command or a user-defined function is executed, the stack level increases by one and decreases correspondingly when an implicit or explicit Quit terminates the execution of this level. It has the value 0 in direct mode prior to execution of the first Do or Xecute or a $$ function. This value is counted in the $STack special variable and indicates the current nesting level.

To provide different routines for error handling at various execution levels, $ETrap can be used as an argument of the New command and then redefined. Thus, when an error occurs and $ETrap has been set, the $ZError special variable is first assigned a corresponding error message. The execution stack is then reset to the level in which $ETrap was defined. Finally, the command contained as a value in the $ETrap variable is executed.

The next example outlines an error handler:

Example

```
P1          //
            ...
            Set $ETrap="Goto ErrorHandler1"
            ...
            Write !,$$F1($Horolog)
            Quit
            // ─────────────
F1(h)       //
            ...
            New $ETrap Set $ETrap="Goto ErrorHandler2"
            ...
            Quit h
            // ─────────────
ErrorHandler1       ...
            Set $ECode="" Quit
ErrorHandler2       ...
            Set $ECode="" Quit
```

Outline of an error handler

In the first line of this routine, $ETrap is set with the code that is to be executed should an error occur. In the example, it is a branch to the

ErrorHandler1 label. The user-defined function F1() uses a New command to save the old value of $ETrap, which it reassigns with the "Goto ErrorHandler2" command. Thus, should an error occur here, a branch is made to another error-processing routine.

In the above example, $STack (after entry into the P1 routine) has the value 1 and the value 2 (after calling the user-defined function $$F1()).

No new level is added

Error processing takes place at the same level in which the error occurred. Thus, no new level is added. This avoids a problem in which the occurring error was initiated through reaching the maximum available stack level.

Each of the two error handlers in the P1 example routine clears the error condition before the terminating Quit command by assigning the null string to the $ECode special variable. The error condition would remain if this was not done.

$STack has a related special variable, $EStack, which also counts the stack level. Normally both values are identical, but in contrast to $STack, $EStack can appear as argument of the New command. This stores the current value for $EStack and restarts the counting at 0.

When an error now occurs during the processing of a routine, the $ETrap contents are executed and the current stack level exited. Both take place implicitly by inserting the following commands in the execution stream:

```
Xecute $ETrap Quit:$Quit "" Quit
```

The first Quit command terminates the execution level with a null string, when the error occurred in a user-defined function and the value of $Quit is TRUE. If this is not the case, an argumentless Quit ends a normal routine call. You are now one stack level higher, and if another (secondary) error occurs, its processing depends on the value of the $ECode special variable in this level—depending on whether a value is present here.

5.4.2.2 Producing an Error

Testing an error handler

To test the logic of an error handler, errors can be produced explicitly by setting the $ECode special variable or with the ZTrap command.

An error occurs whenever the $ECode special variable is assigned a non-empty string. The $ZError variable is then assigned the value <ECODETRAP> and control passes to the error handler, as would be the case for a normal error.

It is sometimes useful to create your own error codes. As mentioned previously, the messages placed in $ECode are enclosed within commas, and begin with a Z (for an implementation-specific error) or with a U (for an application-specific error). The error message "Password expired" could then be assigned to $ECode as follows:

```
Set $ECode=",UPassword expired,"
```

Errors can also be produced with the ZTrap command (abbreviated to ZT). As soon as a ZTrap is executed in a Caché routine, the argument of the command is placed in the $ZError special variable. If ZTrap is used without an argument, $ZError is assigned the value <ZTRAP>. $ECode receives the value ,ZTRAP, in both cases. The execution of the command also causes control to pass to an error handler in the same way as for a normal error.

5.4.2.3 Recording the Error Context with $STack()

The $STack() function (abbreviated to $ST) can be used to record the complete execution environment after an error. $STack in its various forms provides information about the actions that caused the routine to produce the current error, or—should error processing not be active (when $ECode="")—how it reached the last command. $STack() has both single-argument and two-argument forms.

The first argument is always interpreted as an integer value and is greater than or equal to –1. The second argument can consist of one of the following three codes: "PLACE," "MCODE," or "ECODE"; these can be written in either lowercase or uppercase. Table 5.23 shows the single-argument form.

Call	Value
$STack(-1)	Value of the largest stack level that produces a value for the two-argument form of the function.
$STack(0)	Value that shows how this Caché process was started.
$STack(m)	When m is in the range 0<m>$STack(-1), the call returns one of the following values: 1. "DO", when a Do was used to call this stack level. 2. "XECUTE", when an Xecute was used to call this stack level. 3. "$$", when a user-defined function was used to call this stack level.
$STack(n)	Returns the null string when n>$STack(-1)

Table 5.23 Results of the single-argument form of $STack(intexpr)

$STack() can be used to obtain any stack level that was reached during routine execution. The greatest nesting level is stored in $STack(-1). Should error processing not be active (i.e., $ECode=""), $STack(-1) is always equal to $STack. When error handling is active, $STack(-1)> $STack is possible; this is because error conditions of previous stack levels that are larger than the current level have been stored.

$STack(m) (for m in the range of the processed stack levels) displays which call was used to invoke this stack level: with a routine call ("DO"), with an Xecute ("XECUTE"), or with a user-defined function ("$$").

In the two-argument form, the second argument represents a so-called stack code, which can assume one of the three values "PLACE", "MCODE", or "ECODE". All three codes refer to the stack level that was specified in the first argument. Stated very generally, the "PLACE" value provides information about the location of an error, where "MCODE" specifies the Caché code located there and "ECODE" specifies the error message itself.

"ECODE" is the easiest to explain. $STack(2, "ECODE") returns, for example, the error code (provided one is present) at the second stack level, such as ",M9,".

The "PLACE" stack code now returns the location as the line of a routine within the stack level specified as first argument; the location could have the following appearance:

```
L1+3^|"Warehouse1"|MainProg  +5
```

The routine location is specified here with the usual label-plus-offset syntax (L1+3) followed by a routine name and any environment details present (^|"Warehouse1"|MainProg). The value +5 returns the offset to the offending command in the error line. Note that the command Set x=1,y=2 counts as two commands.

A slightly different format is displayed when the error occurs within an Xecute string. In this case, the error line is not specified, but is represented symbolically as an "ə" indirection indicator plus the pointer in this string, as described previously.

The command now actually displayed depends on the value of $ECode at this level. The following table provides an overview.

$STack(m,"ECODE")	$STack(m,"PLACE")
null string	The most recently executed command, when m'=$STack
null string	The currently executed command, when m=$STack
non-null string	The last command in this stack level for which $STack(m, "ECODE") would still have produced the null string

The values in the table can be interpreted as follows. The first two cases indicate that no error occurred at the stack level specified with m. If m does not equal the current stack level, the most recently executed command is executed. If, however, the stack level to be tested equals the current level, the currently executed command is displayed.

If, however, an error is displayed at this stack level (i.e., $ECode'=""), the last correct command is displayed.

For more advanced details about error trapping, please refer to the comprehensive documentation set for Caché, which also describes exotic situations in detail (e.g., when errors occur in an error handler). In particular, refer to the chapters *Error Processing* and *Routine Debugging* in the *Using Caché ObjectScript* manual.

6 Object Access and Persistence

6.1 Objects in Caché ObjectScript

This chapter describes the use of objects in Caché ObjectScript. Caché ObjectScript is a comprehensive object-oriented programming language that was specifically developed to enable the fast creation of database applications. Chapter 5 introduced ObjectScript's basic language elements; this chapter discusses the use of "dot syntax", and explains how to create and manipulate objects in programs.

Object-oriented programming language

6.1.1 Object Identity and Access to Objects

An object is an instance of a specific object class. In the context of Caché ObjectScript, objects can appear in two forms: in the memory of the process that created the object instance and, for instances of persistent object classes, as the stored version in the Caché database.

The way in which an object is referenced also depends on its form. Whereas objects in memory have a temporary object reference (OREF), objects stored in the database have a permanent object identifier (OID).

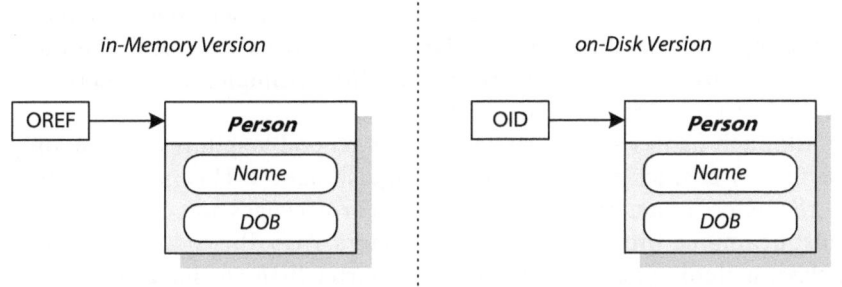

in-Memory Version   *on-Disk Version*

Figure 6.1 OREF object reference and OID object identifier

An OID is assigned to a persistent object when the object is stored in the database the first time. It remains unchanged as long as the object exists.

An OID can be used to locate a persistent object in the database and to load it into memory. As soon as the object has been loaded into memory, the system assigns it an OREF object reference. The application can use this to reference the object, and to access its properties and methods. An OREF is considered to be a *handle* for an object instance, which, however, remains valid only while the instance remains in the process memory. The system assigns a new OREF if the object is reloaded into memory later.

In contrast to an OREF, the OID assigned to an object never changes. That is, the object retains its identity even if the values of all of its properties change over time.

If an object contains references to other persistent objects, these are referenced in memory and in the database using the OREF and the OID of the referenced objects, respectively. Embedded objects are represented in memory with their own object instances and referenced using their OREFs. In the database, they do not have any identity, but are serialized and stored embedded within the receiving object.

An OID is unique throughout a namespace

An important characteristic of an OID is its uniqueness throughout the namespace. To ensure this, Caché forms OIDs from two parts: the object class and an ID (normally numeric) that is unique throughout the class. Caché provides several calls that identify stored objects using the ID part, rather than the complete OID. The following sections describe these calls in detail. Such calls require that the object class can be determined from context.

6.1.2 Naming, Conventions, and Restrictions

The following sections explain the assignment of names in Caché.

6.1.2.1 Uniqueness of Names

All names are "case sensitive"

Generally, all names in Caché ObjectScript (including the names of packages, classes, properties, methods, class parameters, queries, indexes and variables) are *case sensitive*, i.e., the uppercase and lowercase equivalents of an alphabetic character are considered to be two different characters. However, because SQL and ActiveX/OLE are not case sensitive, two names cannot be used that differ in case. Even so, keywords used for declaration, compiler directives, and macro names (for example, #classcontext, ##class, $$$OK) are not case sensitive.

Although names are not subject to any general length restriction, only the first 31 characters are used to distinguish names. This means the first 31 characters of a name must be unique. For packages and classes, names must be unique within the first 25 characters. Also, the complete name of a class, including its package, must be shorter than 56 characters. (Refer to section 4.2.1 for more information about packages.)

6.1.2.2 Use of Uppercase/Lowercase in Names

Caché Objects adopts the following conventions for applying uppercase/lowercase characters to names:

- The names of packages, classes, properties, methods, queries, and indexes are usually written in mixed case. To make the name more readable, the initial character of a word or term is written in uppercase with the remainder in lowercase. Example: IsValidDT().
- Keywords and system variables, such as %this and %val, are written in lowercase.
- The names of class parameters are written exclusively in uppercase.

6.1.2.3 Names and the Percent Sign (%)

Only alphabetic characters and the percent sign (%) are valid as the first character of a name. The package names of the supplied Caché system classes and many of their properties and methods start with a percent sign, e.g., %Library or %New().

Correspondingly, Caché adopts the convention that the percent sign is reserved for system classes and should not be used for the names of user-defined classes and their properties, methods, class parameters, or queries.

Percent sign reserved for system classes

6.1.3 Dot Syntax

As in most object-oriented programming languages, Caché ObjectScript references objects using the dot syntax that specifies the properties, methods and class parameters of individual instances or classes.

To access class methods or objects of non-registered classes, the class type must be specified with the #class declaration or the ##class() macro function. This specification is optional for objects of registered classes. (Refer to Section 6.1.7.)

#class declaration

6.1.3.1 Accessing Properties

The OREF.property syntax references the property of the object to which the OREF object reference applies. Caché signals an error when the dot syntax refers to a property that does not exist.

Internally, Caché uses the two methods OREF.propertyGet() and OREF.propertySet() to reference a property, depending on whether the value of the property is to be read or set, respectively.

Examples

```
Set value=Invoice.Total  →  Set value=Invoice.TotalGet()
Set Invoice.Total=value  →  Do Invoice.TotalSet(value)
```

You can overwrite the original propertyGet() and propertySet() methods (which Caché creates automatically) with methods that you write yourself.

Overwriting propertyGet() and propertySet() methods

6.1.3.2 Invoking Methods

The OREF.method(arg$_1$, arg$_2$,...) syntax references the method() method of the object to which the OREF object reference applies.

Examples

```
Do Invoice.Print()
Set Result=Invoice.AddTax(a,b+2)
```

As this example shows, you can call a method with the Do command or include it as part of an expression. In the latter case, the return value of the method is used to calculate the expression.

Method call with the Do command or as part of an expression

The parameter list enclosed within parentheses follows the method name. Even if a method call does not have arguments, an empty parenthesis-pair () must follow the method name.

The ##class(class).method(arg₁,arg₂,…) syntax calls class methods. This differs from the normal method invocation in that the class methods do not require an OREF. Rather than an OREF, a ##class() declaration makes the reference, as in the following example.

Example

```
Write ##class(Accounting.Invoice).%New()
```

Optionally, as for an instance method, a class method can also be invoked with an OREF. In this case, the OREF merely determines the class. An attempt to call a nonexistent method causes a Caché error.

Creating a new object instance with the %New() class method
An object instance is automatically removed from memory

This example also shows how the %New() class method creates a new instance of a registered or persistent object class in memory.

Caché detects when an object instance is no longer in use and removes it automatically from memory. If you want to force this, you can set the variable containing the OREF to the empty string.

6.1.3.3   Accessing Class Parameters

The special #PARAMETER syntax (when used in method code) refers to a class parameter from its own class. The ##class(class).#PARAMETER syntax can access class parameters from any other classes.

Example

```
If Count>..#MAXCOUNT Set Error="Too many entries!"
```

This restricts a demonstration version of an application to a specific number of data records, which you then specify as a class parameter.

6.1.3.4   Cascading Dot Syntax

The dot syntax can be cascaded to access the properties or methods of embedded or referenced objects.

Examples

```
Vehicle.Manufacturer.Name
```

Following references with cascading dot syntax

Let us assume that the Manufacturer property is a reference to a persistent object or an embedded object. The specified syntax of the Name. property would then correspond to the manufacturer associated with the Vehicle OREF. Similarly

```
Vehicle.Manufacturer.Produce()
```

would be a valid reference to the Produce() method of the associated manufacturer object.

Caché does not limit the number of nesting levels. For example, `Vehicle.Manufacturer.Address.City` refers to the city name of the vehicle manufacturer's address.

6.1.3.5 Relative Dot Syntax

In the context of method code, relative dot syntax (`..`) refers to another method or property of the same object as the most recent reference.

Example

```
Method AgeGet() As %Integer
{
  If ..DOB="" { Quit "" }
  Quit $Horolog-..DOB\365.2425
}
```

In this example, the relative dot syntax accesses the DOB property for the current object instance.

The relative dot syntax depends on the previous `#classcontext` definition. (Refer to paragraph 6.1.7.3.) For method code, this definition is automatically produced by the class compiler.

Here are further examples and their meanings within the `#classcontext Accounting.Invoice`:

Example	Explanation
`..Print()`	Refers to the `Print()` method for the current instance of the `Accounting.Invoice` class.
`..Inum`	Refers to the `Inum` property for the current `Accounting.Invoice` instance.
`..#XYZ`	Refers to the `XYZ` class parameter of the `Accounting.Invoice` class.
`..Manufacturer.Name`	Refers to the `Name` property of that object to which the reference in the `Manufacturer` property for the current instance of the `Accounting.Invoice` class applies.

Table 6.1 Examples of relative dot syntax

The property methods for the conversion and validation of values inherited from the data type classes can also use relative dot syntax to access parameters of properties.

For example, let us assume an active `#classcontext Accounting.Invoice.Inum`. This is automatically the case in property methods such as `InumLogicalToDisplay()`, `InumIsValidDT()`, etc. Because `Inum` is derived from the `%Integer` data type class, this property has a `MAXVAL` parameter that property methods can reference, as shown in the following example:

Example	Explanation
`..#MAXVAL`	References the `MAXVAL` parameter of the `Inum` property.

Table 6.2 Example for accessing property parameters

Although the dot syntax is used mostly within method code, it is also valid outside methods where a valid `#classcontext` declaration exists.

The relative dot syntax is preferred over the ##this syntax

In many cases the relative dot syntax is recommended rather than the ##this syntax.

6.1.4 Using Object References

Object references represent a special case of local variables in Caché (refer to Section 5.1.1). An object reference cannot be constructed in Caché ObjectScript; it can only be obtained using the methods of an object class, such as %New(), %OpenId(), etc.

Under certain conditions, Caché automatically changes an object reference into a regular string:

- output with the Write command—Write OREF
- use in expressions—OREF_" and more"
- creating a list in $LIst format—$LIst(OREF)
- saving in a global—Set ^Global=OREF
- use as a subscript—Set a(OREF)=""

The string has the format number@class, which the Write command shows as follows:

```
>Set pers=##class(User.Person).%New()
>Write pers
1@User.Person
```

The $ISOBJECT *function*

An ordinary string in this format, even if it originated through a type change using OREF, no longer provides a valid object reference. If you try to use it as such, the error <INVALID OREF> occurs. How do you determine whether a variable is a valid object reference? The $ISOBJECT function returns the appropriate truth value, as the following example shows:

```
If $ISOBJECT(pers) { Write pers.%ClassName() }
```

6.1.5 Features of Properties

6.1.5.1 Validation of Property Values

Caché ObjectScript automatically validates the values assigned to the properties of an object class. The PROPERTYVALIDATION class parameter controls this validation.

Table 6.3 Values for the PROPERTYVALIDATION class parameter

PROPERTYVALIDATION	Explanation
0	Perform no validation.
1	The validation is performed immediately when a value is assigned to a property. The status code returned by the corresponding PropertySet() method indicates whether the validation was successful (compare section 6.1.3.1).
2 (default setting)	The validation is performed when the object is stored with %Save(). The status code which the %Save() method delivers as its return value indicates whether the validation was successful.

6.1.5.2 Using Streams

A stream (or BLOB, Binary Large Object) represents a series of characters or bytes; such a stream can be very long. Caché distinguishes between *character streams* and *binary streams*, which consist of characters and binary data, respectively.

Caché further distinguishes between where the stream is stored, whether in a global in the Caché database or in a file at the operating system level.

A number of special methods are available for properties defined as streams. The following table provides an overview:

Method or Attribute	Explanation
Write(data)	Writes the specified data into a stream.
Read(.length)	Reads the specified number of characters or bytes from the stream, and supply them as a method return value. The argument is passed as call by reference; after the method call, it contains the number of read characters or bytes.
WriteLine(data) (for *character streams* only)	Writes the specified data as a separate line of text in the character stream.
ReadLine(.length) (for *character streams* only)	Reads a line of text from the character stream (until the next line terminator is found or the specified length is reached) and supplies the line as a method return value.
Rewind()	Positions the read/write pointer at the start of the stream.
GoToEnd()	Positions the read/write pointer at the end of the stream.
CopyFrom(stream)	Copies a complete stream from another stream. The stream argument is specified as a reference to a valid stream.
OutputToDevice()	Writes the entire contents of the stream to the current device.
LineTerminator (for *character streams* only)	The line terminator used for WriteLine() and ReadLine() (defaults to CR/LF).
AtEnd	True (i.e., 1) if the read/write pointer is at the end of the stream.

Table 6.4 Property methods and properties for streams

The following example assumes that the Person class has a Memo property that is defined as a character stream. This can be used to store text of unlimited length:

```
MemoWrite(ID) //
        Set pers=##class(User.Person).%OpenId(ID)
        Do pers.Memo.WriteLine("This is the first line")
        ...
        Do pers.Memo.WriteLine("This is the last line")
        Do pers.%Save()
        Set pers=""
        Quit
```

Reading from the stream is done similarly. Here, for example, the code reads one line at a time and outputs it directly to the monitor screen:

```
MemoRead(OID) //
        Set pers=##class(User.Person).%Open(OID)
        Do pers.Memo.Rewind()
        WHILE 'pers.Memo.AtEnd {
          Set Length=32767
          Write pers.Memo.ReadLine(.Length),!
        }
        Set pers=""
        Quit
```

6.1.5.3 Using Collections

Collections provide a mechanism for receiving repeated values for a property. Depending on whether these values have a simple sequence or are sorted using a key, a distinction is made between list collections and array collections. The elements in a collection can be literals, references to objects, or embedded objects.

Depending on the type of the collection, various methods are provided to add, find, and delete elements.

The following table provides an overview of the methods for list and array collections:

Table 6.5 Property methods for collections

Method	Explanation	List	Array
Clear()	Deletes all elements of the collection.	Yes	Yes
Count()	Returns the number of elements in the collection.	Yes	Yes
Find(element,key) FindObjectId(id,key)	Searches for the specified element/ OID in the array starting at the position/key. It returns the position/key of the elements found or the "" empty string if the element sought is not present.	Yes	Yes
GetAt(key) GetObjectAt(oid,key) GetObjectIdAt(id,key)	Returns the value/OREF/OID/ID of the elements at the position/key.	Yes	Yes
GetNext(.key) GetObjectNext(.key) GetObjectIdNext(.key)	Returns the value/OREF/OID/ID of the next element after the position/key and updates it.	Yes	Yes
GetPrevious(.key) GetObjectPrevious(.key) GetObjectPreviousId(.key)	Returns the value/OREF/OID/ID of the element before position/key and updates it.	Yes	Yes
Insert(element) InsertObject(oid) InsertObjectId(id)	Inserts the element/OREF/OID/ID at the end of the list collection.	Yes	No
InsertAt(element,key) InsertObjectAt(oid,key) InsertObjectIdAt(id,key)	Inserts the element/OREF/OID/ID at the specified position in the list collection. All other elements are moved by one position.	Yes	No
InsertOrdered(element)	Inserts the element in the list so that all elements for a sequence are sorted according to their values. (Only possible for list collections with literal values, not with references to objects or embedded objects.)	Yes	No

IsDefined(key)	Checks whether an entry exists for the key.	No	Yes
Next(key)	Returns the next position/key after the specified key.	Yes	Yes
Previous(key)	Returns the position/key before the specified key.	Yes	Yes
RemoveAt(key)	Removes the element from the list at the position/key.	Yes	Yes
SetAt(element,key) SetObjectAt(oid,key) SetObjectIdAt(id,key)	Sets the specified element/OREF/OID/ID at the position/key in the collection.	Yes	Yes

For example, use the following code to set the "red" value at the third position of a list collection with the name Colors where palette points to the associated object instance:

Example for the use of collections

```
Do palette.Colors.SetAt("red",3)
```

If the elements are not literals but embedded objects, you must determine whether they have already been instantiated (the OREF object reference exists) or not (the object can be referenced through the OID or ID part, respectively). For example, assume that our Person object class has a list collection, Children, which also contains objects of the Person type. Then, if pers is an object reference of the parent person and child is an object reference of the (possibly just created) child person, the following example sets this child as the first entry:

```
Do pers.Children.SetAt(child,1)
```

You can now use dot syntax to access the properties and methods of the embedded object:

Cascading dot syntax for collections

```
Set pers.Children.GetAt(1).Firstname="Lisa"
```

If you want to use collections of objects that have not been instantiated, you can use the method forms that accept an OID or ID as argument. Similarly, methods that normally return an object reference also have forms that return an OID or ID instead:

```
Do pers.Vaccinations.SetObjectIdAt(VaccId,"2002.08.09")
```

An object is automatically instantiated (so-called *swizzling*) when it is referenced; the attributes and methods then can be used in the familiar way:

Collections and swizzling

```
Write pers.Vaccinations.GetAt("2002.08.09").Type
```

6.1.6 Features of Methods

We have already discussed the general syntax of a method call using dot syntax. For example, if `Invoice` is an OREF that points to an instance of the `Invoice` class, a `Print()` method can be invoked with:

```
Do Invoice.Print()
```

Invoking class methods Class methods can be invoked without an object reference using the `##class()` macro function.

```
Set x=##class(Accounting.Invoice).%OpenId(ID)
```

Parentheses must be specified with a method call, even when no arguments are passed.

6.1.6.1 Use of ##this and %this

Most methods are instance methods and, as such, require a reference to the current object. The OREF is passed implicitly as a parameter to these methods without it being specified in the list of the method's parameters. Within the method, the OREF is available in the `%this` variable. (This variable does not exist in class methods.)

However, `%this` is a system variable and should not be used directly. The built-in `##this` macro function can be used instead.

Example

```
##this.Print()
```

The `##this` macro function is declared implicitly and always contains the object reference (OREF) to the current object. `##this` cannot be used in a class method.

Relative dot syntax is preferable within a method Within methods, you should use relative dot syntax in preference to `##this`. With this syntax, the previous example could have been written as `Do ..Print()`. `##this` is useful to pass an OREF to a routine, as shown the following example.

Example

```
Do Print^InvoiceRtn(##this,30)
```

6.1.6.2 Property and Data Type Methods

Dot syntax permits the use of the special methods that every property inherits from its associated data type class. These special methods are also called *property methods*.

For example, assume that an `Invoice` is an OREF of the `Invoice` class and `Inum` a property of this class of `%Integer` type. The code

```
Set Display=Invoice.InumLogicalToDisplay(Invoice.Inum)
```

uses the `InumLogicalToDisplay()` method, which itself is derived from the `LogicalToDisplay()` method of the `%Integer` data type class.

In general, you can use OREF.PropertyMethod(arg$_1$,arg$_2$,...) to access the property methods inherited from two different sources (also refer to Section 3.3.2.2):

- a method of the property class that determines the behavior of the property
- a method of the data type class that determines the behavior of the data type.

As with instance methods, dot syntax can also be used with property methods. Data type methods can be called directly, without reference to a specific property of a specific class. However, this applies only to executable data type methods—that is, the conversion methods. Validation methods and other methods (which are created only when a method generator compiles the class) are not present as executable code in the data type class.

Invoking property methods

A direct call is made as a class method of the data type class with the syntax ##class(class).PropertyMethod(arg1,arg2,...).

Example

```
##class(User.Person).DOBLogicalToDisplay(+$Horolog)
```

6.1.6.3 In-Memory Values Syntax

To implement a user-written storage strategy that overwrites the %LoadData(), %SaveData(), and %DeleteData() standard methods, the developer needs access to the internal representation of the properties in memory.

Accessing the internal representation of properties in memory

The syntax i%property is used here, where property is the name of the property to be manipulated. Calculated properties cannot be accessed with this syntax.

This example sets the Inum property of an Invoice object:

```
set i%Inum=1234
```

However, this syntax should never be used to access the in-memory values of properties, except within methods for your own storage strategies.

6.1.6.4 Polymorphism

Polymorphism is the hiding of alternative behavior behind a general interface.

Let us assume that the Manufacturer and Vehicle classes each have a Print() method that outputs all values of the properties. You could then easily develop a generally valid print module that is invoked with an arbitrary OREF and that uses the associated Print() method. Polymorphism ensures that this print module does not need to take account of the possible different object types; the following example illustrates this behavior.

Polymorphism and different object types

Example

```
PrintModule(object)  ;
  Open "|PRN|"
  Use "|PRN|"
  Write "Here comes the printout:",!!
  Do object.Print()
  Write !!, "** End of the printout **",#
  Close "|PRN|"
  Quit
```

This print module can now be used in the same way for objects of Manufacturer, Vehicle, or any other type—even for objects defined at a later date.

6.1.7   Declaration and Casting

Create more efficient code

Although dot syntax can normally be used without the declaration of the class to which an OREF refers, Caché Objects can potentially create more efficient code when the exact class has been specified. For non-registered object classes, the class must always be specified explicitly.

There are two different ways of specifying the class that belongs to an OREF:

- Use #class for the declaration of an OREF variable that points to an object of a specific class, e.g., #class User.Vehicle f
- For every call, extend dot syntax with the appropriate class name in the format ##class(class name), such as for
  Write ##class(User.Vehicle)f.Name

For registered classes, these are polymorphous declarations because the object can also be a subclass of the specified class.

6.1.7.1   #class Declaration

A #class declaration appears on its own code line. It remains valid until the end of the routine or until it is revoked with an #endclass declaration.

The syntax takes the form

```
#class class var₁,var₂,...
```

where each var_n is a local variable that is declared as OREF. class is the name of the class that the OREFs reference.

A #class declaration is polymorphous

The class definition is polymorphous, i.e., each var_n element can be either an instance of the specified class or a subclass:

Table 6.6 #class declarations

Example	Explanation
#class User.Vehicle f	Declares the f variable as OREF that points to the User.Vehicle class or a class derived from it.
#class User.Vehicle f1,f2,f3	Declares the f1,f2, and f3 variables as OREFs that point to the User.Vehicle class or a class derived from it.

`#endclass f1,f2,...`	Ends the currently valid `#class` declaration of the listed variables and activates the declarations contained in the stack that these variables had previously.

`#class` declarations can be nested. A nested `#class` declaration rede-clares the variables, and the corresponding `#endclass` re-establishes the previous declaration of the variables.

6.1.7.2 The ##class() Macro Function

The `##class()` macro function extends dot syntax to the specification of a class. In contrast to the `#class` declaration, it is valid only in the exact place where it is used.

Extending dot syntax with a class specification

Examples

```
Set f=##class(User.Vehicle)Vehicle.Name
Set f=##class(User.Person).NameIsValidDT(y)
```

The specification of `##class()` overloads any previous `#class` declara-tion.

6.1.7.3 The #class context Declaration

A `#classcontext` declaration indicates that the following code is per-formed only on a specific class. This declaration influences the meaning of the relative dot syntax and the result of the invocation of the class APIs.

Context of a certain class

The class compiler automatically adds a `#classcontext` declaration at the start of each method. This declaration must be inserted manually into routines that are called by methods when the relative dot syntax is used to access objects.

The `#classcontext` declaration affects all the code that follows, until `#endclasscontext` or the end of the routine is reached. `#classcontext` declarations can be nested. A nested `#classcontext` declaration hides the existing declaration; the associated `#endclasscontext` returns the original declaration.

Class declarations can be changed in different ways, as shown in the following list:

- `#classcontext Invoice` declares that the following code is in the context of the `Invoice` class.
- `#classcontext Invoice.Rnum` declares the following code to be in the context of the property `Rnum` of the `invoice` class, so that `..#MAXVAL` refers to the parameter `MAXVAL` of the property it inherited from its data type class.
- `#classcontext ..Rnum` declares the context of the property `Rnum` of the previous context. If `Invoice` was the previous context, the new context is the same as in the previous example, `#classcon-text Invoice.Rnum`. Relative dot syntax can be used to extend an ex-isting class context.

- #endclasscontext ends the current context declaration and re-activates the previous declaration.

After the declaration of a class context #classcontext Invoice, the use of relative dot syntax, in-memory syntax and ##this all refer to the Invoice class.

6.2   Object Persistence

Caché Objects supports persistent objects, i.e., the ability to write and read objects to and from a database.

Storage strategies as persistence mechanisms

Caché Objects uses so-called "storage strategies" as persistence mechanisms. A storage strategy consists of a name and the specification of a storage class.

6.2.1   Overview

To use the persistence mechanisms provided by the system, a persistent object class must be derived from the %Persistent class. Inheritance provides basic persistence mechanisms. You must create a user-defined storage strategy, if you do not wish to use the standard storage strategy.

Persistent behavior divides into two method groups or interfaces: the persistence interface and the storage interface.

Persistence interface

The persistence interface contains the methods that applications use to directly control the persistence of objects. These include %Open(), %Save(), and %Delete(). The system provides the persistence interface. Application developers cannot change this persistence interface.

Storage interface

The storage interface provides methods that the persistence interface methods use internally to read, store, and delete data. These methods include %LoadData(), %SaveData(), and %DeleteData(). Although method generators typically generate storage interface methods automatically, developers can overwrite the methods provided by the system in order to implement their own persistence behavior.

The following methods of the persistence and storage interfaces cooperate internally:

Table 6.7 Methods of the persistence interface and the storage interface

%Open()	uses	%LoadData()
%Save()	uses	%SaveData()
%Delete()	uses	%DeleteData()

Storage methods are inherited from a separate storage class that is specified as part of the storage strategy.

As an example, consider the CDL code for a Vehicle class for which Caché is to generate all storage code. If you decide to use the standard storage code, Caché automatically performs the storage, loading, and indexing of objects:

```
Class User.Vehicle Extends %Persistent
                    [ ClassType = persistent ] {
```

```
...
}
```

However, the `User.MyVehicle` class requires unique code for storing objects in a database:

```
/// very simple class MyVehicle

Class User.MyVehicle Extends %Persistent
                    [ ClassType = persistent,
                      StorageStrategy = MyStorageCode ] {
...
<Storage name="MyStorageCode">
    <Description>My own storage code</Description>
    <Type>%CustomStorage</Type>
</Storage>
}
```

The developer must also implement the appropriate `%LoadData()`, `%SaveData()`, and `%DeleteData()` methods. (We return to this in Section 6.2.3.1.)

6.2.2 The Persistence Interface

The persistence interface provides the following methods inherited from the `%Persistent` system class:

- the `%Open()` and `%OpenId()` methods
- the `%Exists()`, `%ExistsId`, and `%IsModified()` methods
- the `%Save()` method
- the `%Delete()` method.

These methods are final, i.e., they cannot be overwritten.

6.2.2.1 %Open() and %OpenId()

The `%Open()` method retrieves an object from a database and creates an in-memory version that contains copies of the values for all object properties.

In-memory version of an object

`%Open()` is a class method and uses the OID of the object to be loaded as an argument. `%Open()` returns an OREF that references the memory version (or a null string when the object cannot be found or cannot be loaded for some other reason). If a version of the specified object is already in memory, then `%Open()` only increments the reference counter and returns an OREF that references the previously loaded version.

OID of the object to be loaded

The following code loads a previously stored instance of the `Vehicle` class into memory; `VehicleOid` contains the OID of the vehicle:

```
Set vehicle=##class(User.Vehicle).%Open(VehicleOid)
```

`%Open()` accepts an optional second argument, *Concurrency,* which specifies the behavior for concurrent access to the same object. (Refer to Section 6.2.2.5.)

Second argument Concurrency

Specifying a partial OID (ID part)

A complete OID consists of two components: the specification of the ID part that uniquely identifies an instance of the class and the class name. Normally the %Open() method expects a complete OID with both components as argument. Because the ID part itself is unique within the class, this provides a certain amount of redundancy. Indeed, you can open an object without a complete OID by specifying only the ID part. Assuming that the ID variable contains the ID part of an OID, you can use the alternative method %OpenId() that expects an ID as argument:

```
Set x=##class(User.Vehicle).%OpenId(ID)
```

After the call, x contains an OREF to the opened instance of the Vehicle class. Obviously, you could have formed a complete OID by adding the class name. For example:

```
Set x=##class(User.Vehicle).%Open($LB(ID,"User.Vehicle"))
```

Other than the obvious redundancy through the duplicated specification of the class name, there is another important difference between these variants. We will discuss these in the following section.

OIDs, substitutability and the %OnDetermineClass() method

Principle of substitutability

Using the %Open() and %OpenId() class methods for a specific class does not necessarily mean that an instance of this class will be opened. The principle of substitutability says that instances of subclasses can be used anywhere as instances of a higher-order class. For example, opening a Vehicle could in reality just as well open a Tram or a Bicycle, when these are two associated subclasses, because subclasses have the relationship to the super class: bicycle "is a" vehicle.

This also explains the apparent redundancy in the previous example. Because the instance to be opened could be an instance of any subclass, the complete OID must contain the exact class of the instance to be opened.

Similarly, calling %Open() with a partial OID or for %OpenId() raises a question: What determines the class or subclass of the object to be opened? The %OnDetermineClass() method, which is called internally by %Open() and %OpenId(), determines the final class name.

Determining the final class name

This method is provided automatically for those classes for which Caché Objects maintains OIDs. Because storage strategies generated by Caché uniquely maintain the ID part of OIDs within a class and all subclasses, the %OnDetermineClass() method can easily determine the final class name.

If you wish to use this scheme for user-written storage strategies, you must provide an appropriate %OnDetermineClass() method. If this does not exist, %Open() simply uses the specified class name. However, if it is available, %Open() calls it using the following scheme with the incomplete OID specified as argument:

```
Set status=%OnDetermineClass($ListBuild(ID),.classname)
```

status provides information about the success (or failure) of a method. If the first character is 1, a class name was determined (0 indicates failure).

The original class name (with or without a package name) is passed as a second argument using *call by reference*; this means that the method can change it. For example, if %OnDetermineClass() sets the class name to "bicycle," the %Open() method of the Vehicle class then calls internally the %Open() method of the Bicycle class.

When you write your own %OnDetermineClass() methods, you should always remember that, because this method will be called every time an object instance is opened, performance degradation may result.

Querying OID, ID and class with %Oid(), %Id() and %ClassName()

Determining the OID of an object in memory

You can use the %Oid() method to obtain the complete OID for an object contained in memory. Accordingly, you can use the %Id() and %Class-Name() methods to determine the ID part and the class name. This can also be used to determine the exact class of an opened object:

```
>Set vehicle=##class(User.Vehicle).%OpenId(3712)
>Set oid=vehicle.%Oid()
>Write vehicle.%Id()
3712
>Write vehicle.%ClassName()
User.Bicycle
```

Verifying the existence of an object with %Exists() and %ExistsId()

If you want to verify whether the OID or ID exists before you open an object, use the %Exists() or %ExistsId() method, respectively. For example

```
>If '##class(User.Vehicle).%ExistsId(42) Write "not present!"
```

Verifying changes to an object with %IsModified()

Sometimes it is necessary to know whether an object has been changed. The corresponding information can be examined with the IsModified() method:

```
>If vehicle.%IsModified() Do vehicle.%Save()
```

6.2.2.2 Controlling the Internal Value of a Property

Dot syntax is used to access to the value of a property:

```
Write person.Name
Set person.Name="Smith"
```

In this example, person.Name accesses the Name property of the object referenced by person. Note that ##this.Name or ..Name can also obtain the value of this property within an object method.

Indeed, accessing properties using dot syntax is a simplified notation for access methods. For every property, the system executes internally the oref.propertyGet() or oref.propertySet(new) method for access to oref.property. Thus, the following code is executed in the above examples:

```
Write person.NameGet()
Do person.NameSet("Smith")
```

If a programmer has overwritten the Get() and Set() methods, the programmer's code is used instead of the methods provided by the system.

This is also how you implement calculated properties that do not have a value in memory. In this case, you must provide a Get() method; an additional Set() method is optional.

If, for example, a class Car has a property Power specified in kW:

```
Property Power As %Integer;
```

Calculated property we can then define a calculated property PowerInHP that is not stored.

```
Property PowerInHP As %Integer [ Calculated ];
```

We must now provide a PowerInHPGet() method that calculates and returns (rounded) the horsepower based on the value for Power:

```
Method PowerInHPGet() As %Integer {
    Quit ..Power*1.3596\1
}
```

We can now use the Car class as follows:

```
>Set car.Power=100
>Write car.PowerInHP
136
```

In-memory values syntax If direct access to the value of the property in memory is needed, such as in methods to load and store persistent objects, you can use the *in-memory values syntax*:

```
set i%Power=100
```

However, the use of this special syntax should be restricted to unusual cases.

6.2.2.3 %Save()

%Save() is an instance method that writes into the database the version of an object currently in memory. If the object was stored previously (i.e., it already has an OID), %Save() updates the version in the database. Otherwise %Save() generates a new OID and stores the object. %Save() returns a status code; a 1 as first character indicates that the store operation was successful. (0 indicates that the store operation could not be performed successfully.)

If vehicle represents an OREF to a persistent object, the following code can be used to store it in the database:

```
Set status=vehicle.%Save()
```

The %Save() method is responsible for various tasks such as

- administration of transactions, including the use of `TStart`, `TCommit`, and `TROllback`
- validating the object, including invoking the `%ValidateObject()` method, which in turn invokes the `%OnValidateObject()` method when this is present

- determining the objects in a relationship and, if necessary, invoking the appropriate `%Save()` methods to automatically store these objects
- ensuring that an object points correctly to referencing or embedded objects that have been reloaded automatically
- invoking the `%SaveData()` method to initiate the actual insertion and update of an object and any indexes in the database
- detecting and resolving circular references (recursions of objects linked with each other with references)
- creating an OID for a persistent object.

Shallow and deep save

The `%Save()` method supports an optional argument that specifies how `%Save()` is to handle references to other objects. This argument can assume the following values:

- 0—"Shallow save": store this object independent of whether it has been changed. Referenced objects are also stored only when they have never been stored, namely, do not have any OID. (In this case, storage is required to receive the OID that is to be stored as a reference in the original object.)

- 1—"Deep save": store this object and all related objects that have changed. (This is the default Caché behavior.) In this case, "related" affects all objects in memory that are referenced from the original object or reference it themselves. The original object is written back to the database only if it has been changed.

The definition of "related" relies on swizzling. When, for example, a Vehicle has a reference to a Manufacturer and this was referenced sometime with the syntax

```
vehicle.Manufacturer
```

then a subsequent

```
Do vehicle.%Save(1)
```

causes both `Vehicle` and `Manufacturer` to be stored when they have changed. Namely, an implicit

```
Do vehicle.Manufacturer.%Save(1)
```

is executed.

This applies only when the affected instance of the `Manufacturer` class has been loaded into memory with swizzling, as shown above. If the corresponding instance of `Manufacturer` happens to be in memory independent of a reference from the Vehicle class, even a deep save does not automatically save the Manufacturer instance.

Circular references

The %Save() method automatically discovers and manages circular references between objects. A simple example of such a circular reference involves two objects, A and B, in which object A points to object B and object B points to object A.

Figure 6.2 Circular reference

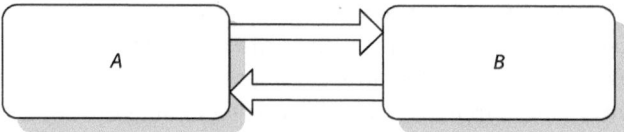

In this case, %Save() stops Caché from entering an endless, recursive loop.

Note that, for circular references, either the reference from A to B or from B to A can be defined as a mandatory property, but never both. %Save() fails when both references are mandatory properties.

Validations during the save operation

%Save() validations

%Save() performs the following checks before it stores an object instance in the database:
- check whether all mandatory properties are present
- check whether the properties values are valid (presuming that the PROPERTYVALIDATION class parameter has been set to the value 2— ValidateOnSave)
- invoke the user-defined method %OnValidateObject(), if it is present
- check values for uniqueness, when these have been marked as *unique* in the class definition. (This is performed internally with the %SaveData() method that %Save() invokes.)

The save operation fails if this validation indicates that a value is invalid. The error status can be obtained as the return value of the %Save() method.

6.2.2.4 %Delete() and %DeleteId()

The %Delete() class method deletes the stored version of a specific object from the database.

```
Do ##class(User.Vehicle).%Delete(oid)
```

However, %Delete() does not delete a version of the object present in memory. Accordingly, the class method %DeleteId() deletes the saved version of an object of which the ID part (and not the full OID) was specified.

System storage classes do not reassign deleted OID values. For user-defined storage classes, the programmer is responsible for assigning or reassigning OID values.

Deleting the full extent

If you wish to delete the full object extent (that is, all instances of an object class including all subclasses), Caché provides the class methods %DeleteExtent() and %KillExtent(). %DeleteExtent() performs a "clean" delete, meaning that transaction processing and locking is used, referential integrity is maintained and any triggers are activated. You can freely use this method in a production environment. On the other hand, %KillExtent() deletes in a "quick and dirty" fashion, and should only be used in a controlled environment (perhaps to delete all test data from a system before it is released into production).

%DeleteExtent() and %KillExtent() methods

6.2.2.5 Concurrency

The %Persistent system class, and thus all persistent objects in Caché, automatically manage concurrency, that is, the concurrent access to objects in a multiuser environment. Concurrency management is achieved with calls of the Caché ObjectScript command Lock. (Please refer to Section 7.3.1 for further information about the Lock command.)

Automatic management of concurrency

There are five different options used to control concurrency. The required concurrency option can be specified as the second argument of the %Open() method when an object is opened.

- 0—"No Locking": no locks are used.
- 1—"Atomic": when an object is loaded, %LoadData() creates a *shared lock* for the object, assuming that the object is stored in more than one node in the database. No locks are created for objects in a single node. The %LoadData() method releases the lock when the loading of the object has completed. When an object is stored for the first time in the database, %SaveData() maintains an exclusive lock during the storage operation should the object be stored in more than one node in the database. %SaveData() does not use any locks when the object is stored in a single node. %SaveData() maintains an exclusive lock during the complete storage operation when an object already stored in the database is being updated.
- 2—"Shared": %LoadData() creates a *shared lock* for an object when it is loaded. The lock is released when %LoadData() has finished the load operation. When an object is stored for the first time in the database, %SaveData() maintains an exclusive lock during the storage operation should the object be stored in more than one node in the database. %SaveData() does not use any locks when the object is stored in a single node. %SaveData() maintains an exclusive lock during the complete storage operation when an object already stored in the database is being updated.
- 3—"Shared/Retained": %LoadData() creates a *shared lock* for an object when it is loaded. The lock is released only after the object has been removed from memory. When an object is stored for the first time in the database, %SaveData() maintains an exclusive lock during the storage operation should the object be stored in more than one

No Locking
Atomic

Shared

Shared/Retained

Exclusive

node in the database. %SaveData() does not use any locks when the object is stored in a single node. %SaveData() maintains an exclusive lock during the complete storage operation when an object already stored in the database is being updated.

- 4—"Exclusive": %LoadData() creates an *exclusive lock* for an object when it is loaded. When an object is stored for the first time in the database, %SaveData() maintains an exclusive lock during the storage operation should the object be stored in more than one node in the database. %SaveData() does not use any locks when the object is stored in a single node. %SaveData() maintains an exclusive lock during the complete storage operation when an object already stored in the database is being updated.

If no concurrency details have been specified, the concurrency default value of the current process is used. The initial value is 1—"Atomic". The following code changes this value to 3—"Shared/Retained":

```
Set oldsetting=$$SetConcurrencyMode^%apiOBJ(3)
```

6.2.2.6 Transaction Mode

The %Persistent system class automatically provides all persistent objects with complete transaction processing, including rollback capabilities. By default, transaction processing is activated as standard for every process. You can use the following code to suppress transaction processing for the current process:

```
Set oldsetting=$$SetTrancactionMode^%apiOBJ(0)
```

You can use the following code to permit transaction processing:

```
Set oldsetting=$$SetTrancactionMode^%apiOBJ(1)
```

Start a transaction

When %Save() saves an object in the database, the method simultaneously starts a transaction (by issuing a TStart command) that contains all changes to the object to be stored and the objects it references. If the %Save() method was successful, it issues a TCommit command to confirm the transaction and to write data to the database.

The following actions are performed if a problem occurs while storing the original object or objects it references:

- Discard all changes made in the database. (Exception: the OID counter managed by the %CacheStorage system class is not reset.)
- Copies of the objects in memory included in the transaction are set back to the state they had before the start of the transaction. This includes resetting to null (" ") all OIDs assigned during the transaction. However, any other changes made to properties during the course of the transaction are not reset.
- The associated %Rollback() method is invoked for every object included in the transaction. The sequence of calls is not defined. %Rollback() invokes the user-written %OnRollback() method, if it exists.

6.2.2.7 Callback Methods

The system automatically invokes callback methods in response to specific actions or events. These methods cannot be called directly.

They are used to include application-specific code that is executed automatically when a specific event occurs. To distinguish this method type from other methods, a name of the form %On*Event* is used here, where *Event* specifies the event that the callback initiates.

For example, the %OnNew() method (if defined) is called automatically from the %New() method when a new object instance is created.

Depending on the type of the object class, different callback methods are available:

Callback methods for registered (transient) objects

Callback method	Invoked by ...
%OnNew()	%New()
%OnClose()	%Close()
%OnValidateObject()	%ValidateObject()

Table 6.8 Callback methods from %RegisteredObject

Callback methods for embedded objects

Callback method	Invoked by ...
%OnDetermineClass(oid,.classname)	%Open(), %OpenId()
%OnOpen()	%Open(), %OpenId()

Table 6.9 Callback methods from %SerialObject

Callback methods for persistent objects

Callback-method	Invoked by ...
%OnAfterSave()	%Save()
%OnBeforeSave()	%Save()
%OnDelete(oid)	%Delete(), %DeleteId()
%OnDetermineClass(oid,.classname)	%Open(), %OpenId(), %Delete(), %DeleteId()
%OnOpen()	%Open(), %OpenId()
%OnRollback()	%Rollback()

Table 6.10 Callback methods from %Persistent

The distinction between system methods and callback methods permits application code to respond to system-initiated events without losing the clear separation of system and application code.

Clear separation of system and application code

Consequently, the affected system methods %New(), %Open(), etc., provided by Caché are final, which means that they cannot be overwritten in application classes. This prevents developers from changing system code and forces every required change or extension to the system behavior to be placed in the appropriate callback method.

6.2.3 The Storage Interface

Through the %CacheStorage storage class, Caché Objects provides a complete storage interface. In addition, developers can create their own storage classes for special application cases that can also be used as storage interfaces. The storage interface consists principally of the following methods:

%CacheStorage storage class

- %LoadData()
- %SaveData()
- %DeleteData()

The following sections describe these methods.

%LoadData()

The %LoadData() method is responsible for loading object properties from the database into the local storage. It is invoked internally by %Open().

%LoadData() can check the value of the %Concurrency special property of the object and implement an appropriate locking strategy.

%SaveData()

The %SaveData() method is responsible for storing in the database the current values of the properties in memory. It is invoked internally by %Save().

If an object has not been stored previously (and thus does not have an OID), %SaveData() assigns an OID and stores the new object with it. Otherwise, the object is stored with the currently existing OID.

%SaveData() can check the value of the %Concurrency property and implement an appropriate locking strategy.

%DeleteData()

The %DeleteData() class method is responsible for deleting an object from the database. It is invoked internally by %Delete().

6.2.3.1 User-defined Storage Interfaces

You can write a user-defined storage interface in two different ways:

- Use %CustomStorage as the storage class and overwrite the storage methods in each individual object class.

Creating a new storage class

- Create a new storage class (e.g., MyStorageClass as a subclass of the system class %CustomStorage) and use this class instead of %CacheStorage to define the persistent object classes. To permit the use of the methods of the storage interface in different persistent classes, these must be implemented as method generators.

The following example illustrates the first variant.

Overwriting methods of the storage interface

Overwriting the storage methods

To implement your own storage interface by overwriting the methods in the specific object class, first define a persistent class with a new storage strategy using the %CustomStorage storage class:

```
/// very simple class MyVehicle
Class User.MyVehicle Extends %Persistent
                [ ClassType = persistent,
                  StorageStrategy = MyStorageCode ] {
```

```
Property Model As %String;
Property Manufacturer As %String;
Property Power As %Integer;
Property Color As %String;

<Storage name="MyStorageCode">
    <Description>My own storage code</Description>
    <Type>%CustomStorage</Type>
</Storage>
}
```

`%CustomStorage` is a storage class with empty implementations of the methods of the storage interface that are overwritten as follows.

%LoadData()

The `%LoadData()` instance method receives as argument the value of the ID of the object to be loaded. The ID is the first part of the OID, which must be unique within a class. How the value of the ID is used and manipulated within the `%LoadData()` method depends entirely on the method's author.

The author of the method can also define how the object is loaded. If the load operation fails, `%LoadData()` should return 0 as the first part of the status value. When the load operation is successful, `%LoadData()` must set the storage values of the properties (except for transient and calculated properties). Typically, the following in-memory value syntax is used:

```
Set i%Name=..NameStorageToLogical(StorageValue)
```

Once all values of the properties have been assigned successfully, `%LoadData()` returns 1 as the first part of the status value.

```
Method %LoadData(id As %String) As %Status [ Private ] {
    /***********************************************************
    Method name:   User-written %LoadData
    Description:   Load the object into storage
    Return value:  %Status
    Note:          id is the ID part of the OID
    ***********************************************************/
    Set $ETrap="Quit $$$ERROR()"

    // Initialize the properties
    Set (i%Model,i%Manufacturer,i%Power,i%Color)=""

    /* Load data from the multidimensional global
       into the properties */

    // Set lock while load proceeding
    Lock +(^MyVehicle(0,id))

    // Extract data from the global
    Set i%Model=$Get(^MyVehicle(0,id,"Model"))
    Set i%Manufacturer=$Get(^MyVehicle(0,id,"Manufacturer"))
    Set i%Power=$Get(^MyVehicle(0,id,"Power"))
    Set i%Color=$Get(^MyVehicle(0,id,"Color"))
```

`%LoadData()` *user method*

183

```
// Release lock
Lock -(^MyVehicle(0,id))

// Return status
Quit $$$OK
}
```

%SaveData()

%SaveData() is an instance method that receives the ID as an argument. (This can also be null when that object has never been stored previously.) All the information that %SaveData() requires is contained in the storage version of the object. %SaveData() returns 1 as first character of the status value when an object has been stored successfully in the database.

%SaveData() is responsible for assigning a unique identifier, if the object is stored for the first time and thus does not yet have an ID.

%SaveData() is also responsible for checking the uniqueness of correspondingly marked indexes. The author of the class can freely define a mechanism for validation. If it is determined that an index is not unique (i.e., it already exists in the class), the storage operation fails, and %Save-Data() returns 0 as first character of the status value.

Finally, the value of the property must be converted into its storage format and then stored.

```
Set StorageValue=..NameLogicalToStorage(i%Name)
```

A simple %SaveData() method could have the following appearance:

%SaveData() *user method*

```
Method %SaveData(id As %String) As %Status [ Private ] {
    /***********************************************************
    Method name:    User-written %SaveData
    Description :   Save the object
    Return value:   %Status
    Note:           id is the ID part of the OID
    ***********************************************************/
    Set $ETrap="Quit $$$ERROR()"

    // Check whether instance exists already
    // if not, create new oid
    If $Get(id)="" {
        Set id=($Order(^MyVehicle(0,""),-1))+1
        Do ..%IdSet(id)
    }

    // Set lock
    Lock +(^MyVehicle(0,id))

    // Save instance
    Set ^MyVehicle(0,id,"Model")=i%Model
    Set ^MyVehicle(0,id,"Manufacturer")=i%Manufacturer
    Set ^MyVehicle(0,id,"Power")=i%Power
    Set ^MyVehicle(0,id,"Color")=i%Color

    // Release lock
    Lock -(^MyVehicle(0,id))
```

```
        // Return status
        Quit $$$OK
}
```

%DeleteData()

An ID is passed as an argument to the %DeleteData() class method. The method deletes all data of the object identified by the ID from the database. %DeleteData() is responsible for executing all actions required to delete the data. If it was successful, it returns 1 as the first character of the status value, otherwise 0 as an error indicator.

```
ClassMethod %DeleteData(id As %String,
        concurrency As %Integer) As %Status [ Private ] {
    /*********************************************************
        Method name:  User-written %DeleteData
        Description:  Delete the object from the database
        return value: %Status
        Note:         id is the ID part of the OID
    *********************************************************/
    Set $ETrap="Quit $$$ERROR()"

    // Set lock
    Lock +(^MyVehicle(0,id))

    // Delete data
    Kill ^MyVehicle(0,id)

    // Release lock
    Lock -(^MyVehicle(0,id))

    // Return status
    Quit $$$OK
}
```

%DeleteData() user method

6.3 Set Operations on Objects

The previous discussions assumed that an OID (or at least the ID part) is known. However, in many practical applications, this is often not the case. To accurately identify an object, a programmer may need to offer the user a selection list (from which he/she selects an object instance to process). This is not necessary when the intended task does not apply to a specific instance, but rather to a range of data—such as print a list, calculate the total for this month's orders, etc.

Caché provides queries as a simple solution for this type of problem. Queries permit set operations on objects.

There are two basic ways of using queries: queries can be predefined in the class definition and then used later as *result sets*, or you formulate queries using SQL embedded within the method or routine code. Because Chapter 8 provides a detailed discussion of embedded SQL, we consider only the object-oriented concept of result sets here.

Result sets or queries with embedded SQL

6.3.1   Result Sets

A result set is the object-oriented interface through which predefined queries in a class definition are used with Caché ObjectScript, Java, or ActiveX. Caché ObjectScript provides result sets as instances of the %ResultSet system class.

Table 6.11 Elements of the %ResultSet class

Type	Name	Explanation
Class methods	%New("class:Query")	The %New() method creates a new ResultSet object. A character string that consists of the class name (or the package name, a period, and the class name), a colon, and the name of the query is specified as argument. Alternatively, the class and query name can be omitted in order to execute a dynamic query of the %DynamicQuery: SQL type. In this case, the SQL code of the query must be specified with the Prepare() method.
Instance methods	QueryIsValid()	Returns 1 when the query is valid, otherwise 0.
	ContainsId()	Returns the number of the associated column when the query returns an ID field for each individual line, otherwise 0.
	GetParamCount()	Gets the number of parameters in the query.
	GetParamName(*Position*)	Gets the name of the parameter at *Position*.
	Prepare(*SQL code*)	The SQL code to be prepared for the dynamic query. Parameters are marked using *?* as a placeholder.
	Execute(*P1,P2,P3,...*)	Executes the query. *P1, P2, P3...* specify the query parameters.
	GetColumnCount()	Gets the number of columns for the query.
	GetColumnName(*column*)	Gets the name of the *column*.
	GetColumnHeader(*column*)	Gets the heading for *column*.
	Next()	Changes to the next line of the query.
	Get(*columnname*)	Gets the value of *columnname* for the current line.
	GetData(*column*)	Gets the value of *column* for the current line.
	Close()	Closes the query.
Properties	AtEnd	Returns 1 when the end of the query is reached, otherwise 0.
	ClassName	The class name of the query.
	QueryName	The name of the query.
	Data(*columnname*)	A multidimensional attribute that contains the values for all columns. This is more efficient than using the Get() or GetData() methods.

Set operations on object instances

A result set enables set operations to be performed on object instances without instantiating each individual object. A programmer works with a result set by writing code that performs the following steps:

Create a new ResultSet object using the %New() class method.
Alternatively: use the QueryIsValid() method to check whether the query is valid, or use the Prepare() method to specify the SQL code for a dynamic SQL query and check the return value if the query is valid.
Prepare the parameters: use the GetParamCount() method to determine the count. GetParamName(Position) contains the associated name. Then invoke the Execute() method with appropriate parameters.
The Next() method fetches the next row. Check the return value to test whether more data are present; otherwise the first character is 0 and the loop must be terminated.
The value of each column can be found in the multidimensional property Data(Column). Display, process, etc., as required.
Finally, do not forget to terminate the query with Close().

This is a very simple means of obtaining values assigned in rows and columns, such as the result of an SQL query. If the query is defined, for example, so that it accepts the initial letter of a name as a parameter and then returns all persons whose name starts with this letter, you can implement a user-parameterized query with little effort.

Values are assigned in rows and columns

However, how do you now establish the connection to the object instances, when, for example, the user has selected a person that he or she now wishes to edit? It is important to know whether and in which column the query result contains the ID field. The ContainsId() method helps here; it returns either 0 or the number of the ID column. By convention, the ID should always be in the first column, so GetData(1) or Data("ID") could be used here. However, it is better not to rely on this, and to access the ID field using the column number determined with the ContainsId() method.

ID is always in the first column with the name "ID"

Once the ID value has been determined, you can open the associated object instance with the %Open() or %OpenId() method of its class; the class name is known, or is otherwise easy to obtain from the ClassName property of the result set.

Example

```
Query  //
       Set rs=##class(%ResultSet).%New("User.Person:All")
       If rs.QueryIsValid() {
         Set status=rs.Execute() // no parameters required
         If 'status Quit
         WHILE rs.Next() {
           Set ID=rs.Data("ID")
           Set Name=rs.Data("Name")
           Set Firstname=rs.Data("Firstname")
           Write ID,?10,Name,", ",Firstname,!
         }
       }
```

```
        Do rs.Close()
        Quit
```

Of course, the same query can be formulated with dynamic SQL:

The example as a dynamic SQL query

```
DynamicQuery  //
        Set rs=##class(%ResultSet).%New()
        If rs.Prepare("Select ID,Name,Firstname
                        From SQLUser.Person") {
            Set status=rs.Execute() // no ? parameter necessary
            If 'status Quit
            WHILE rs.Next() {
                Set ID=rs.Data("ID")
                Set Name=rs.Data("Name")
                Set Firstname=rs.Data("Firstname")
                Write ID,?10,Name,", ",Firstname,!
            }
        }
        Do rs.Close()
        Quit
```

6.4   Using Objects

Examples of the command level in Caché Terminal

In this section we return to the simple Person object class that we developed as the first example in Chapter 1. Again, we use Caché Terminal and the Caché command level discussed in Section 4.4 to illustrate the use of objects.

6.4.1   Practical Use of Objects

```
>Set pers=##class(User.Person).%New()
>Write pers
1@User.Person
```

This creates a new instance of the User.Person class in the memory area of the process. The pers local variable now contains an OREF to the new instance.

```
>Set pers.Name="Muller-Westernhagen"
>Write pers.Name
Muller-Westernhagen
```

This assigns the value "Muller-Westernhagen" to the Name property. The code also validates that the property received the value.

```
>Write pers.Firstname
(empty string)
```

Because we have not yet supplied a value to the Firstname property, it contains the empty string.

```
>Set pers.Firstname="Marius"
```

Here we see how dot syntax makes it very easy to set the Firstname property.

```
>Set sc=pers.%Save()
>Write +sc
1
```

The %Save() method saves the new instance of the object in the database. The status code 1 in the sc variable indicates that the transaction completed correctly.

6.4 Using Objects

```
>Write pers.%Id()
8
>Write pers.%ClassName()
User.Person
```

Saving the new instance in the database

Now that we have saved the object, it has an OID whose elements ID and class name we can query using the %Id() and %ClassName() methods.

```
>Set pers.DOB="that won't take us anywhere"
>Write pers.DOB
that won't take us anywhere
```

Although we have placed an invalid date value in DOB, Caché still appears to accept it. This is also correct, because the PROPERTYVALIDATION class parameter has 2 as default value, which means "validate on save."

```
>Set sc=pers.%Save()
>Write +sc
0
>Do $System.OBJ.DisplayError(sc)
 ERROR: Datatype validation failed: User.Person.DOB
```

When we now attempt to save again, the status code begins with 0, which indicates an error. We can use the $System special object to receive a meaningful error message.

Receiving a meaningful error message

```
>Set dob=pers.DOBDisplayToLogical("12/6/1948")
>Write dob
39421
```

To receive a valid date that we can set in the DOB property, we must first perform the *DisplayToLogical* transformation for the %Date data type. This is easily done with the automatically generated DOBDisplay-ToLogical() properties method. When we consider the internally created value, we determine that Caché stores a date internally in the $Horolog format, which represents the number of days since December 31, 1840.

```
>Set pers.DOB=dob
>Set sc=pers.%Save()
>Write +sc
1
```

The DOB converted into the internal representation still represents a valid object instance; we can now save it without error.

```
>Set pers=""
```

Because the object instance is no longer required in memory, we can now invalidate the pers OREF.

Closing the object instance

6.4.2 Practical Use of Result Sets

Next, let us see how to list all the people stored in the Person class, a task that requires the set approach of a query. We can use the Select query defined in the initial example:

```
>Set rs=##class(%ResultSet).%New("User.Person:All")
>Write rs.QueryIsValid()
1
```

Creating a new result set

The creation of a new ResultSet object was successful, so the query is valid and can be used.

```
>Write rs.GetParamCount()
0
>Set sc=rs.Execute()
```

Because the Select query does not require any parameters, we invoke the Execute() method without arguments.

```
>WHILE rs.Next() { Write rs.Data("Name"),",",rs.Data("First⇦
⇨name"),! }
Adams, Bryan
Bon Jovi, Jon
Ciccone, Madonna Luise
Cocker, Joe
Jackson, Michael
John, Elton
Muller-Westernhagen, Marius
```

Listing all instances of the Person class

We receive a list of all instances of the Person class. This list is sorted alphabetically according to the last name, which is what we specified when we created the query.

```
>Set sc=rs.Execute()
>Set sc=rs.Next()
>Write rs.Data("Name")
Adams
```

A subsequent execution of the query positions the current line again at the start.

```
>Set ID=rs.Data("ID")
>Write ID
5
```

The query contains the ID field, which happens to be 5 for the first person.

```
>Set pers=##class(Person).%OpenId(ID)
>Write pers.Name
Adams
>Write pers.Firstname
Bryan
>Write pers.DOBLogicalToDisplay(pers.DOB)
11/05/1959
```

We can use the ID to reopen the instance and access its properties and methods.

7 Multidimensional Access and Globals

7.1 Multidimensional Variables

Variable types

Caché ObjectScript fully integrates persistent data structures—called global variables or simply "globals"—into the language. As with transient ("local") variables, persistent ("global") variables can exist as either scalar (one-dimensional) or multidimensional structures. As persistent data in the Caché ObjectScript language, global variables enable both permanent object storage and high-performance *multidimensional access*. This chapter covers the latter concept in detail.

Caché ObjectScript uses subscripts to represent individual dimensions, which we refer to as subscripted variables or multidimensional arrays. The next table summarizes the various types of variables.

Variable type	Local	Global
Scalar	Name= Hausmann	^Value= 2
Multidimensional array	var1(ArtNo)= Sweatshirt|Easy Corp.	^ERP.Goods(ArtNo)= Sweatshirt|Easy Corp.

Table 7.1 Different forms of variables

The lower-right-hand cell of the above table (containing a reference to a global, multidimensional array) demonstrates the programming language semantics of this variable form; we will discuss this in detail.

The functions (such as $Get) that Caché ObjectScript provides for processing variables can be used, without exception, for both local and global variables.

Differences between local and global variables

Most commands apply equally to both local variables and global variables. However, the Kill and New commands permit only local variables as arguments in the following two situations:

- Only local, non-indexed variables are permitted as arguments of the New command.
- Only local, non-indexed variables are permitted for the exclusive Kill command. (For example, Kill (a1,a2) deletes all variables except a1 and a2).

Other than these two cases, local and global variables are processed identically, with the obvious proviso that global variables are persistent, whereas local variables are linked to the current process and thus limited in their lifetime.

7.1.1 Arrays with String Subscripts

7.1.1.1 Syntax

The basic syntax for a multidimensional array is simple. Subscripts are enclosed within parentheses and separated by commas.

Example

```
Set x(1)="Monday",x(2,7)="July",x(3,12,25)="Christmas"
```

In the example, the variable x has subscripts enclosed within parentheses denoting three dimensions. However, the inherent simplicity of the syntax seen in this example assumes a special significance in Caché Object-Script:

No dimensioning
- No previous dimensioning is necessary. The Set command defines variables and dimensions as it assigns values to them.

Sparse arrays
- This is made possible by Caché's implementation of *sparse arrays* in which only the defined entries occupy storage space.

In concrete terms, *sparse array* means that the existence of $x(2,7)$ does not automatically imply the existence of any other nodes (such as $x(2,4)$). Only when a node has been defined explicitly does it exist and occupy storage space.

Concept of string subscripts
This comment applies for both local and global variables. Furthermore, both types of variable may have *string subscripts*. Whereas subscripts in most programming languages are exclusively numeric, Caché Object-Script allows both numbers and arbitrary strings as indexes.

Examples

```
Set month("June")=6
Set lvl=Goods(123000,"XL","corn yellow")
```

The second example shows a mixed use of numeric and string subscripts. In this case, the local variable lvl is assigned the value of the three-dimensional variable Goods(123000, "XL", "corn yellow").

In more precise terms, the use of arbitrary strings means that all characters of the base character set (refer to Section 7.1.1.2) can be used as subscripts. The only exception is ASCII NULL; this adopts a special role in the internal representation of indexed variables as a B*-tree. (Refer to Section 7.1.3.1.)

Although there is no direct restriction on the number of subscripts, there is, however, an indirect restriction: the length of the variable name plus the number of all parentheses and commas plus the sum of the length of the individual subscripts cannot exceed 255. The value assigned to a variable (scalar or multidimensional) cannot exceed 32767 characters.

Subscripts can be expressions
Note that individual subscripts can also be represented as expressions.

Example   **7.1 Multidimensional Variables**

```
Set a=3 Set x(2*a,$Length("June"),a)=6
```

This command creates the subscripted variable x(6,4,3) with the value 6.

7.1.1.2 Collation of Multidimensional Arrays

Subscripted multidimensional arrays are automatically sorted in Caché according to a defined collating sequence. The collating sequence is determined by

- the associated character set
- the rule used to sort the individual characters of this set

Caché normally uses the native character set of the computer and the operating system applied according to the Unicode Standard Sorting Sequence. This allows the use of pure (7- or 8-bit) ASCII characters. Furthermore, national character sets with their specific sorting can be processed using Caché's *National Language Support* (NLS). Interested readers should refer to the *Caché Knowledge Base*.

Unicode Standard sorting sequence

Independent of the character set used, the following rule applies to the collating sequence: numerical subscripts come first. In this case, the so-called canonical numbers are sorted first, arranged according to the size of the number from $-\infty$ to $+\infty$. A canonical number is a number from which superfluous signs and zeros have been removed. Whereas ++1, 0.7, and 2.40 are not canonical numbers, 1, .7, and 2.4 have a canonical form. Following numeric subscripts, all other subscripts are sorted in their sequence as strings, including those subscripts that represent a non-canonical number.

Canonical number

Example

```
-100 -5 0 2 2.1 19 "!" "AA" "ZZ" "a" "z"
```

The collation sequence starts with numbers followed by all other indexes, where the exclamation point (ASCII 33) precedes uppercase letters.

Two different sorting operators indicate whether one string follows another in the sorting sequence:

Different sorting operators

- The Follows operator (]) checks for pure string sorting.
- The Sorts-after operator (]]) uses mixed sorting in which numeric subscripts are placed at the start and all other subscripts follow.

Both operators return a Boolean result: 1 for TRUE or 0 for FALSE.

The Follows operator] adheres to the lexicographical order that operates strictly according to the character's ASCII value. Thus, the number 2 follows the number 19, because the ASCII code for 2 (=50) follows the ASCII code for 1 (=49).

In contrast, the Sorts-after operator]] reflects mixed sorting:

Examples

```
>Write 2]19
1
>Write 2]]19
0
```

Mixture of numeric and string indexes

The]] operator is used especially for mixed numeric and string indexes. A numeric comparison (>, <) can be used for purely numeric subscripts; the follows operator can be used for pure string subscripts; the sorts-after operator is appropriate for mixed subscripts.

Numbers with leading zeros

Note that numbers with leading zeros are interpreted as strings, not as numbers. Account and item numbers could use leading zeros as an organizational characteristic. Leading zeros can be easily removed through the use of numeric interpretation: +ArtNo ignores leading zeros to find the number after them.

7.1.2   Global Multidimensional Arrays

Logical extension of the concept of local variables

Simply adding a single character—the global character or caret (^)—suffices to turn a local variable into a global, persistent variable. This is a surprisingly simple concept, which is enabled by sophisticated technology in Caché ObjectScript. The global database is not considered to be a separate entity here, but is a logical extension of the concept of local variables. Nowhere does the programmer need to worry about opening, closing, or defining a global variable.

7.1.2.1   Globals: Persistent Multi-User-Variables

Globals are permanently stored data structures, normally multidimensional, that can be processed in a multiuser environment by various processes. Because of the special importance of this aspect, we will discuss it in detail in Section 7.1.3.2.

The processing of globals in Caché routines is very straightforward. Let us assume that you wish to read the following global entry from the database:

Accessing a global

```
^ERP.Goods(234000)="Trousers|Gentle and Co."
```

It suffices to use it in an expression, such as the assignment to a local variable:

```
Set lv1=^ERP.Goods(234000)
```

The local variable lv1 then contains the string "Trousers|Gentle and Co.". Obviously, the value of ^ERP.Goods(234000) can be referenced directly in an expression, such as in the $ListLength or $LIst list functions:

```
For i=1:1:$ListLength(^ERP.Goods(234000)) {
  Write !,$LIst(^ERP.Goods(234000),i)
}
```

A Set command stores information in the database. Assuming that the
1v2 local variable contains the string "Trousers|Gentle and Co.", the
following Set command stores exactly that information in a global:

```
Set ^ERP.Goods(234000)=1v2
```

An entire global can be deleted with the Kill command. Note that killing
a particular node also deletes values in higher dimensions. To avoid this,
you must use the ZKill variant that deletes only a single value.

Deleting a global

A global record can be changed with the $LIst list function. Assuming
that Gentle and Co. has renamed itself to *Gentle Inc.*, you need only
change the second list element of the ^ERP.Goods(234000) global. The
following Set command does this by referencing the second list element
and overwriting it with the value to the right of the equal sign:

Changing a record

```
Set $LIst(^ERP.Goods(234000),2)="Gentle Inc."
```

This simple and compact syntax executes a number of individual steps:
- Read the data record ^ERP.Goods(234000).
- Change the second list element.
- Rewrite the data record.

7.1.2.2 Semantics for Globals: A Multidimensional Data Model

To fully demonstrate the significance of global variables, we will outline a
material management system for a textile retailer. As in some previous
examples, the ^ERP.Goods global variable uses the ArtNo article number
as a subscript for the first dimension, and the product designation and
manufacturer as value:

```
^ERP.Goods(ArtNo)=<Designation>|<Manufacturer>
```

and as an example for a data record:

```
^ERP.Goods(123000)="Sweatshirt|EASY Corp."
```

In general, a database selects a record according to a unique key. In
Caché, the equivalent of a key is the subscript. The value of a data record
is a list that can be created and analyzed using Caché ObjectScript's list
functions. (Refer to Section 5.1.5.) In the printed examples shown here, we
use the list delimiter | to separate fields within a list. In Caché, the start of
each field is specified internally by storing its absolute position in the list.

Selecting a database record

For example, you could manually add another manufacturer with the
$ListBuild function and then use $LIst to refer to the second list
element:

Example

```
>Set ^ERP.Goods(234000)=$LB("Trousers","Gentle and Co.")
>Write $LIst(^ERP.Goods(234000),2)
Gentle and Co.
```

In this way, the first dimension contains all article numbers, designations, and manufacturers. A selection could have the following appearance:

```
^ERP.Goods(123000)="Sweatshirt|EASY Corp."
^ERP.Goods(234000)="Trousers|Gentle and Co."
^ERP.Goods(345000)="Jacket|Gentle and Co."
^ERP.Goods(456000)="Shirt|Claude Perron Cie."
^ERP.Goods(567000)="Waistcoat|EASY Corp."
^ERP.Goods(678000)="Pullover|Gentle and Co."
...
```

The collation sequence for these numeric subscripts follows an ascending order, proceeding from the smallest to the largest subscript.

The price of an article depends on the size and the article itself, which the article number identifies uniquely. Thus, a value representing the article price is stored in the next (second) dimension identified by the article size.

```
^ERP.Goods(ArtNo,Size)=<Price>
```

And as examples:

```
^ERP.Goods(123000,"L")=22.95
^ERP.Goods(123000,"M")=20.95
^ERP.Goods(123000,"S")=18.95
^ERP.Goods(123000,"XL")=24.95
...
```

The inventory for an article depends on its size and color. We store a value representing this characteristic in the third dimension, as follows:

```
^ERP.Goods(ArtNo,Size,Color)=<Inventory>
```

And as examples:

```
^ERP.Goods(123000,"XL","caribbean blue")=15
^ERP.Goods(123000,"XL","classic beige")=4
^ERP.Goods(123000,"XL","corn yellow")=8
^ERP.Goods(123000,"XL","kiwi green")=8
...
```

A few comments are now appropriate:

- The two first subscripts are each identical in each example above (without, however, being stored more than once). The third dimension defines unique nodes, which (being strings, in these examples) are sorted in string sequence.
- We have produced a data model that can be represented as a multi-dimensional data cube: article number, description, and supplier are in the first dimension, size and price are in the second dimension, and color and inventory level are in the third dimension.
- Caché ObjectScript provides language elements for querying this data structure. The question "Which colors in size 'XL' for article 'Sweatshirt' are currently in stock?" can be answered with a single function, $Order.
- Modeling this simple example in a relational paradigm would require four tables, and the query would need to reference all four to answer

this question. Consequently, many developers of complex applications do not comply fully with the relational model. They often avoid the extremes of normal form in order to preserve database access performance. However, they trade this performance gain for major problems caused by redundant data storage.

7.1.2.3 Managing Globals

Caché comes with a number of utility programs for development and system administration. These include programs for managing globals, which can serve as an example for all other utilities here.

As briefly introduced in Section 4.3, Caché Explorer manages globals. It displays a tree structure for databases and namespaces, providing branches down to the stored classes, routines, and globals stored in a Caché database. Double-clicking the name of a global in Caché Explorer invokes a window with the name *Global View* that lists the structure of that global:

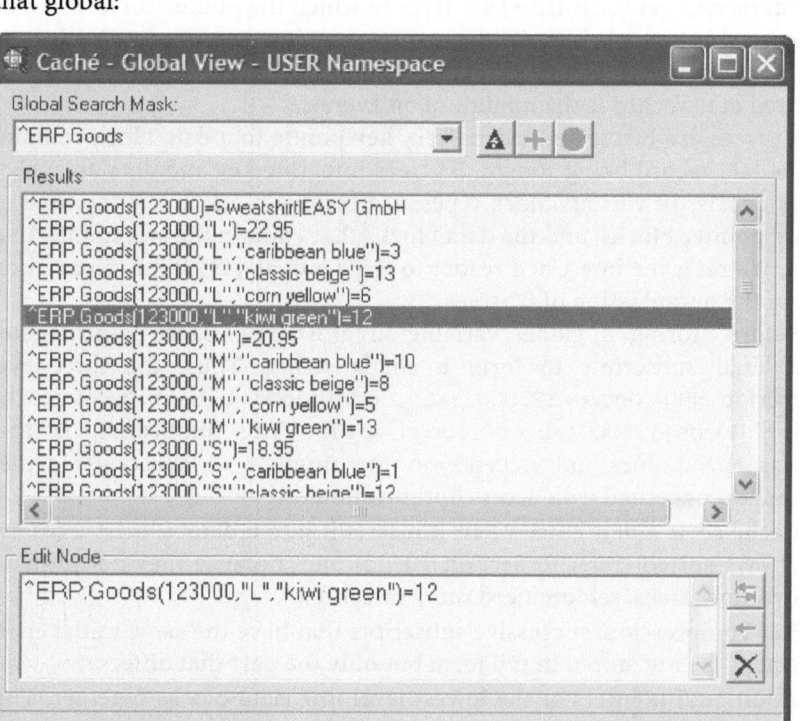

Figure 7.1 Globals in Caché Explorer

When you click a global node, its value is passed to the *Edit Node* field in the lower area where it can be edited. However, you should exercise special care here—it is all too easy to change data inadvertently.

Right-click the *Globals* branch of the associated namespace in Caché Explorer overview to see a options menu. Particularly useful here are the options for exporting and importing globals using operating system files. These options are often used to transfer globals from one Caché system to another.

Individual globals in the list in the right-hand frame of Caché Explorer have a global-specific context menu, also invoked with the right mouse button. In addition to branching in the familiar *Global View*, the *Import* and *Export* options are available here (the use of which is obvious), as is the *Properties* option. The latter opens a new window with further details of a global's characteristics. For more information, refer to the Caché documentation, in particular the *Using Caché Explorer* manual.

7.1.3 File Organization of Globals

7.1.3.1 B*-Trees

Caché stores the globals in B*-trees. Appendix C of the *Caché ObjectScript Reference* contains a detailed description of the basic principles involved and provides many examples. Consequently, this section focuses on general comments about global variables.

Balanced trees

Balanced trees (or B-trees) are trees in which the number of levels to be processed in order to access information remains the same in all subtrees. An advantage of B-trees is that the number of block accesses to find a desired data record is the minimum on average.

B*-trees are B-trees in which every key points to a data block containing a data record being sought. B*-trees integrate key and data areas. B*-trees consist of various block types: a directory block at the top, one or more pointer blocks, and the data blocks that contain the stored information. We refer the interested reader to Härder et al. [1999] for information about the organization of B*-trees.

Globals and B-trees*

Before storing a global variable in a B*-tree, Caché concatenates individual subscripts to form a single string. Thus, the three-level subscript `^ERP.Goods(123000,"XL","caribbean blue")` becomes the string `Goods|123000|XL|caribbean blue`. The implication is that access speed does not depend on the number of subscripts. Other elements concerned with access optimization are:

Properties of B-trees*

- Caché sorts a new entry when it inserts it into a database. B*-trees are always sorted (refer to Section 7.1.1.2) and, because they do not have overflow areas, seldom need reorganization.
- Key compression: successive subscripts that have the same initial characters are not stored in full form but only the part that differs.
- Additional pointers at the lowest level link data blocks together. This optimizes sequential database operations without needing to leave the current data level.
- All blocks in the B*-tree structure are stored in a multilevel cache in memory once a process has read them from the disk. When this is the case, further access to the global avoids accessing the disk. This results in a significant performance improvement.

7.1.3.2 Optimized Setting of Globals with $SORTBEGIN and $SORTEND

Performance problems can occur when transforming a very large number of unsorted or unorganized records into a B*-tree structure, for example by importing data from a sequential file. This is because the corresponding block structure of the B*-tree must be built for each record. The emphasis here is on *very* large. For this case, Caché provides a special mechanism to speed up the global operations by using the $SORTBEGIN and $SORTEND functions.

A special sorting mode collects all data in local memory until the import is complete. A bulk operation is then performed to store the presorted data in the global. This minimizes physical disk access.

Special sorting mode

The sorting mode is initialized with a call to the $SORTBEGIN function with the name of the target global variable specified as argument. No data are physically written to that global until the corresponding $SORTEND function is executed.

$SORTBEGIN and $SORTEND

Example

```
Set X=$SORTBEGIN(^ERP.Goods)
Do Import^Articles           /* many Set commands for
                                ^ERP.Goods occur here, which
                                are buffered in main memory */
Set X=$SORTEND(^ERP.Goods)   /* only now is the imported data
                                physically written into
                                ^ERP.Goods in the correct
                                sort sequence. */
Write X                      /* X contains the number of
                                entries set */
```

7.1.3.3 Globals in Distributed Systems

In the network-centric world we live in, a database management system is judged by its ability to distribute a database in a network configuration and to provide easy access to files or data records at remote computers. Although these considerations are important for a Caché reference book, we can only outline them here. We refer interested readers to Caché documentation, in particular to the *Introductory Guide to Caché System Administration,* which provides a detailed explanation of this subject.

Central to a network configuration (distributed processing) is the concept of a namespace. Objects, routines, and globals in Caché are stored in databases and namespaces. A database corresponds to a system level file with the name cache.dat in a specific directory in the file system.

The namespace concept

A namespace, on the other hand, is a work area in which data and routines *logically* reside. The definition of a namespace maps data and routines to the database in which they are stored. For example, the *Accounting* department of a company could need access to globals contained in different systems or directories. A namespace logically groups all required globals together. This type of grouping is also called *global mapping.*

Figure 7.2 Namespaces in Caché
Configuration Manager

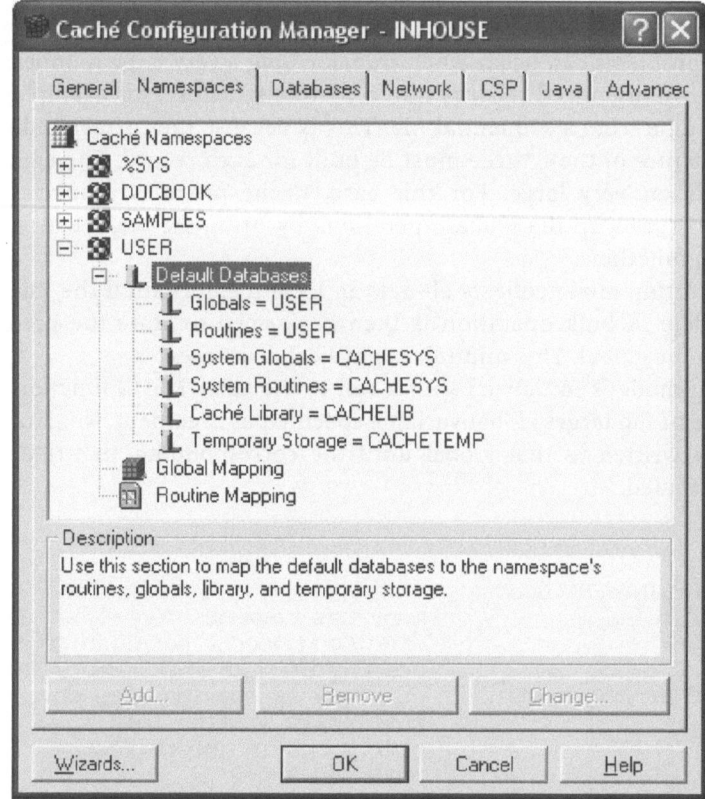

As seen from the viewpoint of globals, the major advantage of namespaces is that the programmer specifies only the names of globals (plus their subscripts) and does not need to know anything about the physical "location" of the global. Indeed, should a global need to be moved to a different computer because of a system failure, Caché ObjectScript routines will continue to operate without change. Furthermore, applications can be developed on a single-user system and the globals at the customer or user location distributed to the appropriate client, application, and database servers; only the namespace definitions need to be changed.

A user who logs in to Caché automatically operates in a specific namespace and has access to its objects, globals, and routines. The standard installation of Caché automatically defines a user namespace with the name USER. System namespaces also exist that contain all % objects, % routines, and % globals. Because these are automatically *mapped*, they can be accessed or processed from other namespaces.

Extended global syntax   We now discuss briefly the extended syntax of globals. (Refer to the *Caché ObjectScript Reference* for more details.) Extended syntax permits references to be made to globals that belong to other namespaces.

In extended syntax, the name of a namespace is specified after the global character, but before the global name, either within square brackets or vertical bars. For example, to reference the ^ERP.Customer global in the MARKETING namespace, you have two syntactical variants:

```
^["MARKETING"]ERP.Customer          // bracketed syntax
^|"MARKETING"|ERP.Customer          // "environment" syntax
```

7.2 Navigating in Multidimensional Arrays

Let us first consider a selection from a three-dimensional array:

```
^ERP.Goods(123000,"XL","caribbean blue")=15
^ERP.Goods(123000,"XL","classic beige")=4
^ERP.Goods(123000,"XL","corn yellow")=8
^ERP.Goods(123000,"XL","kiwi green")=8
...
```

A number of primary evaluations are obvious. We illustrate these in the form of questions:

Evaluating a multidimensional array

1. How many sweatshirts (ArtNo=123000) in size "XL" and color "corn yellow" are currently in stock? (The answer is 8.)
2. Is the color "aubergine" for article number 123000 and size "XL" in stock? (The answer is no.)
3. Which colors for article number 123000 and size "XL" are currently in stock? (The answers are "caribbean blue," "classic beige," "corn yellow," and "kiwi green.")

Let us now examine the methods and language elements that Caché ObjectScript provides for answering these questions.

Methods and language elements

The first question can be answered easily: The number is the value of the global. Thus, it only needs to be referenced with the relevant properties (subscripts):

```
>Write ^ERP.Goods(123000,"XL","corn yellow")
8
```

The second question is essentially an existence question. The general form of this question is: Does a value (entry) exist for a global with the specific subscripts sub_1, sub_2, ..., sub_n? The $Data function answers this question.

The third question is a question for all existing subscripts of a specified global in a specified dimension. The $Order function answers this question.

Functions and some associated topics are described in detail in the following sections.

7.2.1 Existence of Data in the n-th Dimension

$Data (abbreviation $D) is a function with a variable as argument. This variable can be local or global, scalar or subscripted. The value returned by $Data indicates whether the variable specified as argument exists and which data structure is present. $Data returns four different results:

$Data function

- If the result is 0 (or 10), the variable does not exist with the specified subscripts.
- If the result is 1 (or 11), a value with the subscripts exists—namely, the variable contains data.

The following example references the ^ERP.Goods global.

Example

```
>Write $Data(^ERP.Goods(123000,"XL","corn yellow"))
1
>Write $Data(^ERP.Goods(123000,"XL","aubergine"))
0
```

In the first case, the value of the global exists with the three subscripts ArtNo=123000, Size="XL", and Color="corn yellow", hence the result 1 as the value returned by $Data. In the second case, the color "aubergine" is not in stock, and the value of the function call is 0.

Values in higher dimensions
However, $Data can do even more: the function returns the value 10 or 11 indicating whether or not values exist in a subsequent, higher dimension. The result 11 indicates that a value exists with the specified subscripts *and* another value exists at a higher-level dimension. The result 10 indicates that a value exists at a higher-level dimension, but not at the current subscript level.

Examples

```
>Write $Data(^ERP.Goods(123000))
11
>Kill x Set x(1,1)=11 Write $Data(x(1))
10
```

The first example shows that both a value of the ^ERP.Goods global exists for the subscript 123000 and further values exist in the higher dimensions, e.g., ^ERP.Goods(123000,"XL") or ^ERP.Goods(123000,"XL","corn yellow").

In the second example, we have not made reference to the ^ERP.Goods global, because there is no case there for which no data are present at lower dimension level, but are present at a higher level.

The following table summarizes all four values returned by $Data:

Table 7.2 The four possible values for $Data

Variable	No value in a higher dimension	Value in a higher dimension
exists	1	11
does not exist	0	10

Thus, $Data can reliably answer all questions concerning the existence of a variable. Normally a query is made with the If command in the following manner:

Examples

```
If $Data(^ERP.Goods(123000))#10 { Write "article present" }
If $Data(^ERP.Goods(321000))#10=0 {
  Write "article not in stock"
}
```

Query techniques
You can see that modulo division by 10 on the two results from $Data that indicate the existence (namely 1 and 11) returns the value 1. This is

logically interpreted as TRUE. You can achieve something similar with the integer division by 10 to determine whether there are values in a higher dimension: 10 or 11 with integer division by 10 yields 1, however, 0 and 1 with integer division by 10 also yields 0.

The following question often arises: You would like to know whether a value of a global is present, and when yes, you would like to further process the value.

Example

```
If $Data(^ERP.Goods(123000,"XL","corn yellow"))#10 {
  Set number=^ERP.Goods(123000,"XL","corn yellow")
}
```

The number variable then contains the number present in stock for the concrete instance of this article (namely size and color). This previous query avoids a possible <UNDEFINED> error should this article not or no longer exist. The $Get function (abbreviation $G) can greatly simplify this frequently-needed query.

$Get function

Example

```
Set number=$Get(^ERP.Goods(123000,"XL","corn yellow"))
```

If the global exists, this is the result of the function call. However, if it does not exist, the result is the null string, "". This is also the general definition for the single-argument form of $Get. It also exists in a form with a second argument that replaces the default "" with some value when the variable in the first argument does not exist. The next example uses this to assign the correct value 0 (not the null string!) to the number variable should the global not exist.

Example

```
Set number=$Get(^ERP.Goods(123000,"XL","corn yellow"),0)
```

7.2.2 The Next Subscript with $Order

$Order (abbreviation $O) finds the next subscript in the sorting sequence of a local or global subscripted variable. In a loop (such as with the For command), you can obtain the sorting sequence for all defined subscripts within a dimension. To determine the first subscript within a specified dimension, you use a symbolic null string

Next subscript in the sorting sequence

To formulate a simple example, we use the one-dimensional version of the ^ERP.Goods global, namely:

```
^ERP.Goods(123000)="Sweatshirt|EASY Corp."
^ERP.Goods(234000)="Trousers|Gentle and Co."
^ERP.Goods(345000)="Jacket|Gentle and Co."
^ERP.Goods(456000)="Shirt|Claude Perron Cie."
^ERP.Goods(567000)="Waistcoat|EASY Corp."
^ERP.Goods(678000)="Pullover|Gentle and Co."
```

Examples with $Order

Example

```
>Write $Order(^ERP.Goods(345000))
456000
```

The argument for $Order in this example is a concrete instance of the ^ERP.Goods(345000) global and the next existing subscript is returned as result, namely 456000. When you use this as input for the $Order function, you then get the next subscript, etc., until the last subscript. When you use this in the function, it returns the symbolic null string, which you then can use to query the end of the loop. The next example contains a routine fragment that returns all subscripts of the ^ERP.Goods global (and thus all manufacturers).

Example

```
Set x=""
For {
  Set x=$Order(^ERP.Goods(x))
  Quit:x=""
  Write x,?10,^ERP.Goods(x),!
}
```

This example demonstrates a classic use of loops in Caché ObjectScript for *multidimensional access* to globals. Typical variations include:

1. The symbolic subscript x need not exist; the next existing subscript is returned:

```
>Write $Order(^ERP.Goods(222000))
234000
```

Although the value for ^ERP.Goods(222000) does not exist in the example, the result is the next existing subscript 234000.

All subscripts within an interval

2. Frequently you do not want *all* subscripts of a global, but only *all within a range*. For example, you want all ArtNo in the range 300000 to 600000. In this case, you only need to reformulate the start and end condition of the loop:

```
Set x=299999
For {
  Set x=$Order(^ERP.Goods(x))
  Quit:x=""||(x>600000)
  Write x,?10,^ERP.Goods(x),!
}
```

Going backwards through the sort sequence

3. In some cases, it can be useful to go backwards through the sort sequence, for example, to process the most recent entry in chronologically sorted globals. To achieve this, specify $Order with −1 as the second argument.

```
Set x=""
For {
  Set x=$Order(^ERP.Goods(x),-1)
  Quit:x=""
```

```
    Write x,?10,^ERP.Goods(x),!
 }
```

In this example, the article number 678000 is obtained first, followed by subsequent articles in descending subscript sequence through to the first subscript 123000.

To navigate higher dimensions, initially refer to the second dimension of the ^ERP.Goods global for the ArtNo=123000, namely:

Navigating higher dimensions

```
^ERP.Goods(123000,"L")=22.95
^ERP.Goods(123000,"M")=20.95
^ERP.Goods(123000,"S")=18.95
^ERP.Goods(123000,"XL")=24.95
```

How do you obtain the first subscript in the second dimension for the specified subscript 123000? You accomplish this (as demonstrated above) by using the empty string as a symbolic subscript for the second subscript level.

Example

```
>Write $Order(^ERP.Goods(123000,""))
L
```

We now have the means, in the same way as for the first dimension, to obtain all other subscripts in the second dimension:

Example

```
Set ArtNo=123000,x=""
For  {
  Set x=$Order(^ERP.Goods(ArtNo,x))
  Quit:x=""
  Write x,?10,^ERP.Goods(ArtNo,x),!
}
```

We now return to the third question posed at the start of this section: "What colors are currently in stock for article number 123000 in size 'XL'?" By now, the method for answering the question in Caché Object-Script should be straightforward.

Inventory

Example

```
Set ArtNo=123000,Size="XL",x=""
For  {
  Set x=$Order(^ERP.Goods(ArtNo,Size,x))
  Quit:x=""
  Write x,!
}
```

7.2.3 Further Processing of n-Dimensional Structures

The properties of the $Order function make it well-suited to obtain all defined subscripts in a series within a dimension. This is not always the natural sequence for reports. For example, the following representation would provide an overview of article 123000:

```
^ERP.Goods(123000)="Sweatshirt|EASY Corp."
...
^ERP.Goods(123000,"S")=18.95
^ERP.Goods(123000,"S","caribbean blue")=1
^ERP.Goods(123000,"S","classic beige")=12
^ERP.Goods(123000,"S","corn yellow")=7
^ERP.Goods(123000,"S","kiwi green")=3
^ERP.Goods(123000,"XL")=24.95
^ERP.Goods(123000,"XL","caribbean blue")=15
^ERP.Goods(123000,"XL","classic beige")=4
^ERP.Goods(123000,"XL","corn yellow")=8
^ERP.Goods(123000,"XL","kiwi green")=8
```

$Query function

This sequence initially goes down into depth for each article and proceeds by showing the details of the lower dimensions until no further dimension occurs. The next entry in the next higher subscript level is then displayed. This is the so-called "depth-first" search that is enabled in Caché ObjectScript by the $Query function.

In this context, the question of "depth" arises, i.e., the number of possible dimensions. This was not an issue for the simple examples given above. However, it is often frequently asked with regard to complex data structures and can be addressed by the two functions $QLength and $QSubscript, as discussed below.

7.2.3.1 $Query

To introduce $Query (abbreviation $Q), assume the following subview of the ^ERP.Goods global:

```
^ERP.Goods(123000)="Sweatshirt|EASY Corp."
^ERP.Goods(123000,"L")=22.95
^ERP.Goods(123000,"L","caribbean blue")=9
^ERP.Goods(123000,"L","classic beige")=4
^ERP.Goods(123000,"L","corn yellow")=2
^ERP.Goods(123000,"L","kiwi green")=7
```

The result is the full reference

Let us start with a specific reference, namely ^ERP.Goods(123000). From here, $Query obtains the node one dimension deeper, namely ^ERP.Goods (123000,"S"). In contrast to $Order, you receive the full reference as a string.

Examples

```
>Write $Query(^ERP.Goods(123000))
^ERP.Goods(123000,"L")
>Write $Query(^ERP.Goods(123000,"L"))
^ERP.Goods(123000,"L","caribbean blue")
```

```
>Write $Query(^ERP.Goods(123000,"L","caribbean blue"))
^ERP.Goods(123000,"L","classic beige")
```

You can see immediately that you obtain a deeper dimension level in each case, provided it exists. To obtain all defined entries in our small data model, you must use a loop, as usual. Because the result of $Query is a string, you must convert this with the @ indirection operator into an argument format that $Query can use.

Example

```
Set x="^ERP.Goods(123000)"
For  {
  Set x=$Query(@x)
  Quit:x=""
  Write x,"=",@x,!
}
```

In common with $Order, $Query's reference to the symbolic empty string returns the first subscript of the variable's collation order. In addition, specifying –1 as the second argument traverses the collating sequence of subscripts in reverse order.

Extended global syntax

It should also be noted that the $Data, $Get, $Order, and $Query functions all support extended global syntax. This makes it possible (even with multidimensional data structures) to navigate throughout the network to other namespaces.

7.2.3.2 Analysis of Multidimensional Arrays using $QLength and $QSubscript

In some situations, you may wish to investigate the structure of a subscripted variable, whether local or global. This raises two questions:
- How many dimensions does the subscripted variable have?
- What is the value of the ith subscript?

Let us consider the local variable $lv("A",3,7)$. Because the local variable lv has three subscript levels, the answer to the first question is 3. The answer to the second question is 7 when the third subscript is used.

When you write a variable in the symbolic form $Name(s_1, s_2, ..., s_n)$ (with the exception that n=0, if no subscript is used), the result of $QLength(Name(s_1, s_2, ..., s_n))$ is n.

$QLength function

Example

```
>Write $QLength("^ERP.Goods(123000,""S"",""classic beige"")")
3
>Write $QLength("a")
0
```

Note that the variable must be placed within quotes. Thus, the variable name is expected as an argument for $QLength. The function call returns 0, if no subscript exists, as in the second example for the non-subscripted local variable a. The result is an empty string if the argument does not represent a name, as in `$QLength(1)`. `$QLength` can be abbreviated to `$QL`.

`$QSubscript` (abbreviation `$QS`) has two arguments and has the following syntax:

```
$QSubscript(<namevalue>,<intexpr>)
```

As for `$QLength`, the first argument is the name to be investigated, whereas the second argument (interpreted as an integer) specifies which subscript is to be extracted.

When the variable name again takes the form $Name(s_1, s_2, ..., s_n)$, the result of `$QSubscript(`$Name(s_1, s_2, ..., s_n)$`,m)` is the value of the mth subscript, provided m is less than or equal to n. A simple example illustrates the basic concept:

Example

```
>W $QSubscript("^ERP.Goods(123000,""S"",""classic
beige"")",2)
S
```

`$QSubscript` also supplies information for other values of m, as the next table summarizes.

Table 7.3 $QSubscript results

for m	Result of the call
< –1	reserved for future purposes
–1	"environment" (the namespace) of the name
0	name without environment
m'>n	value of the subscript
m>n	null string

When you reference globals in distributed systems (refer to Section 7.1.3.2), extended syntax is considered the norm. A few examples illustrate alternative values for m.

Examples

```
>Set x="^|""remote""|G(1,2,3)"
>Write $QSubscript(x,-1)   // Namespace
remote
>Write $QSubscript(x,0)    // the name of the global
^G
>Write $QSubscript(x,3)    // subscript of the third dimension
3
>Write $Length($QSubscript(x,4))  // null string
0
```

The version with m=0 considers the name of the global, but not the namespace, even when one exists.

7.2.4 Copying n-Dimensional Arrays with Merge

The Merge command (abbreviation M) copies entire subscripted arrays, either local or global.

Its syntax is similar to that of the Set command: the value of a source variable is assigned to a target variable.

Syntax is similar to the Set command

```
Merge <targetvariable>=<sourcevariable>
```

Both source and target variables may be local or global subscripted or non-subscripted variables. As an initial example, we assume that the target variable lvn1 does not exist (namely $Data(lvn1)=0) and that the source variable is a subscripted global variable ^G(i).

Example

```
Merge lvn1=^G
```

This command copies the complete structure ^G into the variable lvn1. The individual values of lvn1(i) and the resulting defined values of all higher dimensions receive the values of ^G(i).

This form of Merge has no problem copying a very large global into another, e.g., with Merge ^GC=^G, where the ^GC global did not exist beforehand. If the ^G global has multiple subscript levels and you wish to copy only the subtree ^G("Sys"), you can use the following command:

Copying very large globals

```
Merge ^GC("Sys")=^G("Sys")
```

Copying large globals can take quite some time to process. As with the Kill command—which, in contrast to the Merge command, operates asynchronously—no accurate statement can be made about the result of terminating the processing, such as with <Control-C>. It is clear that such an interrupt results in a partially copied global; under no circumstances can the result be predicted accurately.

Somewhat more complicated is the copying of a (sub)tree into an existing array structure. Because the formal definition of this operation is not easy to understand, we provide a series of examples to show its main features.

Copying into an existing array structure

The copying of subtrees into themselves is not permitted and produces an error message. Thus, Merge a(1)=a(1,2) is not permitted.

The first example assumes two local, subscripted variables a and b with the following definitions.

```
a(1)=1       a(1,2)=12     b(1)=10
a(2)=2                     b(2)=20
a(3)=3                     b(3)=30    b(3,1)=31
```

Example

```
Merge a=b
```

The array a now assumes the following form:

```
a(1)=10          a(1,2)=12
a(2)=20
a(3)=30          a(3,1)=31
```

You can see that the values for b(i), i=1,2,3 overwrite the original values for a(i), i=1,2,3. The variable a(1,2) is not affected by the Merge and retains its value. Because b(3,1) exists, a(3,1) is added.

For the next example, given an unchanged a, the original structure for b should be extended so that the following array is produced:

```
b(1)=10          b(1,2)=12          b(1,2,1)=121
                 b(1,3)=13

b(2)=20
b(3)=30
```

Example

```
Merge a(1,2)=b(1)
```

Thus, b(1) itself and all subsequent variables should be copied into the a(1,2) array structure. The following assignments determine the resulting array:

```
b(1)            →        a(1,2)
b(1,2)          →        a(1,2,2)
b(1,2,1)        →        a(1,2,2,1)
b(1,3)          →        a(1,2,3)
```

Thus, a dimension change occurs: the original second and third dimensions become a third and fourth, respectively. This causes a to assume the following appearance:

```
a(1)=1          a(1,2)=10          a(1,2,2)=12     a(1,2,2,1)=121
                                   a(1,2,3)=13

a(2)=2
a(3)=3
```

We see here that the substructure b(1) is copied into the substructure a(1,2) in such a way that a(1,2) receives the value of b(1) and the defined values of b(1) expand into the higher dimensions of the variable a(1,2). If a subscript already exists for a that has these subscripts (a(1,2) in the example), it will be overwritten.

The third example again assumes the original value of a. This time b has the form:

```
b(5,6,7)=567         b(5,6,7,1)=5671         b(5,6,7,2)=5672
```

Example 3

```
Merge a(1,2)=b(5,6,7)
```

a(1,2) receives the value of b(5,6,7). The defined values of b(5,6,7) in the fourth dimension are determined by the subscripts 1 and 2, and these expand a(1,2) to a(1,2,1) and a(1,2,2).

Finally, we should note that the Merge command can be used in a distributed environment. Assuming |"Warehouse1"| designates a namespace within the network, the global ^ERP.Goods is copied from that namespace to the local one:

```
Merge ^ERP.Warehouse1=^|"Warehouse1"|Goods
```

Merge *command throughout the network*

7.3   Advanced Global Operations

Caché is a multiuser system. It provides *locking* mechanisms to:

- avoid synchronization problems during concurrent accesses to globals or individual data records by multiple processes
- group together multiple database operations to support transaction processing.

This section provides a detailed description of these processing modes.

Locking avoids synchronization problems and supports transaction processing

7.3.1   Locking Globals

7.3.1.1   Absolute Lock

Global variables are multiuser variables. This means that several processes can have concurrent read and write access to globals. This property gives them their name. However, the multiuser operation, and the resulting possible access of several users to a global variable, can cause synchronization problems. Caché provides a special command—the Lock command—to avoid this problem. This problem can be represented using the classic example of a system-wide unique identification counter.

Global variables support multiuser access

Let us assume that a certain number of Caché routines use a global variable as a unique identifier. This means that each application routine reads the last assigned identification number, increments it by one, and uses it system-wide and network-wide as a unique subscript for a global variable. This situation can often be found in the assignment of unique customer numbers and order numbers, among many other examples.

We will now extend (with the assignment of system-wide unique customer numbers) the material management system used in previous examples of this chapter (refer to Sections 7.1 and 7.2). The global variable ^ERP.Customer(O) stores the most recently assigned customer number. A new customer would receive the customer identification cid incremented by one, as follows:

```
Set cid=^ERP.Customer(O)+1,^ERP.Customer(O)=cid
Set ^ERP.Customer(cid)="data fields"
```

"data fields" here represent some kind of customer-specific data.

In a multiuser environment, the overlapping access of multiple processes can produce inconsistencies when the Lock command is not used to temporarily lock a data record from access by other processes.

Lock *command*

Example

```
Lock ^ERP.Customer(O)
Set cid=^ERP.Customer(O)+1 Set ^ERP.Customer(O)=cid
Lock
Set ^ERP.Customer(kid)="data fields"
```

Notes for the Lock *command*

Some notes are appropriate here:
- A lock created with the Lock command can be requested for both global and local variables.
- The lock remains set until it is explicitly released. The second Lock (without arguments) releases the lock.
- All locks to local or global variables are entered in a so-called lock table. Caché System Viewer can access this table. When a process attempts to lock a variable, Caché first checks in the lock table to see whether an entry is present for this variable. If not, an entry is made in the table. Conversely, the entry is removed from this table as soon as a variable is released.
- When a routine requests a lock, the execution of the routine stops until the variable can be locked. Because, under some circumstances, this can take a long time, a timeout can be specified with the argument of the Lock command. This routine can be accessed using the Else command:

```
Lock ^ERP.Customer:1 Else  Goto Timeout
```

In this example, the routine waits a maximum time of one second for another process to release the possible lock on the ^ERP.Customer global. If this does not occur, the $Test signal variable is 0, the Else command acts, and a branch is made to the Timeout subroutine (in which, for example, the user is requested to first process some other data record).

No unilateral locking

- Locking a variable with the Lock command should be considered as being a convention in the following sense. Once a user has locked a variable, another user cannot lock the same variable, but can access it any way, to change it or even delete it. There is no one-sided locking: the variable is protected only when every process uses Lock to protect its critical routine sections.

Two actions are performed in succession for every Lock command:
1. Release previous locks to other variables.
2. Lock the specified variable (if possible).

Deadlocks are avoided

The automatic release of previously set locks has an important ramification: it is a reliable means of avoiding a concurrency situation for two processes. In such a concurrency situation, called a *deadlock*, each of two processes is waiting for the release of a lock held by the other process.

However, it must be noted that when *local* variables are locked in a namespace, Caché enters variables having the same name in different namespaces with the same name in the lock table that is present just once in the system. This can produce a situation similar to a deadlock.

The release of all previous locks has an interesting consequence should you request multiple locks. If, for example, you want to lock ^A and ^B simultaneously, the command line Lock ^A,^B would seem to suffice. However, this command is equivalent to Lock ^A Lock ^B, where the second Lock command revokes the first Lock command. This has the result that only ^B is locked, not ^A.

Multiple locking

If you want to lock both variables, you must parenthesize the variables to be locked, namely Lock (^A,^B). This locks both variables. You can also specify a timeout here by writing it after the last parenthesis, e.g., Lock (^A,^B):0.

Some of the variables in the list grouped by the parentheses could have already been reserved by another user (process), whereas others are not. This situation is accounted for: a Lock is made on the list only when all variables are "free." Even if just one variable is locked by another user, the complete Lock is delayed until all variables become free or until the timeout written after the parentheses has expired. Timeouts for individual elements of the list cannot be specified.

A lock created with the Lock command always applies to a complete variable structure. Lock ^A also affects the variable ^A(1,2), should it exist. In other words, a lock reference to a non-subscripted global includes all higher dimensions. You can also place the lock on subscripted variables. In this case, the lock affects only the higher dimensions, not the lower dimensions. For example, Lock ^A(1,2) locks the subscripted variable ^A(1,2,4) but not ^A(1). Compared with conventional database systems, this means that locks can be issued for data records in a highly granular manner.

7.3.1.2 Additional Locks

Sometimes it is not desirable to release all previous locks when you want to lock an additional variable. Special forms of the Lock command permit the additional request and the selective release of locks.

A plus character prefixed to an argument locks a variable in addition, whereas a prefixed minus character releases the lock on the variable without affecting other locks.

Syntax for additional locks

Example

```
Lock +^A:0,+^B:0
...
Lock -^B
```

In the example, the first Lock command locks both ^A and ^B, whereas the second Lock command releases the variable ^B (but not ^A). As with a normal Lock, the additional Lock is entered in the Lock table and administered there. Although a deadlock can occur for these forms of the Lock command, you can avoid it through the use of a timeout. This was specified as 0 for these two variables: the new lock is requested only when no previous lock is present for this variable.

We could also have written Lock +(^A,^B) instead of Lock +^A,+^B. However, the two variants differ in that in the first case ^A can be locked when ^B has already been locked by another user. In the second case, either both or no locks are set. Because the probability of a deadlock is somewhat higher in the first case, the second notation is preferred. Furthermore, to avoid unforeseeable problems, every Lock command should include a timeout.

Note that a normal Lock, as previously described, releases all locks, even additional locks requested with the plus character. Only ^X is locked after the following command line:

```
Lock +(^A,^B,^C) Lock ^X
```

7.3.1.3 Shared Locks

Exclusive lock compared with shared lock

The previous locks were all *exclusive*, meaning that if a process holds a lock on a variable, then no other process can request additional locking. However, sometimes you want a process to have a *shared* lock, which does not cause a conflict with other processes. This situation can occur when two processes only read data, but do not change the data. A shared lock can be executed only if no other process has an exclusive lock. The opposite is also true: a shared lock prevents another process from holding an exclusive lock. In addition, a shared lock can be set to an exclusive lock and vice versa.

The type of lock that is desired is indicated in the Lock command after the variable name with a # symbol: Lock ^A#"S" means that the variable ^A is to be locked with a shared lock. "S" stands for *shared*. If the lock type is missing, it is assumed to be an exclusive lock.

A shared lock can also be requested as an additional lock: Lock +^X#"S" indicates that the global variable ^X should be *additionally* locked in *shared* mode. If the variable ^X had already been locked exclusively, then releasing the additional shared lock with Lock -^X#"S" does not release the original exclusive lock.

For more information, refer to Section 7.3.2.4 that provides further details of the special aspects of locking variables within a transaction.

7.3.1.4 $Increment

Specify counter in multiuser systems

We now turn to the classic case of specifying a counter that must be unique in multiuser systems and consequently is protected with a Lock command. (Refer to Section 7.3.1.1.)

The Lock command controls resources system-wide, but it implicitly requires a certain amount of overhead. There are also situations, such as transaction processing (refer to Section 7.3.2.4), in which the lock can be released only at the end of a transaction.

This is the reason why there is a dedicated function for this frequent action, namely $Increment. It can increment or decrement the numeric value of a local or global variable without issuing a lock using the Lock command and without two processes receiving the same counter. The basic definition is:

```
$Increment(variable[,number])
```

where the variable to be incremented does not need to exist. If the variable does not exist, Caché initializes it with the value 0. If the second argument is omitted, the variable is incremented by one.

Examples

```
>Kill ^Counter Write $Increment(^Counter)
1
>Write $Increment(^Counter,-10)
-9
```

In the first case, ^Counter is incremented by 1, and because it was initialized with 0, is assigned the value 1. In the second part of the example, ^Counter is decremented by the value 10.

Thus, the following routine segments are functionally equivalent:

```
Lock ^ERP.Customer(O)
Set (cid,^ERP.Customer(O))=^ERP.Customer(O)+1
Lock

Set cid=$Increment(^ERP.Customer(O))
```

When a process uses $Increment, it does not matter whether a second process locks the counter variable with a Lock command. In this case, $Increment also uniquely increases the counter for this process throughout the system.

$Increment and Lock

We now turn to the particular advantages of the use of $Increment within a transaction.

7.3.2 Transaction Processing (TP)

A transaction is a series of logically related database updates. The withdrawal of an amount of money from an account and the credit of the amount to another account can serve as example in a bank application. Transaction processing observes the "all or nothing principle." Either both entries are made or the state of the database remains unchanged. Expressed more formally, transaction processing satisfies four "ACID" properties.

Atomicity

ACID properties

The result of a transaction is either stored completely in the database or not at all.

Consistency

The result of a transaction must maintain the consistency of a database. This requirement is often also called seriability. It requires that a series of transactions that run concurrently in a multiuser environment produce the same result as when they are performed successively.

Isolation

The result of a transaction becomes visible to other processes only when the complete transaction has finished. This means that a transaction can never have access to *parts* of another.

Durability

The results of a successfully completed transaction should be permanent and survive any subsequent malfunctions of the database, including power failure and hardware faults. Such faults cannot cause data to be lost or transactions to be partially performed. Durability requires, as a minimum, that appropriate measures are taken for data backup. Failure protection for particularly critical data must be included in the considerations.

This section provides a detailed description of transaction processing in Caché.

7.3.2.1 Introduction to Transaction Processing

Within an application routine, a single SQL INSERT, UPDATE, or DELETE statement or a single Set, Merge, or Kill command in Caché Object-Script seldom represents a complete transaction. With transaction processing, a series of commands defines a transaction.

In Caché, use either:

- SQL commands, which are described in detail in Chapter 8
- commands from Caché ObjectScript

The following table provides an overview of the relevant commands in SQL and Caché ObjectScript.

Table 7.4 Overview of transaction commands in SQL and Caché ObjectScript

Command in SQL	Command in Caché ObjectScript	Definition and short description
START TRANSACTION	TStart	Designates the beginning of a transaction.
%INTRANS	$TLevel	Displays whether a transaction is currently being processed.
COMMIT [WORK]	TCommit	Successful end of a transaction.
ROLLBACK [WORK]	TROllback	Unsuccessful end of a transaction; all database operations will be reset.

7.3.2.2 The Transaction Block, TStart and TCommit

Transaction block

In Caché, commands that change globals can be placed in a transaction block. These commands are Set (including Set $Extract, Set $Piece, Set $LIst, and Set $BIT), Merge, Kill, and Read to a global variable. In accordance with the definition of transaction processing, either all global operations are executed completely or not at all. If any error occurs within a transaction, the previously performed global operations of that transaction are reset using special processing.

Two commands, TStart (abbreviated to TS) and TCommit (abbreviated to TC), are central here. They form a transaction block, as the first example shows.

Example

```
TStart
Set ^M(acct)=prec,^PN(nam,acct)=""
TCommit
```

This transaction consists of the two Set commands above. Because they are placed within a transaction block, Caché guarantees that both will be written (but never just one) or (when an error occurs) none are written. We will return later to the consequences of this action for the Lock command.

The following rule of thumb generally applies: only the processing required for a transaction should be performed within a transaction block. Everything else should lie outside. For instance, the Merge and the Kill commands can move or delete large data quantities, and should therefore be used sparingly within a transaction. When possible, commands that communicate with the "external environment" should be avoided in a transaction block. These are the commands Open, Read (also in the form Read ^G), Write, Close, and Job. This reason for this recommendation is that the effects of these commands are immediately visible externally and remain even when the transaction is revoked.

Practical use of transaction processing

In general, a further transaction can be opened within a transaction, even when this violates transaction simplicity. A routine can query the $TLevel (abbreviated to $TL) special variable to determine whether it is currently in a transaction. $TLevel has the value 0 outside a transaction or the value 1 within a transaction; this increases by 1 for each additional level of transaction nesting.

$TLevel special variable

7.3.2.3 Revoking a Transaction with TROllback

A failed transaction ends with a so-called *rollback*. All previously made global changes are revoked, and Locks are reset to the state they had before the start of the transaction. A rollback does *not* reset any local variables that changed during the transaction.

A rollback is requested explicitly with a TROllback command (abbreviated to TRO) or implicitly with a Halt command in the transaction block. In the first case, $TLevel then has the value 0. TROllback does not have an argument.

A rollback is never initiated automatically as the result of an error in a transaction; rather, the error processing for the transaction must initiate rollback explicitly.

Error processing

Example

```
Trans   TStart
        Set $ZTrap="Error"
        Set ^Acct(123999)=100
        Set ^Acct(123999,1)=1
        Set ^Log(123999)=error
        TCommit
        Set ^TP(123999,$Horolog)=1
        Quit
Error   TROllback
        Set ^TP(123999,$Horolog)=0
        Quit
```

In accordance with previous explanations, the $ZTrap variable (refer to Chapter 5) in this transaction is set to the label Error, to which a branch is made if an error occurs. For example, if the local variable error in the fifth line was undefined, it would cause a routine error. All globals set previously are reset in the Error subroutine.

A rollback is performed automatically in Caché in various situations:

Automatic rollback

- At the startup of Caché, when it is determined that there are open transactions.
- If a Halt command is performed, the system will prompt whether open transactions are to be completed or reset. Background processes (i.e., those that were initiated with a Job command) with transactions will be reset without prompting.
- If the system manager stops a process, Caché will ask whether a currently open transaction should be completed or rolled back. A rollback is always performed for background processes.
- %ETN is a utility program for managing error processing. (Refer to Section 5.4.) If its name is placed in the $ZTrap variable, you can determine whether %ETN is to end with a Halt or a Quit in an error situation. A rollback is performed in the first case.
- The system methods for persistent objects automatically handle transaction management.

Particular considerations must be made with regard to transaction processing when you wish to make a system backup or you have activated the journal option. For more information, refer to the *Caché ObjectScript Reference*.

7.3.2.4 Lock and $Increment in Transactions

Let us now return to our example from Section 7.3.1.1 (which assigned the unique identification number cid), but now consider it in the context of a transaction block.

Example

```
Begin    TStart
         Set $ZTrap="Error"
         Lock ^ERP.Customer(0)
         Set cid=^ERP.Customer(0)+1
         Set ^ERP.Customer(0)=cid
         Lock
         Set ^ERP.Customer(cid)="data fields"
         TCommit
         Quit
Error    TROllback
         Quit
```

The following general problem can occur: for concurrent processes in a multiuser environment, process 1 could be just within this transaction block but after the released second Lock. Process 2 comes to the same location and again increments cid by 1, while process 1 enters an error and resets the transaction—and thus ^ERP.Customer(0). Process 3 takes this reset value for ^ERP.Customer(0) and overwrites the data for process 2. This is an obvious error.

Locks are not released before the end of the transaction for this reason: a concurrent process must wait until the transaction has been processed completely or is revoked. This can cause time delays for parallel processes in long-running transactions. There are two methods of avoiding such delays. You can make two transactions out of the one in the above example: one for incrementing the customer number cid, and one for processing the counter. The first transaction can be processed very quickly, making a time delay improbable.

Locks are not released before the end of the transaction

A second method using the $Increment function is more elegant. As you remember (refer to Section 7.3.1.4), it increments (or decrements) a counter without issuing a Lock command. The arguments for $Increment are not considered to be part of the transaction; i.e., should a rollback occur, the counter global is not reset and the problem indicated above cannot occur. However, rolling back a transaction will leave an unused counter.

$Increment function

Finally, we would like to mention that for a Lock command that requests an additional lock (for example Lock +^X), the lock can be released immediately even within a transaction if the additional lock has been requested with a special parameter. The syntax is similar to the one used for requesting a shared lock. The parameter here is "I" (for *immediate unlock*), so the command Lock +^X#"I" indicates that the lock for the global ^X can be released immediately within the transaction, and not only after the transaction completion.

The "I" parameter can be combined with the "S" parameter to obtain a shared lock that can be unlocked immediately. The syntax for this combination is: Lock +^X#"SI".

8 SQL Access and Tables

8.1 Unified Data Architecture

Most applications of any size—even those developed with object technologies—must include a component for reporting and data analysis. In general, developers turn to popular third-party tools for reporting and data analysis, which typically use *Structured Query Language* (SQL) queries to access databases. Hence, an object-oriented database must also support SQL to handle queries that conform to a standard that many tools understand.

Data access using SQL for reporting and analysis tools

On the other hand, few applications commence development from scratch. Often, existing applications and data structures are retained but expanded to fit an object-oriented redesign. In these cases, a database system must import existing table definitions intact and support SQL access to tables for the purposes of query and fast execution of transaction processing.

Transfering existing table definitions

With the Unified Data Architecture (UDA), Caché provides a simple and convincing solution for these two problem areas: by representing data as a standardized class definition, UDA connects the old world (relational tables) with the new world (object-oriented instances).

Modeling is possible in both paradigms, which yields advantages. New development can be object-oriented, yet it can also:

- Automatically support SQL for data access by SQL-based tools.
- Import definitions of existing relational tables using *Data Definition Language* (DDL) to enable the execution of older SQL applications.

In many cases, a substantial increase in performance results when relational applications are transferred to Caché. This is attributed to the fact that a multidimensional database engine is better suited to processing complex transactions. Furthermore, migrating to Caché permits the use of the object technology for new modules or applications, including object-oriented access to existing data.

Multidimensional database engine for the processing of complex transactions

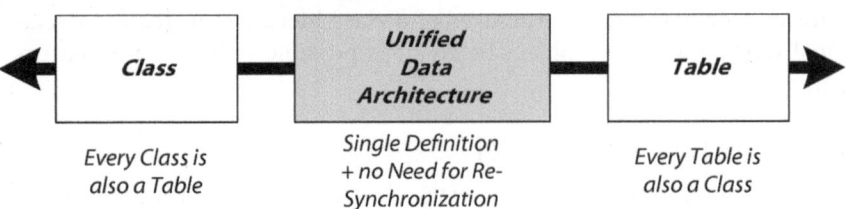

Figure 8.1 Unified Data Architecture

8.1.1   Representation of Classes as Objects and Tables

Within Unified Data Architecture, Caché Objects and Caché SQL represent the class hierarchy modeled in the Caché class dictionary differently: whereas Caché Objects works with objects, Caché SQL uses relational tables. However, there is only a single data definition, and unique data are stored just once.

Figure 8.2 Representing classes as both objects and tables

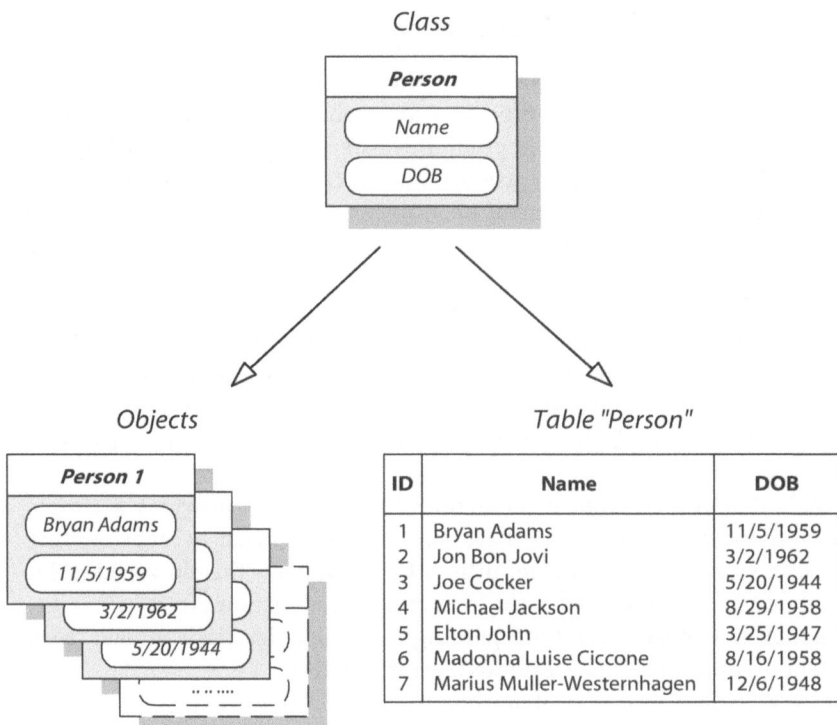

Considered from an object-oriented viewpoint, we see instances of a class. From a relational viewpoint, the data component of the classes become relational tables, whose rows and columns correspond to individual instances and object properties, respectively.

However, not all characteristics of a class hierarchy can be represented in a relational view. One reason is that objects have properties and methods, whereas tables contain just data. Although Caché also correctly represents complex data structures of a class hierarchy in tables, a relational representation of object behavior is possible only to a limited extent.

8.1.2   The Relational Model

The relational model is based on work done at the end of the 1960s by E. F. Codd and Chris Date, who published their findings in Codd [1970] and Date et al. [1996].

Relational theory uses a single construct—a *relation*—to represent the reality to be modeled. This mathematical term designates a subset of the Cartesian product of a list of value ranges *(tuples)*. All relational operations themselves produce relations. Thus, it represents a closed system. (For details about the relational model, consult Kleinschmidt et al. [1997] and Meier [1998].)

For practical use, we consider relations to be *tables* that are built from rows and columns. The *table header* then provides the assignment of properties to *columns*, with individual *rows* being instances or tuples.

Relations as table

Tables (or relations) store data for relational databases. The rows (or tuples) represent individual *data records,* and columns are their *data fields.*

Figure 8.3 A simple table

Table "Customer"

No	Name	City
1	Wollenhaupt	Saint Petersburg, FL
2	Ackerndorf	La Jolla, CA
3	Kleinhaus	Fort Worth, TX
4	Paul & Sons	Alexandria, VA
5	Hesselbach	Frankfurt, Germany

The rows of a table are not sorted as such. This means that the data records have no specific sequence. A specific column or combination of columns forms the *primary key* (or *Row ID*). This is used whenever possible to find a specific row. One table can refer to another when the foreign primary key is used as value in a column. This is then called a *foreign key*.

Primary key to locate a specific row

Foreign key

In addition to basic concepts, the relational model for databases is primarily characterized by normalization rules that define certain uses of tables. These rules define the following *normal forms*:

- The *first normal form* states that all data records of a table must have the same number of fields. It also prohibits multiple values for a field (so-called multiple or repeating fields); thus, all field values must be atomic.

First normal form

- A table corresponds to the *second normal form* when it also ensures that every field depends directly on the primary key (not just on a part of it).

Second normal form

- A table satisfies the *third normal form* when, in addition, no field depends on any field other than the primary key.

Third normal form

Although there are also fourth and fifth normal forms, these have only limited relevance for practical work. A table that satisfies the third normal form is said to be *normalized.*

The standardized *Structured Query Language* (SQL) is the most common method used to access relational databases.

8.1.3 The Projection of Classes to Tables

This section describes how the Unified Data Architecture represents various elements of a class definition as relational tables. We initially provide an overview of how the projection combines different concepts of object and relational worlds:

Table 8.1 Object concepts and their projection to relational structures

From the object concept	To the relational concept
package	SQL schema
class	table
instance	row
object identifier (OID)	ID column as primary key
literal property	column
reference to persistent object	foreign key
embedded object	individual columns
relationship	foreign key / dependent relationship
list collection	column with list field
array collection	child table
stream	BLOB
index	Index
query	optionally: stored procedure or view
class method	optionally: stored procedure

As can be seen from this overview, the relational model does not have an equivalent for class parameters, multidimensional properties, and instance methods. Consequently, the projection does not represent these concepts.

Differences Because no values are stored for transient and calculated properties, they cannot exist within a table and so are also not represented. Calculated fields from SQL can be used as a replacement when they are defined with the appropriate functionality.

In addition to the concepts represented from the object world, Caché also supports triggers that are only present in relational representations.

8.1.3.1 Packages and Schemas

Every package corresponds to a schema. For instance, if a class is called Finance.Accounting (the Accounting class in the Finance package), the corresponding table is Finance.Accounting (the Accounting table in the Finance schema).

The default package name User translates into a default schema name SQLUser. Periods in the package name are replaced by underscores in the schema name. Also, as only the first 25 characters are relevant, they must be unique. For instance, the class name User.Person translates into the table name SQLUser.Person in the relational projection, and Finance.Billing.Invoice becomes Finance_Billing.Invoice.

If a table is referenced without a schema name, the default schema name SQLUser is used. Therefore, the SQL query

```
Select ID, Name from Person
```

```
Select ID, Name from SQLUser.Person
```

8.1.3.2 Table Names

The Caché Objects class compiler automatically creates a corresponding table for all persistent classes derived from the %Persistent system class. This table has the same name as the class or the name specified by the SQLTABLENAME keyword.

Although there are no particular restrictions on the assignment of class names in Caché, there are restrictions on valid names for tables. To avoid conflicts during the interpretation of SQL expressions, a table name cannot be a reserved word in SQL.

Thus, a class whose name corresponds to a reserved word in SQL cannot represent a table unless you specify a different, non-reserved table name. Appendix C contains a complete list of reserved words in Caché SQL.

8.1.3.3 Object Identity

The object identity for individual instances of a class corresponds to the individual rows of a table in the relational representation. These are identified by a primary key. A column for the primary key that contains the ID part of the object identifier (OID) is created automatically for persistent object classes that use the %CacheStorage storage class.

This column is assigned the name ID unless the class already has a property with the name ID. In this case, the column is designated as ID1 (or ID2, if this exists already, etc.).

Also note that the value of the ID column cannot be changed and is managed by Caché. Consequently, SQL cannot be used to set or change the values of this column.

8.1.3.4 Inheritance and Tables

Because the concept of inheritance is not part of the relational model, every table projection corresponds to a flat representation of the higher class hierarchy. Thus, the projected table contains all properties of the class, including those inherited from super classes.

With regard to contained data records, a table that represents a super class contains data for all instances of all subclasses.

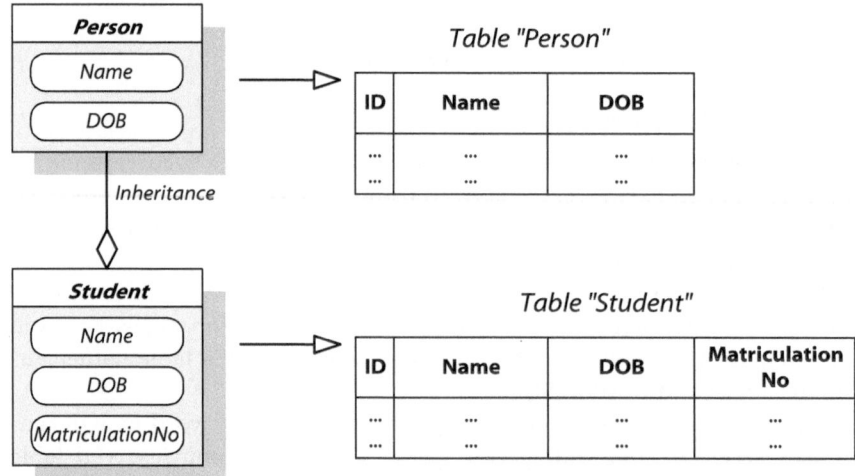

Figure 8.4 Class inheritance projected to relational tables

Thus the Person table in this example contains all persons, including students. In contrast, the Student table contains only students, but for these also the column for the Matriculationnumber property added in the subclass.

8.1.3.5 Literal Properties

SQLFIELDNAME *keyword*

The properties of classes are represented as fields (columns) in relational tables. By default, each field has the same name as the corresponding property. This field name can be overwritten with the SQLFIELDNAME keyword of the property definition. This is necessary, in particular, when the name of the property is a reserved name in SQL. This cannot be used as a field name and must be changed appropriately for the relational projection.

All properties of a class with literal values are projected as table columns in the relational view, but with the following exceptions:

- transient properties
- multidimensional properties
- calculated properties
- private properties

Data types

Data type classes and methods for Caché Objects are applied to a relational projection. This means that the previously discussed conversion and validation mechanisms apply fully, as does the use of the data type parameters described in Chapters 3 and 6. This holds both for data type classes supplied by the system and for user-written data type classes. Thus, user-written *Advanced Data Types* (ADTs) are also available for SQL data access.

The data type definitions made with keywords and class parameters may be used without restriction. For example, a Name property with the following definition

```
attribute Name {type = %String(MAXLEN=30);}
```

represents the Name field of a relational table with the VARCHAR type and a maximum length of 30 characters.

8.1 Unified Data Architecture

No restrictions on data type keywords and class parameters

Calculated properties

Calculated properties are not represented automatically in tables. This is because Caché SQL does not instantiate individual objects and so cannot execute methods used to calculate properties.

If, however, a calculated property is required for SQL, it can be defined as a *calculated field* for the relational projection and specified in the SQL context without instantiating valid code to calculate the value. Thus, a projected property as calculated field can provide both object and SQL functionality.

Object and SQL functionality are offered concurrently

However, because class methods can be invoked from both the object context in the code for calculated properties and the context of the *SQL computed field* specification, the actual calculation should be provided in a class method for such a case.

8.1.3.6 References to Persistent Objects

References to persistent objects are represented in Caché SQL as a foreign key to another table. The ID field that contains the ID part of the OID represents the actual key. Thus, a reference in the VB property to the sales representative stored in a VB object class is also represented in a VB field. This contains an ID, which also provides a valid key for a data record in the VB table. The two tables can be connected in an SQL query using a *join* operation over the foreign key.

Foreign keys to a referenced table

8.1.3.7 Embedded Objects

Properties of embedded objects are projected as individual fields, the names of which are formed from the name of the embedded class and the names of the associated properties. For example, the Street property of the embedded class Address becomes the Address_Street table column.

8.1.3.8 Relationships

Relationships between persistent objects are mapped to Caché SQL as foreign keys to another table. The key is only visible on the side that refers to a single object (meaning *many-* or *child*-page, respectively). Within Caché SQL, the reference can be used as an independent relationship. (See also Section 8.2.2.4.)

8.1.3.9 List Collections

List collections are projected as a single field that contains a list with the values of the collection. Refer to Section 8.2.2.2 for a discussion of processing list fields in SQL.

8.1.3.10 Array Collections

Customer_Invoice child table

Array collections are represented as child tables that are connected with the main table using a foreign key. The name of a child table is formed from the name of the main table, an underscore, and the name of the collection. Thus, an `Invoice` array collection of a `Customer` class creates (in the relational view) a child table with the name `Customer_Invoice`. This child table contains the following fields:

- the foreign key to the main table; the name is that of the main table (e.g., `Customer`)
- a unique key within the child table; the name is always `element_key`,
- the contents of the collection; the name is that of the collection (e.g., `Invoice`).

8.1.3.11 Indexes

In Caché Objects, an object's defined indexes are automatically available in its relational representation. For each SQL access, the *Query Optimizer* automatically selects the appropriate access path from all available indexes.

8.1.3.12 Queries

A class's queries can be made available as either *SQL stored procedures* or as views. The `SQLPROC`, `SQLVIEW`, and `SQLVIEWNAME` keywords are used here in the query definition.

8.1.3.13 Class Methods

Within Caché SQL, class methods can be invoked in the code for calculated fields. This mechanism is also frequently used to represent calculated properties as calculated fields in the relational view.

SQL Stored Procedures

Class methods can also be provided as *SQL stored procedures*. The `SQLPROC` keyword of the method definition is used for this purpose.

8.1.3.14 Triggers

Triggers represent a series of actions

Triggers are available in Caché SQL, in addition to the other relational elements projected from Caché Objects. A trigger is a series of actions that are initiated by various SQL commands. For example, a new row inserted in a table can cause certain actions to occur. Triggers are only relevant for relational access; objects do not use them.

You can define triggers in Caché Object Architect or in Class Definition Language (CDL). Section 4.4.9 describes trigger definitions.

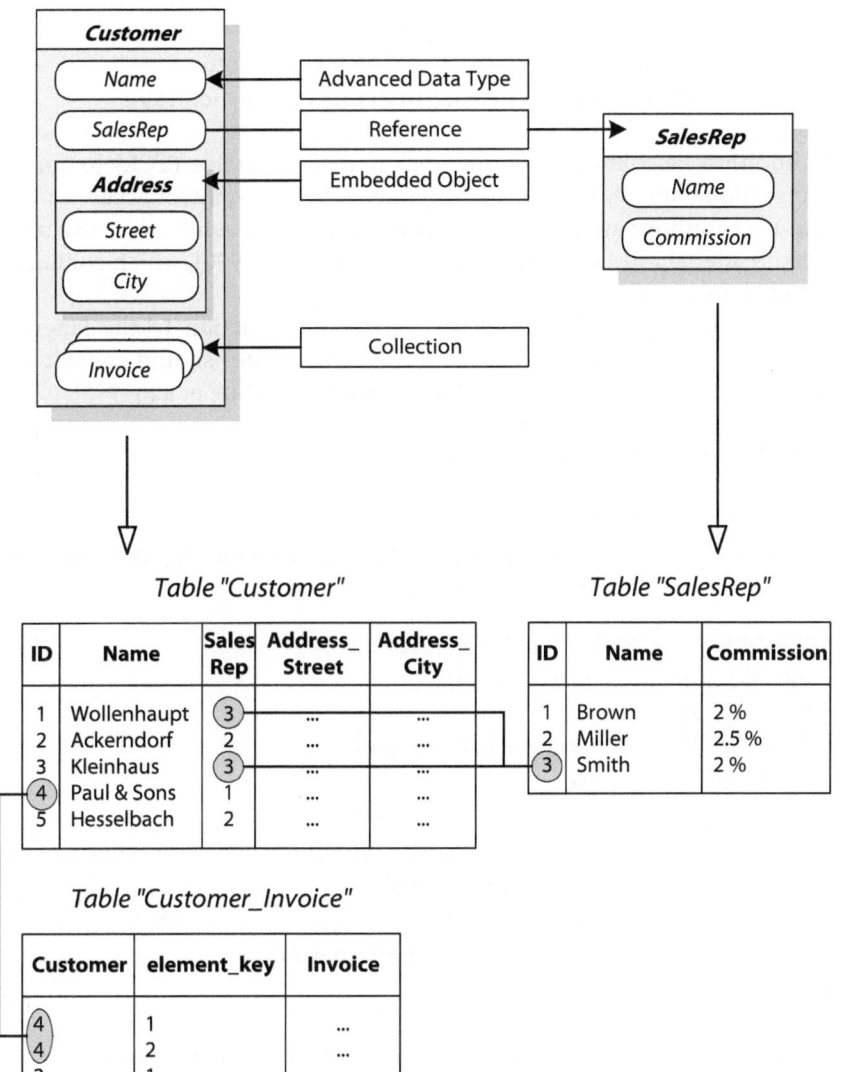

Figure 8.5 Projection of a complex object into multiple tables

Table "Customer"

ID	Name	Sales Rep	Address_ Street	Address_ City
1	Wollenhaupt	3	...	...
2	Ackerndorf	2	...	...
3	Kleinhaus	3	...	...
4	Paul & Sons	1	...	...
5	Hesselbach	2	...	...

Table "SalesRep"

ID	Name	Commission
1	Brown	2 %
2	Miller	2.5 %
3	Smith	2 %

Table "Customer_Invoice"

Customer	element_key	Invoice
4	1	...
4	2	...
2	1	...

8.2 Structured Query Language (SQL)

Structured Query Language (SQL) has established itself as the standard language for database access in relational databases and many other environments. Most tools for report generation, front-end programming, etc., use this popular language to query or change data. Caché SQL supports SQL for queries, as well as for online transaction processing where performance and security are required.

Standard language for database access

8.2.1 ANSI Standard SQL

Caché supports all elements of the ANSI Standards for SQL and SQL2. These are organized into three main areas:

- *Data Query Language* (DQL) to query data
- *Data Manipulation Language* (DML) to process data
- *Data Definition Language* (DDL) to define data structures

In addition, it contains *Transaction Control Language* (TCL) to control transactions and *Data Control Language* (DCL) to control access to data and user authorizations. The last two are not discussed here; the interested reader should consult, for example, Gruber [1990], which contains a detailed discussion.

The following sections provide a short introduction to the language elements of other areas of Standard SQL. The reader should consult specialized literature for a complete description, e.g., Date et al. [1996].

8.2.1.1 Data Query Language (DQL)

The SELECT command

The SELECT command produces an output table containing data from one or more tables as defined by the statement.

SELECT * | { [DISTINCT | ALL] expression,... }
FROM { tablename [aliasname]},...
[WHERE statement]
[GROUP BY { columnname | integer },...]
[HAVING statement]
[ORDER BY { columnname | integer },...]

The columns of the output table follow the SELECT keyword. They can be:
- * (an asterisk, meaning all columns)
- a combination of column names
- table and column names delimited by a period
- expressions

All columns must exist in the tables specified in the FROM clause.

The * represents all columns of the tables specified in the FROM clause, each in the sequence specified by the definition.

Optional parameters   The DISTINCT or ALL parameter is optional. DISTINCT removes duplicate rows from the output table. ALL has the reverse effect, in that all found data are output, even duplicate rows.

Tables from which data are to be fetched follow the FROM keyword. If several table names are specified, this produces the Cartesian product from the columns of all specified tables.

WHERE introduces a truth statement that determines which data are selected from specified tables.

The column names after GROUP BY define row groups with matching values in one or more columns. The statement after HAVING specifies which row groups are selected.

Finally, ORDER BY defines the sorting sequence in which the rows are placed in the output table.

Example

```
SELECT Name,Firstname,DOB
  FROM Person
  WHERE Address_City='Boston'
  ORDER BY Name
```

8.2.1.2 Data Manipulation Language (DML)

The INSERT command

The INSERT command adds a row of data into the specified table.

Inserting a row into a table

INSERT INTO tablename [(columnname,...)]
  { VALUES (expression,...) }
  | query

The command must contain either a VALUES clause or a subquery.

Example

```
INSERT INTO Person (Name,Firstname)
  VALUES('Jackson', 'Michael')
```

The UPDATE command

The UPDATE command changes the values in the fields of one or more rows of a table.

Updating records that already exist in a table

UPDATE tablename
  SET columnname = expression ,...
  [WHERE statement]

If no restricting statement is specified, all rows of the table are updated. The specified columns are assigned a new value for each row that corresponds to the statement.

Example

```
UPDATE Person
  SET Name = 'Michaela'
  WHERE ID = 42
```

The DELETE command

The DELETE command removes one or more rows from a table.

Deleting rows from a table

DELETE FROM tablename
  [WHERE statement]

If no restricting statement is specified, all rows of the table are deleted.

Example

```
DELETE FROM Person
  WHERE ID=42
```

8.2.1.3 Data Definition Language (DDL)

Data Definition Language is the part of SQL used to define data structures. Because relational data models are normally created using tools supplied by a database manufacturer or a third party, the most important application for DDL is the exchange of data definitions between different systems.

Caché supports all DDL commands, including those for views and indexes. At this point we present examples only for the commands to create, change, and delete a table definition.

The CREATE TABLE command

Defining new tables

The CREATE TABLE command creates a new table with specified fields, which, however, do not contain any data.

CREATE TABLE tablename
  (columnname datatype [(length)] [NOT NULL],...)

A column definition specifies the data type of the column's value. The following data types can be used:

Table 8.2 SQL data types

Data type	Explanation
CHAR	String of the specified length
VARCHAR	Variable-length string
LONG VARCHAR	Long string
SMALLINT	Integer values from -32767 to 32767
INTEGER	Integer values from −2147483647 to 2147483647
DECIMAL	Decimal number
DATETIME	Date and time
DATE	Date
TIME	Time
TIMESTAMP	Date and time (timestamp)
FLOAT	Floating-point number
NUMBER	same as FLOAT

You can specify the maximum length of a column's data value.

The ALTER TABLE command

Changing an existing table definition

The ALTER TABLE command changes an existing table definition by removing, adding, or modifying individual fields.

ALTER TABLE tablename
  { DROP columnname }
  | { ADD columnname datatype [(size)] [NOT NULL] }
  | { MODIFY columnname datatype [(size)] [NOT NULL] }

The DROP TABLE command

The DROP TABLE command removes a table definition.

DROP TABLE tablename

When you remove a table from the database, all associated indexes and views are also deleted.

8.2.2 Extensions in Caché SQL

The implementation of Caché SQL provides a number of extensions to ANSI Standard SQL. These extensions support the integration of Caché Objects and Caché SQL, and the inclusion of Caché ObjectScript.

Extensions to ANSI SQL

These extensions fall into the following categories:

- additional Caché operators
- list fields
- joins
- references
- dependent relationships.

8.2.2.1 Additional Caché SQL Operators

Caché SQL provides a number of additional operators compared to standard SQL. These new operators permit more powerful SQL expressions and improve the integration with Caché ObjectScript.

The following table provides an overview:

Symbol	Description
=*	*One-way outer join*
->	*Implicit join* (reference)
_, #	Scalar Caché ObjectScript operators: Concatenation: 'house'_'keeping'='housekeeping' Modulo division: 20#6=2
?, [	Comparison operators: Pattern match: 'DA-JC 345'?1.2A1'-'1.2A1' '1.4N Contains operator: 'DA-JC 345'['JC'
&, !	Caché ObjectScript AND and OR
]	Follows operator: 'B']'A'
%STARTSWITH	Starts with operator: 'Maier' %STARTSWITH 'Mai'

Table 8.3 Additional Caché SQL operators

In addition to single quotes ('...') from ANSI Standard SQL, Caché SQL also permits the use of double quotes ("...") to delimit literals.

Comparison and logical operators can also be negated through the use of a prefixed not.

Negation with not

Example:

```
not= (is equivalent to <>)
not< (is equivalent to >=)
not> (is equivalent to <=)
```

8.2.2.2 Additional Caché Functions

%ID pseudo-column

As a built-in function, Caché SQL provides the %ID pseudo-column which represents the ID field independent of its true column name.

Additional functions can be defined by the programmer. Caché SQL allows the use of any class method as an SQL function, provided they are marked with the SqlProc keyword to indicate a stored procedure. Let us assume that the User.Person class contains the following definition:

Stored Procedure used as an SQL function

```
ClassMethod Reverse(Arg1 As %String)
                    As %String [ SqlName = Reverse, SqlProc ]
{
  Quit $REverse(Arg1)
}
```

Then, with the SQL statement

```
SELECT SQLUser.Reverse(Name) FROM SQLUser.Person
```

you can select a list of reversed names of all persons. Note, however, that the name of the stored procedure specified by SqlName must be unique within the whole SQL Schema and not only within the class as is the case for other, regular methods.

8.2.2.3 List Fields

Caché SQL permits the definition of fields with several values. This concept is known in Caché ObjectScript as a *list*. List fields are useful for storing several pieces of information that relate to a single entity. Typical examples are a multi-line addresses and free-text blocks.

Two formats

SQL projects a list as a single string of serialized data. This string can be stored in two formats:

- $LISt format—the list format specified by the Caché ObjectScript $LISt function; it is managed automatically
- delimited string—the user-managed list format in which the individual elements are separated by a delimiter defined by the developer.

Caché SQL permits the use of list fields for both pure queries (SELECT statement) and database changes (INSERT and UPDATE statements). List collections are represented in the relational projection as list fields. Refer to Section 5.1.5 for the processing of lists in Caché ObjectScript.

8.2.2.4 Joins

Caché SQL extends Standard SQL with two further *join* types:

- *One-way outer join*
- *Implicit join*

One-way outer join

The normal *inner join* from SQL joins rows of one table with rows of a second table. However, in accordance with the definition, it excludes a row of the first table from the selection when there is no corresponding row in the second table.

By contrast, a *one-way outer join* includes all rows of the first table, even when no corresponding row is found in the second table.

The sequence in which tables are specified in the FROM clause determines the definition of a one-way outer join. The first specified table is the source of the join. An outer join is defined through the use of the =* symbol rather than the normal equal sign in the WHERE clause.

The = symbol represents an outer join*

The following example uses the Manufacturer table as a source for a *one-way outer join* operation with the Article table.

```
SELECT Manufacturer.Name, Manufacturer.Location,
Article.Designation
FROM Manufacturer,Article
WHERE Manufacturer.ID=*Article.Manufacturer
```

The Cartesian product for the tables in the FROM clause formed first includes all possible combinations of rows from the Manufacturer and Article tables. The WHERE clause specifies the restricting condition for the *one-way outer join*. Only those rows that satisfy this condition are contained in the query result.

This example returns all manufacturers and the articles supplied by each manufacturer. In contrast to the normal *inner join*, it also contains those manufacturers for which no articles were found.

Implicit join

An *implicit join* designates a join of two tables that are not explicitly specified in the SQL query, but which are implicitly associated by keys in the database. Caché SQL supports two different forms of *implicit joins*: references and dependent relationships.

References and dependent relationships

References

A reference is a relationship between tables in which a field of the table to be referenced contains the primary key (the ID) of a data record for a referenced table. Such a reference is also called a *pointer*.

Caché SQL provides a special *implicit join* syntax that can be used to follow the references. Let us assume there exists an Article table with a single field, Manufacturer, that forms a reference to the Manufacturer table, which itself contains a field Name. Then the syntax Article. Manufacturer->Name specifies the name of the manufacturer of the current article. Thus, Caché SQL takes the implicit insertion of Manufacturer in the FROM clause and insertion of a *join* condition in the WHERE clause.

After resolving the *implicit join* syntax, the following example

```
SELECT Name,Manufacturer->Name
FROM Article
WHERE Type='Tool'
```

is equivalent to:

```
SELECT Article.Name,Manufacturer.Name
FROM Article,Manufacturer
WHERE Article.Type='Tool'
AND Article.Manufacturer=Manufacturer.ID
```

Dependent relationships

One base table row to many child table rows

A dependent relationship is a join between tables in which the existence of rows in a table (the child table) depends on rows in another table (the base table). In other words, the rows of the base table have a one-to-many relationship (1:n relationship) to the rows of the child table.

A child table always references its base table. Thus, a dependent relationship can be considered an implicit reference. However, a dependent relationship is more restrictive than a normal reference, because the *join*-condition specifies that all rows of the child table reference the same row of the base table. Consequently, a dependent relationship satisfies the relational definition of an *inner join*.

The relational projection of embedded objects yields a dependent relationship. A typical example is the relational representation of an invoice with its items that result in two tables: the Invoice base table and the Invoice_Items child table.

There are two types of dependent relationships, namely from the base table to the child table and vice versa.

Child table to base table reference

If B is the base table to the child table C, and F is a field in B, then the *implicit join* syntax C.B->F for a given row points to the value for field F in the row of the base table that belongs to the current row for C. This expression is interpreted as a reference to B.F, where B is implicitly extended to the FROM clause and another *outer join* condition to the WHERE clause.

For an Invoice table with an Invoice_Item child table, the query

```
SELECT Invoice->Date
FROM Invoice_Item
WHERE UnitPrice>100000
```

is equivalent to the query:

```
SELECT Invoice.Date
FROM Invoice_Item,Invoice
WHERE Invoice_Item.UnitPrice>100000
AND Invoice_Item.Invoice=Invoice.ID
```

Base table to child table reference

If B is the base table for C, and F is a field in C, then the *implicit join* syntax B.C->F for a given row from B points to the value for F for all rows of the corresponding child table C. This expression is interpreted as a reference to C.F, where C is implicitly extended to the FROM clause and another *outer join* condition to the WHERE clause.

For example, the following query

```
SELECT Item->UnitPrice
FROM Invoice
WHERE InvoiceNumber=1003274
```

is equivalent to:

```
SELECT Invoice_Item.UnitPrice
FROM Invoice, Invoice_Item
WHERE Invoice.InvoiceNumber=1003274
AND Invoice.ID=Invoice_Item.Invoice
```

8.3 Embedded SQL

To simplify the development of database applications, Caché supports the embedding of SQL in methods and routines. This is called *embedded SQL*, and it can be used in Caché ObjectScript:

- to perform complex database queries
- to bind the results to Caché ObjectScript variables.

8.3.1 Use of Embedded SQL in Method Definitions

Embedded SQL in method definitions is incorporated in the &sql() preprocessor function.

```
ClassMethod Abc()
  {
    &sql(...)
  }
```

In the following examples, this Person class will be used to demonstrate the various possibilities of embedded SQL:

```
Class User.Person Extends (%Persistent)
                              [ ClassType = persistent ]
  {
  Property Name As %String [ Required ];
  Property DOB As %Date(FORMAT = 4);
  ...
  }
```

The FindPerson method uses embedded SQL to search for a person with a specific name. It then opens the corresponding object instance and returns its OREF.

```
ClassMethod FindPerson(name As %String) As %ObjectHandle
  {
    &sql(SELECT %ID into :id FROM SQLUser.Person
        WHERE Name=:name)
```

Embedded SQL—FindPerson

237

```
If SQLCODE<0 Quit ""
Quit ..%OpenId(id)
}
```

A ListPersons method (that uses cursor-based SQL to output a list of the persons) can be defined similarly.

Embedded SQL—ListPersons

```
ClassMethod ListPersons() As %Status
{
    &sql(DECLARE PersCur CURSOR FOR
        SELECT Name, DOB
        INTO :name, :dob
        FROM SQLUser.Person)
    &sql(OPEN PersCur)
    For {
        &sql(FETCH PersCur)
        Quit:SQLCODE
        Write name,?30,dob,!
    }
    &sql(CLOSE PersCur)
    Quit $$$OK
}
```

Embedded SQL can also be used to add new rows to the database.

Embedded SQL—Insert

```
ClassMethod Insert(name As %String, dob As %String)
                                              As %Status
{
    &sql(INSERT INTO SQLUser.Person (Name, DOB)
        VALUES (:name, :dob))
    Write "SQLCODE=",SQLCODE,!
    Quit $$$OK
}
```

Data Definition Language (DDL) can also be used in embedded SQL to define and change relational structures.

Embedded SQL—DefineTable

```
ClassMethod DefineTable()
{

    &sql(CREATE TABLE SQLUser.NewTable
        (Name CHAR(30), Title CHAR(30)))
    Quit $$$OK
}
```

8.3.1.1 Data Formats

Data selected with SQL can be returned in each of the following formats:
- Logical (Default)—returns all values without conversion.
- ODBC—converts all values into ODBC format.
- Display—converts the output values of the SELECT clause into display format, although not for constants or values of variables.

#sqlcompile preprocessor flag

The data format is defined with the #sqlcompile macro preprocessor flag. The following example selects the internal format *(logical format)*:

```
#sqlcompile select=logical
```

8.3.2 Use of Macros in Embedded SQL

Embedded SQL can contain macro references. The macro preprocessor expands these references before the SQL part is translated. This means that macros can be used to generate parts of SQL statements.

The macro preprocessor recognizes the following three constructs:

Construct	Symbol	Description
Preprocessor command	#	Causes the preprocessor to execute the command.
Preprocessor function	## or &	Expands to specific code.
Macro	$$$	Refers to a previously defined macro.

Table 8.4 Macro preprocessor constructs

The following example shows a number of macro definitions and then an SQL command that uses these macros:

```
#define TABLE Person
#define FIELDS Name,Telephone
#define VARS :name,:telephone
#define COND Name %STARTSWITH 'A'
...
&sql(SELECT $$$FIELDS
     INTO $$$VARS
     FROM $$$TABLE
     WHERE $$$COND)
```

The above example resolves to:

```
&sql(SELECT Name,Telephone
     INTO :name,:telephone
     FROM Person
     WHERE Name %STARTSWITH 'A')
```

Macro resolution can also be used to insert an &sql preprocessor function in the code.

```
#define GETNEXT &sql(FETCH xcur INTO :a)
...
For  $$$GETNEXT Quit:SQLCODE=100  Do abc
```

This example resolves to:

```
For  &sql(FETCH xcur INTO :a) Quit:SQLCODE=100  Do abc
```

8.3.3 Cursor and Non-Cursor-Based SQL

Caché ObjectScript supports two types of embedded SQL commands:
- non-cursor-based SQL
- cursor-based SQL

8.3.3.1 Non-Cursor-Based SQL

A non-cursor-based SQL query always returns a single row. If a SELECT command selects more than one data record, only the first record is returned.

```
&sql(SELECT Name INTO :name FROM Person)
```

This command copies the value of the Name field from the first row of the Person table into the name local variable.

8.3.3.2 Cursor-Based SQL

Multiple rows in a result set

Cursor-based SQL permits multiple rows to be retrieved from the result set of a query. A *cursor* is used here as a label for the current row within the query result. The following sequence of commands is executed to implement a cursor:

- Declaring a cursor
- Opening a cursor
- Performing a series of FETCH operations for the cursor
- Closing the cursor

A cursor behaves like a pointer—at any given time, it enables access to the current row and can then be repositioned to the next row.

Declaring a cursor

DECLARE SQL statement

The DECLARE SQL statement declares a cursor. It contains the name of the cursor and a SELECT clause that defines the query to which the cursor refers.

The name of a cursor can consist of an arbitrary number of alphanumeric characters, of which, however, the first character must be a letter and only the first six characters are relevant. The DECLARE command must be placed before all code lines that use the cursor. The OPEN, FETCH, and CLOSE commands can use the cursor once it has been declared. All operations on a specified cursor must be executed within a single Caché ObjectScript routine or method.

```
&sql(DECLARE PersCur CURSOR
     FOR SELECT Name, DOB
         FROM Person
         WHERE Name="Jackson")
```

The above example declares a cursor PersCur that returns the Name and DOB of all rows of the Person table in which the Name field equals "Jackson".

INTO clause

The SQL extensions in Caché SQL support DECLARE commands with the specification of an INTO clause to bind the result of a cursor-based FETCH to local variables.

```
&sql(DECLARE PersCur CURSOR
     FOR SELECT Name, DOB
         INTO :name,:dob
         FROM Person
         WHERE Name="Smith")
```

The cursor declaration in the above example specifies the local variables in which the table fields are to be stored for the subsequent FETCH. The assignment is made using the position in the field or variable list.

Opening a cursor

A cursor must be opened with the OPEN command before it can be used.

```
&sql(OPEN PersCur)
```

FETCH operations for the cursor

The FETCH command stores the field contents of a table row in local variables.

There are two variants of the FETCH command—with and without the INTO clause. If the DECLARE command contains an INTO clause, it is superfluous for the FETCH.

The following example shows how the next row of the PersCur cursor is fetched and the field values assigned to the name and dob variables:

Two variants of the FETCH command

```
&sql(FETCH PersCur INTO :name,:dob)
```

Because the variables have already been determined with the DECLARE command, the &sql(FETCH PersCur) command would also have sufficed here.

Each FETCH command can use its own INTO clause to store data in the appropriate variables.

Closing the cursor

The CLOSE command closes a cursor that is no longer required:

```
&sql(CLOSE PersCur)
```

8.3.4 Evaluating Query Results

8.3.4.1 Retrieving Query Results into Local Variables

The INTO clause specifies the local variables in which the query results are stored. It can be specified as part of either the DECLARE or the FETCH command.

```
&sql(DECLARE PersCur CURSOR
     FOR SELECT Name, DOB
          INTO :name,:dob
          FROM Person
          WHERE Name="Smith")
&sql(OPEN PersCur)
&sql(FETCH PersCur)
...
&sql(CLOSE PersCur)
```

In this example, the FETCH command stores the field contents for Name and DOB in the local variables name and dob, respectively. Alternatively, the following code can be specified:

```
&sql(DECLARE PersCur CURSOR
     FOR SELECT Name, DOB
          FROM Person
          WHERE Name="Smith")
&sql(OPEN PersCur)
```

```
&sql(FETCH PersCur INTO :name,:dob)
...
&sql(CLOSE PersCur)
```

Here, the INTO clause is specified in the FETCH command instead of in a cursor declaration. This has the advantage that each FETCH can specify different variables in which to store field contents.

8.3.4.2 Retrieving Query Results into Multidimensional Arrays

INTO clause with target array

The result of an SQL query can also be bound to a local subscripted variable. This is specified as a target variable in the INTO clause; the last subscript must not be specified:

```
&sql(FETCH PersCur INTO :e("query-result 1",))
```

Caché stores the values of the individual columns of the query result in these indexed variables; the column number is used as index for the last dimension. Thus, when we execute the query

```
&sql(SELECT * INTO :e() FROM Person WHERE Name='Smith')
```

on a Person table with the ID, Name, and DOB columns, the ID, the Name, and the DOB are stored in e(1), e(2), and e(3), respectively.

8.3.4.3 Retrieving Query Results into Objects

As we have seen, embedded SQL can store data fields in variables. However, the use of dot syntax for objects is not permitted in embedded SQL. If you wish to combine object properties with SQL, you must do this indirectly using Caché ObjectScript variables. Simple Caché variables are then used in SQL commands and their values assigned to the corresponding object properties outside the SQL context.

Indirectly using Caché ObjectScript variables

```
&sql(SELECT Name FROM Person INTO :name WHERE ID=4711)
Set supplier.Name=name
```

In this example, the value of the Name field from the Person table is first assigned to the name local variable. Then, outside SQL, the value of the name variable is assigned to the Name property of the object that is identified by the supplier OREF.

8.3.5 Inserting and Updating Values

8.3.5.1 Inserting and Updating from Variables

You can also add new records and update old ones using variables (in the same manner as explained in the above sections) with the INSERT and UPDATE commands, respectively:

```
Set name=employee.Name
&sql(INSERT INTO Person (Name) VALUES (:name))
```

8.3.5.2 Inserting and Updating from Multidimensional Arrays

Caché SQL supports subscripted variables as passed values in embedded INSERT and UPDATE commands. The last subscript of the array must not be specified here. For example, the command

```
&sql(INSERT INTO Person VALUES :pers("Profile",))
```

sets every field of a row of the Person table into the value of pers("Profile",<column number>).

Caché SQL does not need a list of field names after the table name when an indexed variable is used to pass the values. Internal field numbers are used to assign the values to the table fields.

8.3.5.3 Inserting and Updating from Objects

Because the dot syntax for objects is not available within embedded SQL, inserting and updating values from objects must also be performed indirectly using local variables. Local variables are assigned values using object syntax (outside of embedded SQL code) and then used in SQL commands, as shown in the following example:

```
Set name=customer.Name,firstname=customer.Firstname
&sql(INSERT INTO Person (Name, Firstname)
    VALUES (:name, :firstname))
```

8.3.6 Return Values and Error Messages

Each execution of an embedded SQL command returns values in a number of local variables. These variables can be checked to determine whether the operation was successful.

One of the local variables is %ROWCOUNT that contains the number of rows changed after executing the embedded SQL. The value is overwritten after each execution of embedded SQL. After INSERT operations, there is another variable %ROWID that contains the ID of the newly inserted row. You can use its value to process a new record immediately without needing to execute a further SELECT statement. Such processing could be to instantiate the object with the %OpenId() method.

The SQLCODE variable returns a numeric value. This value indicates one of the states shown in the following table:

SQLCODE	Meaning
0	Successful completion.
100	Successful completion but no (further) row satisfied the query condition.
<0	Error condition. The Caché system documentation contains a complete list of the SQLCODE error numbers.

Table 8.5 Values for SQLCODE after executing embedded SQL

8.4 Caché SQL Manager

Often, it is desirable to use relational tables to quickly view the data stored in Caché, perhaps to assist with testing and debugging. Also, there are administrative tasks related to SQL access that need to be done. Caché SQL Manager is the right tool for such purposes. Developers and administrators can use it to inspect table definitions, manage SQL users, create indexes or views, and import/export data.

Figure 8.6 Caché SQL Manager

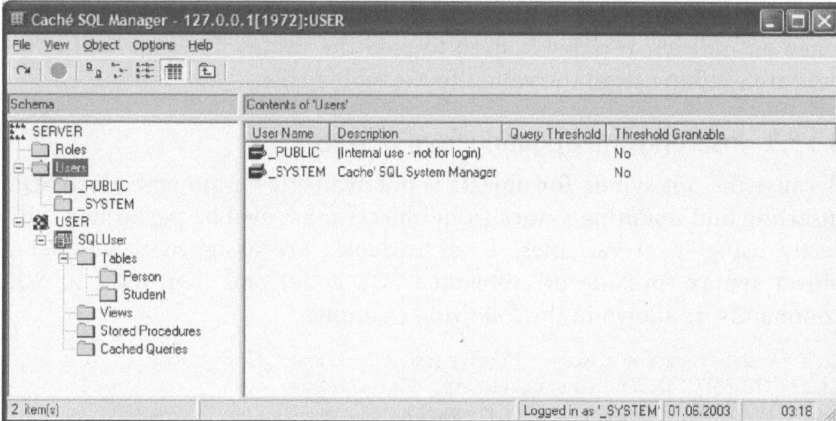

In the tree structure on the left-hand side, you can click *Tables* to see all tables in the current namespace. When you click a specific table, you can inspect its details. Besides these basic features, Caché SQL Manager offers a choice of options related to SQL access:

- You can look directly at the data in a typical table view.
- You can look at all properties of tables such as triggers, indexes, stored queries, and compiler information.
- The *Cached Queries* task folder displays ODBC queries that are currently cached, and allows you to access and edit them.
- The *Roles* task folder provides a list of roles currently defined on the system; you can then access and edit them.
- The *Users* task folder allows you to edit users on the system. You can assign individual privileges and grant table and role access.
- The *Views* task folder provides stored table views.
- By means of two wizards, you can easily export and import data to and from ASCII files.

Access to external relational databases with the SQL Gateway

Two menu options in the *File* menu are especially interesting: *Link Table* allows you to link into Caché tables stored in external relational databases and access them from within Caché ObjectScript. Because this uses standard ODBC connections, almost any relational database can be reached and integrated.

Porting relational applications to Caché

Data Migration works very similar. However, the data definition and data are totally integrated in Caché. This means applications that previously worked with other relational databases can continue to be used with Caché.

Finally, after selecting the *Execute Query* tab for a table, you can enter a free-text SQL query and execute it immediately to see the results:

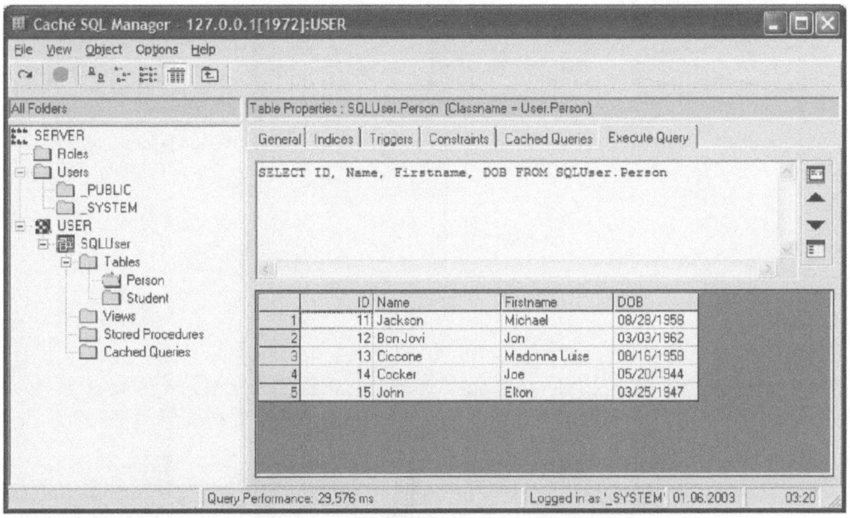

Figure 8.7 *Execute Query* tab with a free-text SQL query

8.5 Caché SQL Server—Access Using ODBC

An important application of SQL is to enable access to a database from external systems such as list generators, reporting tools, relational applications, etc. Caché SQL Server provides this relational access for external systems. It offers various application interfaces (APIs), of which only ODBC, being the most important, is discussed here.

Giving external systems access using ODBC

For a database to be reachable using ODBC, it must supply client systems with a so-called ODBC driver. This is database-specific and allows applications to issue certain software-vendor-independent SQL calls defined by the ODBC standard. The interested reader should consult Geiger [1995] as a standard work on ODBC.

To check that the Caché-supplied ODBC driver has been automatically installed and is registered correctly in a Windows client system, open the *Control Panel* and double-click the *ODBC* menu icon. The *ODBC Data Source Administrator* window appears. Select the *System-DSN* register tab, and check to see that the Caché ODBC driver is available in the list of data sources.

Ensuring that a Windows client has the right ODBC driver

Figure 8.8 The ODBC Data Source Administrator from the Windows control panel

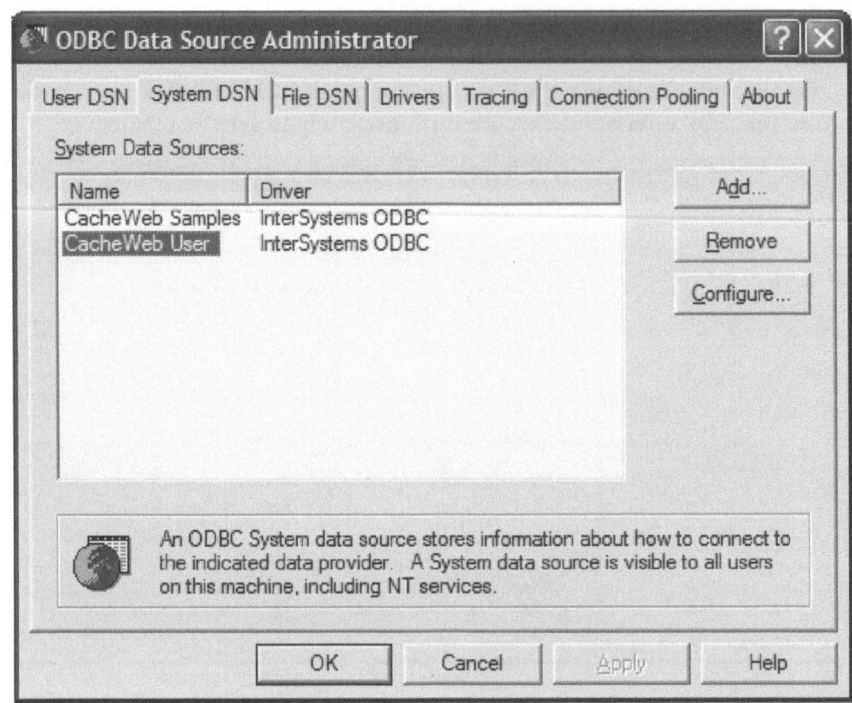

As you can see, the Caché installation has created two system data sources for you, named "CachéWeb Samples" and "CachéWebb User" for the Samples and User namespaces, respectively. You can just use them, or click the *Add* button to create a new data source using the Caché ODBC driver.

Figure 8.9 Selecting the Caché ODBC driver

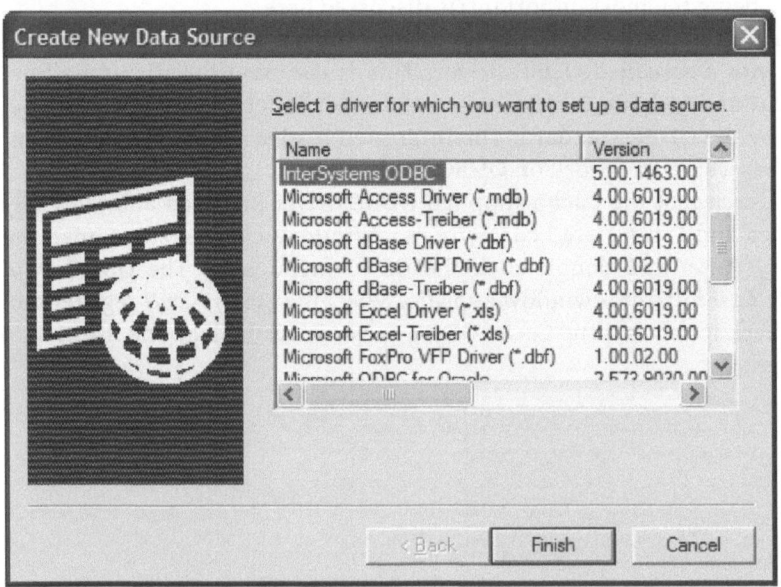

A list of all installed ODBC drivers appears. The driver for Caché has the designation "InterSystems ODBC."

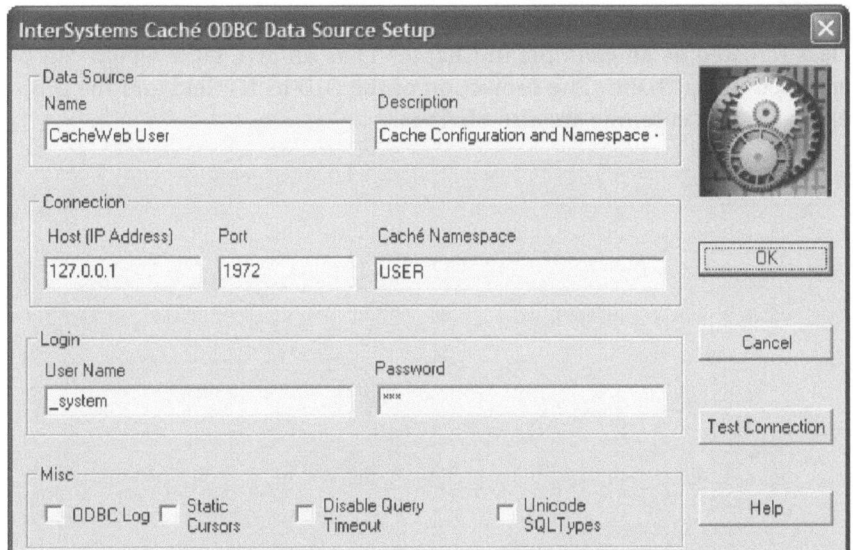

Figure 8.10 Setting up the Caché ODBC driver

The setup of the driver requires only a few details. First, specify an arbitrary (but unique) *Data Source Name (DSN)*. *IP Address* and *Port* access the local Caché system at the default settings 127.0.0.1 and 1972, respectively. USER, or another namespace created by the user that contains the data, is set as *Caché Namespace*. Unless you have created your own SQL users in Caché SQL Manager, the *User ID* and *Password* are _system and sys, respectively.

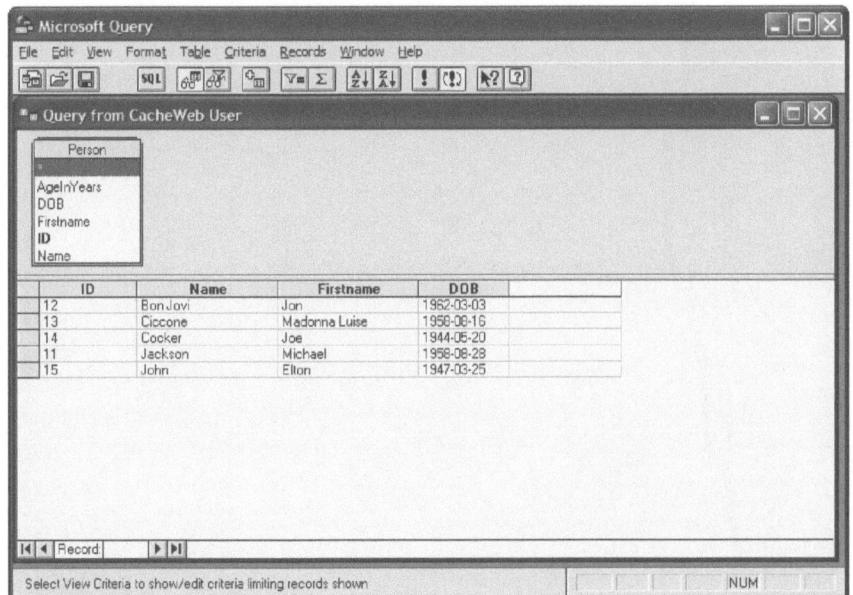

Figure 8.11 Query result in Microsoft Query

Caché is now defined as an ODBC data source and is available for access by all Windows applications on the client computer. The example shows a query performed with Microsoft Query on this data source.

You can see immediately that Caché SQL represents the Person object class (created as an example in Chapter 1) as an SQL table which can be accessed using ODBC. The projection of the OID as ID field and the properties as table columns are also obvious.

9 Programming with ActiveX

ActiveX, a component of every 32-bit Windows system, is a standard means for communication between object-oriented components under Microsoft Windows. Usually a Windows application consists of a number of ActiveX components provided as DLL or OCX files. The application itself can also be an ActiveX component—familiar examples of this are the programs in the Microsoft Office suite. Each of these applications can be controlled by ActiveX and thus enables the creation of complex application packages. The fundamentals of ActiveX programming and its uses are described in detail in Chapell [1998].

ActiveX as a Windows component

9.1 Overview

The communication using ActiveX involves two partners: the component that calls another object (the *master*), and the object that is called and controlled (the ActiveX *server*). Caché can be used in both roles. Visual Caché makes it possible to access database objects using ActiveX. In this case, Caché acts as the ActiveX server. Using the Caché Activate gateway, Caché can itself control other applications using ActiveX. In this case, the applications properties and methods can be accessed and modified from Caché ObjectScript.

Visual Caché and the Caché Activate gateway

The *ActiveX Automation* mechanism can be used to remote control components. Because this mechanism is available not only in a wide variety of development environments, but also from various scripting languages, it is eminently suitable for controlling Caché applications from scripts.

ActiveX Automation

In addition to controlling components, Active X Automation also gives access to their properties and methods, provided the component makes them available in the form of a *type library*. Development environments use this information to support the developer in using the components. For example, names of properties and methods can be selected from a list or their correct spelling and number of parameters checked.

Type library

In this chapter we demonstrate not only how ActiveX can be used to access Caché and Caché objects, but also Caché can be used to access other ActiveX components.

9.2 ActiveX Connections with Caché

The ActiveX interface provides a large palette of client applications and development tools that can be used with Caché database objects. The architecture of Caché's ActiveX interface is shown below:

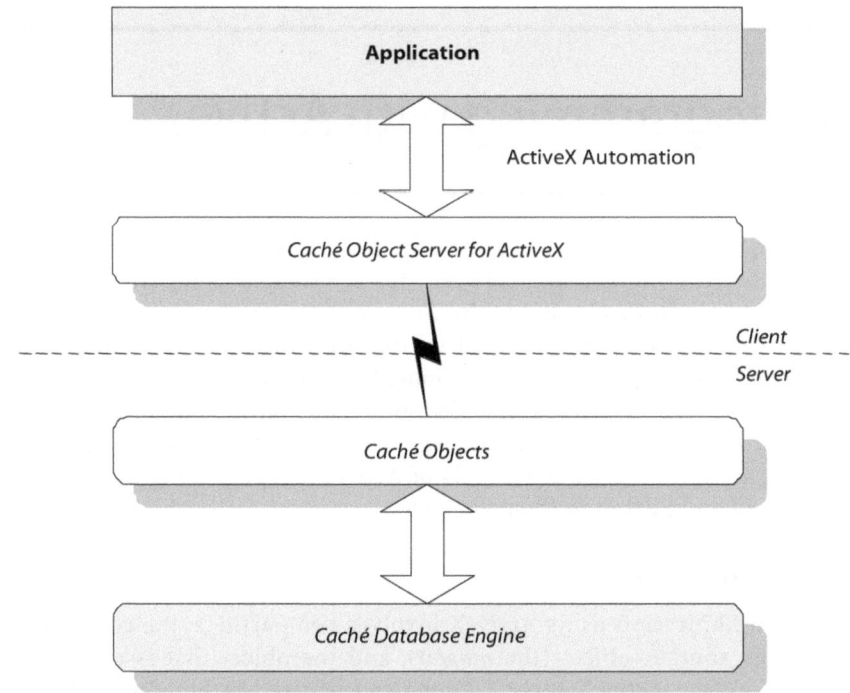

Figure 9.1 Caché Object Server
for ActiveX

ActiveX components   As the figure shows, the Caché Object Server for ActiveX is the central component for communication between applications and the Caché database. In addition, Caché Objects has other components that can be used for the development of the user interface. An overview of all components follows:

- Caché Object Server for ActiveX: This is an automation server that presents Caché objects as ActiveX objects.
- Caché Query Control: This helps in the creation of search forms for queries in Caché.
- Caché List Control: This component is a display element that presents the results of a predefined query in a tabular format. It can be used to display query results without requiring any programming.
- Caché Form Wizard: An Add-In for Microsoft Visual Basic that allows the automatic creation of forms for accessing and editing Caché object data.

9.2.1 Caché Object Server for ActiveX

Access to server based   The Caché Object Server for ActiveX is a full ActiveX Automation Server.
Caché objects   It gives client applications access to server-based Caché objects. Internally, Caché Object Server creates ActiveX objects that represent a mirror image of a Caché object of the server. Properties of Caché objects are represented as ActiveX properties and the methods correspondingly as ActiveX methods. When such an ActiveX method is invoked, its execution is internally delegated to the Caché Server.

Each Caché object on the client has a corresponding object on the server. Several client objects can have the same associated server object. In this case the object reference counter is incremented by one for each connected client object.

The Caché object on the client is an ActiveX object and refers to the relevant server object:

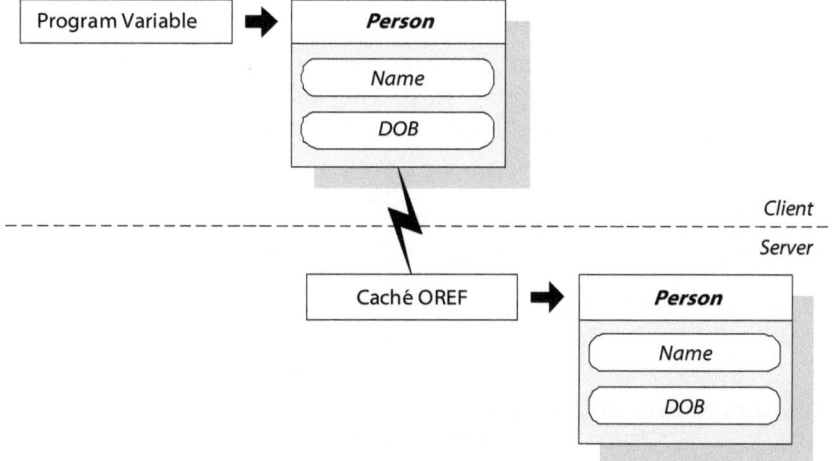

Figure 9.2 ActiveX objects and server objects

Normally all objects that can be reached using ActiveX must be registered on the system on which they are used. To do this, all information concerning an ActiveX component must be stored in the Windows system registry. The Caché Object Server spares the user the need to register each object class defined on the Caché server on each and every client system. Instead it makes the class information available at runtime and thereby makes it possible to establish large systems with many client computers, without the need to administer many registry entries.

9.2.1.1 Caché ActiveX Objects

For accessing a Caché system, Caché Object Server for ActiveX provides six classes of ActiveX objects:

- Caché ObjInstance: This class represents the control object for a Caché server object needed by the client. Each Caché server object used by a client application has an instance of the ObjInstance class.
- Caché Factory: This class is the connection to the Caché server and acts as the object factory, which the application uses to create and manage Caché objects. An application needs only a single instance of the Factory class.
- Caché ResultSet: This class manages the result sets of database queries and allows them to be easily searched and fetched.
- Caché BinaryStream: This class reads and writes large blocks of binary data to and from the database.

- Caché CharacterStream: Similar to BinaryStream, this class manages large text blocks.
- Caché SysList: This class contains functions to process data in Caché's special list format. Applications can use it to produce the Caché lists needed for method calls or to analyze the Caché list returned from methods.

9.2.1.2 First Step: JavaScript

Windows Scripting Host

Windows contains a system that can execute scripts in different languages—the Windows Scripting Host. The following example list.js shows a simple access to the Caché database from JavaScript.

```javascript
// This script lists all persons
// in the database

var factory = new ActiveXObject("CacheObject.Factory")

var connStr = factory.connectDlg();

if( connStr != "" )
{
  factory.connect( connStr );
  var rs = factory.ResultSet("User.Person", "All");
  rs.execute();

  while( rs.next() )
  {
    WScript.echo( rs.Data("Name"));
  }
}
```

This program can be started from the command line as follows (in this case, the sample file must be in the current directory):

```
C:\>cscript list.js
```

Connection dialog

A connection dialog appears where you can create or select a connection to the Caché database. A list with names then appears in the input request window. The program ends here. However, let us look in detail how the output was created:

To be able to use Caché Object Server, we must first create an instance of the Factory class; the following code is used in JavaScript:

```
Var factory = new ActiveXObject("CacheObject.Factory")
```

Connection string

In order to establish a connection, Caché Object Server needs a connection string. This string can be provided by the application or created dynamically by calling the ConnectDlg method, which lets the user select a connection. In either case, the connection string is passed to the Connect method that connects the factory with the Caché server:

```
var connStr = factory.connectDlg();
...
factory.connect( connStr );
```

The `ResultSet` function returns an empty result set for a query stored in the object class:

```
var rs = factory.ResultSet("User.Person", "All");
```

The result set is filled when we invoke the `Execute()` method. In the next step, we can loop through the result line-by-line and output each single name.

```
rs.Execute();

while( rs.Next() )
{
  WScript.echo( rs.Data("Name"));
}
```

This example shows how easy it is to create a small database application using ActiveX. The following sections describe the development of database applications with Visual Basic, where the developer can also use the other ActiveX components of Caché Objects.

9.3 Caché Objects and Visual Basic

Generally speaking, any application that supports ActiveX can easily obtain access to Caché through the Caché Object Server for Active X. However, because there are a few special tools available only for Visual Basic, we will use Visual Basic for all examples in this chapter. Caché Objects can be used from Visual Basic without requiring any further configuration. In this case, Caché Object Server is dynamically loaded and accessed. This dynamic behavior is typical when ActiveX is used in scripting languages. To try the following example under Visual Basic, start a new *Standard EXE* project and double-click the form window. Now enter the code below in the `Form_Load()` function and start the application by selecting *Start* from the *Run* menu.

Creating a new project as Standard EXE

```
Private Sub Form_Load()

  Dim connStr As String
  Dim factory As Object
  Dim rs As Object

  Set factory = CreateObject("CacheObject.Factory")

  connStr = factory.ConnectDlg

  If connStr <> "" Then
    factory.Connect connStr

    Set rs = factory.ResultSet("User.Person","All")
    rs.execute

    While (rs.Next())
      Debug.Print rs.Data("Name")
    Wend
```

```
        End If
End Sub
```

You can view the program's output, which is identical to that of the JavaScript program, by selecting the *Direct window* from the *View* menu.

9.3.1   Installing a Visual Basic Project

Early binding compared with late binding

In the previous examples, we used ActiveX Automation with *late binding*. With this procedure, the application has no information about which ActiveX server is available. Therefore all commands to be executed on the object must be sent as plain text without knowing, for example, whether the called method exists. To support the developer during the writing of programs, ActiveX offers another mode, so-called *early binding*. Here, a *type library* provides information about the methods and properties that are available in an object class. This speeds up the application because the method calls need no longer be sent as plain text. In addition, a development environment such as Visual Basic can present the developer with a list of an object's properties and methods and so help with writing the code. To do this, one must register all object classes to be used with the development environment. In Visual Basic, this is done with references to the associated ActiveX libraries.

9.3.1.1   Adding Caché Object Server to the Project References

To use early binding, the classes of the Caché Object Servers must be added to the Visual Basic Project.

1. Use the *Project|References* menu option to open the *References* window.
2. Activate the checkbox to the left of the entry `CachéObject` and, if necessary, invoke the `CacheFormWizard` (see Section 9.3.3.3).

Figure 9.3 Adding ActiveX References

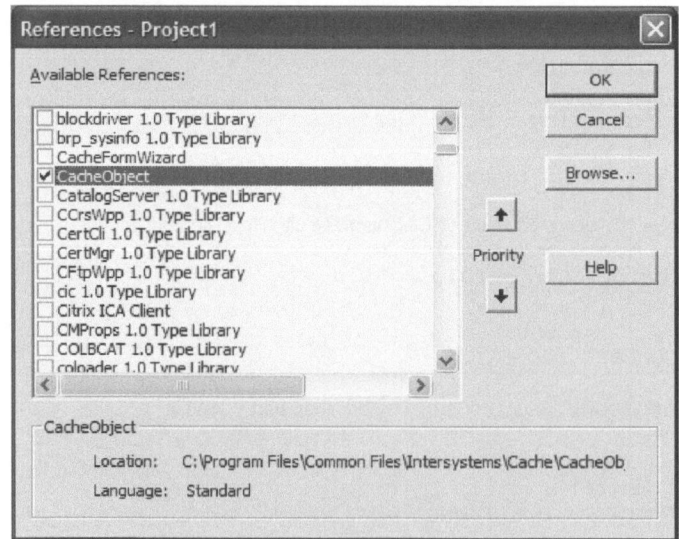

The effect of early binding is immediately visible in our example when the declaration of the `factory` variable in our example program is changed from `Object` to the correct type `CacheObject.Factory`. If you now enter `CacheObject.`, a window appears with the possible object types:

Figure 9.4 The effect of early binding

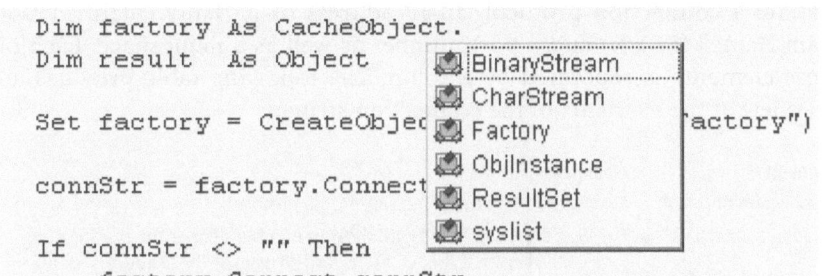

```
Dim factory As CacheObject.
Dim result  As Object              BinaryStream
                                   CharStream
Set factory = CreateObjed         Factory    actory")
                                   ObjInstance
connStr = factory.Connect         ResultSet
                                   syslist
If connStr <> "" Then
      factory Connect connStr
```

After changing the declaration as follows, the development environment will list the method and property names available for all variables.

```
Dim factory As CacheObject.Factory
Dim rs As CacheObject.ResultSet
```

Adding Caché object servers to the project reference makes the creation of objects considerably easier. The `new` operator can now be used instead of `CreateObject`:

```
Set factory = new CacheObject.Factory
```

As we have seen, adding Caché Object Server to the project references greatly simplifies working with Caché server objects.

9.3.2 Working with Caché Objects in Visual Basic

The following sections describe the most important steps necessary to work with Caché objects in Visual Basic:

- Connecting to a server
- Creating a new object instance
- Saving an object
- Opening an existing object
- Closing an active Caché object
- Using Caché objects in Visual Basic
- Executing a query from Visual Basic
- Error handling in Visual Basic

9.3.2.1 Connecting to a Server

As we saw previously, the `Factory` object must be used to create a connection before the Caché Server can be accessed. To do this, you must create a new instance of the *Factory* class using the `new` command or `CreateObject`:

```
' Use of early binding
Set factory = new CacheObject.Factory
```

```
' Use of late binding
Set factory = CreateObject("CacheObject.Factory")
```

Next, the connection must be established using the Connect() method. This method requires a connection string containing the following information: a connection protocol, an IP address or a "Fully Qualified Domain Name" (FQDN) and a port number as well as a namespace. Each of these elements is separated by a colon. The following table provides an overview of the elements of the connection string:

IP address and port number to specify the Caché Server

Table 9.1 Elements in the connection string

Element	Meaning
Connection protocol	Always cn_iptcp to indicate TCP/IP protocol.
IP address or FQDN	The IP address combined with the port number defines the specification for a Caché server. 127.0.0.1 can be used as the IP address for the local system.
Port number	The port number (usually 1972, the registered port number for InterSystems) is indicated in square brackets and immediately follows the IP address or the FQDN.
Namespace	The namespace in which the Caché object are stored. If it is omitted, the application is connected to the standard namespace (the namespace in which the server process is running).

A complete example for the connection string is:

Examples of connection strings

```
cn_iptcp:127.0.0.1[1972]:USER
```

The connection string can be coded in the application or obtained from the user by calling the Factory object's connection dialog:

Figure 9.5 The connection dialog

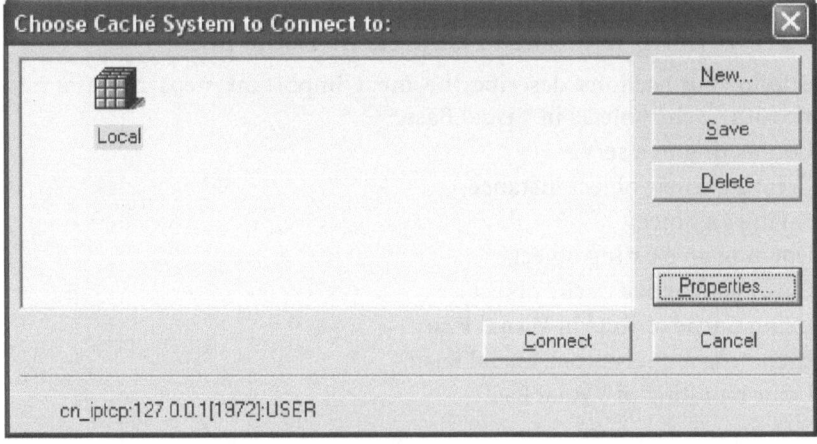

Invoking the method ConnectDlg() displays the dialog. Optionally, a non-standard window title can be set. As a result of the method call, a valid connection string is returned or the empty string if the user did not make any selection.

```
connStr = factory.ConnectDlg("Please connect me to...")
```

The following example shows a possible implementation of a central function that manages the Factory object of a Visual Basic application (the Visual Basic application establishes a connection to the Caché server when needed):

```
Dim factory As CacheObject.Factory

Private Function getFactory() As CacheObject.Factory

   Dim connStr As String
   Dim success As Boolean

   ' Creates an instance of the Factory object
   ' To allocate a object value, "Set" must be used

   If factory Is nothing Then
     Set factory = CreateObject("CacheObject.Factory")
   End If

   ' If no connection to the server exists, establish one
   If Not factory.IsConnected() Then
     ' The string with the connection parameter can be
     ' explicitly specified:
     connStr = "cn_iptcp:127.0.0.1[1972]:USER"

     ' Alternatively a pop-up dialog box can be used
     ' This method returns the connection string
     connStr = factory.ConnectDlg()

     success = factory.Connect(connStr)
   End If

   Set getFactory = factory
End Function
```

You can use the `IsConnected()` method to check whether a factory object is connected to a Caché Server. This method returns `true` if a connection has been established.

The Caché factory object creates a connection to the server when the `Connect()` method is called as follows:

```
success = factory.Connect(connectstring)
```

The return value of `Connect()` is `true` if a connection to the server has been established; otherwise, the `false` value is returned.

9.3.2.2 Creating a New Object Instance

The `New()` method of the Caché factory object creates a new instance of any Caché object:

```
Dim person As Object
Set person = factory.New("User.Person")
```

The name of the Caché class for which a new instance is to be created is specified as an argument of the `New()` method. `New()` performs the following actions:

Complete VB example for the connection development

New() method of the Caché Factory object

- It creates a new instance of the specified class on the server. This is equivalent to the Caché call ##class(User.Person).%New(). It returns the value of this server object's OREF to the client.
- It creates a new instance of an ActiveX object on the client connected to the server object. A reference to the new ActiveX object is returned to the client application.
- If New() cannot create the object, an error is reported (refer to Section 9.3.2.8).

9.3.2.3 Saving an Object

An instance of a persistent object can be saved with its %Save() method (sys_Save in Visual Basic). The sys_Save method belongs to a Caché object, not to the Factory object:

```
Dim success As String
success = person.sys_Save
```

9.3.2.4 Opening an Existing Object

The Caché factory object's Open() method loads an existing object from the database:

```
Dim person As Object
Set person = factory.Open("User.Person", oid)
```

Open() needs two arguments

Open() has two arguments: the name of the Caché class to be opened and the OID associated with the saved object. The value for the OID is specified in Caché list format (provided the standard storage strategy was used). Open() does the following:

- It loads the object into the server's memory. This corresponds to executing ##class(User.Person).%Open(oid) in Caché. The value of the server object's OREF is returned to the client.
- It creates a new instance of an ActiveX object on the client connected to the server object. A reference to the new ActiveX object is returned to the client application.
- If Open() could not open the object, an error condition is returned (refer to Section 9.3.2.8).

OpenId() method of the Factory object

Use the OpenId() method of the Caché Factory object to open an object with a "manually" created value for the ID part of an OID:

```
Dim person As Object
Set person = factory.OpenId("User.Person", "12")
```

OpenId() uses the class name and the passed ID part to create a full OID (in this case, $ListBuild(12, "User.Person")).

9.3.2.5 Closing an Active Caché object

Objects are automatically closed by the system when they are no longer referenced. To explicitly close a reference using Visual Basic, set the variable to the `Nothing` value:

```
Set person = Nothing
```

9.3.2.6 Using Caché objects in Visual Basic

Once an instance of a Caché object has been created in Visual Basic using the `New()` or `Open()` methods of the Factory object, this instance can be used like any other object, for example to set or read the value of properties:

```
Dim name As String

name = person.Name
person.Name = name
```

The methods of an object can be called (methods are always executed on the server):

Methods are executed on the server

```
Dim age As Integer
age = person.Age()
```

Because the % character used by Caché to indicate system functions for a class is not allowed in Visual Basic, the Caché Object Server automatically replaces it with the prefix `sys_`:

Caché ObjectScript	Visual Basic	Comments
person.%Save()	person.sys_Save	Methods starting with "%"start with "sys_" in Visual Basic.

Table 9.2 Method name difference between Caché ObjectScript and Visual Basic

9.3.2.7 Executing a Query from Visual Basic

Caché contains an object-oriented interface for executing queries provided as the special result set object. Result set objects exist only temporarily on the client; they have no corresponding object instance in the Caché database. Each result set object is associated with a specific query in the Caché class definition.

Object-oriented interface for executing queries

The following example executes the `All` query in the `User.Person` class.

```
Dim Counter As Integer
Dim Columns As Integer
Dim rs As CacheObject.ResultSet
' Select query
Set rs = factory.ResultSet("User.Person", "All")

' Determine how many columns the data has
Columns = rs.GetColumnCount()
' Execute query
rs.Execute

' Loop through all columns to list their name
```

259

```
For Counter = 1 To Columns
   Print rs.GetColumnName(Counter); Tab(20);
Next Counter
Print

' Loop through all rows returned
While rs.Next()
   For Counter = 1 To Columns
      Print rs.GetData(Counter); Tab(20);
   Next Counter
   Print
Wend

' Close the ResultSets
rs.Close
```

The query returns all instances of the User.Person class, assuming that the User.Person class in Caché has a query All with SQL code such as SELECT ID, Name, Firstname, DOB FROM User.Person ORDER BY Name . At the end, the result set is closed using the Close method.

9.3.2.8 Error Handling in Visual Basic

Visual Basic errors

If an error condition occurs, the factory object returns a Visual Basic error. Visual Basic can use the Err object to obtain further information about the error.

```
Private Sub OpenObject(oid As String)
   ' set up error handling
   On Error GoTo error_trap:

   ' Try to open a nonexistent object
   Dim person As Object
   Set person = Factory.Open("User.Person", oid)
   Exit Sub

error_trap:
   ' error handling (display error in a dialogbox)
   Dim ErrMsg As String
   ErrMsg = Err.Number & " : " & Err.Description
   MsgBox ErrMsg, vbCritical, Err.Source

End Sub
```

There are three categories of Caché errors in ActiveX:

Table 9.3 ActiveX error codes

Error code	Description
9990	An error occurred during the attempt to create an object. The most common reason is that the class to be accessed does not exist in the given namespace of the server.
9991	An error occurred in Caché.
9992	A method with a return type of %Status has returned a status code of false.

9.3.3 Graphic User Interfaces with Visual Caché

There are other Caché ActiveX components that help you create user interfaces. To use the control elements of Visual Caché, they first must be added as components to the project.

1. Select the *Components* option from the *Project* menu to open the dialog box shown below.
2. Activate the checkboxes next to the following selections:
   - CachéList ActiveX Control Module
   - CachéQuery ActiveX Control Module.

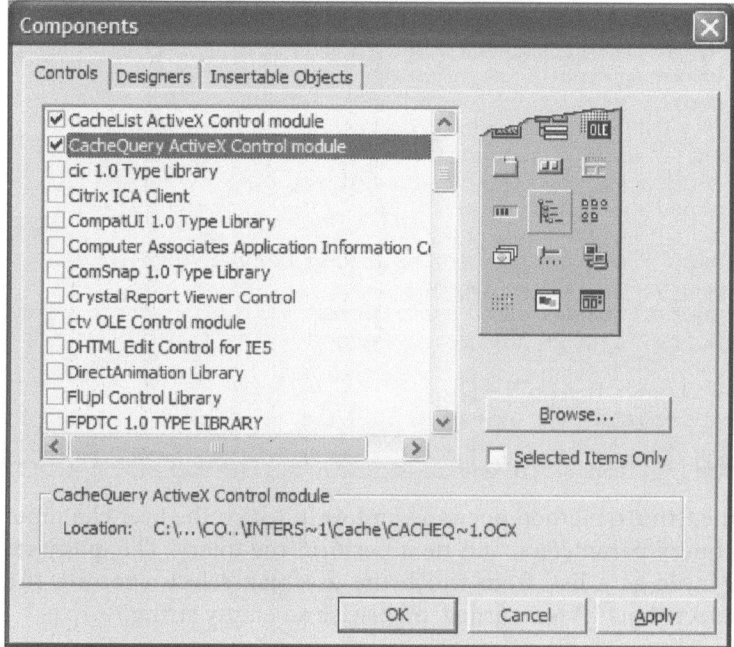

Figure 9.6 Selecting ActiveX components

The toolbar now contains these new icons:

  CacheQuery ActiveX Control Module

  CacheList ActiveX Control Module

9.3.3.1 The CacheQuery Control

The CacheQuery control offers an easy way to create fast and powerful search forms for a precompiled query in Caché. To use the CacheQuery control, a corresponding control element must be created on a form. This symbol is visible only at design time and disappears during program execution. The required parameters must be set before the CacheQuery control can be used.

Creating search forms for a query

The properties can be set either during the development phase using the property editor or during program execution with program code. The mandatory parameters for the CacheQuery control are:

- Class name
- Query name
- Factory

In addition to these parameters, the execution requires an active connection to a Caché server. This uses the familiar Factory object to which the CacheQuery object is connected by setting its property Factory.

Let us assume that there is a CacheQuery control on the form called cacheQuery. The query window called with the following code prompts the user to select a person object from the list:

```
Dim Factory As New CacheObject.Factory
Dim connStr As String
Dim idPerson As String

' as always, create a connection...
connStr = Factory.ConnectDlg("Connecting...")
factory.Connect connStr

' The necessary properties of the CacheQuery control
Set cacheQuery.Factory = factory
Set cacheQuery.ClassName = "User.Person"
Set cacheQuery.Title = "Select a Person"

' Show the Query Dialog
idPerson = cacheQuery.FindId

MsgBox "The following ID was selected: " & idPerson
```

Invoking the FindId method opens a window in which the user can input or change query parameters, and then perform the query. The query result is displayed as a list, from which the user can select a record. If a record is selected, its ID is returned, otherwise an empty string.

Figure 9.7 The CacheQuery control in action

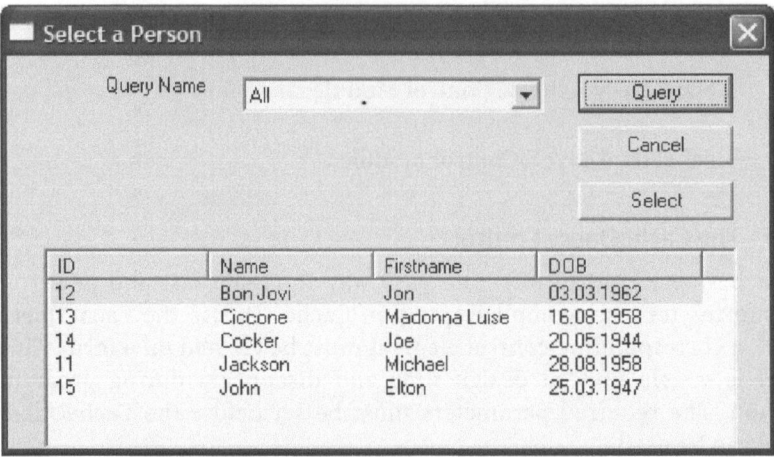

9.3.3.2 The CacheList Control

The additional CacheList control provided for those cases where the CacheQuery control does not suffice allows a more flexible data presentation.

To use this control, you place the control element on a form and set its size as needed. Assuming that the inserted control element has the name cacheList, the following program displays a list of all persons:

```
Public Sub Form_Load()
  Dim factory As New CacheObject.Factory
  Dim connStr As String
  Dim idPerson As String

  ' As always, establish the connection...
  connStr = factory.ConnectDlg("connecting...")
  factory.Connect connStr

  ' Set the connection of the CacheList controls
  Set cacheList.Factory = factory

  ' Display the Query dialog
  success = cacheList.ResultSet("User.Person", "All")
  cacheList.Run
End Sub
```

Sample for your own development projects

By reacting to events like OnClick, OnDblClick, OnKeyPress, and OnKey-Down, it is easy to program display and selection dialogues with individual behaviors:

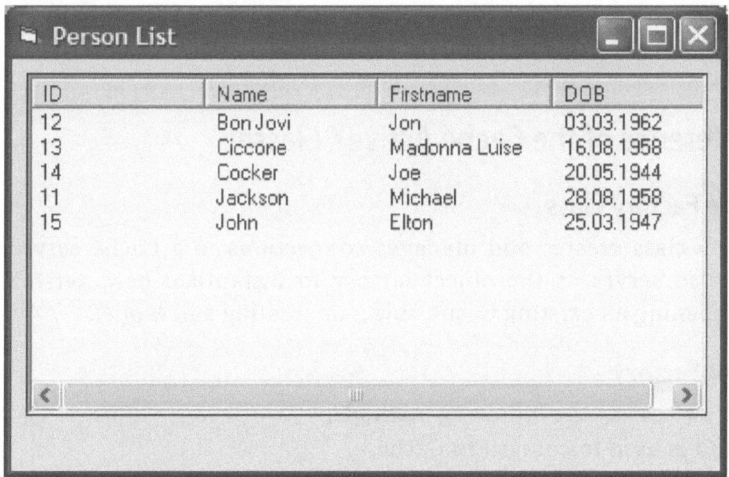

Figure 9.8 A person list created with the CacheList control

9.3.3.3 The Caché Form Wizard

The *Caché Form Wizard* is an easy-to-use Visual Basic add-in. It automatically generates Visual Basic forms that can be used to view, edit or add new instances for data stored in a Caché class. You can select the properties from the object class and its connected classes to be contained in the form as well as the queries to be used to fetch instances.

Automatically generated Visual Basic forms

The Caché Form Wizard must be loaded as a project reference (refer to Section 9.3.1.1). It is then available by selecting *Caché Form Wizard* from the *Add-Ins* menu.

The Caché Form Wizard is not only provided to create forms with little programming effort. The automatically generated Visual Basic form and code can also be examined as samples for your own development projects. Forms created by the Caché Form Wizard internally use the Caché

Object Factory to access Caché objects. With a little reworking, it can therefore be used as the foundation for more complex applications.

Figure 9.9 Form generated by the Caché Form Wizard

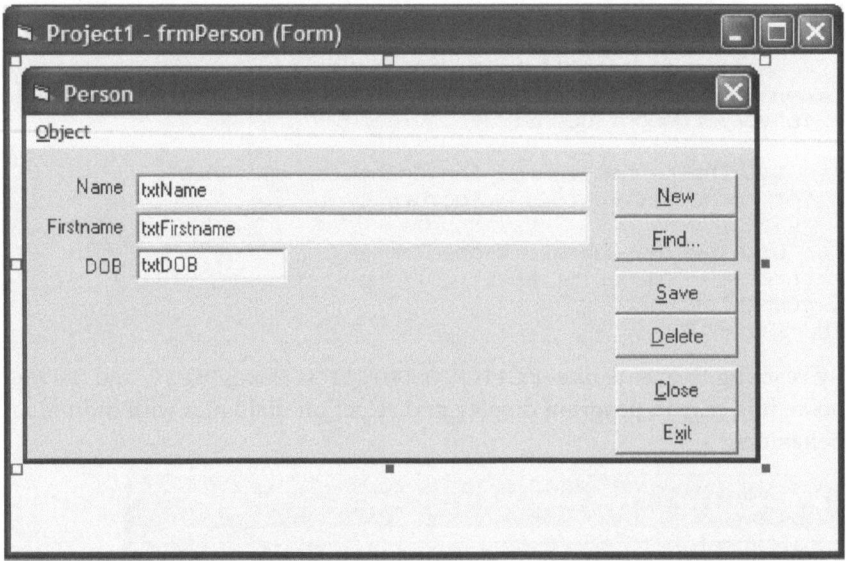

9.3.4 Reference of the Caché ActiveX Classes

9.3.4.1 The Factory Class

Creating and managing a connection to a Caché Server

The factory class creates and manages connections to a Caché server. This class also serves as the object factory to instantiate new ActiveX objects by opening an existing Caché object or creating a new one.

Elements of Factory

The factory class has the following methods:
- Connect() is used to connect to Caché,
- ConnectDlg() opens a window for the connection dialog,
- Disconnect() closes a connection to Caché,
- IsConnected() checks whether a connection exists,
- New() creates a new ActiveX object,
- Open() opens an existing object using the OID,
- OpenId() opens an existing object using the class name and the ID,
- SetLogMask() is used for debugging,
- Static() is used to execute class methods.

The Connect() method

The Connect() method of the Factory object creates a connection to the given namespace of a Caché Server. The complete syntax for Connect() is:

```
Boolean Connect(String Connectionstring)
```

An example of its use:

```
' Create a connection to a server
Dim strConn As String
Dim success As Boolean

strConn = "cn_iptcp:127.0.0.1[1972]:USER"
success = Factory.Connect(strConn)
```

We already know the format of the strConn string from previous sections.

The ConnectDlg() method

The ConnectDlg() method of a Factory object opens a window with a connection dialog. It allows the user to select a connection and returns a connection string that can be passed to the Connect() method. The complete syntax for ConnectDlg() is:

```
String ConnectDlg(String Title)
```

An example of the use of the method:

```
strConn = factory.ConnectDlg()
Dim success As Boolean
success = factory.Connect(strConn)
```

The optional Title parameter can be used to specify the window title for the connection dialog box. If it is not specified, a standard title appears.

The Disconnect() method

The Disconnect() method of a Factory object closes a connection that was previously established with Connect(). It can be used as follows:

```
factory.Disconnect
```

Before the connection is disconnected, all open objects used in the connection must be closed. If this is not the case, an error will occur indicating that there are still open references.

The IsConnected() method

The IsConnected() method returns true if a connection exists, and false if no current connection exists:

```
If Not factory.IsConnected() Then
  Dim connStr As String
  Dim success As Boolean
  connStr = "cn_iptcp:127.0.0.1[1972]:USER"
  success = factory.Connect(connStr)
End If
```

The New() method

The New() method simultaneously creates a new ActiveX object instance on the client and a corresponding Caché object instance on the server. It is used as follows:

```
Dim obj as Object
Set obj = factory.New(classname,initvalue)
```

Where *classname* is the name of a valid class on the Caché Server and *initvalue* an optional value used at the time of initialization of the new instance and passed to the %New() method of the Caché class.

The Open() method

The Open() method creates a new ActiveX object that represents the data of a corresponding object on the Caché Server. The complete syntax for Open() is:

```
Open(String classname, String OID)
```

It can be used as follows:

```
Dim obj as Object
Set obj = factory.Open(classname,oid)
```

Classname and OID

Where *classname* is a valid Caché class and *oid* is a valid OID.

This call specifies the object class twice—in its first argument and then again in the second as part of the OID. This is similar to the Caché Object-Script syntax ##class(classname).%Open(oid). The class specified in an OID can be either the same as the *classname* of the indicated class or a subclass.

The OpenId() method

The OpenId() method creates a new ActiveX object that represents the data of the corresponding Caché Object. The complete syntax for OpenId() is:

```
OpenId(String classname, String ID)
```

It can be used as follows:

```
Dim obj as Object
Set obj = factory.OpenId(classname,id)
```

Where *classname* is a valid Caché server-defined class and *id* is the ID part of a valid OID.

In contrast to Open(), the classname is specified only once. The OpenId() method can be used when the ID part of an OID is known, for example, from a ResultSet.

The Static() method

The Static() method returns a static object that can be used for executing class methods. It cannot be used to execute instance methods or access properties.

An example of its use:

```
Dim obj as Object
Set obj = factory.Static(classname)
text1.txt = obj.ClassMethod()
```

9.3.4.2 The SysList Class

Caché uses a special format for lists. Many Caché methods either return the value in $LIst format (represented by data type %List) or expect arguments to be passed to them in this format. Furthermore, OIDs are saved in this format when the standard storage strategy is used. The Visual Basic SysList class can be used to analyze or change such lists independently of the Caché Object Server.

Caché supports two formats for lists in Visual Basic: strings in $LIst format and SysList objects. Strings in $LIst format are displayed as the %String data type and handled as a unit, without allowing operations on individual elements within the list. SysList objects are displayed as %List data type and allow operations on individual elements within the list. The Get() and Set() methods can be used to convert SysList objects between the two formats.

Elements of SysList

The SysList class has the following elements:

- The Count property contains the number of elements in the list,
- the Item property contains every non-$LIst element in the list,
- the ItemList property contains every $LIst element in the list,
- the Add() method appends a new element at the end of the list,
- the Clear() method removes all elements from the list,
- the Get() method returns the internal string representation of the list,
- the Remove() method removes an element from the list,
- the Set() method assigns a string to a list object.

The Count property

The Count property of a SysList object returns the number of elements in the list. An example of its use:

```
' The FavoriteColors properties has the type %List
Dim color as CacheObject.SysList
Set color = onePerson.FavoriteColors
Dim count as Integer
count = color.Count
```

The count variable now contains the number of elements in the list.

The Item property

The Item property of a SysList object can be used to extract or set values for each element in the list. The following example shows how the list can be unpacked:

```
' MyList is a list with two elements
Dim Item1 as String
Dim Item2 as String
Item1 = MyList.Item(1)
Item2 = MyList.Item(2)
```

This method can also be used to create new or modify existing lists:

Functions to manage lists

Number of elements in a list

Extract or set the list

```
' Creating a new color list
Dim Colors as CacheObject.SysList
Set Colors = new CacheObject.SysList

Colors.Item(1) = "Red"
Colors.Item(2) = "Blue"
Colors.Item(3) = "Green"

' The FavoriteColors property has the type %List
aPerson.FavoriteColors = Colors
```

The ItemList Property

The ItemList property of a SysList object makes it possible to read or set values in a list that are themselves elements of a SysList object. For following example shows its use to unpack SysList objects embedded in other SysList object:

```
' The List colorList contains three further lists
Dim color1 as CacheObject.SysList
Dim color2 as CacheObject.SysList
Dim color3 as CacheObject.SysList

Set color1 = colorList.ItemList(1)
Set color2 = colorList.ItemList(2)
Set color3 = colorList.ItemList(3)
```

Where color1, color2, and color3 are SysList objects that can be un-packed with Item and ItemList.

ItemList can also be used to enter elements into a list:

```
' Create a new ColorList that contains the
' SysList objects color1 and color2
Dim ColorList as CacheObject.SysList

Set ColorList = new CacheObject.SysList
Set ColorList.ItemList(1) = color1
Set ColorList.ItemList(2) = color2
```

The Add() method

Adding elements at the end of the list

The Add() method adds elements at the end of the list:

```
' We use again the list colors1
colors1.Add("yellow")
' If yellow is added at the end of the list, it becomes the
fourth element in this list.
Dim Color4 as String

Color4 = color1.Item(4)
' Color4 has the value "yellow"
```

The Clear() method

Removing all elements from a SysList object

The Clear() method removes all elements from a SysList object:

```
' Remove the data from SysList object color1
color1.Clear()
' color1 is now an empty SysList object.
```

The Get() method

The `Get()` method is used to convert a Caché list into a string. It is used as follows:

```
' We use again the color list
Dim colorString as String
colorString = color1.Get()
```

The Remove() method

The `Remove()` method removes an element from the list. The empty space is then filled by moving up the successive list elements. For example:

```
' And again the list color1 with the elements
' Red, Blue, Green and Yellow

colors1.Remove(2)

' This call removes blue from the list and makes green the
second and yellow the third element in the list
Dim color1 as String
Dim color2 as String
Dim color3 as String

color1 = colors1.Item(1)
color2 = colors1.Item(2)
color3 = colors1.Item(3)

' color1 is red, color2 is green, color3 is yellow
```

The Set() method

The `Set()` method is used to convert a string in `$LIst` format into a Caché list. It is used as follows:

```
' x is a string

Dim NewList as CacheObject.SysList
Set NewList = new CacheObject.SysList
NewList.Set(x)
```

9.3.4.3 The ResultSet Class

Caché provides the special class `ResultSet` as an interface for executing predefined queries. Each `ResultSet` object is connected to a specific query from the Caché class definition.

A single `ResultSet` object controls the execution of a query and is also used to examine its results.

Elements of ResultSet

The `ResultSet` class has the following elements:

- The `GetParamCount()` method returns the number of possible parameters in a query,
- the `GetParamName()` method returns the name of a specific parameter,

Converting a Caché list into a string

Removing an element from the list

Converting a string into a Caché list

Executing a query and examining the result

- the `Execute()` method executes the query to which the `ResultSet` object refers,
- the `GetColumnCount()` method returns the number of the columns in a result set,
- the `GetColumnName()` method returns the name of a column,
- the `Next()` method accesses the next row with data,
- the `GetData()` method returns the data of the referenced column,
- the `Close()` method closes a result set.

The GetParamCount method

Maximum number of parameters

The `GetParamCount()` method returns the maximum number of parameters expected by the query. The complete syntax of this method is:

```
Short GetParamCount()
```

An example of its use:

```
Dim Args As Integer
Set rs = factory.ResultSet("User.Person", "All")

' How many parameters are allowed for this query?
Params = rs.GetParamCount()
```

The GetParamName method

The `GetParamName()` method returns the name of a parameter at the specified position. The complete syntax for `GetParamName()` is:

```
String GetParamName(Short ParamNumber)
```

The following example uses the positions of the parameters in the parameter list as argument to retrieve the associated parameter name:

```
Dim Args As Int
Set rs = factory.ResultSet("User.Person", "All")

' How many arguments are allowed for this query?
Args = rs.GetParamCount()
Dim i as Integer

For i = 1 To Args
  Print rs.GetParamName(i)
Next i
```

The Execute() method

Executing the query

The `Execute()` method of a ResultSet object executes the query that was specified when the object was created. All specifiedparameters are passed to the query:

```
Dim rs As CacheObject.ResultSet
Set rs = factory.ResultSet("User.Person", "All")

' Execute the query now
' This query returns all persons
rs.Execute
```

The GetColumnCount() method

The `GetColumnCount()` method returns the number of columns in the result set.

```
' assuming the ByName has four columns

Dim Columns as Integer

Columns = rs.GetColumnCount()
' Columns = 4
```

The GetColumnName() method

The `GetColumnName()` method returns the column name.

```
' assuming column 2 is "Name"

Dim ColumnName as String
ColumnName = rs.GetColumnName(2)
' ColumnName has the value "Name"
```

The Next() method

The `Next()` method positions the pointer to the next row with data. It returns `true` if further rows in the result set contain data, otherwise `false`. The `Next()` method must be called once to position the first row with data before the `GetData()` method can be used. Typically both methods are combined in a loop, as shown below:

```
While rs.Next()

    ' Loop over all columns of a row

    For Counter = 1 To Columns
        Print rs.GetData(Counter)
    Next Counter
Wend
```

The GetData() method

The `GetData()` method returns the data for the current row. Its use has been seen in the previous example.

The Close() method

The `Close()` method closes the result set if it is no longer needed. It is used as follows:

```
rs.Close
' rs contains now no data of the previous query
```

9.3.4.4 The BinaryStream and CharStream Classes

The special `BinaryStream` and `CharStream` objects provide an ActiveX interface for the use of streams (BLOBs). Each of these objects is connected with a specific stream type in Caché.

Elements of BinaryStream and CharStream

The BinaryStream and CharStream classes have the following elements:

- The Data property contains the stream data,
- the Oref property is for internal use by Caché,
- the FileRead() method reads data from a file,
- the FileWrite() method writes data into a file,
- the GetPicture() method delivers data from a binary stream ready for use as a Visual Basic picture object,
- the Read() method reads data from a stream,
- the Rewind() method sets the read/write pointer back to the beginning of the stream,
- the SetPicture() method stores the contents of a Visual Basic picture object in a binary stream,
- the Write() method writes data to a stream.

The Data property

Stream data

The Data property contains the complete stream data. An example of its use:

```
' Assuming person has a property Picture,
' which is defined as a binary stream.

string = person.Picture.Data
' string now contains the binary data of the picture
```

The FileRead() method

Reading a file as a stream

The FileRead() method reads an operating system file and converts it into a stream. An example of its use:

```
' Assuming, person has a property Picture,
' which is defined as a binary stream.
person.Picture.FileRead("c:\My Files\photo.Jpg")
```

The FileWrite() method

Saving a stream as a file

The FileWrite() method saves the content of a stream into a file at the operating system level. An example of its use:

```
' Assuming Person has a property Memo,
' which is defined as a Character Stream.

Person.Memo.FileWrite("c:\own data\memo.txt")
```

The GetPicture() method

Picture object of Visual Basic

The GetPicture() method is available only for streams of the *binary stream* type. It prepares the stream's data so they are suitable for use in a Visual Basic picture object. The following example shows the principle:

```
' Assuming person has a Picture property,
' which is defined as a binary stream.

Set Photo.Picture=person.Picture.GetPicture
```

The Read() method

The `Read()` method reads the specified number of characters or bytes from the stream and delivers them as its return value. An example of its use:

```
' Assuming person has a property Memo,
' which is defined as a character stream.
' Read 100 characters of text
Text1.Text=person.Memo.Read(100)
```

The Rewind() method

The `Rewind()` method moves the read/write pointer back to the start of the stream. The following example illustrates its use:

```
' Assuming person has a Memo property,
' which is defined as a character stream.
' Back to the start of the stream
Person.Memo.Rewind
```

The SetPicture() method

The `SetPicture()` method is available only for b*inary streams*. It saves the data of a Visual Basic picture object into a stream. The following example shows its use:

```
' Assuming person has a property Picture,
' which is defined as a binary stream.

Set pic = Photo.Picture
person.Picture.SetPicture pic
```

The Write() method

The `Write()` method writes data into a stream. It is used as follows:

```
' Assuming person has a Memo property,
' which is defined as a character stream.

person.Memo.Write(data)
```

9.3.5 Caché ActiveX Controls Reference

9.3.5.1 The CacheList Control

The CacheList control is a control element used to display query results. The control has a result memory that can be filled in one or more consecutive query executions. This gives the user maximum control over the displayed data.

Elements of the CacheList control

The CacheList control has the following elements:

- The `MinToDisplay` property sets the minimum number of rows to be displayed,

- the `MaxToDisplay` property sets the maximum number of rows to be displayed,
- the `Factory` property contains the Factory object that manages the Caché connection,
- the `HideId` property controls whether or not an ID column is to be displayed,
- the `HideSelection` property controls the behavior of the list when the focus changes,
- the `HideColumnHeaders` property controls whether or not the column headers are to be displayed,
- the `Connect()` method initiates a connection to the Caché Server,
- the `Clear()` method clears the display area of the controls,
- the `ClearData()` method deletes the data in the result memory of the CacheList control,
- the `GetData()` method determines the value of a row using the column and row index,
- the `GetDataByName()` method determines the value of a cell using the row index and column name,
- the `GetSelectedIndex()` method returns the index of the selected row,
- the `SetAlignment()` method sets the alignment of a column,
- the `SetColumnWidth()` method sets the width of a column,
- the `ResultSet()` method binds a compiled query to the control element,
- the `Run()` method executes the selected query,
- the `GetColumnCount()` method returns the number of result columns,
- the `GetColumnName()` method returns the name of a result column,
- the `GetColumnHeader()` method returns the name of a result column header,
- the `GetParamCount()` method determines the number of query parameters,
- the `GetParamName()` method returns the name of a query parameter,
- the `GetIndexCount()` method determines the number of rows in the result memory,
- the `AutosizeColumnByHeader()` method sets the column width based on the column header,
- the `AutosizeColumnByData()` method sets the column width determined by the contained data,
- the `GetIdColumn()` method returns the index of the ID column,
- the `DynamicSQL()` method prepares a dynamic SQL query for execution.

The MinToDisplay property

Number of rows to display   The `MinToDisplay` property determines the minimum number of rows to be displayed.

The MaxToDisplay property

The MaxToDisplay property determines the maximum number of rows to be displayed.

The Factory property

This property contains the Factory object for the current connection to the Caché Server. It can be read as well as written, for example, to reuse a connection established with the Connect() method in your own code (refer to Section 9.3.4.1).

The HideColumnHeaders property

When this property is set to true, column headers will not be displayed.

Suppressing column headers

```
' Display column headers
cacheList.HideColumnHeaders = false
```

The HideId property

When this property is set to true, the ID column will not be displayed.

Displaying the ID column

```
' The user should not see the ID column
cacheList.HideId = true
```

The HideSelection property

This property controls whether a selected row stays marked even if the CacheList control element loses its input focus:

```
' Selected elements should stay selected if focus gets lost
cacheList.HideSelection = false
```

The Connect() method

The Connect() method establishes a connection to the Caché Server. It is equivalent to the Connect() method of the Factory object (refer to Section 9.3.4.1).

The ClearData() method

The results of queries executed using Run() are always appended to the data already present in the result memory. To delete this list, use the ClearData() method that deletes the internal result memory of the CacheList control.

Deleting result memory

```
' Empty the result memory...
cacheList.ClearData

' ...and fill with new queries
cacheList.Run "Jack"
```

The Clear() method

This method deletes the display area of the CacheList control.

Clearing the display

```
cacheListe.Clear
```

Neither the data in the database nor the instances of objects created in memory are changed.

The GetData() method

The `GetData()` method returns the value of a single cell in the result memory. The desired cell can be addressed by specifying the row and column indexes:

```
' What is in the 2nd row in the 3rd column?
value = cacheList.GetData(2,3)
```

The GetDataByName() method

The `GetDataByName()` method returns the value of a single cell in the result memory using the column's name:

```
' What is in the 2nd Row in "Name" column?
value = cacheList.GetDataByName(2, "Name")
```

The GetSelectedIndex() method

Currently selected row

The `GetSelectedIndex()` method returns the row index of the currently selected row. After executing a query, the first row of the newly returned data is selected.

The SetAlignment() method

Column alignment

This method controls the horizontal alignment of the contents of a column. The contents can be aligned left, right, or centered.

```
' Selecting a column's alignment
'    0 = left (default)
'    1 = right
'    2 = center

' Sets the 2nd column to be right aligned
cacheList.SetAlignment 2, 1
```

The SetColumnWidth() method

Column width

This method changes the width of a column:

```
' Sets width of the first column to 20 twips
cacheList.SetColumnWidth 1, 20
```

The ResultSet() method

The `ResultSet()` method selects a precompiled query for execution using the `Run()` method. Both the class containing the query and the name of the query must be specified.

```
Boolean ResultSet(String Classname, String QueryName)
```

The `All` of the `User.Person` class query can be selected as follows:

```
Dim found As Boolean

' Prepare the compiled query
found = cacheList.Resultset("User.Person","All")
```

The Run() method

Once a precompiled or dynamical query is selected, it can be executed with the Run() method. Any necessary query parameters are specified as arguments of the Run() method. The query result is then appended to the result memory of the CacheList control:

```
Dim found As Boolean

' Prepare the compiled query
found = cacheList.Resultset "User.Person","All"
  cacheList.Run
end if
```

The GetColumnCount() method

The GetColumnCount() method returns the number of result columns. In connection with our previous example, it has the following form:

```
Dim columns As Integer

columns = cacheList.GetColumnCount
```

The GetColumnName() method

This method returns the name of a column specified by its column index:

```
Dim columns As Integer
Dim column As Integer

' We output a list of column names
columns = cacheList.GetColumnCount

For column = 1 to columns
   Print cacheList.GetColumnName(column)
Next column
```

The GetColumnHeader() method

This method is functionally identical to the previously described GetColumnName() method.

The GetParamCount() method

This method returns the number of required parameters required by a query. This is particularly useful when working with dynamic SQL queries.

The GetParamName() method

This method returns the name of a query parameter:

```
Dim params As Integer
Dim param As Integer

cacheList.ResultSet "User.Person", "All"

' We write out a list of the parameter names
params = cacheList.GetParamCount
```

```
For param = 1 to params
   Print cacheList. GetParamName(param)
Next param
```

The GetIndexCount() method

Number of rows

This method returns the number of rows in the result memory.

```
' How many rows do we have?
rows  = cacheListe.GetIndexCount
```

The AutosizeColumnByHeader() method

This method sets the width of the column so that the complete column header is displayed:

```
Dim columns As Integer
Dim column As Integer

' Autosize each column by its header
columns = cacheList.GetColumnCount

For column = 1 to columns
   Print cacheList.AutosizeColumnByHeader(column)
Next column
```

The AutosizeColumnByData() method

This method works similarly to `AutosizeColumnByHeader()`, except that the width of the column is determined so that all the values are completely visible.

The GetIdColumn() method

Determining the ID column

This method returns the column index of the ID column in the result memory:

```
Dim idColumn As Integer

idColumn = cacheList.GetIdColumn
```

The DynamicSQL() method

Dynamic SQL query

This method prepares a dynamic SQL query for execution. Placeholders can be used for query parameters; they are marked in the SQL text with question marks (?):

```
Dim valid As Boolean

' Prepare the query...
valid = cacheList.DynamicSQL("SELECT ID, Name
         FROM User.Person WHERE Name %STARTSWITH ?")

if valid = true then
   cacheList.Run "Kü"
end if
```

9.3.5.2 The CacheQuery Control

The CacheQuery control makes it easy to develop sophisticated selection windows that can be filled with the result of object queries and presented to the user to select individual records.

Elements of the CacheQuery control

The CacheQuery control contains the following elements:

* The MaxToDisplay property sets the maximum number of rows to be displayed,
* the Factory property contains the Factory object with the connection to Caché,
* the HideId property controls whether or not the ID column is displayed,
* the HideSelection property controls the behavior of the list if the focus changes,
* the ClassName property sets the name of the class that contains the query to be executed,
* the QueryName property sets the name of the query to be executed,
* the QuerySelection property shows whether the user can select from the available queries,
* the Title property sets the window title,
* the WaitForUserInput property controls whether the query is to be executed before it is displayed,
* the FindId() method calls the query window and returns the user-selected ID,
* the SetParam() method sets a query parameter.

The MaxToDisplay property

The MaxToDisplay property returns the maximum number of rows to be displayed.

Number of rows to display

The Factory property

This property contains the Factory object for the current connection to the Caché server. This property must be set before invoking FindId() (refer to Section 9.3.4.1):

```
' Establish the
factory.Connect(connStr) connection

' and add it to the CacheQuery control
Set cacheQuery.Factory = factory
```

The HideId property

Setting this property to true suppresses the display of the ID column.

Displaying the ID column

```
' The user should not see the ID column
cacheQuery.HideId = true
```

The HideSelection property

This property controls whether a selected row stays marked even if the CacheQuery control element loses its focus:

```
' Selected rows should stay selected even if focus is lost
cacheQuery.HideSelection = false
```

The ClassName property

Class name of query

Specifies the originating class for the query:

```
cacheQuery.ClassName = "User.Person"
```

The QueryName property

Query name

Determines the query to be executed.

```
cacheQuery.QueryName = "All"
```

The QuerySelection property

Query selectable by user

Determines whether the user is presented with a list of all queries from which the required class is to be selected:

```
' The user can select query
cacheQuery.QuerySelection = true
```

The Title property

Sets the title of the query window:

```
' The user should read this:
cacheQuery.Title = "Please select a person:"
```

The WaitForUserinput property

Immediately executing a query

Determines whether the query is to be executed immediately using the preset parameter values so that the query results are displayed when the window opens:

```
' The list should be filled:
cacheQuery.WaitForUserInput = false
```

Otherwise the user must explicit invoke the query by pressing the corresponding button.

The SetParam() method

Supplying parameters with values

The SetParam() method is used to set parameter values before the query is invoked by FindId. If the query is to be executed when the window is displayed (WaitForUserInput = false), the parameters must be set before calling FindId() otherwise their default values will be used.

The FindId() method

Executing the query

This method opens the query window, executes the query to fill the list if WaitForUserInput = false, and waits for the user to select an object from the list or terminate the operation. In the last case, the FindId() method returns an empty string, otherwise the ID of the selected object:

```
set cacheQuery.Factory = factory

cacheQuery.ClassName = "User.Person"
cacheQuery.QueryName = "All"
 cacheQuery.WaitForUserInput = false

Dim id As String
id = cacheQuery.FindId
```

9.4 Accessing ActiveX Server with Caché Activate

As described in the overview, Caché can also control other ActiveX components. The following example shows how Internet Explorer can be controlled by Caché.

Example for controlling ActiveX components

9.4.1 Creating the ActiveX Classes

To access the classes of an ActiveX component, Cache must first create the wrapper classes that represent the properties and methods of the corresponding class in the ActiveX component. The *Caché Activate Wizard* helps by determining the methods and properties of the ActiveX *type-library* and creating the necessary classes directly in Caché.

Type library

You can start the wizard by selecting the *Activate Wizard...* option from the *Tools* menu in Caché Studio. After a welcome screen, which can be skipped, a list appears with all components registered in the system that can be controlled using ActiveX automation.

Check the name of the ActiveX type library on which you wish to work. You must also specify the name of the package under which the classes will be created.

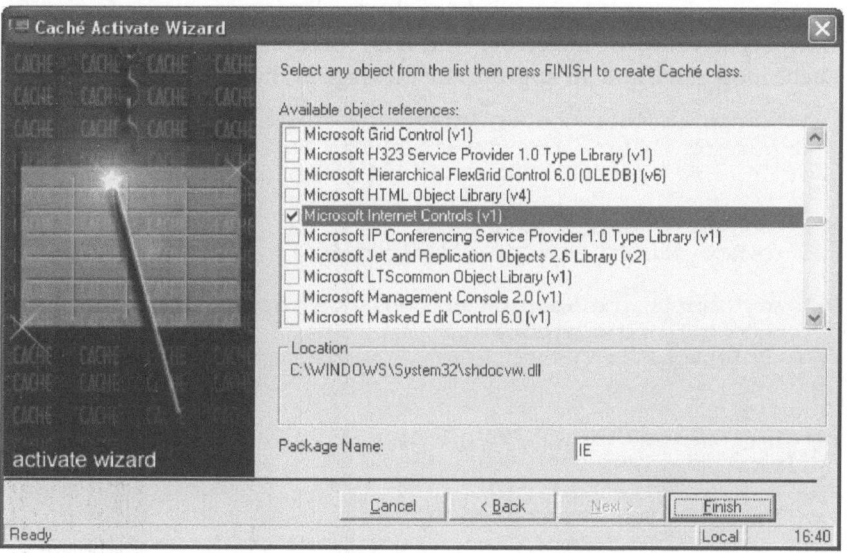

Figure 9.10 The Caché Activate Wizard

If your input is correct, click *Finish* to start the wizard. The wizard reads the information from the library and creates the needed classes.

Figure 9.11 Successful result of the Caché Activate Wizard

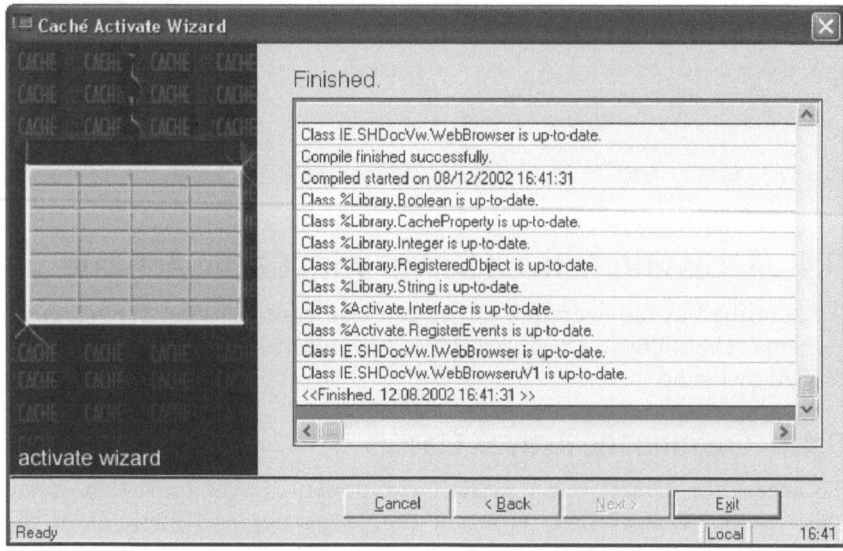

The creation of the wrapper classes is now complete, and you can begin with the ActiveX programming from Caché.

9.4.2 Programming with ActiveX Components

Calling an URL in Internet Explorer

The following small Caché program uses the previously created classes to create an object reference to Internet Explorer and calls its Navigate() method to load an Internet address.

While the Web page loads, the Busy property of the Internet Explorer object is true and the Caché program simply outputs dots to the screen. As soon as the page has loaded (or the loading process terminates, for example, because of an error), the Busy property becomes false, the Caché loop ends, and an appropriate message is shown.

```
/* Create an instance of Internet Explorer,
   by instantiating the generated Caché class */
Set ie = ##class(IE.SHDocVw.InternetExplorer).%New()

// Load an Internet page
Do ie.Navigate("http://www.synerva.de")

/* Wait until the loading process has completed,
   meanwhile output dots (.)  */
WHILE ie.Busy
{
  Write "."
}
Write !

// Then display Internet Explorer.
Set ie.Visible = 1
```

10 Object Interaction with Java

In addition to the platform-independent development of user interfaces, Java is also increasingly being used for the development of application logic (refer to Eckel [1998].) Caché's Java binding permits developers to write complex transaction processing applications in Java that work with a Caché database server.

The developer can choose between objects whose behavior is completely application controlled, and persistent objects, so-called *Entity-Beans*, which are managed through an Enterprise JavaBeans container such as JBoss or BEA WebLogic. In both cases, Caché's Java binding delivers the required classes without requiring any additional programming effort.

Java objects or EJB EntityBeans

10.1 Overview

Java clients can be connected to Caché using the Caché Object Server for Java, which automatically creates Java classes that provide transparent access to the objects of a Caché Server. In addition to object-oriented access, the Caché Java also provides relational access through JDBC to the same data. The object-oriented binding is conceptually similar to the ActiveX binding introduced in Section 9.2.

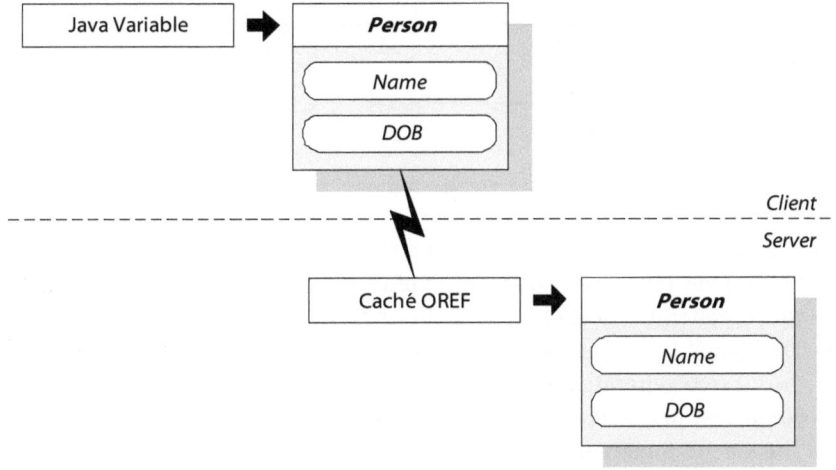

Figure 10.1 Structure of the Caché Java binding

Caché Studio can automatically create Java classes that reflect a Caché class structure in a process called projection. For the development process, this means that Java files representing the Caché classes are generated at design time and can be compiled together with the application program code. Together with the Caché Java classes, provided as a CacheDB.Jar archive, they allow Caché data to be accessed through JDBC and as objects.

Figure 10.2 Components of the Caché Java binding

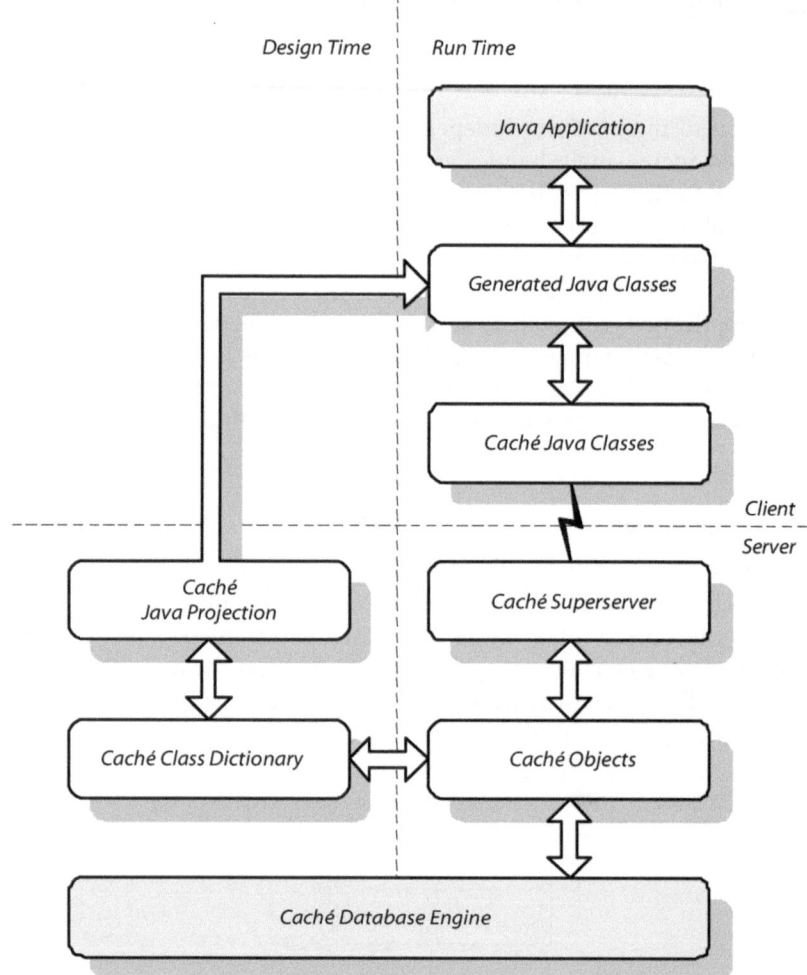

The Caché Object Server for Java consists of the following components:

- The Caché Java Projection, an extension to the Caché class compiler, which generates Java class definitions from Caché class definitions.
- The Caché Java Classes, a set of Java classes, which work together with the classes generated by the Caché Java Projection to provide transparent access to Caché database objects.
- The Caché Superserver, a powerful server component, which handles communication between Java clients and the Caché database using TCP/IP.

10.2 Creating Java Classes

Before a Caché class can be used in Java, a projection must be added to the class definition. This is done in Caché Studio similar to defining a method or property: the *New Projection Wizard* can be started by either right-clicking the source code of a class and selecting it from the context menu or by choosing *Add|New Projection Wizard* from the Class menu.

The projection is selected in the dialog box that opens. A single Caché class can have more than one projection, for example one for Java and another one for C++.

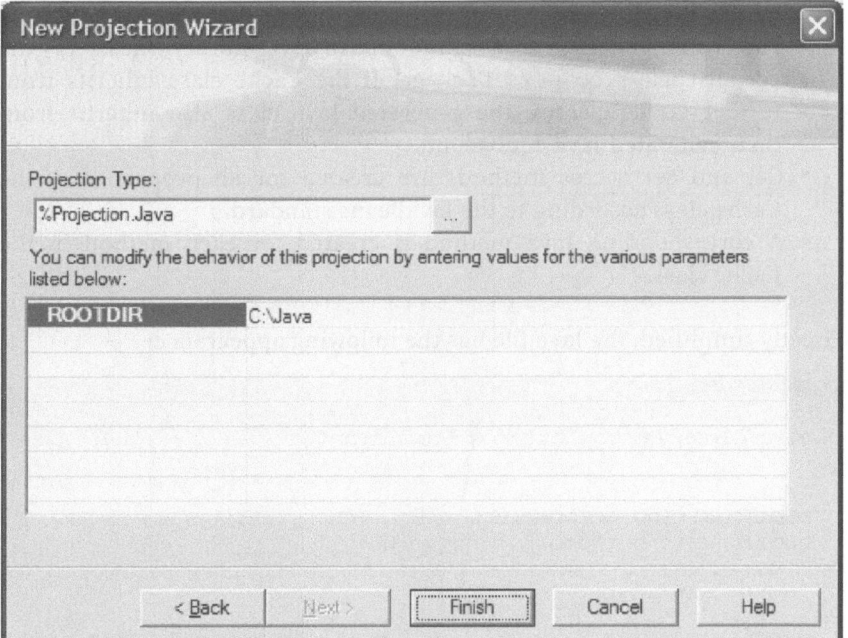

Figure 10.3 Creating a projection in Caché Studio

The projection of a class, i.e. creating files with Java source code, is controlled by a projection class in the Caché class library. Each projection of a class can use a different projection class. In addition to Java, there are projection classes for Enterprise JavaBeans and C++.

Projection classes typically have a number of class parameters that influence the projection. The %Projection.Java class must be given the name of a directory in which the Java files will be created. The generated Java class receives the package name for the Caché class that it represents.

```
Projection Test As %Projection.Java(ROOTDIR = "C:\Java");
```

The wizard finishes by adding a line to the source code of the Caché class describing the projection.

10.2.1 Structure of the Generated Java Classes

Each time the Caché class compiler compiles a class, the associated projections are automatically executed, and the generated Java files updated.

This means Java and other language bindings are always kept current when the class definition changes.

If a Caché class User.Person has a Java projection %Projection.Java with the parameter ROOTDIR = "C:\Java", the projection works as follows:

The package name becomes a subdirectory

- The package name of the Caché class becomes one or more subdirectories below the root directory specified by the ROOTDIR parameter.
- A Java file is created whose name corresponds to that of the Caché class. The following also apply:
  - The package name of the Java class also corresponds to the package name of the Caché class.
  - The class inherits from the Persistent library class in the com.intersys.objects package. If the Caché class inherits from further Caché classes, the generated Java class also inherits from their generated Java equivalent.
  - Get and Set access methods are created for all properties of the Caché class according to the JavaBeans standard.
  - A corresponding Java method is created for each method in the Caché class.

Greatly simplified, the Java file has the following appearance:

```
package User;
...
public class Person extends Persistent
{
    ...
    public String getName() ...
    public void setName(String value) ...
    ...
    public int Age() ...
    ...
}
```

10.2.2 Rules for the Caché Java Projection

The different syntax rules of Caché and Java mean several conversions take place during projection. The rules are described in the next sections.

10.2.2.1 Identifiers

% character is converted to "_"

Java identifiers are usually directly taken from Caché. The only exception is the % character often used for marking Caché system methods and properties, which is converted to the _ (underscore) symbol. The details of changes made during projections follow:

Class names

Class names usually remain unchanged. The same is true for package names, which are used for the package definition of the Java file and to build the directory path to the generated file.

The only exceptions are the classes of the Caché `%Library` system library, which are reflected in the `com.intersys.objects` package. These classes already exist in the `CacheDB.jar` library. Consequently, the created classes contain an import instruction to reference this package:

```
import com.intersys.objects.*;
```

Properties

Java property names are also taken directly from Caché; the % symbol is converted to the _ (underscore) symbol.

Two accessor methods, for reading and for writing, are created for each property. (No writing method is created for a *read-only* property.)

```
Property Name As %String;
```

becomes in the generated Java class:

```
public void setName(String value) throws CacheException
public String getName() throws CacheException
```

If the identifier corresponds to a reserved Java keyword, its name receives a prefixed _ symbol.

Reserved keyword as identifier

```
Property int As %String;
```

becomes:

```
public String get_int() throws CacheException
```

Methods

Caché methods retain their name in the Java projection. A method name that starts with the % symbol is converted to `sys_`. For example

```
Do Person.%Save()
```

becomes:

```
Person.sys_Save(int depth)
```

Formal parameter

Names of formal parameters follow the same rules as property names.

10.2.2.2 Specifying a Java Package

A package can be specified for a generated Java class. Although this is not necessary, it can sometimes make it easier to manage classes in a complex project.

The JAVAPACKAGE class parameter in the Caché class definition is used to specify a package name:

```
class User.Person
{
  Parameter JAVAPACKAGE = "cache.book.example";
  ...
}
```

Dot syntax for packages

The original package name of the class is User in this example. The added parameter makes the Java projection generate a class with the package structure cache.book.example. As the example shows, packages can contain subpackages, whose names are separated from the super packages by a dot.

Packages must be defined at the very beginning of the class definition; in other words, the JAVAPACKAGE class parameter may only be preceded by comments.

10.2.3 Caché Java Classes

Caché provides a set of Java classes that work with the classes generated by the Caché Java class generator. They provide a transparent connection to objects stored on a Caché server.

The Caché Java classes can be found in the CacheDB.jar Java archive. Amongst other, this archive contains the following classes important for the Java binding:

Table 10.1 Important Caché Java classes

Class name	Description
com.intersys.objects Database	The Database class defines the method interface to a Caché database.
com.intersys.objects CacheDatabase	The CacheDatabase class is the object factory that creates new instances of the database connection.
com.intersys.objects Persistent	Similar to the Caché class library, this is the super class of all persistent Caché classes.
com.intersys.objects CacheException	The CacheException exception is thrown when an error occurs accessing the Caché database.

Combining object access and JDBC

The Caché Java binding uniquely combines object-oriented access to object properties and methods with relational access using JDBC. For this reason, classes of Caché the object binding are closely related to the classes of the standardized JDBC framework (refer to Section 10.4.2).

10.3 Using Caché Objects and Java

The following sections show the steps required to access objects and relations in the Caché database.

10.3.1 Setting Up a Java Project

Before the Caché Object Server for Java can be used, the following path must be added to the CLASSPATH environment variable of the Java system:

```
SET Cache=C:\CacheSys
SET CLASSPATH=%Cache%\Dev\Java\Lib\CacheDB.jar;%CLASSPATH%
```

Alternatively, you can specify the path as a parameter when you start the Java Virtual Machine (JVM).

```
C:\>Java -cp %Cache%\Dev\Java\Lib\CacheDB.jar
```

10.3.2 The Caché Object Server for Java

To improve performance, Caché Java Classes implement a distributed client-side object cache. This minimizes repeated server calls with the consequent performance improvement; the actual improvement depends on the application. This *caching* is performed automatically and remains totally transparent to the developer.

Distributed object cache

10.3.3 Connecting to a Server

In order to access server objects, a Java application must first connect to the Caché server using the getDatabase() static method of the Cache-Database class:

```
// Java Code
String strCon = "Jdbc:Cache://127.0.0.1:1972/USER";
Database db = Database().getDatabase(strCon," SYSTEM","SYS");
```

The format of the connection string is the same as the one needed by a JDBC database connection. This means that it starts with Jdbc and the name of the database driver to be used, in this case Cache, separated by a colon. Similar to an Internet address, the next component is another colon and two slashes, followed by the server address and IP port to be used. Another slash follows, and finally the associated namespace.

Connection is specified by a JDBC connection URL

Element	Description
URL prefix	jdbc: and the name of the database driver: Jdbc:Cache://
IP address or FQDN	IP address and port number together form a distinct specification for a Caché server. For the local system, the special IP address 127.0.0.1. can be used.
Portnumber	The port number (normally the InterSystems registered port number 1972) is separated from IP –address or the FQDN by a colon.
Namespace	The namespace in which the Caché objects reside. If omitted, the application is connected with the standard namespace (i.e., the namespace in which the server process runs).

Table 10.2 Elements of the Java connection string

To retain compatibility with previous version, the connection string format of the ActiveX binding (refer to Section 9.3.2.1) can also be used, however, it should no longer be used.

In addition to specifying a connection string, user name, and password, the CacheDatabase class provides other means of creating a Database object. One of the most important methods is to reuse an existing JDBC connection to Caché server:

Reusing an existing JDBC connection

```
Database db = Database().getDatabase(JdbcConnection)
```

10.3.4 Creating Object Instances in Java

A new instance of a Caché object can be created from Java with the new operator and passing it a reference to an active Database object.

The Java new operator

For example, the following code establishes a connection to a Caché Server and creates a new instance of the Caché Person class:

```
String strCon = "jdbc:Cache://127.0.0.1:1972/USER";
Database db = Database().getDatabase(strCon,"_SYSTEM","SYS");
Person aPerson = new Person(db);
```

The aPerson variable now refers to a new instance of the Person class. The instance's properties are preset to the default values from the Caché class definition.

Opening an existing Caché object

In the same way, the _open() static method opens an existing Caché object. For this to occur, a valid OID of a previously saved Caché object must be specified. Alternatively, the ID of a saved object can be used. The object instance is brought into the server's memory and its OREF value returned to the Java client. Here, a new instance of the corresponding Java object is created and passed back to the server object. The Java application can work with that object just like any other Java object.

The following example illustrates this scenario:

```
String strCon = "jdbc:Cache://127.0.0.1:1972/USER";
Database db = Database().getDatabase(strCon,"_SYSTEM","SYS");

Oid oid = new Oid("1","User.Person");
Person a Person = (Person) Person._open(db, oid);
```

The following example is equivalent, but uses the ID of the saved object.

```
// id is the ID part of an OID
Id id = new Id("1");
Person a Person = (Person) Person._open(db, id);
```

10.3.5 Using Caché Objects within Java

If an instance of a Caché object has been created in Java, it can be used just as any other Java object. As mentioned previously, the Java projection mechanism creates the properties and the methods using specific rules. For example, the properties of the previously created Person class can be set and retrieved as shown in the following example:

```
String name = a Person.getName();
...
a Person.setName("Jackson");
```

Methods are executed on the Caché server

In a similar way, the methods of the Caché object can be called from Java. Methods are always executed on the Caché server:

```
int theAge = aPerson.age();
```

In Java, properties are not directly accessed but rather using generated accessor methods that ensure the data values are valid. This means that object trees stored in the database can be parsed from Java without difficultiy. References to persistent objects can be used in the same way as any regular property value:

```
name = aPerson.getFather().getName();
```

10.3.6 Multi-value Properties

Now that we have seen the use of simple properties, let us now look at multi-value properties. These, in Caché, can exist as collections (list or array) or as bidirectional relationships between persistent objects. For such properties, the projection mechanism creates accessor methods that return the corresponding value holder objects which contain the object set. A Java implementation appropriate for the set is used:

Type of object set	Projection
Array collection	Are the elements of the set... • ...Objects? → `ArrayOfObjects` • ...Literals? → `ArrayOfDataTypes`
List collection	Are the elements of the set... • ...Objects? → `ListOfObjects` • ...Literals? → `ListOfDataTypes`
One-to-many relationship	`RelationshipObject`
Parent-child relationship	`RelationshipObject`

Table 10.3 Java projection of multi-value properties

The `ArrayOfObjects` and `ArrayOfDatatypes` classes implement the `Java.util.Map` standard interface. This means they can be processed in Java as usual and converted into `Collection` objects of the Java library.

In a similar fashion, the corresponding classes for list properties, `ListOfObjects` and `ListOfDataTypes`, implement the `List` and `Collection` interfaces of the `Java.util` standard package.

Relationship properties are different; they exist as a *parent-child relationship* or as a *one-to-many relationship*. Here, the Caché `RelationshipObject` class is used, which has special methods to insert, shift, remove and count the contained objects.

Multi-value properties implement the interface of the `Java.util` package

10.3.7 Accessing Streams from Java

Caché supports the concept of streams to accommodate large blocks of unstructured data such as pictures or very long text. Depending on the content they can store, streams exist as character streams or as binary streams:

Stream content	Projection
Binary data	CacheInputStream extends java.io.InputStream CacheOutputStream extends java.io.OutputStream
Character data	CacheReader extends java.io.Reader CacheWriter extends java.io.Writer

Table 10.4 Java projection of streams

For example, the following code reads a long message from a character stream:

```
CacheReader reader = aPerson.getNote();
String line = null;

do {
  line = reader.readLine();
```

```
  if( line != null )
    System.out.println( line );

} while (line != null);
```

10.4 Queries and ResultSets

Java's JDBC framework is useful for executing queries that process objects stored in the Caché database. A predefined ResultSet object accommodates the query result and provides special functions for the processing the result data.

10.4.1 Using Queries

Execution of a Caché query returns a JDBC result set

The Java object binding contains the CacheQuery class that can be used to access queries specified in class definitions on the Caché server. This method executes a specified query and returns a JDBC ResultSet:

```
String strCon = "jdbc:Cache://127.0.0.1:1972/USER";
Database db = Database().getDatabase(strCon,"_SYSTEM","SYS");

// Open precompiled Query
CacheQuery qrq=new CacheQuery(db,"User.Person","All");

// Execution
ResultSet rs = qry.Execute();

// Release of data sets
while( rs.next() )
{
  System.out.println( rs.getString("Name"));
}
```

The close integration of object and JDBC access means a wide range of existing Java libraries and visual Java Beans can be used to display data; furthermore, a range of libraries and visual JavaBeans can be used "of the shelf" with Caché.

10.4.2 Relational Access using JDBC

Dynamic SQL queries with JDBC

As previously mentioned, JDBC and object access are very tightly connected. In the following example, a JDBC query with dynamic SQL code is used to obtain a list of objects. Each object is then immediately instantiated so that its methods can be called:

```
String strCon = "jdbc:Cache://127.0.0.1:1972/USER";
String strQuery = "SELECT ID, Name FROM User.Person";

// Here the JDBC driver is loaded.
Class.forName("com.intersys.jdbc.CacheDriver");

// Create the server connection
Connection dbconn = DriverManager.getConnection(strCon,
                                  "_SYSTEM", "sys");
// Prepare and execute the SQL statement
```

```
PreparedStatement stmt = dbconn.prepareStatement(strQuery);
ResultSet rs = stmt.executeQuery();
' Create an Object connection
Database objConn = new Database().getDatabase(dbConn);

User.Person person = zero;
String id;

// Output results
while( rs.next() )
{
  System.out.print( rs.getString("Name"));

  id = rs.getString("ID");
  person = User.Person._open(objConn, new Id(id));

  System.out.println(" Age: " + person.getAge());
}
```

Thanks to the Unified Data Architecture, we can access all data in a relational or an object-oriented way as appropriate.

10.5 Caché Object as Enterprise JavaBeans

Enterprise JavaBeans are the standard Java-based middleware created to facilitate the operation of complex, distributed Java applications.

10.5.1 Concept

A distributed application consists of three layers:

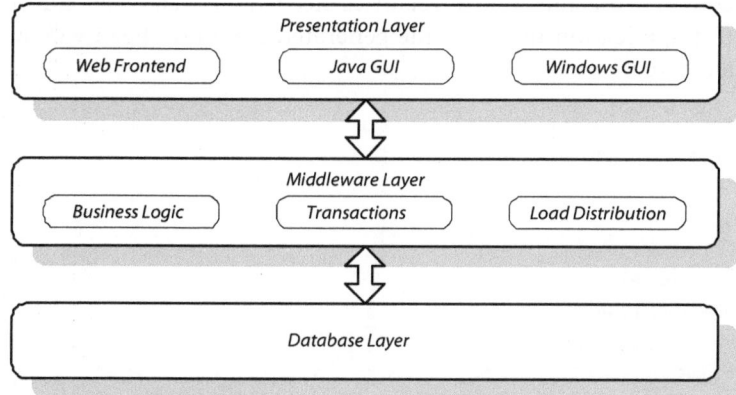

Figure 10.4 The three layers of the EJB model

As the diagram shows, the middleware is not only responsible for implementing the business logic but also for structural measures such as transaction processing and load distribution. The Enterprise JavaBeans specification defines a standard for a corresponding middleware system. One of the services an EJB-conforming middleware offers is to fetch data objects from the underlying database layer, so-called *EntityBeans*.

Caché enables the user to create EJB EntityBeans from objects defined in the Caché database. These EntityBeans are then made available by an

EJB Container. Caché automatically generates all necessary operations and implements all required interfaces in accordance with the EJB specification.

10.5.2 Projection

EJB EntityBeans are created using the previously discussed projection mechanism. For the EJB projection, the %Projection.EJB projection class (refer to Section 10.2) is used. As mentioned, this projection requires more parameters than the simple Java projection.

Creating an EJB projection

The following example shows the definition of an EJB projection for the User.Person class:

```
Projection projEJB As %Projection.EJB
(
    APPLICATIONDIR = "C:\Jdk\Jboss2.4.4\deploy",
    APPSERVERHOME = "C:\Jdk\Jboss2.4.4",
    BEANNAME = "Person",
    CACHEPATH = "C:\CacheSys\dev\Java\lib",
    CLASSLIST = "User.Person",
    CLASSPATH = ...
    DRIVERMANAGER = 0,
    JAVAHOME = "C:\JDK\JDK1.4.0",
    PACKAGE = "Example",
    PATH = "C:\Jdk\Jdk1.4.0\bin;",
    ROOTDIR = "C:\Java",
    SERVERTYPE = "JBOSS"
);
```

After compiling the class, the directory specified with the ROOTDIR parameter contains the files and directories needed to create the EJB archive. A test application that uses the generated EJB EntityBean will also have been created.

Figure 10.5 Output of the EJB projection

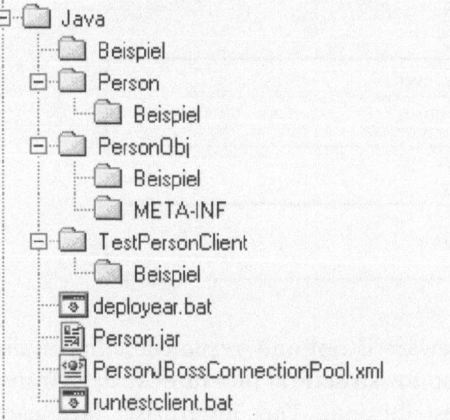

Using the generated script to deploy the EntityBeans

The deployear.bat batch program must be executed to deploy the projected EntityBean. The program compiles all Java files, bundles them with the deployment descriptor ejb-jar.xml and container-specific configuration files (such as jboss.xml or weblogic.xml) to produce a Bean archive which is then copied into the EJB container's deployment directory.

A second batch program created with the `runtestclient.bat` name executes a generated test program. This program tries to load the referenced EntityBean with the primary key 1. In addition to testing the function of the generated EntityBeans, this small application is also a good example of how to work with EntityBeans.

The EJB projection is extremely complex and requires detailed knowledge of the function and structure of Enterprise JavaBeans, and the associated EJB server. The meaning of some parameters for the EJB projection may vary slightly depending on the type of EJB container:

Parameter	Meaning
ROOTDIR	The base directory under which all files for the EJB projection are created.
SERVERTYPE	The associated EJB container. The following server types are supported: • BORLAND — Borland Application Server • WEBLOGIC — BEA WebLogic 6.x • JBOSS — Jboss • PRAMATI — Pramati Server
APPLICATIONDIR	The directory in which the generated EntityBean archive should be copied so it can be installed by the EJB server.
APPSERVERHOME	The base directory of the application server.
BEANNAME	The name of the generated EntityBean.
CACHEPATH	The directory that contains the Caché Java library CacheDB.jar.
CLASSLIST	A comma-separated list of all Caché classes that the projection is to produce.
CLASSPATH	The Java classpath to be used in the generated shell scripts.
DRIVERMANAGER	Defines whether or not the Drivermanager is to be used: 0 do not use Drivermanager 1 use Drivermanager
JAVAHOME	The base directory of the JDK installation.
PACKAGE	The package name to be used.
PATH	The path that contains the JDK tools (javac and jar).

Table 10.5 Parameters of the EJB projection

295

11 Web Programming with Caché Server Pages

11.1 Introduction

Databases have become an indispensable enabling technology for dynamic Web content, on both the Internet and company intranets (cf. Atzeni et al. [1999]). This chapter describes how Caché and a Web server can dynamically create content by retrieving up-to-date information from a database and presenting it in a browser. The base technology required to achieve this involves Caché Server Pages (CSP), which Caché has supported since version 4. CSP offers an elegant means of producing high-performance, highly scalable Web applications in a short time. They also simplify the subsequent maintenance and the further development of such applications.

Caché Server Pages (CSP)

Caché Server Pages enable the providing of dynamic Web contents depending on time, relationships within the saved data, user entries, etc., even contents that were generated coincidentally. This is based on the concept of HTML pages with specific tags that are executed on the Caché server each time the page is called and return individual content, namely the Caché Server Pages. CSP can integrate not only HTML, but also XML, images, and any other binary files.

Support for HTML, XML, pictures and other binary data

Generally, Caché Server Pages can be developed in two different ways:

- As HTML or XML files with embedded special CSP tags and other CSP language elements. Caché automatically translates such CSP files into class definitions and compiles them into executable method code when they are first called (and after any change).
- Directly as Caché classes that are subclasses of %CSP.Page. The execution logic and the required HTML or XML tags are coded in the On-Page() method.

Based on the coding approach used, the first method is also referred to as *tag-based development* and the second one as *code-based development*.

Tag- and code-based development

These two methods are favored by the two groups of developers that usually work closely together on comprehensive Web applications: the Web designers and the programmers. Whereas the Web designers who mainly take care of the pages' appearance and the Web applications' interface favor a tag-based development approach, the programmers responsible for the business logic and for providing contents from the database prefer the code-based approach.

CSP technology provides appropriate tools for both groups and guarantees their smooth interaction. While programmers create CSP classes and write business logic in Caché Studio as usual, CSP files can also be edited with any normal HTML or text editor. But above all, Web designers can continue to use their preferred design tool and just include the business logic created by the programmer. This is possible thanks to the use of standard HTML code in which special CSP tags in the style of XML extensions are directly inserted.

*CSP plug-in for
Macromedia Dreamweaver*

Caché provides a special plug-in for a design tool very popular with professional Web designers—Dreamweaver from Macromedia. Once the plug-in is installed, the special CSP tags and other CSP language elements can be inserted and managed conveniently (*Caché CSP* on the *Insert* menu).

11.2 CSP Basics

*Microsoft IIS, Apache Web Server,
and others are supported*

For a Caché server and Web server to work together, you must install an interface to Caché on the Web server. Caché provides such a Web gateway for Microsoft IIS and the Apache Web Server, among others.

Once the CSP Web gateway is installed on a Web server, it can forward Web browser requests to Caché. The gateway uses the file extension to determine whether a request is intended for the Web server itself or for Caché; requests for the files extensions .csp or .cls are forwarded to Caché.

The data forwarded by the browser is then evaluated by the Caché server. The Caché application uses this data to generate the HTML code (XML code or other data types) that is returned by the Web server for display on the browser.

Figure 11.1 Integration of Web server and database server for processing CSP pages

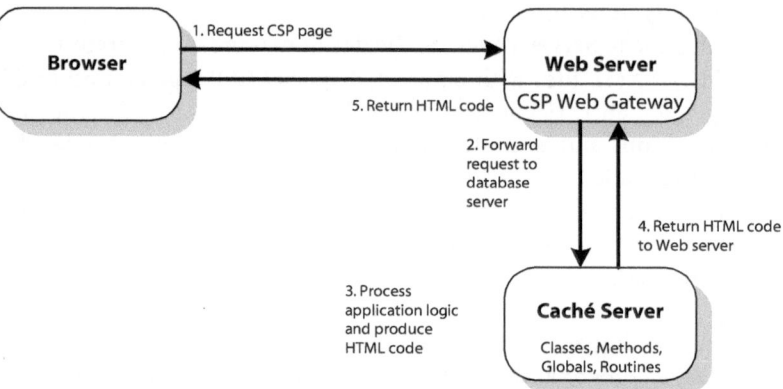

The Web server and database server can be located on the same or different machines in the network. In either case, they communicate with each other using the TCP/IP protocol. For development and test environments it is often convenient to install both servers on the same PC, and also run the browser on that machine.

Caché's own Web server

Because a Web server is not part of every development configuration, Caché comes with its own Web server. However, because, the Caché Web server implements only the minimum HTTP protocol and does not support the state-aware mode that is described later, it is meant only for test cases in a single-user environment. The Caché Web server is automatically installed during the Caché installation, and can be reached using the InterSystems port number 1972. The examples in this chapter use this configuration.

11.3 Setting Up CSP

11.3.1 Configuring CSP Web Gateway

For configurations in which a professional Web server is used instead of the built-in Caché test server, Caché includes *CSP Web Gateway Management,* a Web-based front end for configuring and setting up applications. The URL to call the start page when using the Microsoft Internet Information Server is:

```
http://localhost/csp/bin/CSPmsSys.dll
```

and

```
http://localhost/cgi-bin/nph-CSPcgiSys
```

when using the Apache server under UNIX, assuming that the Web server is on the same machine as the calling browser. (Otherwise, the name localhost must be replaced with the actual IP address of the Web server.)

Web Gateway Management allows you to configure different aspects of the connection between the Web Server and Caché. If Caché has detected a running Web server during installation, the CSP Web Gateway should have been correctly installed and have a minimum configuration. The Caché documentation contains detailed information about possible configurations; refer to the *CSP Programmer's Guide.*

Installing and managing connections between a Web Server and Caché

11.3.2 Configuring CSP

Caché itself contains several settings for CSP. These are combined in *Caché Configuration Manager* (in Caché Cube) under the *CSP* tab. One of its functions is to configure CSP applications for different namespaces.

Figure 11.2 CSP tab in Caché
Configuration Manager

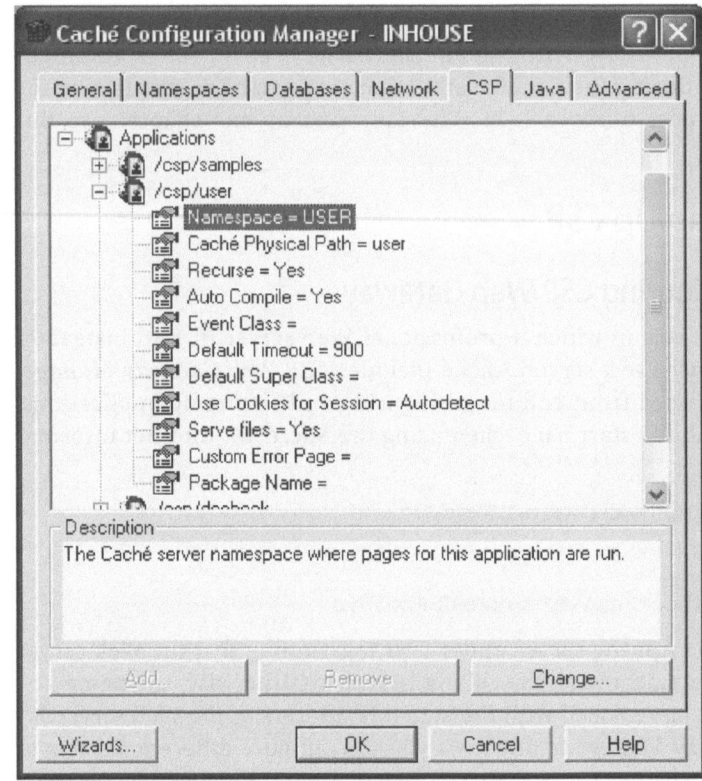

As you can see, Caché automatically assigns an application with the name
/csp/namespace to each namespace, where namespace is replaced by the
actual namespace name. You can assign other applications here; these
must be made known to the associated Web Server and connected using
the CSP Web Gateway Configuration.

Each application has a number of parameters:

Table 11.1 Properties of a CSP
application definition

Parameter	Meaning
Namespace	The namespace in which the application is to operate
Caché Physical Path	The path on which CSP files are to be physically accessed by the Caché server, either on the server itself or on a mapped network drive of the Web server
Recurse	Indicates whether subdirectories are also to be included
Auto Compile	Indicates whether changes to CSP page cause the corresponding class in the database to be recompiled automatically
Event Class	Name of the CSP class whose methods are called for certain events within the application, for example, for a timeout
Default Timeout	The time for the session timeout in seconds (for example, the value 900 means that the session is terminated when the user has not responded within 15 minutes)
Default Super Class	Super class whose properties and methods all CSP classes inherit that are automatically generated from .csp files. No entry here means that the super class is %CSP.Page
Use Cookies for Session	Indicates whether or not CSP's automatic session

	management uses cookies
Serve files	Indicates whether the Caché server should also serve static HTML pages and other files contained in the application directories (useful for graphic files, start and end page of the application, etc.)
Custom Error Page	A user-defined error page
Package Name	The package name to which the CSP classes belong. Default: csp.

Normally you set only the first two parameters; the default settings can be used for the other values. To change a parameter, double-click the corresponding line.

Default value and changing the parameter settings

11.3.3 CSP File Names, URLs and Classes

The browser requests a CSP page using an URL of the form:

```
http://<hostname>/<path>/<filename>.csp[?...]
```

`<hostname>` represents the Web server and `<path>` represents a virtual directory on this Web server that has been associated with a defined CSP application (or one of its subdirectories).

However, the `<filename>.csp` file does not need to physically exist in one of the Web server's directories. Internally, every CSP "page" corresponds to a class in the Caché database. Each of these classes can be created as usual in Caché Studio. Alternatively, it is also possible to generate and update classes dynamically. In this case, the CSP code is simply stored as a file with the extension .csp in the associated directory. The naming conventions of the corresponding operation system apply. Since a Cache class is created for each CSP page, the chosen names must also represent valid Caché class names.

Every CSP "page" corresponds internally to a class in the Caché database

The complete name of the class is created from the package name csp (or the package name specified when the CSP application was defined), the names of the subdirectories below the index path indicated for the CSP application and finally the file name (without the extension .csp). So the following URL

Forming class names from URLs

```
http://localhost:1972/csp/user/example.csp
```

results in the use of class csp.example in the USER namespace, and

```
http://localhost:1972/csp/user/Accounting/Invoice.csp
```

means that the CSP class csp.Accounting.Invoice within the same namespace is to be used.

When Caché determines (during the first call) that a page is not present as a class, Caché compiles it to produce such a class. The compilation and the storage on the database server causes all following calls of this page (class) to execute much faster than the first call. A change to the original page causes recompilation.

If a page is not yet present as a class or its content is not current, Caché compiles it automatically

The second syntax using the file extension .cls allows more flexibility in the choice of class names. The complete file name (possibly with package name) without the .cls suffix is used as the class name here.

Therefore,

```
http://localhost:1972/csp/user/User.CSPExample.cls
```

corresponds to the User.CSPExample CSP class.

Accessing static files

CSP also serves—unless this has been turned off in the application definition—static HTML pages, XML documents, images, or other data. Consequently, the URL

```
http://localhost:1972/csp/user/Bild.jpg
```

can be used to view the JPG file stored in the \CacheSys\csp\user directory.

11.4 Developing in CSP

11.4.1 The CSP Object Model

The %CSP.Page system class

CSP is completely integrated in Caché's object model. Each CSP page, whether created as a .csp file and automatically compiled or directly programmed in Caché Studio, is always a subclass of %CSP.Page. However, neither the system class itself nor the derived CSP classes are ever instantiated. This is not necessary because the complete functionality is implemented in class methods, which can be executed without instantiating the classes.

Caché automatically instantiates the other three system classes relevant for CSP and makes a corresponding object reference available to the programmer. This object reference then can be used to reference the respective instances, as shown in the following table:

Table 11.2 %CSP classes and their OREF

Class	OREF	Description
%CSP.Request	%request	Information about the HTTP method called, including passed CGI variables, form elements, and query strings.
%CSP.Session	%session	The properties of the current CSP session including application data.
%CSP.Response	%response	The properties that influence Caché's response to a Web Browser.

11.4.2 Syntax Elements in CSP Pages

Generating dynamic content for page elements

In addition to traditional HTML code, CSP pages are characterized by elements that generate dynamic content. Such dynamic data are provided as Caché objects, result sets, variables, and other elements. In addition to HTML tags, the following code elements appear in CSP pages:

- Expressions of the form #(...)# are replaced by their value at runtime during page generation.
- Expressions of the form ##(...)## are replaced by their value when the CSP class is compiled.

- CSP tags of the form `<CSP:xxx ...>` provide built-in and user-defined functionality.
- CSP attributes of the form `CSPxxx` extend HTML language elements with CSP functionality.

Executing code written in Caché ObjectScript

- Caché scripts execute code written in Caché ObjectScript to generate pages at runtime. They are enclosed within script tags of the form `<script language=cache runat=server> ... </script>`
- A further type of Caché script is executed once during the compilation of a page to store it in a database. The code is generally the same as previously; the header tag of the script has the form `<script language=cache runat=compile>`
- Page references to other CSP pages in the form `#url(...)#` or just by using the URL.
- Calls to subroutines stored on the server in the two forms `#server(...)#` and `#call(...)#`.

11.4.3 Application State Modes

Operating an application in state-aware mode

CSP allows an application to operate in *state-aware mode*. In this mode, a private session exists between the Web server and the database. The main advantage is that each user's request can be served in its own Caché server process, with the consequence that resources do not need to be shared with other users. This not only improves performance and security, but also simplifies application programming because the program context can be maintained between invocations.

"Stateless" mode

In contrast, the standard *stateless mode* allows several users to share a single connection. The status parameter specified by the programmer is used to control the two modes. For more information, refer to Section 11.6.3.

11.4.4 A First Example

As a simple first example, we program a CSP page in Caché Studio. First click on *New* in the Caché Studio's *File* menu. A dialog appears in which we can select the type of the new file. We select *Caché Server Page* to generate a CSP standard page with the placeholder "My page body" as body text.

The example adds the current date to a welcome string. The code fragment:

```
<h2 align=center>Hello and welcome to our eShop</h2>
<h2 align=center>on #($ZDate($Horolog,9))#.</h2>
```

contains a value substitution that itself uses the `$Horolog` and `$ZDate` database elements to provide and format the current date, respectively.

Evaluation of expressions on the Caché server

The syntactic construct `#(...)#` is one of the fundamental elements of CSP technology. This character sequence in an HTML page informs the Web server that the Caché server will return the contents of the brackets after evaluating the enclosed expression. The code:

```
$ZDate($Horolog,9)
```

calls the $ZDate Caché ObjectScript function to return a formatted date. Two function arguments are used in the above case: the $Horolog special variable that returns the current date and time as two integers, and the "9" formatting option that informs $ZDate to output the month, day, and year as shown in Figure 11.3. The *Caché ObjectScript Reference* supplied in Caché's online documentation provides detailed descriptions of $ZDate and $Horolog.

The code must be compiled to display the pages. We are prompted for the name to be used to save the CSP page; we use the name welcome.

Within a few seconds, the class is compiled and the new CSP page is ready to use. We can call it by entering its URL into the browser's address line:

```
http://localhost:1972/csp/user/welcome.csp
```

or by selecting *View|Webpage* from the Caché Studio menu.

A browser window similar to the following appears:

Figure 11.3 HTML page with dynamically generated content

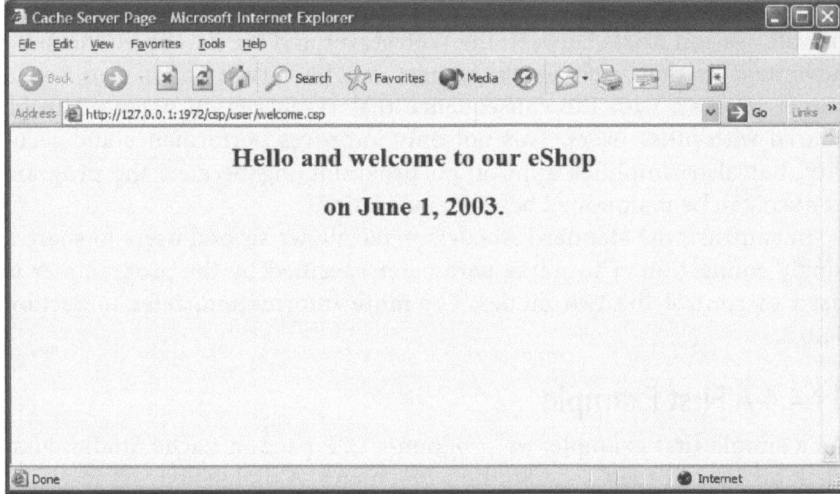

Displaying source text in a browser

We can use the "show source" menu option of the browser to view the source code that the Web server has delivered; we will find pure HTML text here. Instead of the two lines of code that we entered in the CSP page, you see something like this:

```
<BODY>
<h2 align=center>Hello and welcome to our eShop</h2>
<h2 align=center>on June 1, 2003.</h2>
</BODY>
```

Thus, page source text made visible in the browser for CSP pages never supplies the original page, but always the dynamically generated content.

11.5 Creating Dynamic Content

Caché Server Pages provides various ways to include variable content in Web pages. It comes with a series of language elements to facilitate the development of sophisticated procedures for selecting and presenting data. Such elements are:

- Value substitution (introduced in the previous example)
- Executing scripts
- Calling server methods
- Predefined database queries
- Dynamic database queries
- Loop constructs
- Branching code

11.5.1 Value Substitution

CSP permits the use of variable names that are automatically replaced with their current values at runtime. The Web designer can freely specify general conditions, such as position, format and representation of each individual variable, without being concerned about the source of runtime values. Instead, this is the task of the programmer, who provides the designed pages with elements of application logic and so makes them operational.

Current values replace variable names at runtime

11.5.1.1 Simple Value Substitution

An example of value substitution through the specification of functions or special variables has already been shown with the use of the date in the previous section. The sample method can be used to add the contents of user-defined variables at any position in a CSP page.

Special variables and user-defined variables

Let us assume that a person's date of birth is stored in the DOB variable. Then

```
#(DOB)#
```

at any position in the page formulates a simple reference to this variable. Instead of the reference, Caché substitutes the current contents of the variable at runtime, and returns it (together with other page text) by the Web server to the requesting browser.

Any type of HTML formatting can be used in the environment of the reference to lay out the appearance of the displayed value. For example, the date can be shown italicized or formatted as a heading. Note that the formatting must apply to the complete expression (including the enclosing brackets and hash characters).

Using HTML formatting for variable values

Because no restrictions are placed on the use of variables, they can also be placed within URLs or used as parameters in HTML tags.

If the referenced variable is not defined at runtime, no substitution occurs and an error message appears in the browser. If, however, the vari-

Including variable values from a database

able exists but has no value, no content will be displayed. Should such a variable form the only content of a line, this line will not be written.

11.5.1.2 Using Global Variables

In addition to local variables that exist only within a session, global variables from the database can be included in CSP in the same manner. A *hit counter* (that counts the accesses to a specific page) is a simple application example. The Caché ObjectScript function $Increment accommodates the calculation right within the variable substitution:

```
You are visitor number #($Increment(^VisitNumber))# to this
page. <br>
```

11.5.1.3 Object References as Data Source

Accessing properties and methods of objects

Caché allows the use of scalar values in Web pages at runtime, as in the two previous examples, and it provides significant capabilities for accessing class instances stored in a database. Both properties and methods for objects can be a data source for an application at runtime.

The welcome page of an electronic bookstore that promotes a certain book each week serves as example. The data for all books are stored as the Book class that provides the required properties and methods. Let us consider the following code fragment:

```
<CSP:OBJECT Name="BookOfTheWeek" Class="Book" ObjectId="1">
Our book of the week:
#(BookOfTheWeek.Cover)#
<a href=#url(BookInfo.csp?ISBN=#(BookOfTheWeek.ISBN)#)#>
#(BookOfTheWeek.Title)# by #(BookOfTheWeek.Author)# </a>
```

The line #(BookOfTheWeek.Cover)# is similar to a simple variable reference. However, it is a reference to the Cover property of the BookOfTheWeek object (i.e., it is not a reference to a variable). The latter is provided by a CSP:OBJECT tag as an instance of the Book class. As a property of the BookOfTheWeek object, which itself represents an instance of the Book class, Cover can be displayed like any other variable within the page.

Hyperlinking to a dynamically selected page

The code line that follows the variable reference contains a hyperlink to the information page of the purchased book. The href value for the link uses the #url(...)# syntax from CSP. This allows to formulate a hyperlink to a dynamically selected page. For even greater flexibility, CSP pages can be called with query strings, namely, name/value pairs appended with a question mark to the page name. In the example, it is the ISBN and #(BookOfTheWeek.ISBN)# name/value pair. The use of #(BookOfTheWeek.ISBN)# within the #url()# construct is an example of nested references that CSP supports.

Using the CSP:Object tag

The CSP:Object tag provides data for the Caché object. This tag causes an object from the database to be opened and assigns it a name for use within the Web page. The first parameter Name represents this name, whereas Class designates the object class (here: Book). The third argument is the ID used to store the object in the database, in our case, a unique integer that identifies the desired book. As we know, every object can be identified uniquely in Caché using its class name and its ID. Object IDs are assigned automatically when a class object is created and are stored permanently for this object in the database.

The last code line (Author and Title) provides additional examples for the reference to properties of the Book class.

11.5.1.4 Value Substitution at Compile Time

All forms of value substitution can be modified so that the value substitution does not take place at runtime (i.e., each time when the CSP page is displayed), but only once when the corresponding CSP class is compiled. For this, the substitution is included in a ##(...)## construct, using two # symbols instead of one. This construct allows a CSP application to change its behavior according to client-specific parameter settings without any performance degradation.

##(...)## construct

11.5.2 Executing Scripts

It is only a short step from value substitution, to performing calculations or executing code for some other purpose. This can be done with the script tag, as shown in the following example:

```
<script language="cache" runat="server">
  Set (Name,Firstname,DOB)=""
  If ID'="" { Do ..Find(ID,.Name,.Firstname,.DOB) }
</script>
Found Person: #(Name)#, #(Firstname)#, #(DOB)#
```

The first line introduces the script code. The language parameter sets the language to Caché ObjectScript. Alternatives are basic for Caché Basic and SQL for Caché SQL (both can also be executed on the Caché server), or JavaScript for JavaScript and VBScript for Microsoft's VBScript; both are executed in the client browser and can be used in the framework of CSP pages.

Suitable language for the script code

runat="server" tells CSP that the script should be executed at runtime by the Caché Server. Other choices are runat="compile", which tells Caché to execute the script only once when the classes are compiled, and the omission of the *runat* parameter, which causes execution on the client computer. The latter works only with the JavaScript and VBScript browser supported languages. The </script> tag is the closing bracket for the script code.

Execution of script code on the server

Scripts executed on the Caché Server can use the Write command to output text. This text then becomes part of the HTML page that the browser sees; the following example outputs a list with twenty numbered list entries:

```
<ul>
<script language="cache" runat="server">
  For i=1:1:20 { Write "<li>List entry #",i,"<br>",! }
</script>
</ul>
```

Finally, there is a special syntax for the script tag used to define methods of the CSP class. If you write

```
<script language="cache" method="list"
arguments="number:%Integer" returntype="%String">
  For i=1:1:number {
      Write "<li>Element #",i,"<br>",!
  }
  Quit ""
</script>
```

then the defined method list() can be used anywhere within the value substitution page:

```
<ul>
#(..list(10))#
</ul>
```

Attention must be paid to the relative dot syntax that the ..list() method call uses to correlate to its own (CSP) class. The same way, methods can be written which deliver a return value instead of outputting text. Such methods then can be inserted in a CSP page using value substitution.

11.5.3 Calling Server Methods

The previously discussed mechanisms for value substitution and executing scripts allow Caché code to be executed either once when the CSP class is compiled or each time the CSP page is displayed. However, to execute server methods as a response to client-side events such as data entry in a form field or clicking a button, we need a different mechanism: calling server methods.

#call and #server

Actually, CSP comes with two such calls: #call and #server. Although they are fairly similar, there have significant differences: the functionality of #server is based on a small Java applet that Caché automatically loads into the browser. As this applet must be executed by the browser, it can cause problems with some browsers and security settings. #call, on the other hand, works without applets with pure HTML. However, the asynchronous nature of #call calls means they cannot return any values.

Embedded JavaScript syntax &js<...>

Both call types can use Caché's special "Embedded JavaScript" syntax &js<...> to return JavaScript code to the browser and to invoke any actions there. The following example illustrates this mechanism:

```
<form name="Customer" method="post">

Please enter an existing customer number:
<input type="text" Name="CustNo" onChange=
    #server(..CheckCustNo(document.Customer.CustNo.value))#>

</form>

<script language="cache" method="CheckCustNo"
    argument="CustNo:%String">
 If '##class(User.Customer).%ExistsId(CustNo) {
```

```
    &js<alert('Customer #(CustNo)# does not exist!');>
  }
</script>
```

11.5.4 Predefined Database Queries

A typical application for a database query is the bestseller list of an electronic bookstore. This is normally a list of available titles in which the user can click an interesting list entry to obtain an information page that presents further details about the book. Because such a bestseller list can change continuously, it is a good example for the use of dynamic content in Web pages.

Example: Bestseller list for an electronic bookstore

CSP technology provides a simple means using the previously mentioned Book class. To generate the bestseller list, every Book object has a SalesSuccess property, which is an exponentially weighted moving average of sales volume over time. This value makes it easy to determine the bestseller property of a book.

Book object and SalesSuccess *property*

The hyperlinks to the information pages of the individual bestsellers are generated from a list of titles that is obtained from the database using a predefined SQL query. Caché enables this using the CSP:QUERY tag. Such a tag in a CSP page tells the database the class (for which data should be provided) and the name of the associated special query. This query is part of the class definition in the database. (Refer to the example in Chapter 1.) In our case, it would be useful to have a ShowBestseller query defined for the Book class.

Execute a predefined SQL query from the database

The CSP:QUERY tag is one of the most important CSP language elements. It enables a dynamic presentation of data based on highly-variable and sophisticated criteria. In a nutshell, SQL queries are embedded directly in HTML pages. The Caché server handles the preparation and execution of the database query at the start of page processing, and automatically closes the query at the end of processing. More specifically, the CSP:QUERY tag performs the following tasks:

The CSP:QUERY *tag*

- connecting to the selected Caché class
- executing the specified query
- passing a *result set* to the CSP page.

The CSP:QUERY tag performs a database query and assigns a name to the result set. This allows the result set to be used within the page. The CSP:QUERY tag has three properties (parameters):

- NAME is the name of the ResultSet object.
- CLASSNAME designates the Caché class that contains the query definition.
- QUERYNAME specifies the name of the query to be executed.

The name of the result set is Bestseller in the example. The ShowBestseller query in the Book class could be defined as follows:

```
SELECT TOP 10 BookTitle FROM SQLUser.Book
  ORDER BY SalesSuccess DESC
```

The CSP:QUERY call takes the following form:

```
<CSP:QUERY NAME=Bestseller CLASSNAME=Book
QUERYNAME=ShowBestseller>
```

The query shown here has no parameters; it always returns the ten best-selling books. The Caché online documentation describes how extensions with parameters can be used to make handling more flexible.

Filtered data are stored in the result set

Once the request has been processed, the filtered data results are stored in the named result set associated with the calling page. The results can now be used freely and presented in the page. For example, we could reference the result set object and extract the BookTitle column to simply display it:

```
#(Bestseller.Data("BookTitle"))#
```

A hyperlink to an information page passing the book ID can be written as:

```
<a href=BookInfo.csp?ID=#(Bestseller.Data("ID"))#>
```

The section after the next one shows how this can be extended to produce a table.

11.5.5 Dynamic Database Queries

Dynamic Query with SCRIPT LANGUAGE="SQL"

In addition to executing a predefined query from the class definition, CSP allows execution of a dynamic query by enclosing the SQL code of the query in a script bracket. Otherwise, the functionality is identical. The following example illustrates this:

```
<script language="SQL" name="Bestseller">
SELECT TOP 10 ID, BookTitle FROM SQLUser.Book
  ORDER BY SalesSuccess DESC
</script>
```

11.5.6 Loop Constructs

Accessing data records individually or cyclically

A result set normally consists of several data records. We need a method to access these records individually or cyclically, and output them successively as HTML code in a Web page.

Similar to a programming language, CSP provides tags to produce variable program procedures. One of these is the CSP:WHILE tag. It permits the cyclical processing of a part of page generation depending on whether or not a condition is satisfied. Such a condition could be "end of the result set reached."

CSP:WHILE tag

The CSP:WHILE tag includes the CONDITION parameter, which specifies the control condition of the WHILE loop. All items used to generate the final HTML page entered after this tag are to be executed the same number of times as the loop is performed. The </CSP:WHILE> tag closes the block.

Thus, the code fragment for a line output of the bestseller list from the previous section has the following form:

```
<CSP:WHILE CONDITION=Bestseller.Next()>
<a href=BookInfo.csp?ID=#(Bestseller.Data("ID"))#>
  #(Bestseller.Data("BookTitle"))#</a><br>
</CSP:WHILE>
```

11.5.7 Branching Code

In addition to the cyclical generation of parts of a Web page, CSP can perform individual branches of the creation process depending on specific conditions. Also similar to popular programming languages, it provides IF and ELSE tags with the corresponding "closing brackets." The following section considers a more comprehensive example of its use.

IF and ELSE tags

An electronic bookstore again serves as starting point. Depending on upcoming holidays, an appropriate welcoming text should appear on the screen so that special books can be promoted. For example, a visitor on Valentine's Day receives an appropriate message when he or she arrives at the starting page of the bookstore, and—because it is the day of love—possibly also a reference to romantic literature.

Internally, such a display is generated as follows:

```
<CSP:IF CONDITION="..IsAHoliday($Horolog)">
  <CSP:OBJECT NAME="Holiday" CLASS="Promotion"
              ObjectID="#(..IsAHoliday($Horolog))#">
  #(Holiday.Greeting)# <br>
  We have something special for this #(Holiday.Name)#: <br>
  <a href=#url(BookInfo.csp?ISBN=#(Holiday.Book.ISBN)#)#>
    #(Holiday.Book.Title)# by #(Holiday.Book.Author)#
  </a>
<CSP:ELSE>
  <!-- on normal days the usual promotions, see above -->
  Our book of the week:
  #(BookOfTheWeek.Cover)#
  <a href=#url(BookInfo.csp?ISBN=#(BookOfTheWeek.ISBN)#)#>
  #(BookOfTheWeek.Title)# by #(BookOfTheWeek.Author)# </a>
</CSP:IF>
```

Let us consider this code more closely. The CSP:IF tag, the first line, together with the /CSP:IF tag, the last line, encloses the scope of the conditionally executed CSP code. CSP:IF introduces a part that is processed only when the contained condition is satisfied. The part introduced by CSP:ELSE is bypassed when the evaluation of the condition produces the *false* value.

The condition itself is specified by the CONDITION argument of the CSP:IF tag. The user-defined method ..IsAHoliday() determines whether the current date (found in $Horolog) is a holiday.

Specifying a CONDITION argument

If this is the case, the current holiday promotion is fetched as an object from the database:

```
<CSP:OBJECT NAME="Holiday" CLASS="Promotion"
            ObjectID="#(..IsAHoliday($Horolog))#">
```

The ..IsAHoliday() method returns an object ID. Thus, this method determines whether today is a holiday, as well as which holiday it is. This can be achieved simply when the method is programmed. You need only ensure that the method passes a valid object ID as return value that refer-ences an associated instance in the Promotion class. A null value is re-turned for non-holidays.

Once the object is provided, its properties control the display of infor-mation. Familiar Caché ObjectScript syntax is used here. The lines:

```
#(Holiday.Greeting)# <br>
We have something special for this #(Holiday.Name)#: <br>
```

output the contents of Greeting and Name that have been specially cre-ated for this advertising in instances of the Promotion class, whereas the following two lines obtain their data from an object of the Book class as-sociated with the provided object of the Promotion class.

As known from other chapters of the book, every Caché class can be used as data type (property) in any other class. Such a multilevel access is referenced with the usual Caché ObjectScript dot notation:

```
<a href=#url(BookInfo.csp?ISBN=#(Holiday.Book.ISBN)#)#>
 #(Holiday.Book.Title)# by #(Holiday.Book.Author)# </a>
```

The section following the CSP:ELSE tag is the usual advertising used when there is no special promotion for the day.

The </CSP:IF> tag completes the block.

11.6 Interaction with CSP

Presenting variable content is just one aspect of dynamic Web pages. Another is interaction between user and server. For example, the user's input can strongly affect content displayed in a browser. Sometimes, the user can even change the contents of the associated database.

In this regard, the areas of interest are the use of CSP with forms, the management of requests and sessions, and the authorization of users for various levels of interaction with a database Here are the basic steps in which Caché processes any request passed from the Web server:

- A new request object is created and its OREF assigned to the %request variable.
- If this is the first request of a session (i.e., several requests from the same browser), a new session object is created and its OREF assigned to the %session system variable. Otherwise, the current session object for the currently running session is assigned.
- Caché calls the Page() method of the CSP class that is associated with the called URL.
- The Page() method itself now successively calls various other meth-ods:
  - OnPreHTTP() initializes the page and generates the HTTP headers that are sent over the Web server to the browser
  - OnHeaders() transfers the generated headers
  - OnPage() creates the actual page content (HTML, XML, binary file)
  - OnPostHTTP() performs the required cleanup.

- A session object exists until the session is terminated by the application or a timeout occurs. The end method is called in both cases to properly close the session object.

11.6.1 Using Forms

The text that a user enters in a form can be transferred to the Web server using the HTTP protocol in two ways:
- with the GET method as part of an URL
- with the POST method in the body of an HTTP request.

Thus, the following URL:

```
http://myfirm.com/info/LoginStatus.csp?CustomerID=47110815
```

passes a specific login ID of the customer using the GET method.

11.6.1.1 The Request Object

In compliance with HTML standards, every form input consists of a name/value pair. These do not necessarily result from a user's keyboard input (consider hidden form fields). However, the term "form input" is well established for this type of stream, which is why we use this term here.

Form input consist of name/value-pairs

It is quite possible that several values exist for a specified name. These can be used, for example, for text boxes that provide multiple selections. Together with some general information about the associated request, the form input is passed to the CSP class in the database that corresponds to the calling CSP page. This is performed using a %CSP.Request object whose OREF is supplied by Caché in the %request system variable.

Multiple values for a specified name

Thus, for the above-mentioned URL, the request object receives a property URL with the value http://myfirm.com/info/LoginStatus. csp plus a PageName property with the value LoginStatus.csp and a data entry with the name CustomerID and the value 47110815.

Typically, form input is generated from HTML forms. In the case of the POST method, this means that when the form is transferred, the request object receives four form input elements: CustomerID, Name, Address and City.

Important: The names of Caché-specific data elements, such as CSPToken, start with the characters "CSP". To avoid conflicts, you should not use these characters at the start of names for your own data entries.

The names of Caché-specific data elements start with "CSP"

The following table provides a complete overview of the properties of the request object.

Name	Data type	Description
CharSet	%String	Font corresponding to the HTTP header
ContentType	%String	File type corresponding to the HTTP header
Cookies	Array of string values	Cookies that the browser sent (returned) to the Web server

Table 11.3 Properties of the request object

CgiEnv	Array of string values	The complete set of CGI environment variables (including their content)
Data	multidimensional property of %String values	The full set of data elements (including their content)
GatewayApplication	%String	Name under which the Caché application was created in the *Web Gateway Manager*
GatewayConnectionName	%String	Name of the server connection (Caché server) established for the application
Method	%String	HTTP method (e.g., GET or POST)
NewSession	%Boolean	TRUE for the first request of a session, FALSE for all other requests
PageName	%String	Name of the CSP page, e.g., Login.csp
URL	%String	URL for the specified page, including page name and extension, but without any (CGI) query string that exists
User Agent	%String	Type of browser that sent the request; this corresponds to the contents of the HTTP user agent header

11.6.1.2 Using Request Data

The request object provides three basic types of data: data elements, CGI environment variables, and cookies. Data elements are contained in the multidimensional property Data. The complete format is:

```
%request.Data(Name,IndexNumber)=value
```

This property is used as described in detail in Chapter 5 for multidimensional variables. This way, the existence of a certain name/value pair can be checked with the Caché ObjectScript $Data function or the next element can be searched with the $Order function. For both other data types (CGI environment variables and cookies), the request object provides corresponding methods. The following table summarizes these methods.

Table 11.4 Methods of the request object

Name	Return value	Function	Argument(s)
Count-Cookie	%Integer	Number of values for a specified cookie name	Name of the cookie (%String)
Get-CgiEnv	%String	Data value of an environment variable that was provided with the request	Name of the data element (%String), default value (%String, optional argument, defaults to "")
Get-Cookie	%String	Data value of a cookie that was provided with the request	Name of the cookie (%String), default value (%String, optional argument, defaults to ""), index number (%Integer, optional argument, defaults to 1)
IsDefined-CgiEnv	%Boolean	Information on whether the environment variable is defined	Name of the environment variable (%String, optional argument, defaults to all)

IsDefined-Cookie	%Boolean	Information on whether the cookie is defined	Name of the cookie (%String, optional argument, defaults to all), index number (%Integer, optional argument, defaults to all)
Next-CgiEnv	%String	Used to loop through all environment variables; returns the name of the next element	Name of the current environment variable or "" (%String)
Next-Cookie	%String	Used to loop through all cookies; returns the name of the next element	Name of the current cookie or "" (%String)

If a CSP page with URL

```
http://mycompany.com/client/info/Status.csp?clientID=47110815
```

is called, `%request.Data("clientID",1)` contains the value `47110815`. Note that the names of data elements are *case sensitive*; this means you must distinguish between upper- and lowercase. Accordingly, in the example above, `%request.Data("clientid",1)` would not be defined.

If data values are to be retrieved, the existence of which cannot be guaranteed or if an optional default value is to be specified that is used for unspecified values, use the Caché ObjectScript `$Get` function, as shown in the following example: *Default value as second parameter of `$Get`*

```
$Get(%request.Data("numbercopies",1),1)
```

In this case, the value of `numbercopies` is used if it exists, otherwise `1`.

11.6.1.3 Multiple Data Elements

Under some circumstances, multiple data elements occur in request objects. In this case, several values are associated with a single name. This occurs when: *Multiple data elements: multiple values with one name*

- a single form element returns several values, as for multiple selections in SELECT tags
- a form element (usually a text input field) returns a value longer than 32 KB. Caché automatically divides this into multiple data elements.
- a form contains several input fields with the same name
- a constructed URL contains the same data element name more than once. Although this is normally the result of a programming error, it is sometimes intentional and useful.

If such multiple data elements (multiple values) occur in a request object, they can be identified by their different values on the second subscript level; for example, `%request.Data("CustomerID",1)` can be used to access the first instance of `CustomerID` and `%request.Data("Customer-ID",2)` for the second instance. *Accessing a specific data element*

If all values are to be processed, you can start with a loop at 1 and continue executing it until no further value exists, as shown in the following code fragment: *Determining the number of values*

```
For i=1:1 {
  Quit:'$Data(%request.Data("CustomerID",i))
  Set ID=%request.Data("CustomerID",i) ...
}
```

11.6.1.4 A Journey through the Form

Traversing the data entries of a form

The Caché ObjectScript $Order function provides another powerful construct to evaluate user entries. You can use it to traverse data entries that the form returns to the Web server.

Assume that the following URL is transferred:

```
http://myfirm.com/info/LoginStatus.csp?Status=s&CustomerID=47
110815
```

A call to:

```
$Order(%request.Data(""))
```

then returns the name of the first data element, here CustomerID.

The data are sorted according to their name

Why is CustomerID the first data element and not Status? The storing sequence in the request object does not always correspond to the occurrence of the individual elements in the request. Rather, the data are sorted by name, more specifically, in the *collating sequence* that the database administrator specified during the installation of Caché. Normally this will be a sequence appropriate for the English alphabet. If you wish to test this setting, you can easily create a test page.

The call:

```
$Order(%request.Data("CustomerID"))
```

returns Status, the name of the next data element. Finally,

```
$Order(%request.Data("Status"))
```

returns the value " " because no further data element follows Status.

11.6.1.5 Manipulating the Request Object

Setting or changing a data element value

Not only names and values can be read from a request object, but also specific data stored in the object can be changed. It is possible to modify existing values and even create or delete data elements. For example, the statement:

```
Set %request.Data("Length",1)=12
```

changes the value of the Length data element to 12, if it exists. Otherwise, a new element is created with the name Length and set to the value 12.

The call:

```
Kill %request.Data("Length")
```

Removing a data element and all its values

removes the Length data element with all values from the request object. Alternatively, when a second subscript is specified, the Kill command explicitly removes individual instances of multiple data elements. Any remaining values are renumbered. This means that there are not any gaps in the instance numbering after such a step.

The call:

```
Kill %request.Data
```

removes all existing data from the request object.

11.6.2 Binding Forms to Objects

The CSPBIND attribute provides an elegant means of obtaining data from Caché and updating the database with modifications. It is an attribute included as an additional feature to the familiar HTML tags.

The CSPBIND *attribute*

CSPBIND makes it possible to directly bind HTML forms to Caché objects. Because no additional actions or methods need to be written, this is the easiest programming technique for handling object data in a Web application. Let us consider the following page fragment:

Binding HTML form fields directly to Caché objects

```
<CSP:OBJECT NAME=CurrentCust CLASSNAME=Customer
            OBJECTID=#(%request.Data("CustID",1))#>
<FORM NAME=CustomerForm CSPBIND=customer>
Name: <INPUT TYPE=TEXT NAME=Name CSPBIND=Name>
First: <INPUT TYPE=Text NAME=Firstname CSPBIND=Firstname>
Address: <INPUT TYPE=TEXT NAME=Address CSPBIND=Address>
...
Credit card: <INPUT TYPE=TEXT NAME=CCard CSPBIND=CCard>
...
<INPUT TYPE=BUTTON VALUE="Save" NAME=Save
 OnClick=CustomerForm_save();>
</FORM>
```

The CSPBIND attribute is used both in the form header and in the individual input fields. It is used in the header to bind the form to a concrete data object. This was generated here with CSP:OBJECT after the CustID object ID was obtained in some manner (not described here) and was transferred with the pending request. CSPBIND is used in the individual fields to represent and/or actively change the properties of the object. The programmer does not need to do anything else here.

Using CSPBIND *in the form header and in individual input fields*

During compilation of the CSP class, Caché creates some JavaScript elements that are responsible for validating and processing the form elements. The CSPREQUIRED attribute can be used to inform them that a certain form field requires an entry for the form to be valid. In the example, this is shown with form field Name.

To ensure the content of the object is updated in the database when the save button is clicked, it is also possible to use the JavaScript method formname_save() that is also automatically generated by Caché (for formname the actual name of the form is to be inserted).

Saving with the JavaScript method formname_save()

However, this technique works only when the variable contents of individual properties can be displayed directly in a corresponding input field. If additional conversions are required for added flexibility, conventional methods of form processing must be used.

Conversions require conventional methods of form processing

11.6.3 Session Management

A feature that makes working with CSP really effective is its ability to track (on a page-by-page basis) the status of a session involving user, browser, Web server, and database. The concept of *sessions* allows one set of data to be applied over the complete session. For example, when a customer makes a purchase online, you can manage input data and transaction data as one set, even though it may be generated over several Web pages. Sessions supply the programming infrastructure required for providing customer-related functionality in a Web application.

Managing a session with a session object

The session object is the central element of session management with CSP. Similar to the request object (described in detail above), Caché automatically creates a session object where it stores name/value pairs that contain certain information about the user session. However, in contrast to the request object, it is not reassigned for every browser request, but is retained over the complete session. This, however, does not mean that specific data in it cannot be changed during the session.

Caché creates a session object when a user first accesses a CSP page with a browser. This object is retained until the application or a timeout ends the session. In this case, the session object is destroyed and the occupied memory space released. If the same user accesses another page of the application while the session object still exists, this request is assigned to the current session; the data of the session object is available for this request.

11.6.3.1 Processing a User Session

The following internal actions are performed when processing a user session:

- The user with a browser accesses the starting CSP page that he reaches with a virtual directory of his Web server.
- The Web server forwards the CSP request to the associated Caché database server.
- Caché receives the request, creates a request object, and assigns it the data that the browser supplied with the Web server, as described in the previous section.

Activating the existing session object or creating a new object

- If the user is already in a session, Caché activates the existing session object that was created for this user. Otherwise, a new session object is created at this time and populated with data.
- Only now does Caché call the page() method of the class that corresponds to the requested CSP page. For example, if the page Login-Status.csp was requested, the page() method of the LoginStatus class will be processed.
- The LoginStatus.page() method generates HTML code that the Web server sends to the user's browser.
- Caché deletes the request object.
- If the application ends the user session during the course of the page call, the session object is also now deleted. In all other cases, it is just

deactivated up to the next request by the same user or until a timeout cancels the session.

11.6.3.2 An Example

Similar to the request object, user variables that control the session can also be saved in a session object. Assume for our electronic bookstore that the customer order to be processed is to be identified with a data element named OrderID. The order data are stored in a dedicated object of the Order class identified uniquely by the OrderID. The following code fragment written in Caché ObjectScript is embedded between script tags in a CSP page:

Saving user variables in the session object

```
If $Data(%session.Data("OrderID")) {
  Set ordr=##class(Order).
        %OpenId(%session.Data("OrderID"))
} Else {
  Set ordr=##class(Order).%New()
}
```

Within the If condition, the $Data function tests whether a data element named OrderID exists in the current session object. If yes, the value of OrderID is used to fetch the associated object of the Order class from the database and provide it in the ordr variable. If the data element is not yet present in the session object, the associated Order object also does not yet exist. The %New() method of the class creates it.

Checking whether a data element is already present in the current session object

At a later place in the code, the data element OrderID must be created and assigned the OID of the newly created Order object as value:

```
Set %session("OrderId",1)=ordr.%Id()
```

The %Id() method of the ordr object of the Order class is used here.

11.6.3.3 Properties of the Session Object

The session object provides predefined data elements that can be used for CSP programming. Every call of a page() method produces a session object with the current session parameters. The following table summarizes the predefined properties of the %CSP.session class.

Name	Data type	Description	Default value
AppTimeOut	%Integer	Time in seconds that the application waits for the next user input	900
EndSession	%Boolean	Indicator whether the application is to be closed after processing the page	False
onAppTime-OutMethod	%String	Name of the method to be executed after an application timeout	
onEndMethod	%String	Name of the method to be executed after normal completion of the application	

Table 11.5 Properties of the session object

Preserve	%String	Specifies which context is to be preserved from one request to the next one (meaning: 0—only the session object, 1—also all local variables and open objects, 2—full context)	0
SessionId	%Integer	Unique ID for the session (read-only value)	
Data	multidimensional	Stored user data	

Some properties of the session object can be used to evaluate the system settings for the session and use these to control the processing of the user application.

However, the far more frequent and interesting use concerns the multidimensional property Data. As we have already seen in the previous example, it can be used to store and process user data application-wide and forward these data between the individual page calls.

The Data property behaves like a multidimensional array and can be used in the same way. For example, when a user logs in to the application and enters a user name in a form, this name can be recorded in the session object of the user session.

```
Set %session.Data("username")=%request.Data("name",1)
```

At a later point in time—possibly within a completely different Web page—this recorded name can be retrieved and used:

```
Hello, #(%session.Data("username"))#!
```

The $Order, $Data, and $Get functions and the Set, Merge, and Kill commands help in using the multidimensional property. For further details, refer to Chapter 5.

11.6.3.4 Preserving Context

A session represents a permanent information exchange between user and database. Therefore, it is often advantageous to have the context of a session preserved from one request to the next. Caché provides mechanisms for automatically storing and retrieving the session context. The server uses the value of the %session.Preserve property at the end of processing each page to determine the amount of data that needs to be saved. Two cases should be noted:

- Value 0: The content of the session object is saved automatically and restored at the next page call of the session.
- Value 1: The complete context of the current Caché server process is saved, in addition to the previously mentioned data; this includes locks and opened device/files.

The programmer can freely change the value of %session.Preserve at any point in the application. It would be conceivable to set a state 0 at the beginning when the user passively reads the page contents, and increase it to 1 as soon as the user starts to interact with the database and to initiate transactions.

The %session.Preserve=1 value means that the next request of the same session is served by the same server process as the current request and no session of a different user can use this process in the time between the requests. If the value of %session.Preserve=0, the next request for the same user session is served by either the same or another process. The user and the programmer have no influence here. Although Caché will attempt to reuse the same process, because this is more efficient than the assignment of a new server process, there is no guarantee. In addition, processes can only be used jointly by those sessions that exhibit the same security characteristics.

Let us take an e-commerce application as an example of a browser session using previously stored customer data and a shopping basket object in which the user can enter his/her order details. Let us also assume that we have previously defined classes for Customer and Order in the database, and that an existing Customer object is opened when a user logs in. Later, when the first article is added to the customer's shopping basket, we create a new object for the Order class. Two outcomes are possible. Firstly, the customer completes the order at some time, in which case the Order object is stored in the database. Secondly, the customer decides otherwise and discards the order or does not make any further input. In the second case, the Order object would be closed without any data being stored.

Such an application is simple to implement using either Preserve=0 or Preserve=1. These differ in the storage location used for data during session.

%session.Preserve=1 lets us retain object references to the open Customer and Order objects in local variables, such as:

```
Set Cust=##class(User.Customer).%OpenId(…)
Set Ordr=##class(User.Order).%New()
```

Caché manages these (local) variables, and also the objects they reference, between the individual CSP pages of the application.

Things are somewhat different with %session.Preserve=0. The Customer and Order objects are stored and closed in the database at the end of a page. The associated object IDs are retained in the session object. The corresponding objects must be opened and closed every time an application request is processed. The data stored in the session object of the session (in our case, the OIDs) are the only means of communicating between individual pages.

An error occurs when, on completion of a page, the value for %session.Preserve is 0 and the Caché process still holds locks or is running a database transaction.

The request object is an exception for passing objects. Regardless of the Preserve value in the session object, it is *never* passed to another

Preserving a server process for a unique user session

Retaining object references and local variables

Retaining only the session object

Request object is always current

page. Rather, every page request starts with a newly initialized request object that contains only data for the current request.

11.6.3.5 Terminating a Session

There are three ways to terminate a user session:

- Executing the Halt command in Caché ObjectScript.
- Setting the %session.EndSession property to TRUE within the page() method.
- Running into a timeout condition.

Every time a session is terminated using the EndSession parameter, Caché calls the method specified in the %session.onEndMethod object property to complete the session. When, however, the session is terminated using Halt, the method is no longer called.

If the page() method terminates while EndSession=0, Caché waits until either a new request for the same session arrives or until the time specified by the value of the %session.AppTimeOut property has expired. If the latter occurs, the method for the name specified in the %session.onAppTimeOutMethod property is also called.

Terminating a session with a timeout

The expiration of the timeout interval does not itself terminate the user's session. Rather, the decision is made in the onAppTimeOutMethod code and thus can be controlled by the programmer. An actual end of the session is realized by setting %session.EndSession=1 within the method code. If this does not occur, the timeout counter restarts at zero.

11.6.4 Concepts for User Management

Generating personalized data based on user (customer) properties

In e-commerce, it is important to present data and logic for its manipulation according to the properties of users (who are customers). Procedures must be provided to allow the system to recognize a customer and to generate data that is uniquely personalized for him/her (such as outstanding orders, etc.).

Mechanisms that protect the user's data from access by other users are, of course, mandatory. This begins at the user session and extends over the complete "lifetime" of all customer-related data in the database.

11.6.4.1 Saving Customer Data

Assigning transactions to a customer account

It is normal for a user who often works with a database to be given a user name and password. The latter identifies the user to the system as the person who is authorized to passively or actively access a specific area in the database. It is desirable to store details, such as user name and password (together with e-mail address, credit card data, etc.) in a Customer object managed by Caché. This gives the system a means of identifying a specific customer over session limits and to assign transactions to a customer account. Here, a customer account can be considered similar to a user account for a multiuser operating system.

CSP pages and embedded forms can provide a login mechanism for a Caché application that requests a user name and password from a customer. They also pass the details to the database server. Verification of the passed data (normally with a script) and further processing of the application is performed there. A common example would be the user querying the database for a list of outstanding orders. Based on the content of this list, he/she may wish to change some of the records, for example, to direct delivery at a different address or to increase the quantity requested. The Caché online documentation describes the details of how this can be implemented.

11.6.4.2 Private CSP Pages

How is it possible to guarantee that each registered user can view and change only the data from his/her own customer account?

Normally, the customer sees a hyperlink similar to My Customer data on a Web page. If the customer clicks this while not yet "logged in," he/she receives a form to identify himself/herself with user name and password. After a successful login, there is another form that displays the user data and allows the user to edit it when necessary. If, however, the user is already in the "logged in" state when clicking My Customer data, the system presents the form with the user data immediately. The page is a dynamically generated object, presented in this form only for this one customer. This is a so-called *private page,* which is another powerful CSP concept for generating user-related content and increasing data security.

A private CSP page has the following characteristics:

Characteristics of private CSP pages

- A new session cannot be started. (The user can reach here only when logged in.)
- To avoid hacker attacks, the URL for access to this page is valid only for the current session.
- It cannot be reached using the browser's read-characters function (same advantage as previous).
- It cannot be called directly from the browser, but only as a hyperlink from another CSP page.

A CSP:CLASS tag is used to define a page as being private:

Defining the CSP:CLASS *tag*

```
<CSP:CLASS PRIVATE=1>
```

To access such a page, you see an URL of the following form in the browser:

```
...Cache.csp?CSPToken=ER45678IJY6T5RF
```

Here, Cache.csp identifies the page as a CSP page, whereas the string ER45678IJY6T5RF (or similar) represents a *token* that further identifies the desired page. This is a hash value formed from the name/value pairs that produce the query string for a public page, such as user name, password, and so on. This coded value is valid only for the current user ses-

Token valid only for the current user session

sion. Using this value in a browser after the end of the session would produce a *Page not found* error.

11.6.4.3 Linking to Private Pages

A hyperlink to a private CSP page can be formulated using the #url()# syntax from CSP:

```
<a href=#url(Acct.csp?Cust=#(%request.Data("CustID",1))#)#>
My customer data</a>
```

Encrypted page names and parameters

The page name and parameters placed within the #url()# brackets are automatically encrypted when a private page is called. Thus, the browser's address line shows, for example, the URL:

```
http://www.myfirm.com/Acct.csp?CSPToken=ER45678IJY6T5RF
```

When the same link is followed during a later session, this character string would accordingly appear different.

11.7 A Sample Application

The application shown here uses only a few of the wide-ranging capabilities that CSP provides for programmers and users. This application has the advantage that, despite all simplifications, it is a complete application that can be reproduced at any time and is built from examples already seen in this book. More extensive solutions can be found in Röhrig [2000] and [2001], the online documentation supplied on the accompanying CD-ROM, and the SAMPLES namespace of the installed Caché database.

Sample application with HTML code, CSP tags, and embedded Caché ObjectScript code

Our small application consists of three CSP pages with HTML code, CSP tags, and embedded Caché ObjectScript lines:
- the First.csp start page with hyperlinks to the other pages
- the Second.csp page to display a selection list of all persons stored in the database with hyperlinks to process the individual person entries
- the Third.csp page to process a selected data record ("person details")

Initially, let us make a few observations about the functionality of the application. The application is invoked with the following hyperlink:

```
http://localhost:1972/csp/user/First.csp
```

The First.csp start page appears with a simple selection menu:

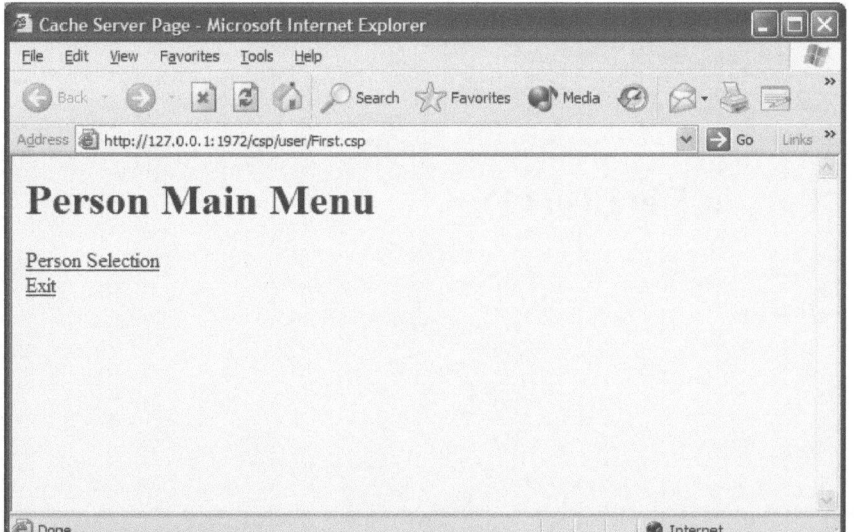

Figure 11.4 Main menu for the sample application

When the user clicks the `Select Person` menu item, the `Second.csp` page appears, providing "Person Selection."

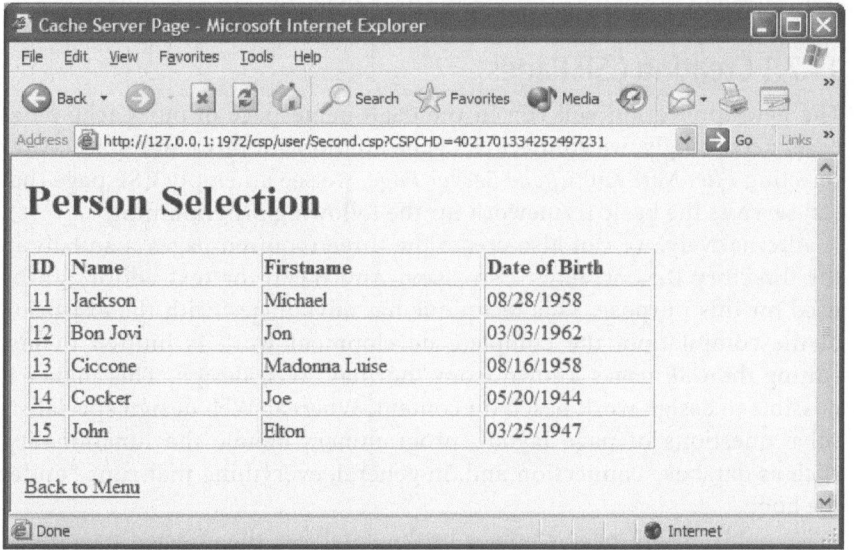

Figure 11.5 `Second.csp` page— person selection

This page shows the ID, name, first name, and date of birth for all persons stored under the `Person` object class in the database. The ID field is provided as a hyperlink. When you click an ID, the `Third.csp` page opens to process data for this person.

Figure 11.6 Third.csp page—
person details

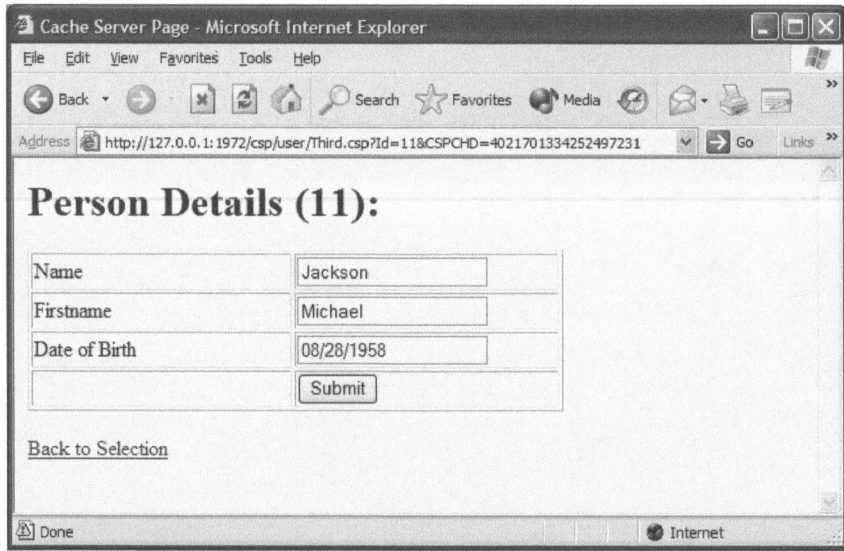

This page contains a form that displays the details for the selected person. The data fields can be overwritten by user inputs. The changed values are transferred to the database when the user clicks the Submit button.

11.7.1 Creating CSP Pages

Creating the basic structure of CSP pages in Caché Studio

The new application will run in the USER namespace of our Caché database. Accordingly, we connect in Caché Studio with this namespace. After selecting *File, New* and *Caché Server Page,* we see an empty CSP page that can serve as the basic framework for the following programming.

Alternatively, we can also create the three required pages manually in the directory C:\cachesys\csp\user. Any HTML or text editor can be used for this purpose. This technique has advantages: with the exception of the compilation, the complete development work is limited to just editing the CSP pages known from "normal" Web design. This makes it possible to assign work based on content. Whereas Web design specialists solve questions of page layout, programmers handle the functionality, such as database connection and, in general, everything that runs "under the hood."

CSP pages recompile automatically after every change

To apply HTML page changes to the database, the affected page must be recompiled. This is also the case for new pages. However, Caché itself ensures that stored classes are up-to-date, so a programmer does not need to take any action. A slight delay in response to a browser-based request is the only sign of automatic compilation.

The First.csp page

With the exception of its extension, the First.csp page has no special features. It is a purely static HTML page. Other than the headers, which an HTML editor can add automatically, its code has the following general form:

```
<body>
<h1>Person Main Menu</h1>
<a href=Second.csp> Person Selection </a> <br>
```

```
<a href=http://www.intersystems.com> Exit </a> <br>
</body>
```

`Second.csp` creates a table with two lines and four columns following the "Person Selection" heading. The fields of the first line have the entries `ID`, `Name`, `Firstname`, and `DOB`. The table heading has bold formatting and a "Back to Menu" hyperlink entered at the end of the page.

The Second.csp *page*

The preliminary result, the static part of this page (again without header), is shown in the following listing:

```
<body bgcolor="#FFFFFF">
<h1>Person Selection</h1>
<table border="1" width="81%">
  <tr>
    <td width="6%"><b>ID</b></td>
    <td width="31%"><b>Name</b></td>
    <td width="36%"><b>Firstname</b></td>
    <td width="27%"><b>DOB</b></td>
  </tr>
  <tr>
    <td width="6%"></td>
    <td width="31%"></td>
    <td width="36%"></td>
    <td width="27%"></td>
  </tr>
</table>
<p><a href="First.csp">Back to Menu</a>
</body>
```

The further work in `Second.csp`, the addition of the tags that organize the database access, is performed in the HTML source text mode of a Web editor. Section 11.7.2 provides further details.

But first, `Third.csp` must be created. The page has "Person Details (#(%request.Data("Id",1))#)" as headline. This causes the person ID selected as hyperlink in `Second.csp` to be entered every time the page is invoked. The request object of the page call performs the transfer. A form with a table is created to display the remaining data. The table contains text input fields with label and a Submit button (Figure 11.9). The label and designation of the fields correspond to the variable names in `Second.csp`, which themselves are derived from properties of the `User.Person` class.

The Third.csp *page*

Figure 11.7 Input form for person
details in Dreamweaver

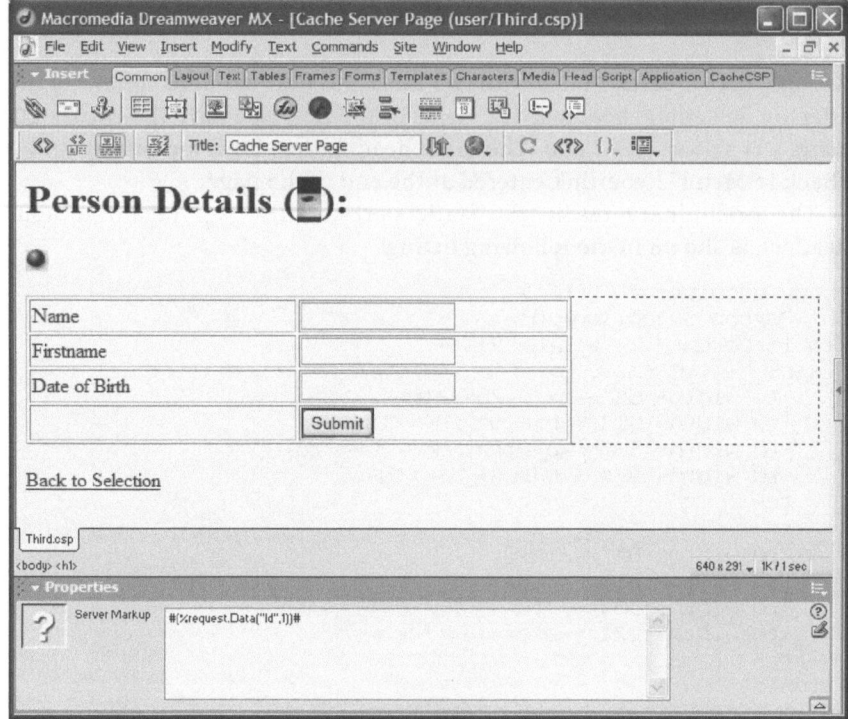

11.7.2 Connecting to the Database

*Populating a table with content from
a database*

The actual work of the Second.csp page (populating a table with content
from a database) is performed by just a few code lines. It must be ensured
that the All query of the User.Person class is executed and all data of the
result set written successively in the lines of the HTML table. This is easy
to solve with two CSP tags and corresponding value references.

Technically, this involves editing the second table line in the previously
created HTML page. The result follows:

```
<CSP:QUERY NAME="pers" CLASSNAME="User.Person"
          QUERYNAME="All">
<CSP:WHILE CONDITION=pers.Next()>
  <tr>
    <td width="6%"><a href=Third.csp?Id=#(pers.Data("ID"))#>
                                #(pers.Data("ID"))#</a></td>
    <td width="31%">#(pers.Data("Name"))#</td>
    <td width="36%">#(pers.Data("Firstname"))#</td>
    <td width="27%">#(pers.Data("DOB"))#</td>
  </tr>
</CSP:WHILE>
```

*Performing a query and assigning
the result to the ResultSet object*

The CSP:QUERY tag after the table heading ensures that the predefined
Select query of the Person class is executed on the complete data and
the result assigned to the pers result set object. The following WHILE
loop outputs the data line-by-line. It uses the Next() method of the result
set as a break condition. This method returns a null value when no further data records exist. Provided this is not the case, the associated prop-

erties of an object of the Person class are available. They are taken from the multidimensional Data property of the result set object and made visible one after the other each in a line of the HTML table. We already know the #(...)# referencing for Caché values in HTML pages.

Clicking the hyperlink in the Id column of the table initiates a request to the Third.csp page and concurrently transfers the Id parameter with the value of a person ID, in particular, that for which processing is required.

Two tasks must be solved in the Third.csp page:
- the presentation of data for display in the form
- a method that updates the corresponding object in the database when the Submit button is clicked

Displaying data requires only that an object of the User.Person class be fetched from the database, in particular, the one identified by the ID transferred from Second.csp. The CSP:OBJECT tag is used here. In addition, we need a form that must be connected to the person object with its entry fields. For this purpose, we use the CSPBIND attribute; for the name, without which no person shall be saved, expanded by CSPREQUIRED.

The resulting page code has the following appearance (table and form have already been created with the HTML editor):

```
<body>
<h1>Person Details (#(%request.Data("Id",1))#):</h1>
<CSP:OBJECT NAME="pers" CLASSNAME="User.Person"
           OBJID=#(%request.Data("Id",1))#>
<form method="POST" name="PersDetail" CSPBIND="pers">
  <table border="1" width="69%">
    <tr>
      <td width="50%">Name</td>
      <td width="50%"><input type="text" name="Name"
                  size="20" CSPBIND=Name CSPREQUIRED></td>
    </tr>
    <tr>
      <td width="50%">Firstname</td>
      <td width="50%"><input type="text" name="Firstname"
                  size="20" CSPBIND=Firstname></td>
    </tr>
    <tr>
      <td width="50%">DOB</td>
      <td width="50%"><input type="text" name="DOB"
                  size="20" CSPBIND=DOB></td>
    </tr>
    <tr>
      <td width="50%"> </td>
      <td width="50%"><input type="submit"
                  value="Submit" name="submit"></td>
    </tr>
  </table>
</form>
<p><a href="Second.csp">Back to Selection</a></p>
</body>
```

The second task—saving the data in the database—requires a method that is invoked when the user presses the Submit button.

As we know, Caché provides such a method as a standard for all forms that are connected to object classes with the CSPBIND attribute. Consequently, we need only use this method and expand the definition of the send button accordingly:

```
<td width="50%"><input type="button"
          value="send" name="send"
          OnClick=PersDetail_save();></td>
```

Call application using URL or Caché Studio

The example application is now ready to be used. We can start it from its URL `http://localhost:1972/csp/user/First.csp`. It is also possible to select *Web Page* from the *View* menu once the page `First.csp` has been loaded in Caché Studio.

12 XML and Web Services

The eXtended Markup Language (XML) has rapidly become a standard for the platform-independent exchange of any type of complex data. There are scarcely limits on the deployment of XML: because XML documents are simple text files, they can easily be transmitted between, and understood by, different systems. Accordingly, XML provides a powerful basis for platform-independent data exchange and automatic processing of the included data. For information on the basics of XML, refer to Kazakos [2002].

12.1 Introduction

Primarily, XML is a specially formatted text file. The XML structure is similar to that of an HTML page, but subject to considerably stricter structure rules. An example of a simple XML document:

```
<data>
  <person firstname="John" name="Dow">
    <car>VW beetle</car>
  </person>
  <person firstname="Joseph" name="Miller">
    <car>Indy car</car>
    <bike>Folding bike</bike>
  </person>
</data>
```

12.1.1 Well-formed XML Documents

The primary requirement on an XML document is that it be well-formed; this consideration refers to the basic structure of the document.

Basically, an XML document consists of elements and attributes. The structure of an XML document is a hierarchical tree, the nodes of which correspond to the elements in the XML document. Accordingly, a document structured through the concatenation and the nesting of so-called XML *tags*.

XML can depict any hierarchically structured data

Although there are no restrictions placed on tag names, you might consider using names appropriate for the application in which the document is to be deployed. You must close each opened tag with the corresponding tag. The content of the element is located between the opening and the closing tags. The explicit closing tag is identical to the opening tag, except that it is prefixed with the / character.

Opening and closing XML tags

```
<element>Content</element>
```

If an element has no content, you can close it implicitly by prefixing the second angle bracket with the / character:

```
<element />
```

An element can specify attributes, possibly with value, in the opening tag:

```
<element attribute="value" attribute2="value2" />
```

In addition to text, an element can contain additional elements. This allows any desired structure to be formed:

```
<element>
  Text
  <sub-element>Text</sub-element>
  <sub-element>Text</sub-element>
</element>
```

The only requirement for the structure of an XML document is that it can have only one node at the top level of the hierarchy. An XML document that complies with the above syntax requirements is called a *well-formed document*.

12.1.2 Correctness of XML Documents

A well-formed XML document can be processed by so-called XML parsers. Although a document must be well-formed, this does not guarantee the document's usability for a certain area of deployment. For example, although the following two XML documents are both well-formed, and their information content is identical, a processing routine that can interpret one of the two formats will scarcely also understand the other:

```
<person>
  <name>Cocker</name>
  <first name>Joe</firstname>
  <dob>1944-05-20</dob>
</person>
```

```
<person    name="Cocker"
           firstname="Joe"
           dob="1944-05-20" />
```

Thus, the XML parser requires further information regarding its planned use before it can evaluate the structure of an XML document. For this purpose, two different form of additional information can accompany an XML document: the document type definition (DTD) and the XML schema.

12.1.2.1 Document Type Definition

Originally, only the document type definition (DTD) was available to specify the document structure. The DTD describes the structure of an XML document by specifying the corresponding tags, the associated subtags, and the allowed content. An example of a DTD is shown in the example below:

```
<!ELEMENT Person (Name?,Firstname?,DOB?,
FavoriteColors ?) >
<!ELEMENT Name (#PCDATA) >
<!ELEMENT Firstname (#PCDATA) >
<!ELEMENT DOB (#PCDATA) >
<!ELEMENT FavoriteColors (favoritecolorsItem*) >
<!ELEMENT FavoriteColorsItem (#PCDATA) >
```

DTDs have the deficiency that although they provide information regarding the structure of a document, they do not adequately provide semantic details, such as data types or cardinalities. In addition, a DTD itself is not a well-formed XML document, a fact that unnecessarily complicates processing. The XML schema specification was defined to overcome these DTD disadvantages.

12.1.2.2 XML Schema

An XML schema definition is itself a well-formed XML document, which, for example, can define and use cardinalities and data types:

```
<s:complexType name="Person">
  <s:sequence>
    <s:element name="Name" type="s:string" minOccurs="0" />
    <s:element name="Firstname"
        type="s:string" minOccurs="0" />
    <s:element name="DOB"
        type="s:date" minOccurs="0" />
    <s:element
        name="FavoriteColor"
        type="ArrayOfFavoriteColorItem" minOccurs="0" />
    </s:sequence>
</s:complexType>

<s:complexType name="ArrayOfFavoriteColorItem">
  <s:sequence>
    <s:element name="FavoriteColorItem"
        type="s:string" minOccurs="0"
        maxOccurs="unbounded" nillable="true" />
  </s:sequence>
</s:complexType>
```

12.2 Caché and XML

As the previous example of XML schema shows, the representation is very similar to a class definition. XML schema have the only weakness that they cannot be used to describe methods. Caché makes it possible to export objects as XML documents or import XML documents to create Caché objects without making any major changes to the existing class definition.

To convert the Caché classes into XML-enabled classes, they must inherit from the %XML.Adaptor system class that contains the functionality needed for the interaction with XML. The class definition of User.Person changes to:

```
Class User.Person Extends (%Persistent, %XML.Adaptor)
```

The following two parameters and five new methods are available after the class has been compiled:

Table 12.1 Parameters and methods from the *%XML.adaptor* class

Name	Description
Parameter XMLENABLED	This parameter has the value 1 and indicates that the class is XML enabled.
Parameter XMLNAME	This is the name of the XML tag that has been created for this class object.
Method XMLSchema()	Creates an XML schema definition for the class and all referenced data types.
Method XMLDTD()	Creates a DTD for the class.
Method XMLExport()	Creates an XML document that contains the current object as well as all reachable XML-enabled subobjects.
Method XMLImport()	Imports an XML document and builds the contained object tree in memory.
Method XMLNew()	An internal function called by Caché during an import; it should not be called by the user.

12.2.1 Creating XML

XML with Caché Server Pages

Caché Server Pages (CSP) can be used to output members of the Person class saved in the database as an XML document. The following CSP page executes a database query that outputs all persons. The objects found are output in sequence by the XMLExport() method; the individual person documents are combined using the persons tag as root element:

```
<?xml version="1.0" encoding="UTF-8" standalone="yes" ?>

<csp:content type="text/xml">

<script language="sql" name="rs">
  SELECT ID FROM SQLUser.Person
  ORDER BY Name
</script>

<persons>
<csp:while condition=" rs.Next()">
<script language="Cache" runat="Server">
  set person= ##class(User.Person).%OpenId(rs.Data("ID"))
  Do person.XMLExport()
</script>
</csp:while>
</persons>
```

In addition, to allow the Internet Explorer to automatically format the document display as a tree, the document content type is changed to text/xml:

Tree representation of XML documents

```
<?xml version="1.0" encoding="UTF-8" standalone="yes" ?>
<persons>
  <Person>
    <Name>Bon Jovi</Name>
    <Firstname>Jon</Firstname>
    <DOB>1962-03-03</Birthdate>
```

```
    <FavoriteColors>
      <FavoritecolorItem>Blue</FavoriteColorItem>
      <FavoritecolorItem>Red</FavoriteColorItem>
    </Favoritecolors>
  </Person>
  <Person>
    <Name>Ciccone</Name>
    <Firstname>Madonna Luise</FirstName>
...
  </Person>
</persons>
```

12.2.2 Adapting the XML Projection

The XML output created above is a standard projection that has been automatically created. You can use the class and property parameters to customize the XML output to meet a wide range of special requirements.

12.2.2.1 Suppressing Output

If you do not wish a property to appear in the XML projection, you can suppress it by changing the XMLPROJECTION parameter, as shown in the following example:

```
Property DOB As %Date(XMLPROJECTION = "NONE");
```

12.2.2.2 Element Names

Classes and properties have an XMLNAME parameter that can be used to change the tag name used to publish the property or the class:

```
Property DOB As %Date(XMLNAME = "Birthdate");
```

The output changes to:

```
    <Birthdate>1962-03-03</Birthdate>
```

12.2.2.3 Projection Type

The properties of a class can be created as either a sub-element or an attribute of the class element. To create a separate sub-element, the XMLPROJECTION parameter must have the value ELEMENT:

```
Property Name As %String(XMLPROJECTION = "ELEMENT");
```

The same output ensues as before the change:

```
    <Name>Bon Jovi</Name>
```

If the value is changed to ATTRIBUTE, the property is exported as an attribute of the class element:

```
Property Name As %String(XMLPROJECTION = "ATTRIBUTE");
```

The previous definition creates the following XML output:

```
    <Person Name="Bon Jovi">
```

12.2.2.4 Multi-value Properties (Collections)

Several parameters control the projection of multi-value properties:

Parameter	Description
XMLPROJECTION	This parameter must have the value COLLECTION for a collection.
XMLNAME	The name of the XML tag that will be created for the collection property.
XMLITEMNAME	The name of the XML tag that will be created for every element in the collection.
XMLKEYNAME	The name of the attribute that will contain the key used to save the element in the array collection.

The following definition shortensthe descriptors for the `FavoriteColor` property to `colors` and `color`, respectively:

```
Property FavoriteColors As %String(
    XMLITEMNAME = "Color",
    XMLNAME = "Colors",
    XMLPROJECTION = "COLLECTION");
```

The output changes to:

```
<Colors>
    <Color>Blue</Color>
    <Color>Red</Color>
</Colors>
```

12.2.3 Importing XML

Importing existing XML documents into Caché objects

The Caché XML interface can also be used to import existing XML documents and convert them into Caché objects. The imported document must have the same structure that would be produced by the corresponding class.

The `%XML.Reader` class used to retrieve the XML document reads a document from a file, a string variable or a stream. The imported document can be browsed node-by-node and converted into Caché objects.

Correlation map

To enable `%XML.Reader` to correlate a node to a Caché class, a table must be provided that associates the node names with the corresponding Caché classes. This table, called the `Correlation-Map`, can include several entries. Each entry consists of one node name and one class name. Each node name must be unique. A Caché class, on the other hand, can be assigned to several node names. The `Correlation-Map` is populated with the `Correlate()` method of the `%XML.Reader` class:

```
// Associate a class name with the XML element name
Do reader.Correlate("Persons","User.Person")
Do reader.Correlate("Users","User.Person")
```

Retrieval in Caché object-by-object

The actual import takes place object-by-object. This means if an XML document contains several objects, each one is read in an individual processing step. The importing routine provides a reference for the retrieved object. Any existing sub-objects are also retrieved during the retrieval process. The returned object reference then can be used to access the other objects:

```
// Start a new XML Reader
Set reader = ##class(%XML.Reader).%New()

// Open the XML Data
Do reader.OpenFile("persons.xml")

// Connect the Person node name with the class
// User.Person.
Do reader.Correlate("Person","User.Person")

// Import the contained objects
set person =""
WHILE( reader.Next(.person) )
{
  ' Save the object and all sub-objects
  Do person.%Save()

  ' Display progress on screen
  Write "Person ",person.Name," read in",!
}

// Done.
```

Because the objects retrieved in this way currently exist only in memory, you must explicitly save them in the database. This separation between retrieval and saving enables you to access objects and perform any changes.

Note that the XML import is not limited to persistent classes, but can be performed with any XML-enabled Caché class.

Import is not limited to persistent classes

12.3 Caché Web Services with SOAP

The Simple Object Access Protocol (SOAP) uses XML to code function calls that can be exchanged between any systems. Because a SOAP message is also an XML document, it is particularly well-suited for being sent to a Web server to request special services there. We call these special services *Web services*.

12.3.1 Introduction

Web services are based on a number of XML-related standards. The Web Services Description Language (WSDL) not only calls Web services using SOAP but also provides an exact description of the provided Web services so that clients can create the necessary calls using SOAP. In this respect, WSDL is similar to a type library in ActiveX (refer to Section 9.3.1.1).

SOAP, XML, and WSDL

With the help of CSP Web Gateway, Caché can publish any class method as a Web service. The only requirement is to add the WebMethod keyword to the method definition. An example for a simple Web service follows:

```
/// Simple Web service example

Class User.SOAPService Extends %SOAP.WebService
{
  /// Name of the Web service.
  Parameter SERVICENAME = "SOAPService";

  /// URL for the Web service
  Parameter LOCATION = "http://localhost:1972/csp/user";

  /// SOAP namespace for user datatypes
  Parameter NAMESPACE = "localhost";

/// Load the specified person from database
ClassMethod LoadPerson(Id As %Integer)
                        As User.Person [ WebMethod ]
  {
    quit ##class(User.Person).%OpenId(Id)
  }

/// Negate the specified number
ClassMethod Minus(Number As %Integer) As %Integer [WebMethod]
  {
    quit -Number
  }
}
```

When the Caché class compiler compiles the class, it creates an specific class for each method marked as a WebMethod. The created class provides the operations required to create WSDL, to decode and perform the SOAP calls, and to return the result as a SOAP message.

12.3.2 Using Web Services

The use of SOAP as a communication protocol allows the provided services to be accessed from a wide range of programming languages and platforms. The following examples demonstrate several possible ways of using Web services created with Caché.

Usually, access to Web services is provided with an additional library that handles any conversions. For each example, we specify the library used at the beginning of the corresponding section.

12.3.2.1 CSP Gateway

The easiest way to test a newly created Web service is to use the Caché's CSP Gateway. In this case, no further library is necessary. However, this function mainly serves to test a Web service. Once the class has been opened with the corresponding Web service in Caché Studio, the overview page for the opened Web service can be displayed in the Web browser by clicking *Web Page* in the *View* menu. Both the WSDL description of the service and the associated methods can be called directly from the overview page:

Web Service User.SOAPService

The following operations are supported. For a formal definition, please review the **Service Description**.

- **LoadPerson**

- **Minus**

12.3 Caché Web Services with SOAP

Figure 12.1 The CSP overview of a Caché Web service

For each method, a separate HTML page is generated that provides a form in which all parameters of the method can be entered:

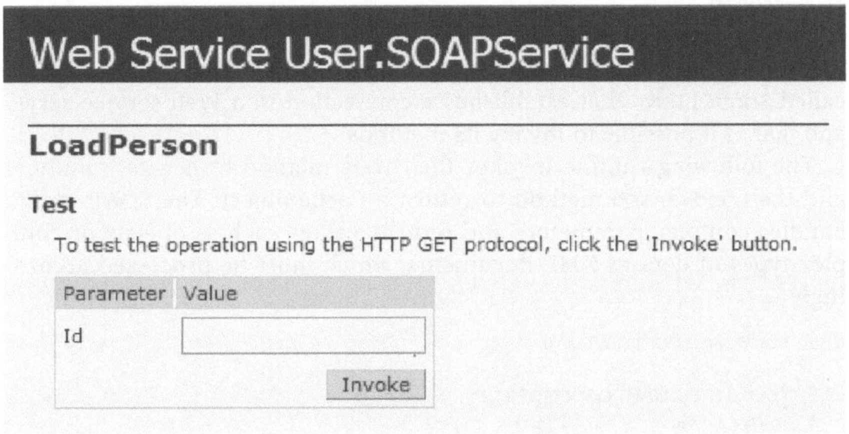

Figure 12.2 Invoking a Web method

Web Service User.SOAPService

LoadPerson

Test

To test the operation using the HTTP GET protocol, click the 'Invoke' button.

Parameter	Value
Id	

Invoke

Once the parameter values have been entering, the method can be invoked by clicking *Invoke*. The method call returns a SOAP message that the browser displays appropriately formatted:

Result of a method invoked using the CSP gateway

```
<?xml version="1.0" encoding="UTF-8" standalone="no" ?>
<SOAP-ENV:Envelope
  xmlns:SOAP-ENV="http://schemas.xmlsoap.org/soap/envelope/"
  xmlns:xsi="http://www.w3.org/2001/XMLSchema-instance"
  xmlns:s="http://www.w3.org/2001/XMLSchema">
  <SOAP-ENV:Body>
    <LoadPersonResponse xmlns="localhost">
      <LoadPersonResult>
        <Name>Jackson</Name>
        <Firstname>Michael</Firstname>
        <DOB>1958-08-29</DOB>
        <FavoriteColors>
          <FavoriteColorsItem>Blue</FavoriteColorsItem>
          <FavoriteColorsItem>Red</FavoriteColorsItem>
        </FavoriteColors>
      </LoadPersonResult>
    </LoadPersonResponse>
  </SOAP-ENV:Body>
</SOAP-ENV:Envelope>
```

12.3.2.2 Visual Basic 6.0

Microsoft offers a SOAP toolkit for download that makes it easy to invoke Web services from Visual Basic 6.0. The current version of the toolkit can be downloaded from the following Internet address:

```
http://msdn.microsoft.com/soap
```

Once you have installed the SOAP toolkit, you must add references to the following new libraries to the Visual Basic project (refer to Section 9.3.1.1):

- Microsoft Soap Type Library
- Microsoft XML

Aside from many additional ActiveX classes, the toolkit contains a class called SoapClient that establishes a connection to a Web service server and makes it possible to invoke its methods.

Return values can be XML documents

The following routine invokes the Minus method to negate a number and the LoadPerson method to return a Caché object. The SOAP toolkit handles complex parameters and returns values such as objects or complex types of data as XML documents, which must be processed accordingly:

```
Dim soap As SoapClient

' Establish SOAP connection
Set soap = New SoapClient
soap.mssoapinit
   "http://127.0.0.1:1972/csp/user/User.SOAPService.CLS?WSDL"

' First, print a negated number
Print soap.Minus(1000)

' The person object is a list with XML nodes
Dim result As IXMLDOMNodeList

' Load the User.Person object with ID = 4
Set result = soap.LoadPerson(4)

' Print the XML result
Print result.xml

' Print nodes individually
Dim length As Integer
length = result.length

While length > 0
  length = length - 1
  Print result.Item(length).text
Wend
```

12.3.2.3 Visual Basic .net

Because SOAP forms a central communications protocol in .net technology, all libraries needed for access exist once the .net framework has been installed.

Add WSDL reference as Web reference

In Visual Basic .net, Web services are integrated similarly to libraries, and can be directly used as classes. In a new Visual Basic .net project for a Windows application, the WSDL reference is inserted into the project using the *Add Web reference* item in the *Projects* menu. The following dialog box shows the URL of the WSDL description in the address field and prompts for confirmation. The Web service can be added once the WSDL file has been downloaded.

The reference can now be used in the .net application as follows (the example assumes that the Web service reference is named `CacheService`):

```
Dim soap As CacheService.SOAPService

soap = New CacheService.SOAPService()
Debug.WriteLine(soap.Minus(1000))

' Load person
Dim person As CacheService.User_Person
person = soap.LoadPerson(4)

' Write properties
Debug.WriteLine("Name: " + person.Name)
Debug.Write("FavoriteColors: ")

Dim i As Integer

For i = 0 To person.Colors.Length - 1
  Debug.Write(person.Colors.GetValue(i) + " ")
Next
```

This example shows how the .net framework uses the type information of a WSDL file similar to early binding in Visual Basic (refer to Section 9.3.1.1).

12.3.2.4 Java

Java has many libraries available for SOAP access. The most popular implementation is offered by the Apache Software Foundation. Its Axis Project offers a complete open source implementation. Axis libraries are available at the following address:

```
http://xml.apache.org/axis/index.html
```

Axis libraries

The Axis toolkit provides a number of ways to access Web services. The following example shows how the Java classes to generated from the WSDL definition of the Web service can be used in a Java application to invoke the Web service methods. The basic steps are:

- Generating Java class files with the `wsdl2java` tool.
- Integrating the libraries and the generated classes in the application.

341

Generating Java class files

If the required libraries have been added to the CLASSPATH (consult the Axis toolkit documentation for detailed information), the wsdl2java tool can be invoked with the following statement:

```
java org.apache.axis.wsdl.WSDL2Java <WSDL-URL>
```

When applied to this example, the program will generate the following six Java files. The file and class names of these files are derived from the referenced Web services:

Table 12.3 Java files for the SOAP example

Name	Description
SOAPServiceSoap.java	Contains the interface with the methods of the Web service.
SOAPServiceSoapStub.java	Encapsulates the functions necessary for invoking the Web service and implementing the above interface.
ArrayOfLieblingsfarben.java	A class for implementing the FavoriteColors collection property of the User.Person class.
UserPerson.java	Implements a Java class that acts like User.Person.
SOAPService.java	An interface definition of the ServiceLocator for making the connection to the Web service and returning a reference for an object that implements the appropriate Web service methods (see SOAPServiceSOAP.java).
SOAPServiceLocator.java	Implements the above interface.

Classes generated using this procedure can then be used in a Java program with the help of the Axis library:

```
package sample;

import org.apache.axis.client.Call;
import org.apache.axis.client.Service;
import javax.xml.rpc.namespace.QName;

public class SOAPExample
{
  public static void main(String[] args)
  {
    try {
      SOAPServiceSoap soap = new
               SOAPServiceLocator().getSOAPServiceSoap();
      System.out.println(soap.minus(new Long(1000)));

      UserPerson person = soap.LoadPerson(new Long(4));
      System.out.println("Person: " + person.getName());
    } catch (Exception exAny) {
      System.err.println(exAny.toString());
    }
  }
}
```

13 Device Management

Caché is available on various operating systems such as Windows, UNIX (including Linux), and OpenVMS. For each of those platforms, the input/output (I/O) programming provides commands and procedures for controlling devices as diverse as terminals (monitor screens), printers, magnetic tapes, sequential files, and spool devices. I/O programming also controls the TCP connections for client/server systems.

13.1 Input/Output

Despite this range of operating systems and devices, Caché pursues a standardized concept for input/output. This section introduces the fundamental side of the concept. Because of the limited space available here, we can explain only the basics involved. The interested reader should consult the Caché documentation for further details and examples, in particular *Using Caché ObjectScript*, which provides a very detailed description of the input/output programming in the section *I/O Devices and Commands*.

Standardized concept for the input and output

13.1.1 Basic Characteristics of I/O Programming

Generally, input/output devices are addressed and specified in two ways:

- Calling the %IS utility program. Refer to the *Using Caché ObjectScript* manual.
- Using the Open, Use and Close commands. In this case, devices are named using Caché-specific device designations. The Read and Write commands perform the actual input/output.

%IS utility program

Open, Use, and Close commands

Each Caché process has a main input and output device, which are identical and become the *principal device* at login to Caché from a terminal. The $Principal special variable contains the name of this device, which it retains until the process ends. The $Io special variable initially also contains this value, but it can change should the I/O device change. Thus, $Io always reflects the value of the *current* device, which obviously can differ from the *principal device*.

The Use command and the specification of a device can be used to address a different output device. Whereas the *principal device* of a process can be addressed with an Open command using Use $Principal (or its equivalent Use 0), all other devices must be reserved beforehand

Principal device

with the Open command. However, in certain situations an automatic switch is made from the current device to the *principal device*:

- when the current device is closed with a Close command ,
- when an error occurs in the program processing, but no error trap has been set,
- when the command shell is entered in programming mode.

Null device

A so-called *null device* exists in addition to the *principal device*. The *null device* is used primarily when output is not to be routed to the terminal screen. An Open command with the designation nul: opens a null device under Windows, /dev/null under UNIX, and NL: under OpenVMS. Read commands to the *null device* receive the null string; Write commands send nothing and terminate immediately.

Processes initiated with a Job command

Processes initiated with a Job command have the *null device* as the *principal device*. This ensures that the creation of a new Caché process using the Job command does not fail only because a *principal device* has already been reserved by another process.

A Halt command terminates a Caché process and releases all devices allocated to it.

13.1.2 Input/Output-specific Special Variables

Several input/output operations affect the values of certain special variables, which themselves can be used to control input/output.

The following table summarizes device-specific special variables. Chapter 5 and the Caché documentation provide further details.

Table 13.1 Device-specific special variables

Special variable	Description
$Io	The current device
$Key	Contains the character that ended the last Read command
$Principal	The *principal device*, which remains unchanged during the lifetime of the process
$X	Contains the current column number of the used device
$Y	Contains the current row number of the used device
$ZEOF	Indicates that the end of file was reached while reading a sequential file
$ZMode	Shows the parameter that was used in an Open or Use command for the current device
$ZPOS	Contains the current file position for a sequential file

To some extent, because $Test can be used to check the *timeout* for Open and Use, it is also a device-specific variable.

13.2 The Open, Use, and Close Commands

13.2.1 Formal Definition

The Open, Use, and Close input/output commands can reserve (i.e., open an I/O channel to the specified device), use, write to, read from, and close devices. To reroute an input/output operation to a certain device, you must perform the following actions:

Routing input/output operations to a specific device

- If the required I/O device is not already the *principal device*, use an Open command to reserve the device for this process. No other process can reserve this device after a successful reservation. Sequential files are an exception.
- A Use command makes the reserved device the current device.
- A Read command can read from this device; a Write command writes to it.
- Once output operations have completed, a Close command releases the reservation so that another process can issue a reservation.

The I/O commands have the following formal definitions:

Open device[:[specs][:[timeout][:"mnespace"]]
Use device[:[spec][:"mnespace"]]
Close device[:specs]

All three commands can have a postcondition. The following section provides details of the device designations for device. The following table provides information on the form of the supplementary parameters. A colon is used as delimiter between the individual parameters.

Argument	Explanation
specs	Detailed description of the reserved device, e.g., the type of access for sequential files. Also refer to Section 13.3.1.
timeout	The number of seconds that a process waits for the release of the device currently reserved by another process. If the reserve is successful within this interval, the $Test special variable is set to 1, otherwise it is zero and the Else command can respond appropriately. An Open command without timeout always waits until the requested device becomes free. This can result in the process hanging, which, for example, can be terminated with <Ctrl-C>.
mnespace	A mnemonic space is a Caché routine that performs device-specific actions. These include, for example, cursor movements on a screen (refer to Section 13.3.2). The mnemonic space addressed with label is executed with Write /label.

Table 13.2 Parameters for input/output commands

Examples

```
Open "LPT1:" Use "LPT1:"
```

Open and use the printer attached to LPT1:.

Examples of I/O commands

```
Open "c:\folder1\test.out":(/CREATE:/STREAM):5
```

Open a sequential file. (Refer to Section 13.3.1.)

```
Open "|PRN|":"W"
```

Open the Windows default printer for writing.

```
Open "|PRN|HP LaserJet 5P"
```

Open the Windows printer with the designation "HP LaserJet 5P" instead of the default printer.

```
Set Pipe="ls —l" Open Pipe Use Pipe Read x
```

Open a pipe to the UNIX command ls —l and read the first line of its output.

13.2.2 Device Designations

Symbolic names are used for most device classes, although device designations can be taken from the base operating system (such as for a sequential file under Windows: \directory\filename.ext; refer to Section 13.3.1). The following table shows device designations used in Caché:

Table 13.3 Device designations

Device designation	Explanation
|TRM|:*process*	Caché terminal window under Windows, e.g., |TRM|:42.
|PRN|*printer*	Windows printer, e.g., |PRN|\\marketing\printer1.
|TNT|*node:port*	Device attached using telnet, e.g., |TNT|192.9.200.167:4.
|LAT|*node:port:service*	Device attached using LAT, e.g., |LAT|Server_A:Port_8. Only one of the designations port or service can be used, not both together.
|TCP|*idnum*	Connection to a TCP socket, e.g., |TCP|1. IP address and socket number are specified as parameters.
|NPIPE|*idnum*	Named pipe, e.g., |NPIPE|2. The name of the pipe is specified as parameter.
drive:\dir\file.ext */path/file* *drive:[dir]file.ext;version*	File in the operating system (Windows/UNIX/OpenVMS), e.g., c:\Myfiles\Letter.doc, /usr/winfried/appointments or DUAO:[usr]myfile.txt;2.
device: */dev/device* *device:*	Device in the operating system (Windows/UNIX/OpenVMS), e.g., COM2:, /dev/tty07 or LTAO:.
UNIX command	Pipe to a UNIX command, e.g., ls —l /usr/winfried/t*.

The *Using Caché ObjectScript* manual contains complete definitions for all supported operating systems.

13.3 Practical Use of Input/Output in Caché

13.3.1 Sequential Files

Read and write access to files is a common operation. Caché supports sequential files (in all operating systems) and the special RMS file format in OpenVMS. Although the two access modes have minor differences, sequential files—to which we restrict ourselves—have a number of parameters not available for RMS files.

Read and write access to files

The Open command in the following general form opens a sequential file:

Open file[:[(parameter[,parameter ...])][:timeout]]

The specified parameters have the following meaning:

Parameter	Description
/APPEND	Append the data records at the end of an existing file.
/CREATE	Open a file for writing. The file will be created if it does not exist.
/FIXED	Data records have a fixed length that is specified with the /RECORDSIZE parameter.
/NEW	Open a new file. If a file with the same name exists, it will be deleted.
/READ	Read access to a file.
/RECORDSIZE=n	The length of the data records for the /FIXED format.
/STREAM	The file behaves as a stream. Individual records are separated using Write !.
/VARIABLE	Each Write creates a data record in the *variable length* format.
/WRITE	Write access to a file.

Table 13.4 Parameters for sequential files

The Use command with the form Use file:(/position=position) can move a point to a position within a file. The following example reads the third, fourth, and fifth data records with the fixed record length of 100 characters from the "Fixed.len" file.

Positioning within a file

Example

```
Set file="Fixed.len"
Open file:(/FIXED:/RECORDSIZE=100)
Use file:(/POSITION=200)
Read record(3),record(4),record(5)
```

Two parameters can be specified when a sequential file is closed: /DELETE and /RENAME=filename. In the first case, the file will be deleted after it is closed. In the second case, the file will be renamed to the specified name.

Closing a sequential file

13.3.2 Printers and Terminals

Accessing printers and terminals (the two are syntactically equivalent in Caché) has the same importance as accessing files.

The Open command (in the following general form) opens a printer or terminal. At this time, or with a subsequent Use command, parameters can be specified to select certain options:

Specifying parameters for opening printers and terminals

Open device[:[(parameter[,parameter ...])]][:timeout][:"mnespace"]]
Use device[:[(parameter[,parameter ...])]][:"mnespace"]]

The specified parameters have the following meanings:

Table 13.5 Parameters for printers and terminals

Parameter	Description
/BREAK	Allow the use of Ctrl-C to interrupt the program execution. It can be disabled with /BREAK=O.
/CRT	Specify that the device is a screen. In contrast, /CRT=O identifies the device as a printer.
/ECHO	Activate echo, namely the display of the entered characters (active as default). /ECHO=O deactivates the echo.
/EDIT	Allow the use of cursor keys to edit inputs. This option can be deactivated with /EDIT=O.
/MARGIN=n	Set the right-hand margin. If $X exceeds the specified value, Caché automatically performs a line feed. The specification of O as argument inhibits an automatic line feed.
/TERMINATOR=s	Specify the character that terminates an input. Any string of control characters can be specified for s, default is $Character(13,27).
/UPPER	Automatically convert entered lowercase letters into uppercase letters. This option can be deactivated with /UPPER=O.

Example

```
Use $Io:(/ECHO=O:/UPPER)
Read "Please enter your password: ",Password
Use $Io:(/ECHO:/UPPER=O)
```

Converting input characters into uppercase letters

In this example, the echo has been deactivated for the current device and the conversion into uppercase letters activated before the request for the password is made. The parameters are then reset.

13.3.3 Input/Output at Terminals

Under some circumstances, programming an output device with escape sequences can be useful. This affects both printers and ASCII screens that are attached serially or asynchronously. Caché supports this form of terminal programming in various ways.

ANSI X3.64 is a standard for these escape sequences. A typical sequence for positioning the cursor at the coordinates x,y has the form:

Example

```
Set X=10,Y=20
Write *27,*91,Y,*59,X,*72
```

The * character prefixed to a number converts it into the corresponding ASCII code, for example, *27 converts into the Escape character. Note that the y-coordinate precedes the x-coordinate.

Representing cursor position with $X and $Y

Changing the cursor on the output screen does *not* change the values of $X and $Y. You can set the values for $X and $Y in accordance with the last cursor movement. In the above example, Set $X=X-1,$Y=Y-1 would suffice. The subtraction of -1 for the coordinates results from the coordinate origin being (0,0) in Caché rather than (1,1) as in ANSI X3.64.

Rather than direct programming, it is usually better to use so-called *mnemonic namespaces* for terminal programming. We have already mentioned mnemonic namespaces in conjunction with the formal definition of the Open and Use commands. The *mnemonic namespace* of interest here is ANSI X3.64, which standardizes terminal programming. Because Caché provides this system-wide as a default for terminals, the following formal specification is superfluous as an argument for either the Open or Use command:

Mnemonic namespaces

Example

```
Use $Io::"%X364"
Open "/dev/tty06":"%X364"
Open "|PRN|" Use "|PRN|":"%X634"
```

As an example, we will demonstrate a typical use of the Write command. The cursor positioning specified above is represented using the CUP(y,x) mnemonic and initialized with a Write command with a slash, in the following manner:

Positioning a cursor

Example

```
Set X=10,Y=20
Write /CUP(Y,X)
```

The following table contains the most important control mnemonics from the ANSI-X3.64 standard. The *Using Caché ObjectScript* manual contains a complete list.

Mnemonic	Explanation	Changed
/CUB(columns)	Cursor back	$X
/CUD(rows)	Cursor down	$Y
/CUF(columns)	Cursor forward	$X
/CUP(y,x)	Cursor positioning	$X, $Y
/CUU(rows)	Cursor up	$Y
/DCH(number)	Delete characters	
/DL(number)	Delete lines	
/ECH(number)	Erase characters	
/ED(parameter)	Erase display (0=cursor to end, 1=start to cursor, 2=complete)	
/EL(parameter)	Erase line (0=cursor to end, 1=start to cursor, 2=complete)	
/ICH(number)	Insert characters	
/IL(number)	Insert lines	
/SGR(parameter)	Select graphic rendition (0=normal, 1=bold, 4=underlined, 5=flashing, 7=reverse)	

Table 13.6 Important control mnemonics from the ANSI-X3.64 Standard

Appendix A. Caché ObjectScript Reference

Commands

Command	Description
Break[:cond]	Interrupt execution of the current routine for debugging purposes.
Break[:cond] [status]	Activate or deactivate user interrupts.
Close[:cond] device[:parameter]	Close the device, make it available again for other users and, possibly, set the device characteristics.
CONTINUE[:cond]	End the current execution of the code block of a For, WHILE, or Do/WHILE loop and check the condition to determine whether a further iteration follows.
Do[:cond] Do[:cond] {…} WHILE expression	Invoke a subroutine or code block and continue the program processing with the next command after completion.
Do[:cond] entryref[(parameter)] [:cond]	Invoke a subroutine, pass the optional parameter and continue the program processing with the next command after completion.
Else	Execute the following commands only if the value of $Test is 0.
Else {…}	Execute the following code block only if none of the preceding If and ElseIf conditions were true.
ElseIf expression {…}	Execute the following command block only if none of the preceding If and ElseIf conditions were true and expression is true.
For For {…}	Execute the remainder of the line or the following code block until a Quit or Goto command ends the loop.
For variable=expression[,…] For variable=expression[,…] {…} For variable=start:increment:[end] For variable=start:increment:[end] {…}	Repeat the execution of the following commands in the routine line or the following code block for different values of a local variable.
Goto[:cond]	Resume the normal execution of a routine that was interrupted with the Break command.
Goto[:cond] location[:cond]	Continue the program execution at another line or in another routine.
Halt[:cond]	Terminate the current Caché job and close the terminal session.
Hang[:cond] seconds	Suspend routine execution for the specified time.
If	Execute the following commands only if the value of $Test is true.
If expression If expression {…}	Test the expression and execute the remainder of the line or the following code block if the result is true.
Job[:cond] routine[:cond][(routine-parms)][:[process-prams] [:timeout]]	Start execution of a new Caché process.

351

Command	Description
Kill[:cond] Kill[:cond] variable Kill[:cond] (variable)	Delete all variables, only the specified variables, or all except the specified variables.

Lock[:cond]
Lock[:cond] [+/−]variable[,...]
  [:timeout]
Lock[:cond] [+/−](variable[,...])
  [:timeout]
	Set or remove locks on local or global variables.

Merge[:cond] target=source	Copy variable trees.
New[:cond] New[:cond] variable[,...] New[:cond] (variable[,...])	Hide all, the specified, or all except the specified local variables in a subroutine.
Open[:cond] device[:(parameter)] [:timeout][:"mnespace"]	Open a device for later use and optionally set the device characteristics.
Print [line1[:line2]]	Output the specified routine lines to the current device.
Quit[:cond]	End the execution of a subroutine invoked with Do, Xecute, or For.
Quit[:cond] expression	End the execution of a user-defined function and return the value of the expression as result.

Read[:cond] [f,][string,][f,]
  variable[:timeout]
Read[:cond] [f,][string,][f,]
  *variable[:timeout]
Read[:cond] [f,][string,][f,]
  variable#n[:timeout]
	Read information from the current device.

Set[:cond] variable=expression Set[:cond] (variablelist)=expression	Assign a value to one or more variables.
TCommit[:cond]	Confirm the current transaction and make all database changes permanent.
TROllback[:cond]	Abort the current transaction and revoke all database changes.
TStart[:cond]	Mark the start of a transaction.
Use[:cond] device[:(parameter)] [:timeout][:"mnespace"]	Make a previously opened device the current device and optionally set the device characteristics.
View block View offset:mode:length:new-value	Modify a memory location or read and write database blocks. Reserved for internal use by Caché.
WHILE expression {...}	Repeat execution of the following code block until expression evaluates to false.
Do {...} WHILE expression	Define the end condition after a Do/WHILE code block.
Write[:cond] [f,]expression Write[:cond] [f,]*expression	Output characters to the current device.
Xecute[:cond] expression[:cond]	Execute Caché ObjectScript code that is stored as data.
ZBreak	Set a break point for debugging purposes.
ZInsert "code"[:location]	Insert a line into the routine currently being edited.
ZKill variable	Delete a local or global variable without deleting its child nodes.
ZLoad [:cond] ZLoad routine	Load a routine for editing.
ZNspace expression	Change the current namespace.
ZPrint ZPrint line1[:line2]	Output the specified routine lines to the current device.

Command	Description
ZQuit ZQuit[:cond] expression	Remove all or a specified number of execution levels from the execution stack.
ZRemove ZRemove line1[:line2]	Delete all or the specified lines from the routine currently being edited.
ZSave ZSave routine	Store the routine (possibly with a different name).
ZSYNC	Ensure that all logical transactions have also physically completed.
ZTrap[:cond] ZTrap[:cond] expression	Force an error with the specified message or with the default message <ZTRAP>.
ZWrite ZWrite variable	Write the values of all local variables or of the specified local or global variable to the current device.
ZZDUMP (expression)	Write the string as hexadecimal dump to the current device.

Functions

Function	Description
$Ascii(expression[,position])	Return the ASCII code of a character.
$BIT(bitstring,position[,bitvalue])	Create a new bit string if needed and optionally set the bit value at the specified position.
$BITCOUNT(bitstring[,bitvalue])	Count the number of bits in the bit string, either all or those with the specified bit value.
$BITFIND(bitstring,bitvalue[,startpos])	Search for a bit value in a bit string and return that position.
$BITLOGIC(bitstring_expression [,length])	Perform a bit logic operation on the bit string.
$CASE(expression,result:value,...)	Evaluate expression and return the value after the result that applies.
$Char(expression[,...])	Produce a string with the specified ASCII code from a list of integers.
$Data(variable)	Specify whether a variable reference is defined, has successors, or both or none applies.
$Extract(expression[,from[,to]])	Return apart of a string from a start position to an end position.
$Find(string,substring[,position])	Return the end position of the substring in a string.
$FNumber(number,format[,decimal])	Return the value of an expression in the format specified by the user.
$Get(variable[,default])	Return the value of a variable if it exists.
$Increment(variable[,num])	Increment the specified variable by 1 or the specified value.
$INumber(number,format[,erropt])	Check a number for the specified format and convert it into the internal representation.
$ISOBJECT(variable)	Check whether the specified variable is a valid OREF.
$Justify(expression,width[,decimal])	Return a right-justified value and optionally format and round it numerically.
$Length(expression[,delimiter])	Return the length of a string in characters or the number of substrings separated by the specified delimiter.
$LIst(list[,from[,to]])	Return the list elements in the specified range.
$ListBuild(element,...)	Create a list with the elements specified as arguments.

Function	Description
$ListData(list[,position])	Test whether an element in the list is present and has a value.
$ListFind(list[,value [,start]])	Search for a value in a list beginning at the specified start position.
$ListGet(list[,position[,default]])	Return the value of a list element if it exists.
$ListLength(list)	Return the number of elements in a list.
$NAme(variable[,number])	Return the name of variable in canonical form with at most the specified number of dimensions.
$Next(variable)	Return the next index of a variable in the specified dimension.
$NUMber(number[,format[,min [,max]]])	Validate a number and convert it into the canonical Caché format.
$Order(variable[,direction])	Return the next or previous index of a variable in the specified dimension.
$Piece(expression,delimiter [,from[,to]])	Return one or more substrings separated by the specified delimiter.
$QLength(reference)	Return the number of dimensions for the indexed variable.
$QSubscript(reference,number)	Extract the specified number of dimensions from the indexed variable.
$Query(reference[,direction])	Return the next or previously defined reference for an indexed variable.
$Random(range)	Return a pseudo random number in the specified range.
$REverse(string)	Return the characters of the string in reversed sequence.
$Select(expression:value,...)	Return the value after the first expression that evaluates to TRUE (i.e., 1).
$SORTBEGIN(global)	Start a special sorting mode for the specified global.
$SORTEND(global[,save])	End the sorting mode for the global and save any updated data.
$STack(context_level[,code_string])	Return information about the active execution context on the call stack.
$Text(location)	Return the source text of a routine line.
$TRanslate(string,replace[,by])	Return a string in which specified characters were replaced by other specified characters (or were removed).
$View(address[,mode,length])	Return the contents of a memory location.
$ZABS(n)	Return the absolute value of a number (without sign).
$ZARCCOS(n)	Return the arccosine of a number between −1 and 1.
$ZARCSIN(n)	Return the arcsine of a number between −1 and 1.
$ZARCTAN(n)	Return the arctangent of a number.
$ZBITAND(bitstring1,bitstring2)	Return a bit string that results from the logical AND operation on two bit strings.
$ZBITCOUNT(bitstring)	Return the number of set bits (bits with the value 1) in the bit string.
$ZBITFIND(bitstring,value[,position])	Return the position after the first occurrence of the value (0 or 1) in the bit string, possibly from the specified position.
$ZBITGET(bitstring,position)	Return the bit value (0 or 1) of a specified position in the bit string.
$ZBITLEN(bitstring)	Return the length of a bit string.
$ZBITNOT(bitstring)	Return a bit string that results from the logical NOT operation on a bit string.

Function	Description
$ZBITOR(bitstring1,bitstring2)	Return a bit string that results from the logical OR operation on two bit strings.
$ZBITSET(bitstring,position,value)	Return a changed bit string in which the bit at the specified position is set to the specified value (0 or 1).
$ZBITSTR(size,value)	Return a bit string of specified length in which all bits have the set value (0 or 1).
$ZBITXOR(bitstring1,bitstring2)	Return a bit string that results from the logical XOR operation on two bit strings.
$ZBOOLEAN(arg1,arg2,bit-op)	Return a bit string that results from the specified logical operation on two bit strings.
$ZConVerT(string,mode)	Return a string processed according to the specified mode.
$ZCOS(n)	Calculate the cosine of an angle specified as radians.
$ZCOT(n)	Calculate the cotangent of an angle specified as radians.
$ZCSC(n)	Calculate the cosecant of an angle specified as radians.
$ZCrc(string)	Return the CRC checksum for the specified string.
$ZDate(Hdate[,format[,monthlist [,yearopt[,start[,end[,mindate [,maxdate[,erropt]]]]]]]])	Format the date specified in the internal $Horolog format as output in accordance with the parameters.
$ZDateH(date[,format[,monthlist [,yearopt[,start[,end[,mindate [,maxdate[,erropt]]]]]]]]	Format the date specified in the internal $Horolog format as output in accordance with the parameters.
$ZDateTime(Hdatetime,dformat [,zformat[,precision[,monthlist [,start[,end[,mindate[,maxdate [,erropt]]]]]]]])	Format the date/time combination specified in the internal $Horolog format as output in accordance with the parameters.
$ZDateTimeH(datetime,dformat [,zformat[,monthlist[,start[,end [,mindate[,maxdate[,erropt]]]]]]]])	Format the date/time combination specified in the output into the internal $Horolog format in accordance with the parameters.
$ZEXP(n)	Calculate the exponential function for n.
$ZF(-1,"commandline"[,args])	Execute the command line at the operating system level.
$ZHex(parm)	Convert a hexadecimal number into a decimal number, or vice versa.
$ZIncrement(variable[,num])	Increment the specified variable by 1 or the specified value. Identical to $Increment.
$ZLASCII(string[,position])	Calculate a numeric value from the first four bytes of the string or the four bytes at the specified position.
$ZLCHAR(n)	Calculate a four-byte-long string from the specified number.
$ZLN(n)	Calculate the natural logarithm of the specified number.
$ZLOG(n)	Calculate the logarithm of the specified number to the base 10.
$ZNext(reference)	Return the next defined reference of an indexed variable.
$ZOrder(reference)	Return the next defined reference of an indexed variable.
$ZPOWER(num,n)	Exponentiation—calculate the n-th power of the specified number.
$ZPrevious(reference)	Return the previously defined reference of an indexed variable.
$ZSEarch(target)	Return on a Windows platform the path and name of the specified operating system file or group of files.
$ZSEC(n)	Calculate the secant of an angle specified as radians.

Function	Description
$ZSEEK(offset[,mode])	Set the current device to a specific offset.
$ZSIN(n)	Calculate the sine of an angle specified as radians.
$ZSort(variable[,direction])	Return the next or previous index of a variable in the specified dimension.
$ZSQR(n)	Calculate the square root of the specified positive number.
$ZTAN(n)	Calculate the tangent of an angle specified as radians.
$ZTime(Htime[,format[,precision [,erropt]]])	Format as output the time specified in the internal $Horolog format in accordance with the parameters.
$ZTimeH(time[,format[,erropt]])	Format the time specified in output format into the internal $Horolog format in accordance with the parameters.
$ZTSRT(tlist[,delimiter])	Convert the specified list from the "tlist" format into the "plist" format.
$ZWAscii(string[,position])	Calculate a numeric value of the first two bytes of the strings or the two bytes at the specified position.
$ZWChar(n)	Calculate a two-byte-long string from the specified number.

Special Variables

Special variable	Description
$Device	Indicates whether the last input/output operation was successful.
$ECode	If an error has occurred, contains a list of one or more error codes delimited by commas.
$EStack	The number of stack levels that have been buffered for error handling.
$ETrap	A string containing Caché ObjectScript code to be performed should an error occur.
$HALT	User-defined program that is to be executed when a Halt command is issued for the process.
$Horolog	The current date and time.
$Io	The identification of the current device.
$Job	The identification of the user Caché job (process).
$Key	The control sequence that ended the last Read command.
$Principal	The identification of the main device of the user job.
$Quit	Contains 1 when the current context must be ended with a Quit command with argument, otherwise 0.
$STack	The number of execution levels contained in the stack for the user job.
$Storage	The number of bytes currently available for the user job to store local variables.
$SYSTEM	Contains the OREF of the system object with method. This provides programming information and control over the system, object, SQL, and CSP environment of Caché.
$Test	The result of the last If condition or the timeout.
$TLevel	The current nesting level of transaction processing.
$X	The number of the output column of the current device.
$Y	The number of the output line of the current device.

Special variable	Description
$ZA	Contains device-specific information about the current device.
$ZB	Contains device-specific information about the current device.
$ZChild	The identification of the last job created with the Job command.
$ZEOF	Indicates whether the end of file has been reached after reading from a sequential file. −1 indicates *end of file*.
$ZError	The text for the last error message.
$ZHorolog	The number of seconds elapsed since the last Caché system start.
$ZIo	Contains detailed information about the current device. If the current device is a terminal with remote connection, it contains information about the connection.
$ZJob	Status information about the current job.
$ZMode	Parameters specified for the current device with the Open or Use command.
$ZName	The name of the routine currently being executed.
$ZNSpace	The name of the current namespace.
$ZOrder	Returns the value of the next defined global reference.
$ZParent	The identification of the higher-level job that created the user job with the JOB command.
$ZPI	The value of the pi constant (3.141592653589793).
$ZPOS	Indicates the current file position within a sequential file.
$ZReference	The global reference last used by the job.
$ZStorage	The (parameterizable) size of the partition for the current job in KBs.
$ZTimeStamp	The current date and time in $HOROLOG format for the normalized UTC time.
$ZTimeZone	Contains the local time zone.
$ZTrap	The current error handling routine.
$ZVersion	The designation and version number of the Caché system currently running.

Structured System Variables

Structured system variable	Description
^$[|namespace|]Global(global name)	Provides information about globals.
$Data(^$[|namespace|]Global (global name))	Returns a numeric value that specifies whether a global exists in the namespace: 0 = global does not exist 10 = global exists
$Order(^$[|namespace|]Global(global name)[,direction])	Returns the name of the next or previous global in the namespace. 'direction' specifies the search direction: 1 = next global −1 = previous global
$Query(^$[|namespace|]Global(global name))	Returns the ^$Global reference of the next existing global in the namespace.
^$Job(job number)	Provides information about Caché jobs (processes).

Structured system variable	Description
$Data(^$Job(job))	Returns a numeric value that specifies whether a job exists: 0 = job does not exist 10 = job exists
$Order(^$Job(job)[,direction])	Returns the identification of the next or previous job. 'direction' specifies the search direction: 1 = next job −1 = previous job
$Query(^$Job(job))	Returns the ^$Job reference of the next existing job.
^$[|namespace|]Lock(lock name)	Provides information about locks (that were set with the Lock command).
$Data(^$[|namespace|]Lock(lock name))	Returns a numeric value that specifies whether a lock exists in the namespace: 0 = lock does not exist 10 = lock exists
$Order(^$[|namespace|]Lock(lock name)[,direction])	Returns the name of the next or previous lock in the namespace. 'direction' specifies the search direction: 1 = next lock −1 = previous lock
$Query(^$[|namespace|]Lock(lock name))	Returns the ^$Lock reference for the next existing lock in the namespace.
^$[|namespace|]Routine(routine name)	Provides information about routines.
$Data(^$[|namespace|]Routine(routine name))	Returns a numeric value that specifies whether a routine exists in the namespace: 0 = routine does not exist 10 = routine exists
$Order(^$[|namespace|]Routine(routine name[,direction]))	Returns the name of the next or previous routine in the namespace. 'direction' specifies the search direction: 1 = next routine −1 = previous routine
$Query(^$[|namespace|]Routine(routine name))	Returns the ^$Routine reference for the next existing routine in the namespace.

Operators

Operator	Operation
+	Plus: Force the numeric interpretation of the operands.
-	Minus: Invert the sign of the operands and force the numeric interpretation of the operands.
+	Addition: Add two operands interpreted as numbers. Example: 12+8 produces 20.
-	Subtraction: Subtract the second operand from the first operand after both have been interpreted numerically. Example: 20-8 produces 12.
*	Multiplication: Multiply the numeric value of the first operand with that of the second. Example: 10*2 produces 20.
/	Division: Divide the first operand by the second. Example: 40/2 produces 20. Division by zero is not permitted and produces an error message.
**	Exponentiation: Calculate the operand$_2$-th power for operand$_1$. Example: 2**3 produces 8.
\	Integer division: Perform the integer division of the numerically interpreted operands. Example: 22\5 produces 4. Division by zero is not permitted and produces an error message.

Operator	Operation
#	Modulo: Perform the remainder division of the first operand by the second. Example: 22#5 produces 2. Division by zero is not permitted and produces an error message.
<	Less than: Perform a less-than comparison of the two numerically interpreted operands. Example: 4<7 produces 1 (true).
>	Greater than: Perform a greater-than comparison of the two numerically interpreted operands. Example: 4>7 produces 0 (false).
=	Equals: Compare two operands for identity. Example: "xyz"="xyz" produces 1 (true).
[	Contains: Check whether the second operand is contained in the first. Example: "xyz"["a" produces 0 (false).
]	Follows: Check whether operand$_2$ follows operand$_1$ in the ASCII sorting sequence. Example: "def"]:"abc" produces 1 (true),"2"]"12" produces 1 (true).
]]	Sorts after: Check whether the second operand is sorted after the first operand. The collation sequence starts with the null string, then all canonical numbers, and finally all strings in alphabetic sequence. Example: 2]]"A" produces 0 (false). 12]]2 produces 1 (true)."ABC"]]"AABC" produces 1 (true).
?	Pattern match: Check whether the operand corresponds to a specified pattern. Example: "02745"?5N produces 1 (true) because the string consists of five digits.
_	Concatenation: The concatenation operator appends the second operand at the end of the first operand. Example: when var1="HI", var1_" THERE" produces "HI THERE".
& &&	And: Perform the Boolean And operation (AND) on operands interpreted as truth values. Example: (4<7)&(7>5) produces 1 (true). The && operator does not evaluate the right-hand operand unnecessarily.
! ||	Or: Interpret the two operands as truth expressions and perform the Boolean Or operation (OR). Example: (4<7)!(7>5) and (4<7)!(5>7) both yield 1 (true). The || operator does not evaluate the right-hand operand unnecessarily.
'	Not: Invert the function of an operator or the truth value of the operand. Example: 12'=(4*4) and '(12=(4*4)) yield 1 (true), 12'=(4*3) and '(12=(4*3)) yield 0 (false).
@	Indirection: Interpret the operand and replace this with its value.

Pattern Match Characters

Character	Meaning
A	Represents all 52 ASCII uppercase and lowercase letters ("A" to "Z" and "a" to "z").
C	Represents the 33 ASCII control characters (ASCII codes 0 to 31 and 127).
E	Represents any character.
L	Represents all 26 ASCII lowercase letters ("a" to "z").
N	Represents all 10 ASCII digits ("0" to "9").
P	Represents any of the 33 ASCII punctuation characters (ASCII codes 32 to 47, 58 to 64, 91 to 96 and 123 to 126).
U	Represents all 26 ASCII uppercase letters ("A" to "Z").

Appendix B. CDL Reference

Keywords for Classes

Keyword	Default	Explanation
Class	--	Defines a data type class or object class.
Abstract	FALSE	Specifies that the class is abstract. Abstract object classes cannot be instantiated. Abstract data type classes cannot be used to define properties.
ClassType	--	Class type. Possible values: *datatype*, *persistent*, *serial*, *view* and *csp*.
ClientDataType	VARCHAR	Must be specified for data type classes (ClassType= datatype); specifies the data type for Java and ActiveX clients.
CompileAfter	--	Specifies that this class is to be compiled only after the other listed class(es) have been compiled.
Ddl Allowed	FALSE	Indicates whether a class definition can be changed using SQL DDL commands.
Extends	--	List of the super classes from which this class inherits.
Final	FALSE	Specifies that the class is final. Subclasses cannot be derived from final classes.
Hidden	FALSE	Indicates that a class does not appear in the class directory.
Import	--	List of packages in which class names without a given package name are expected.
IncludeCode	--	List of Include files (delimited by commas) with external code to be inserted in the class definition for method code.
IncludeGenerator	--	List of Include files (delimited by commas) with external code to be inserted in the class definition for method generator code.
Language	cache	Indicates the standard language for the class method code. Possible values: *cache*, *basic* and *java*.
Odbctype	VARCHAR	Must be specified for data type classes (ClassType= datatype); indicates the data type for ODBC accesses.
Owner	_SYSTEM	Specifies the owner of persistent classes and the related SQL table.
ProcedureBlock	TRUE	Defines that a method code in this class is standardized as an encapsulated procedure.
PropertyClass	--	Used by Caché classes to define property methods .
SqlCategory	STRING	Mandatory for data type classes (ClassType=datatype); specifies the SQL category for the data type.
SqlRoutinePrefix	--	Prefix for automatically generated Caché routines for SQL queries to this class.
SqlRowIdName	ID	Alternative name for the ID field in the SQL projection.
SqlRowIdPrivate	FALSE	Indicates that the ID field in the SQL projection is to be viewed only when it is specifically selected.
SqlTableName	(class name)	SQL name of the table that represents the object class .

Keyword	Default	Explanation
StorageStrategy	Default	The storage strategy to be used for the persistent object class.
System	0	A value of 1 defines the class as an internal Caché system class.

Keywords for Properties

Keyword	Default	Explanation
Property	--	Defines a simple property.
Relationship	--	Defines a property as a bidirectional relationship between persistent objects.
Calculated	FALSE	Specifies that the value of the property is not stored but calculated when needed.
Cardinality	--	The cardinality of a relationship between persistent objects. Possible values: *one*, *many*, *parent* and *child*.
Collection	--	Defines a property as a collection and specifies the type. Possible values: *list* and *array*.
Final	FALSE	Specifies that the definition of the property is final and cannot be changed in subclasses.
Inverse	--	Defines the opposite sides of a bidirectional relationship between persistent objects by specifying the name of the corresponding property of the other class.
Multidimensional	FALSE	The marked property behaves like a multidimensional field.
Private	FALSE	Specifies that the property is private. Private properties are visible only within the own class and subclasses.
Required	FALSE	Specifies properties that must be set before storing the instance. Ignored for transient classes.
SQLCollation	--	Specifies sorting for SQL access. Possible values: *EXACT*, *SQLSTRING* and *SQLUPPER*.
SQLColumn-Number	--	Specifies the SQL column sequence, which is usually automatic.
SQLComputeCode	--	Specifies the code that determines the value of a calculated field in SQL.
SQLComputed	FALSE	If present, this property is represented as calculated field in SQL.
SQLFieldname	(property name)	Specifies the name of the field in SQL.
Transient	FALSE	Marks individual properties of a persistent or embeddable class as transient. Transient properties are not stored.

Keywords for Methods

Keyword	Default	Explanation
[Class]Method	--	Defines a (class) method for the class.
Abstract	FALSE	Indicates that the method is abstract.
CodeMode	code	Indicates how the method is implemented. Possible values: *call*, *code*, *expression*, and *objectgenerator*.
Final	FALSE	Specifies that the method is final. Final methods cannot be overwritten in subclasses.
GenerateAfter	--	Specifies that a method generator is only executed after the other indicated methods have been generated.

Keyword	Default	Explanation
Language	(from class definition)	Specifies the language in which the method is implemented: *cache*, *basic*, or *java*.
NotForProperty	FALSE	Specifies that this method of a data class is not used for the generation of a property method.
PlaceAfter	--	Determines that the generated code for this method is to appear after the code for the other specified method.
Private	FALSE	Marks the method as private. Private methods can only be invoked within their own class or in subclasses.
ProcedureBlock	(from class definition)	Indicates that the method code should be encapsulated as a procedure block.
PublicList	--	Lists the public variables that are visible in the method.
ServerOnly	FALSE	Indicates that the method should not be part of the Java or C++ projection of the class.
SqlName	(method name)	Specifies an alternative name for the SQL projection used as a stored procedure.
SqlProc	FALSE	Specifies that the method can be called from SQL as a stored procedure (permitted only for class methods).
WebMethod	FALSE	Specifies that the method can be called as a Web method using SOAP (permitted only for class methods).

Keywords for Class Parameters

Keyword	Default	Explanation
Parameter	--	Defines a class parameter.
Default	--	Specifies the value of the class parameter.

Keywords for Queries

Keyword	Default	Explanation
Query	--	Defines a query for the object class.
Final	FALSE	Specifies that the query is final. Final queries cannot be overwritten in subclasses.
Private	FALSE	Marks the query as private. Private queries can only be invoked within their own class or in subclasses.
SqlName	(query name)	Specifies an alternative name for the SQL projection of the query as a stored procedure.
SqlProc	FALSE	Specifies that the query can be called from SQL as a stored procedure.
SqlQuery	--	Contains the executable SQL code of the query.
SqlView	FALSE	Specifies that the query can be called from SQL as a view.
SqlViewName	--	Defines the name of the view when the SqlView keyword is specified.

Keywords for Indexes

Keyword	Default	Explanation
Index	--	Defines an index for the object class.
Condition	--	For a conditional index, specifies the condition for a record to be included.
Data	--	Specifies a list of properties that are to contain additional data values in the index.

Keyword	Default	Explanation
Extent	FALSE	Specifies that the index defines an object container [extent]. Extent indexes do not contain any properties as key or additional data values.
IdKey	FALSE	Specifies that the index forms the Idkey. Such an index is then responsible for managing the object identity and is always "unique." The property values used to form the index cannot be changed during the lifetime of an object instance.
PrimaryKey	FALSE	Specifies that the index forms the primary key.
SqlName	(index name)	Specifies the name of the index in its SQL projection.
Type	--	Specifies the index type: *index* or *bitmap*.
Unique	FALSE	Specifies that no two object instances can have the same values for the index properties.

Appendix C. SQL Reference

Data Query Language (DQL)

```
SELECT * | { [DISTINCT | ALL] expression,... }
  FROM { tablename [aliasname]},...
  [ WHERE condition ]
  [ GROUP BY { columnname | integer },...]
  [ HAVING condition ]
  [ ORDER BY { columnname | integer },...]

  [{ UNION [ALL]

SELECT * | { [DISTINCT | ALL] expression,... }
  FROM { tablename [aliasname]},...
  [ WHERE condition ]
  [ GROUP BY { columnname | integer },...]
  [ HAVING condition ]
  [ ORDER BY { columnname | integer },...]

  }]...
```

Parameter	Definition
Expression	Expression that produces a value. Can contain a *columnname* or consist of one.
Tablename	Name or synonym for a table or a view.
Aliasname	A temporary synonym for a *tablename* defined here and is valid only in this command.
Condition	A condition that is true or false in the FROM clause for every row or row combination of the table(s).
Columnname	Name of a column of a table.
Integer	Integer that determines an *expression* using its position in the SELECT clause.

Data Manipulation Language (DML)

INSERT INTO *tablename* [(*columnname,...*)]
  { VALUES (*expression,...*) }
  | *query*

UPDATE *tablename*
  SET *columnname = expression ,...*
  [WHERE *condition*]

DELETE FROM *tablename*
  [WHERE *condition*]

Parameter	Definition
Tablename	Name or synonym for a table or a view.
Columnname	Name of a column of a table.
Expression	Expression that produces a value. Can contain a *columnname* or consist of them.
Query	A valid SELECT clause.
Condition	A condition that is true or false in the FROM clause for every row or row combination of the table(s).

Transaction Control Language (TCL)

```
%BEGTRANS
```

```
%INTRANS
```

```
COMMIT [WORK]
```

```
ROLLBACK [WORK]
```

Data Definition Language (DDL)

CREATE TABLE *tablename*
...(*columnname datatype* [(*length*)] [NOT NULL] ,...)

ALTER TABLE *tablename*
...{ DROP *columnname* }
  | { ADD *columnname datatype* [(*length*)] [NOT NULL] }
  | { MODIFY *columnname datatype* [(*length*)] [NOT NULL] }

DROP TABLE *tablename*

CREATE VIEW *viewname* [(*columnname* ,...)] AS *query*

ALTER VIEW *viewname* [(*columnname* ,...)] AS *query*

DROP VIEW *viewname*

CREATE [UNIQUE] INDEX *indexname*
  ON *tablename* (*columnname* ,...)

ALTER [UNIQUE] INDEX *indexname*
  ON *tablename* (*columnname* ,...)

DROP INDEX *indexname*

Parameter	Definition
tablename	Name of a table.
columnname	Name of a column of a table.
datatype	Data type for the values of the column. Possible data types are CHAR, VARCHAR, LONG VARCHAR, SMALLINT, INTEGER, DECIMAL, DATETIME, DATE, TIME, TIMESTAMP, FLOAT and NUMBER.
length	Maximum length for the values of the column.
query	A valid SELECT clause.
viewname	Name of a view.
indexname	Name of an index.

Reserved Words in Caché SQL

The following table contains all words reserved in Caché SQL. Irrespective whether written in uppercase or lowercase, these words cannot be used as designators for tables, columns, views, etc.

%AFTERHAVING	%ALPHAUP	%ALTER	%ALTER_USER
%BEGTRANS	%CATALOG	%CHECKPRIV	%CREATE_ROLE
%CREATE_USER	%DELDATA	%DESCRIPTION	%DROP_ANY_ROLE
%DROP_USER	%EXACT	%EXTERNAL	%FILE
%FOREACH	%GRANT_ANY_PRIVILEGE	%GRANT_ANY_ROLE	%INSTALL
%INTERNAL	%INTEXT	%INTOBUILD	%INTRANS
%INTRANSACTION	%MCODE	%MULTILINE	%NAME
%NOCHECK	%NODELDATA	%NOINDEX	%NOLOCK
%NUMBER	%NUMROWS	%ODBCOUT	%ROUTINE
%ROWCOUNT	%STARTSWITH	%STRING	%THRESHOLD
%UPPER	%YESNO	ABSOLUTE	ACTION
ADD	ALL	ALLOCATE	ALTER
AND	ANY	ARE	AS
ASC	ASSERTION	AT	AUTHORIZATION
AVG	BEGIN	BETWEEN	BIT
BIT_LENGTH	BOTH	BY	CASCADE
CASE	CAST	CATALOG	CHAR
CHARACTER	CHARACTER_LENGTH	CHAR_LENGTH	CHECK
CLOSE	COALESCE	COLLATE	COMMIT
CONNECT	CONNECTION	CONSTRAINT	CONSTRAINTS
CONTINUE	CONVERT	CORRESPONDING	COUNT
CREATE	CROSS	CURRENT	CURRENT_DATE
CURRENT_TIME	CURRENT_TIMESTAMP	CURRENT_USER	CURSOR
DATE	DEALLOCATE	DEC	DECIMAL
DECLARE	DEFAULT	DEFERRABLE	DEFERRED
DELETE	DESC	DESCRIBE	DESCRIPTOR
DIAGNOSTICS	DISCONNECT	DISTINCT	DOMAIN
DOUBLE	DROP	ELSE	END
ENDEXEC	ESCAPE	EXCEPT	EXCEPTION
EXEC	EXECUTE	EXISTS	EXTERNAL
EXTRACT	FALSE	FETCH	FILE
FIRST	FLOAT	FOR	FOREIGN
FOUND	FROM	FULL	GET
GLOBAL	GO	GOTO	GRANT
GROUP	HAVING	HOUR	IDENTITY
IMMEDIATE	IN	INDICATOR	INITIALLY
INNER	INPUT	INSENSITIVE	INSERT
INT	INTEGER	INTERSECT	INTERVAL
INTO	IS	ISOLATION	JOIN
KEY	LANGUAGE	LAST	LEADING
LEFT	LEVEL	LIKE	LOCAL

LOWER	MATCH	MAX	MIN
MINUTE	MODULE	NAMES	NATIONAL
NATURAL	NCHAR	NEXT	NO
NOT	NULL	NULLIF	NUMERIC
OCTET_LENGTH	OF	ON	ONLY
OPEN	OPTION	OR	ORDER
OUTER	OUTPUT	OVERLAPS	PAD
PARTIAL	POSITION	PREPARE	PRESERVE
PRIMARY	PRIOR	PRIVILEGES	PROCEDURE
PUBLIC	READ	REAL	REFERENCES
RELATIVE	RESTRICT	REVOKE	RIGHT
ROLE	ROLLBACK	ROWS	SCHEMA
SCROLL	SECOND	SECTION	SELECT
SESSION_USER	SET	SIZE	SMALLINT
SOME	SPACE	SQL	SQLCODE
SQLERROR	SQLSTATE	SUBSTRING	SUM
SYSTEM_USER	TABLE	TEMPORARY	THEN
TIME	TIMESTAMP	TIMEZONE_HOUR	TIMEZONE_MINUTE
TO	TRAILING	TRANSACTION	TRANSLATE
TRANSLATION	TRIM	TRUE	UNION
UNIQUE	UNKNOWN	UPDATE	UPPER
USAGE	USER	USING	VALUE
VALUES	VARCHAR	VARYING	WHEN
WHENEVER	WHERE	WITH	WORK
WRITE	ZONE		

Glossary

Abstract class

An object class that cannot be instantiated or a data type class that cannot be used for characterizing literals. Abstract classes serve as templates used to derive subclasses.

ActiveX/COM/DCOM

Interface defined by Microsoft for communication among objects.

Advanced Data Type (ADT)

Data type defined by the user that describes the syntax and semantics of operations that can be applied to the data type. ADTs extend the base data types supplied with Caché and can be used in place of them.

C++

Object-oriented programming language that is a further development of C.

Caché

Postrelational database from InterSystems. It contains a multidimensional data server and an application server with *Unified Data Architecture*.

Caché Basic

An implementation of the programming language Basic available in Caché as an alternative to Caché ObjectScript.

Caché Objects

Collective designation for the object-oriented functionality of Caché. The most important components include Caché Studio and the Object Servers for Java, ActiveX/COM/DCOM, and SOAP.

Caché Object Server

Responsible for making Caché objects available for applications and tools written in Java or C++ or use the ActiveX/COM/DCOM or SOAP interfaces.

Caché ObjectScript

The object-oriented programming language of Caché. It supports direct, object, and SQL access to the database, and allows the inclusion of embedded SQL, HTML, and JavaScript code.

Caché Server Pages (CSP)

Caché technology that can dynamically generate HTML or XML pages for the development of Internet and Intranet applications. CSP is based on a number of Caché system classes and special HTML/XML tags.

Caché SQL

Collective designation for the relational functionality of Caché. The most important components are Caché SQL Server and Caché SQL Gateway.

Caché SQL Gateway

Caché SQL component that forwards Caché internal data accesses to other relational databases.

Caché SQL Server

Caché SQL component that enables relational applications or tools to access Caché data using SQL. The supported interfaces include ODBC and JDBC.

Caché Studio

Graphical development environment for Caché class hierarchies, routines, and CSP pages.

CDL

The Class Definition Language of Caché.

Class

A class groups objects of the same type. Caché classes are used both as object factory (i.e., they contain a constructor function to create new instances) and as object container (i.e., they allow set operations on their instances).

Collection

Structure that can accept a group of repeated elements within an object instance. Collections can contain any number of literals, references to objects, or embedded objects. Caché distinguishes between array collections (sorted using a key) and list collections (simple list).

Data Access Modes

Method used by application logic to access data. Caché supports three different access modes: object, SQL, and multidimensional access.

DDL

The Data Definition Language for SQL. It defines relational tables, views, and indexes. From DDL code, Caché can automatically create table and object definitions for Caché's Unified Data Architecture.

ECP

The Enterprise Cache Protocol for Caché. The special communications protocol that optimizes the performance and scalability of multilevel client/server configurations using strategies for distributed data and object caching.

Embedded Object

An object that can only exist embedded in another, persistent object.

Final Class

The class whose elements cannot be changed in derived subclasses.

Global

A global variable in Caché ObjectScript. A global variable forms the basis for data storage in Caché.

Inheritance

The derivation of a new, more specialized class (subclass) from an existing class (super class), where the subclass inherits all elements, such as properties and methods, from the super class. These can be changed (overwritten) and new elements can be added that are only defined in the subclass.

Instance

A copy of a class, or simply an object. It exists at runtime and occupies memory. Caché distinguishes between transient objects (temporary) and persistent objects (stored permanently in the database).

Java

A platform-independent object-oriented programming language, developed by Sun Microsystems.

Method

A public interface of an object that hides private code implementing the object's behavior.

Message

Objects interact using standardized messages, which normally contain a call to a specific method.

Namespace

Typically, each namespace contains all the objects, data, and routines of a specific application. In a Caché system, the names of packages/classes, routines, and globals within a namespace are unique.

Object

An instance (an individual example) of a class. It exists at runtime and occupies memory. Caché distinguishes between transient objects (temporary) and persistent objects (permanent, stored in the database).

Object Technology

The method that application developers use to model the real world as object classes and their instances. The knowledge and behavior of objects from the real world are represented in the properties and methods of objects, the internal implementation of which is hidden by encapsulation.

ODBC

Open DataBase Connectivity. The standard interface for SQL communication, originally developed in Windows environments, but also available under UNIX and other operating systems.

ODMG

The Object Database Management Group. ODMG defines the ODMG standard for object-oriented database systems on which Caché is based.

Package

A way to group related classes under a common name. If no package name is specified, Caché assumes User as the package name for user-defined classes and %Library for Caché system classes.

Persistence

The property that defines a class of objects as being permanent. Persistent objects exist after a session ends, until they are explicitly deleted. Caché makes persistent objects permanent by storing them in a database with all their properties for multiuser and client/server support, transaction processing, etc.

Polymorphism

The initiation of different actions by an identical message when they are sent to objects in different classes.

Postrelational Technology

The database technology that excels in representing complex structures because it is not restricted to two-dimensional tables. Caché postrelational technology is based on a multidimensional database engine and object technology for real-world modeling of complex structures.

Property

A data value (an attribute or a relationship) stored in an object instance. It can be a literal, a reference to an object or an embedded object, as well as a bidirectional relationship between persistent objects.

Relationship

A special type of property that defines a bidirectional connection between two persistent objects. Relationships automatically provide referential integrity.

Routine

A collection of lines containing Caché ObjectScript or Caché Basic code that is stored in a namespace under a unique routine name.

Schema

A way to group related tables under a common name.

SOAP

The Simple Object Access Protocol, an XML-based mechanism for remote procedure calls, with which different applications can be tied together over the Internet.

Subclass

A class derived from a super class using inheritance.

Super class

Class from which a subclass is derived using inheritance.

Unified Data Architecture

The data definition layer (repository) in the Caché system architecture. It permits a uniform definition of classes and tables without paradigm breaks or the need for manual synchronization.

Visual Caché

The component that integrates Caché with Visual Basic's development environment.

Web Service

A distributed application component whose communication is based on XML and SOAP, and can be transacted over the Internet. Caché allows any class method to be published as a Web service.

Bibliography

Achtert, W.: Objektorientierte Software-Entwicklung. Von der Strukturierung zur Migration. 2nd Edition, Munich: Computerwoche-Verlag, 1997

American National Standards Institute: ANSI/MDC X11.1-1994: M Programming Language. Silver Spring: M Technology Association, 1994

Atkinson, M.P., Welland, R. (eds.): Fully Integrated Data Environments. Persistent Programming Languages, Object Stores, and Programming Environments. Esprit Basic Research Series. Berlin Heidelberg New York: Springer, 2000

Atzeni, P., Mendelzon, A., Mecca, G. (eds.): The World Wide Web and Databases. Lecture Notes in Computer Science, Vol. 1590. Berlin Heidelberg New York: Springer, 1999

Blaha, M., Premerlani, W.: Object-Oriented Modeling and Design for Database Applications. Upper Saddle River: Prentice Hall, 1997.

Booch, G.: Object-Oriented Design with Applications. 2nd Edition, New York: John Wiley & Sons, 1996

Cattel, R. G. G., Barry, D. K., Bartels, D.: The Object Database Standard: ODMG 2.0. San Francisco: Morgan Kaufmann, 1997

Codd, E.F.: A Relational Model for Large Shared Data Banks. Commun. ACM 13:6, 377-387 (1970)

Conrad, S.: Föderierte Datenbanksysteme. Konzepte der Datenintegration. Berlin Heidelberg New York: Springer, 1997

Currier, R.: The Emergence of Postrelational Databases. Changes in DBMS Technologies Occurring in Response to a Shift to the Third Computing Paradigm. Park City: Strategic Marketing, 1997

Cymanek, J.: Caché verbindet Welten: Objekte multidimensional gespeichert. Objekt Fokus 3–4/98, 24–29 (1998)

Date, C. J., Darwen, H.: A Guide to the SQL Standard. Reading: Addison-Wesley, 1996

Dick, K.: InterSystems' Caché: New Object Database Technology Meets the Challenge of Business Complexity. Palo Alto: Kevin Dick Associates, 1998

Eckel, B.: Thinking in Java. Upper Saddle River: Prentice Hall Computer Books, 1998

Geiger, K.: Inside ODBC. Redmond: Microsoft Press, 1995

Gruber, M.: Das SQL Buch. Düsseldorf: Sybex, 1990

Härder, T., Rahm, E.: Datenbanksysteme. Konzepte und Techniken der Implementierung. Berlin Heidelberg New York: Springer, 1999

Hesse, S., Kirsten, W.: Einführung in die Programmiersprache MUMPS. 2nd Edition, Berlin New York: Walter de Gruyter, 1989

Ihringer, M.: Unified Data Architecture. Datenbank Fokus 12/98, 29–31 (1998).

Ihringer, M.: Auf dem Weg von der relationalen in die objektorientierte Welt. Computerwoche 29/98, 48 (1998)

Ihringer, M.: Das Objekt-Modell der Caché-Datenbank: DB-Entwicklung ohne Paradigmenbrüche. Objekt Fokus 11–12/98, 72–76 (1998)

InterSystems Corp. (ed.): Caché Knowledge Base. Version 5. Cambridge: InterSystems, 2002

Bibliography

InterSystems Corp. (ed.): Caché ObjectScript Reference. Version 5. Cambridge: InterSystems, 2002

InterSystems Corp. (ed.): Introductory Guide to Caché System Administration. Version 5. Cambridge: InterSystems, 2002

InterSystems Corp. (ed.): Using Caché Multi-Dimensional Storage. Version 5. Cambridge: InterSystems, 2002

InterSystems Corp. (ed.): Using Caché Explorer. Version 5. Cambridge: InterSystems, 2002

InterSystems Corp. (ed.): Using Caché ObjectScript. Version 5. Cambridge: InterSystems, 2002

Kießling, W., Köstler, G.: Multimedia-Kurs Datenbanksysteme. Berlin Heidelberg New York: Springer, 1998

Kirsten, W.: Von ANS MUMPS zu ISO M. Darmstadt: Epsilon, 1993

Kleinschmidt, P., Rank, C.: Relationale Datenbanksysteme. Eine praktische Einführung. Berlin Heidelberg New York: Springer, 1997

Lang, S. M., Lockemann, P. C.: Datenbankeinsatz. Berlin: Springer, 1995

Maurer, H., Scherbakow, N., Halim, Z., Razak, Z.: From Databases to Hypermedia. Berlin Heidelberg New York: Springer, 1998

Meier, A.: Relationale Datenbanken. Leitfaden für die Praxis. 4th Edition. Berlin Heidelberg New York: Springer, 2001

Orfali, R., Harkey, D., Edwards, J.: The Essential Distributed Objects Survival Guide. New York: John Wiley & Sons, 1996

Patrick, J.J.: SQL Fundamentals. Upper Saddle River: Prentice Hall, 1999.

Poo, D.C.C., Kiong, D.B.K.: Object-Oriented Programming and Java. Singapore: Springer, 1998

Röhrig, B.: Futter für die Schnellen—Teil III. Toolbox Magazin 06/00, 76-80 (2000)

Röhrig, B.: Futter für die Schnellen—Teil IV. Toolbox Magazin 01/01, 76-80 (2001)

Schader, M.: Objektorientierte Datenbanken. Die C++-Anbindung des ODMG-Standards. Berlin Heidelberg New York: Springer, 1997

Taylor, D. A.: Object-Oriented Technology: A Manager's Guide. Reading: Addison-Wesley, 1990

Taylor, D. A.: Business Engineering with Object Technology. New York: John Wiley & Sons, 1995

Thalheim, B.: Entity-Relationship Modeling. Foundations of Database Technology. Berlin Heidelberg New York: Springer, 2000

Vaskevitch, D.: Two Steps Forward, One Step Back. Byte Magazine 5/92, 43–46 (1992)

Vossen, G.: Datenmodelle, Datenbanksprachen und Datenbank-Management-Systeme. 2nd Edition. Bonn Paris Reading: Addison-Wesley, 1994

Whitehorn, M., Marklyn, B.: Inside Relational Databases – with Examples in Access. London: Springer, 1998

Index